ONE DAMN THING AFTER ANOTHER

ONE DAMN THING AFTER ANOTHER

HUGH GARNER

McGRAW-HILL RYERSON LIMITED

Toronto   Montreal   New York   London   Sydney
Johannesburg   Mexico   Panama   Düsseldorf
Singapore   Sao Paulo   Kuala Lumpur   New Delhi

ONE DAMN THING AFTER ANOTHER

Passage quoted on pp. 67-69 taken from *The Far Distant
Ships* by Joseph Schull, pp. 139-142, published by the
authority of the Minister of National Defense, Ottawa, 1961.
Reproduced by permission of Information Canada.

Photograph of the Abraham Lincoln Battalion © Hazen
Sise. Reproduced with the permission of Hazen Sise.

ISBN 0-07-077618-0
2 3 4 5 6 7 8 9 10   D-73 10 9 8 7 6 5 4 3
Printed and Bound in Canada

To Robbie Garner, my fifth grandchild,
and the youngest Garner of them all.

The next thing most like living one's life over
again seems to be a recollection of that life,
and to make that recollection as durable as
possible by putting it down in writing.

Benjamin Franklin

AUTHOR'S PREFACE

There is no such thing as a "born writer." There are, however, people who, from an ingrained love of literature, a childhood conditioning to reading as entertainment or relaxation, and a driving, inexplicable urge to express themselves through the written word, sometimes become writers. The three conditions outlined above may not be true of all writers, but they were true of me.

There are all sorts of writers, for the word "writer" has become a generic term; it includes poets, journalists, playwrights, advertising copywriters, historians, biographers, and writers of fiction. When I speak of writers I am speaking of fiction writers, those who use the novel and short story as their means of self-expression.

The reasons for any person becoming a writer are probably as varied as the number of writers since writing began. For most it is either a craving for fame, a seeking of wealth, a quenchless urge to express themselves, an attempt to make contact with society, a realization that writing offers them the easiest or only means to make a living, or a combination of all these things. My own reasons for becoming a writer were the urge to express myself and the realization that fiction writing and journalism offered me a rewarding way to make a living. This, however, did not occur to me until some time after I had become a writer. My approach to what was eventually to become a full-time career was lackadaisical, and during my teens and twenties was abandoned much of the time.

The best ways for a poor, uneducated person to escape his poverty and class are to become a professional athlete, a theatrical personality, or an artist. These three lines of endeavor are above or outside class society, and they allow the athlete, actor, or artist to meld into a group of classless individuals who are acceptable in all social strata. To attain prominence in these things does not require a social background, financial backing, or a long, formal education. What it does need is determination, training, and the development of certain talents.

In the case of a writer, who is a literary artist, his training (whether he is conscious of it or not) starts at a very early age when he develops a love for the written word. During his schooldays and from his reading, he discovers that sub-consciously, subliminally, call it what you will, he is able to write stories or essays with greater ease than most of his classmates, and crude though they may be they are likely to be the best handed in to the teacher. This invariably happened to me. I always stood at the top of the class in English composition, while near the bottom in English grammar.

My deficiency in grammar (it was the only subject I failed in my Grade 8 high school entrance examinations) was the result, I think, of the uninteresting way it was presented. I could write a grammatical sentence, but I could not analyze why it *was* grammatical. I still can't. To use a bad analogy, I could see the beauty in a well-written sentence or a pretty girl, but could not analyze their beauty as a grammarian or a physiognomist can. Years later a drinking companion of mine, then a high school teacher, said to me after reading my first published novel, *Storm Below,* "I found a couple of grammatical errors in your book." "Is that all?" I asked him. "Anyway, who cares? I'm not writing grammar, I'm writing literature." He repeated this many times to people, until his death a few years ago.

Like some jazz musicians who cannot read a note of music I am able to write without knowing the rules of grammar, syntax, or composition. I am still unable to explain why a piece of writing is good or bad, including my own, but I *know* when it is one or the other, and when it is bad I sense why, and am able to change it. Literary explanations and educated criticism are the forte of teachers and professors; writing is the job of the writer. According to a scholarly essay I once read, writers, including the best ones, are seldom if ever intellectuals; literary critics are, at least by their self-admission, always intellectuals. Because I admit to being self-taught—and which writer isn't?—book reviewers and critics have sometimes called me a "natural writer," often using the description in a pejorative sense. As there are no "born writers" there are also no "natural writers."

I said or wrote once that I was descended from a long line of Yorkshire woollen weavers, drunkards on the male side and temperance fanatics on the female. I carried on the male tradition, but as a writer I am a mutant from the Garners, Fozards, and Stephensons who were my closest ancestors.

The only books in our house that I remember were *A Mother's Recompense,* and *The Way Of All Flesh* by Samuel Butler, which my mother had received as Sunday school prizes during her childhood. As a small boy I received Christmas presents of the G.A. Henty books, *A Boy's Own Annual,* and others from my maternal grandmother in England. Later on, long before I was old enough to join the public library, I bought weekly issues of English public school story papers with names like *Triumph* and *Magnet,* in which I vicariously associated myself with the British aristocracy. My favorite character was a smoking and drinking incorrigible named "The Bounder," who nevertheless would often come through in the clutch and do brave or decent things for his schoolmates in the Lower Fourth. The Bounders of this world have always been my favorite people.

As a child I also read the Tom Swift and Frank Merriwell books, thinking, even then, that their authors were mental basket cases. I scoffed at the prissy little Fauntleroys in such Horatio Alger Junior type books as *By Luck And Pluck, Joe The Shoeshine Boy* and other such pieces of "inspirational" claptrap. I was always wishing the runaway horse pulling the carriage carrying the rich man's daughter would trample the hero to death, or that the rich little girl our hero saved from the millrace would have bad breath and acne, and would marry the works superintendent's son.

In my late pre-teens my awakening sex drive made me seek out the women's underwear pages of department store catalogues, and read the less-than-fulfilling fantasies contained in *True Story* magazine. It was a case of the written fantasy assuaging the personal one.

During puberty sex, or at least my sexual fantasies, took me over completely. I surreptitiously read *Louis Beretti, Kings Back To Back*, the sexual references and stories in *The Bible*, Erskine Caldwell's *Tobacco Road*, and every other dirty book I could lay my hands on. Most of these books were obtained from an Owl Drugstore lending library at 3¢ a day. One day I rented *Lady Chatterley's Lover* from beneath the drugstore counter, at 5¢ a day. I suppose that during this period I was also reading such classics as *Huckleberry Finn, The Swiss Family Robinson, Treasure Island, Robinson Crusoe* and others, but to me they were kids' adventure books, and remain so to this day. At an early age I also read Henry Miller's *Tropic of Cancer* and *Tropic of Capricorn*, and they were more my meat. I can truthfully say that sex drove me to a love of literature, and vice versa. At the age of seventeen I made love to a girl for the first time, in Toronto's Don River Valley at the lower end of the Rosedale Ravine, in a spot where the Bayview Extension now runs. (Many years later, as a newspaper columnist, I wrote a column pointing this out, and wondering why the Metro Toronto roads department didn't erect a cairn on the spot. My editors couldn't see the joke, and killed the column.) From the night of my deflowerment my fantasies began to give way to sexual reality, though I remained a pornography fan. I still believe that a seeking-out of pornography to give substance to or relief from a young person's sexual fantasies is as good a way to get them reading as anything else.

A favorite question of interviewers is: "How did you learn to write?" My answer has always been that I learned to write by giving in to a voracious appetite for reading during my youth; by a cultivated ability to absorb what I had read, seen or experienced; by noting, perhaps subconsciously, how good writers wrote; and finally by living many of the things I later wrote about.

Some time ago an actor who has read many of my short stories on CBC radio wondered aloud to someone how Garner knew so much about gauges, calipers and parts-inspection procedures in a story about a farm implement factory, called "E Equals MC Squared." There's no secret about it; I worked once as an inspector in the punch-press department of the Massey-Harris company. I've also been asked where I learned about "priming" tobacco leaves, working in a carnival, crossing the ice of a Quebec river, life on a wartime Canadian corvette, selling products door-to-door, or whatever. My answer has been, "By doing those things," and sometimes adding, "from sheer necessity."

Thought I wasn't aware of it in my younger days, it seems that most of my jobs, travels, love affairs, wars, and living in general, were preparations for writing. I can depict with reasonable accuracy the life-style and speech of prostitutes, housewives, downtown landladies, nuns, policemen, soldiers, sailors, prison inmates, Indians, schoolteachers, con artists, bartenders, librarians, pimps, drunks, and suburbanites of both sexes. With the help of textbooks or trade manuals, and by keeping the jargon to a minimum, I can also reproduce various professional speech patterns. My main problem today is reproducing the slang dialogue of youth; I offer no geriatric excuse for this, it is one of the penalties of growing old. Like most writers my age I avoid as much as possible using today's young people as protagonists, and like other writers my novels and stories tend to use youth in the past tense.

Some critics have said I have a fairly good ear for dialogue—though, I think, not as good as John O'Hara had—but this is a trade skill I learned from listening to all sorts of people talking and absorbing what they said and how they said it.

There is a *canard* spread by the over-educated and by academics (after all, professors make a living by keeping students in school as long as possible) that writing belongs to those, and those only, especially in Canada, who have the best educations. In fiction writing the very opposite is true, as any perusal of an author's list or literary *Who's Who* will easily prove. The formal education a fiction writer needs, and many of the better ones haven't even had this, is a grade school ability to spell the words of his language, the skill to place them in a sentence one after the other, the sentences into paragraphs, and in the case of a novel, the paragraphs into chapters and the chapters into a book.

Though I have a natural disinclination to read about the childhood experiences of other people and an even stronger disinclination to write about my own, my editor insists that I do so. For those readers like myself who think such things belong in the "Bright Sayings Of Children" section of family digest magazines I promise to keep my own to a bare minimum.

My three earliest childhood recollections, which must have occurred between the ages of three and five, are the following: being sent on my third birthday to Parish Church School in Batley, Yorkshire, England; singing *There Is A Green Hill Far Away* before a Sunday School assembly in a Protestant chapel (I had been baptised in the Church of England, but my mother, and probably all of her family, had switched from established church to chapel in the manner of many English working class); and being promised a motorbike by some neighborhood lout, whom I believed. I distinguished my first day at school by messing my knee-length trousers in class; I waited patiently but in vain for the promised motorbike; and I astounded the Sunday school by remembering and delivering all the words of the Christian hymn, singing it with a complete lack of shyness but with a toddler's aplomb.

These three unconnected events I now realize were significant to the extent of exhibiting my personality: a complete disrespect for scholarship and such, a cynicism towards all promises and towards my fellow man, and a complete knowledge of my abilities and an immodest surety in delivering them despite the doubts of audiences or individuals. These three things: vulgar scorn for established authority, a mistrust of other people, and a determination to show my disbelievers or detractors they are wrong, are the dominating facets of my psychological make-up to this day.

I was maritally but not physiologically a seven-month baby, which I was not aware of until my early teens when I compared my birth certificate with my parents' marriage licence. My father, Matthew Garner, who was born in the nearby town of Dewsbury, was perhaps an unwilling groom in a marriage I have no doubt I brought about. In 1913, the year of my birth, my father emigrated to Canada to the vicinity of London, Ontario. I haven't the faintest idea what type of work he was engaged in there, but know only that he joined up as a bandsman, playing a tenor horn at the outbreak of World War One, in the 18th Battalion of the Canadian Expeditionary Corps. After he and his unit arrived in England there was either a reconciliation between my mother and him, or my mother foolishly followed him around England. I remember we lived "as paying guests" in the house of a Belgian refugee family named Vandervelde in the Brixton borough of London during the zeppelin raids, and for a time, perhaps it was only a day or two, in Folkestone. At sometime during the war my father fathered my brother Ronald, four years younger than me.

Except for brief periods in the early years of their marriage my mother and father did not live together, and my home, or what I vaguely remember as my home, was that of my maternal grandmother, a tall, dignified lady, a widow named Martha Anna Fozard. Her husband James (I don't even know the Christian name of my paternal grandfather) was a worker in Taylor's woollen mill, which along with other mills and coal mines justified my birthplace being stuck in the West Riding of Yorkshire. I learned later that both my father and paternal grandfather had played in the Batley Brass Band, and even later still that Batley had once been famous for its rugby teams. My mother's father, James, was, according to my mother who had signed the temperance pledge at the age of eight and never took an alcoholic drink in her life, a notorious boozer. In one of her nostalgic moments she told me of him once spending most of his week's wages in the local pub and with what was left buying a whole sheep which he carried home triumphantly on his shoulder.

My Grandma Fozard's family had been sent to Germany in her childhood, so that my great-grandparents, the Stevensons, could teach woollen weaving to the new German woollen mill workers. As a consequence of living much of her girlhood in Germany and going to school there my Grandma was completely bilingual in English and German.

I sneaked, rather shamefacedly, into the world on February 22nd, 1913, in a row of houses built back-to-back with another row on Henrietta Street. The house was No. 7 Back Henrietta Street, to distinguish it from No. 7 Henrietta Street proper, on the street behind us. It was a typical English industrial-town working-class house of the type I recognized in D. H. Lawrence's *Sons And Lovers* and later saw in such movies as *Room At The*

Top and *Saturday Night And Sunday Morning*. Our house had one big room on the ground floor which served as kitchen, dining and living room, and which opened to a wooden porch with steps leading down to a bricked-in front (back?) yard complete with a brick outside loo.

A narrow set of inside stairs led up to a bedroom on the second floor and again to a bedroom on the third floor. The "bathroom" was the kitchen sink and a washtub of water on Saturday night in front of the fireplace, which had a built-in cooking stove.

Across a narrow laneway outside the back brick wall stood an Irish Catholic Club. The Irish, who had emigrated to Batley either to work in the mills or in the coal pits, certainly couldn't have been living on any lower level than we were, but I still remember, that they were looked down upon by the English natives.

When my father returned to England from France, I think but am not sure, he had wangled himself a cushy job in the Canadian Army Pay Corps. This might have come about because he had gone on from the parish or council elementary school to what was then called a grammar school in England, the equivalent I suppose of our public high schools. Somewhere along the line he had made the transition from mill-hand to auditor, but how or when it came about I have no idea, and really no interest.

He returned to Canada in 1919, and my mother, brother and I followed in a shipload of British war brides on the *S.S. Melita*, arriving in Quebec City in July, 1919. Our first night in Canada was spent under the ministrations of the Salvation Army in the Immigration Building in Quebec City, and the next day we travelled from there to Toronto by train.

We lived first in a rather large old slum house on Ontario Street just north of King, I suppose with friends of my mother's from England. Who they were or what their name was I have long forgotten. The house has been torn down now for a long time and the head office of the Drug Trading Company occupies the site.

Having started school at the age of three I already had a Standard Two primary education, and when the Toronto schools started up after the summer vacation in September I was enrolled in Junior First class at Duke Street Public School, equal to today's Grade One. Duke Street School has been long gone, and now so has Duke Street itself, called Adelaide Street East today. The only things I remember about my first year in a Canadian school are being the best reader in the class, thanks to my three-year jump on the other kids, writing our sums and sentences on slates rather than in workbooks, and hitching rides to and from school standing on the back runners of horse-drawn sleighs, which were endemic to the Toronto of the time. Perhaps my most vivid recollection is an olfactory one: the vinegar smell that permeated the air at the corner of Duke and Sherbourne Streets from the vinegar works on the northeast corner.

I suppose that in those days I spoke with a Yorkshire accent you could cut with a letter-opener, and I distinctly remember learning to use Canadian expressions from my classmates such as "You did so!" and "Oh, I never did!" My mother's first job in Canada was in a shoe factory on Sherbourne Street, where they turned out women's long laced and buttoned boots. Behind our house on Ontario Street was a small stable from which the owner rented out draft horses and what were then called "hoosier wagons," high-sided dump carts the bottoms of which could be tripped open with a lever, dropping their load of sand, gravel or whatever to the ground.

Those years should have been lonely ones for I cannot remember ever being more than casually acquaintanced with the other boys in that neighborhood or the neighborhoods that followed up to my teens. I wasn't lonely however, for I had something going for me: I could play by myself for hours with small stones in an empty field behind the Berkeley Street firehall, creating with the stones and my imagination armies of British and German troops or cowboys and Indians. I never tired of this, and years later when I had almost finished public school I still made up imaginary casts of armies, posses, and Indian bands out of crayonned small squares of paper on the floors of wherever we were living at the time. I would speak to my characters, giving them orders, telling them to charge or retreat, cautioning them against an ambush or an artillery barrage. I was a contented loner, militarily oriented, and in certain ways have remained so all of my life.

From Ontario Street we moved to a two-room flat on Wascana Avenue in old Cabbagetown, into a house whose bottom floor was occupied by the Britt family. Mr. Britt was a conductor on the Toronto Street Railway, and the Britt's eldest boy Fred was in my class at Park School. Park School is still there, on what is called Shuter Street now, and Wascana Avenue is part and parcel of the narrow unreconstructed belt of Cabbagetown that lies between Shuter Street on the north, Queen Street on the south, from Parliament Street to the Don River. Most of Cabbagetown was eradicated after World War Two and replaced by government-subsidized housing known as Regent Park North and Regent Park South. I used an amalgam of Wascana Avenue and Blevins Place, a couple of blocks north of it running east from

4

Sumach, as "Timothy Place" in my novel *Cabbagetown*. In 1972 I revisited Wascana to find several of the row houses, including the one I lived in, torn down and replaced by a trucking yard.

It's not quite coincidental that so many of the houses I lived in during my childhood have since been torn down. My birthplace, 7 Back Henrietta Street, which I took my wife to see and which I hoped to photograph a few years ago, has been torn down to make a parking lot for the Irish Club, rebuilt since I was there during World War Two. Houses I lived in on Sumach and Ontario Streets have gone too. Other houses I lived in on Steiner Street, Metcalf, Wellesley, Berkeley, and other "inner city" streets have either been torn down or have been completely forgotten by me. A year ago a *Globe & Mail* reporter, a photographer, and I took a long stroll through old Cabbagetown's rebuilt and unreconstructed sections. I told the reporter that Wascana Avenue, on which we happened to be standing at the time, was the "Timothy Place" of *Cabbagetown*.

"Don't you feel an affinity for it?" he asked. "Hasn't it any nostalgic memories for you after using it as Ken Tilling's street in your novel?"

"No," I said.

"Doesn't it remind you of anything?"

"Oh sure. All the old streets I once lived on down here do."

"And what's that?"

"Bedbugs," I told him.

The two things I hated most during my childhood were bedbugs and social workers. About the first, there were many slum housewives, my mother among them, who could smell bedbugs. In those days before DDT and other insecticides, the best way to attack them was to soak the metal beds and bedsprings with kerosene, called "coal oil," which might hold them at bay for a short time. The social workers, like the schoolteachers and librarians of the day largely untrained and uneducated, were not as numerous as the bugs but too numerous for *my* comfort at least.

At the western extremity of the Queen Street bridge across the Don River Valley stood the Evangeline Settlement House, a neighborhood building which contained a preventive medicine clinic, more social workers, and, though I only presume this, classrooms in which baby-care, hygiene, and crafts were taught. I have a hazy recollection of going there once to get an inoculation against one of the contagious diseases that spread in annual epidemics throughout Cabbagetown and across the river in Riverdale. In those days every house that held a child suffering from measles, diphtheria, whooping cough, mumps, or chicken-pox had its front door plastered with a quarantine sign, with a colour to differentiate the disease, which listed in small type the fines for violations of the city's contagious disease ordinances. What this really meant was that none of the children in the house or family (and in most houses there was more than one family) were allowed out of the house or backyard until an arbitrary length of time was over.

If I remember correctly the longest quarantines were for diphtheria and scarlet fever, while smallpox, which was still around in those days, must have meant something like a life sentence. It's an exaggeration of course but almost every summer of my childhood was marked by either me or my brother catching one or more of the diseases, sometimes consecutively. I spent more summer holidays in my backyard than anyone I ever knew, afraid to venture out of the back gate in case a health inspector spotted me or I was fingered by a bitchy neighbor. I didn't know it then, and wouldn't have appreciated it if I had known, but my meagre diet and susceptibility to *all* the childhood diseases filled my bloodstream with antibodies and kept my arteries free of the build-up of cholesterol. For instance, during the 1940s and 50s there were far more middle-class kids crippled by polio than there were working-class slum kids; most of us had probably had "infantile paralysis" in its mild form and had built up an immunity against the disease.

The only serious illness of the many I had as a child was scarlet fever, which I picked up at a 6¢ Saturday matinee at a small movie house on Queen Street west of Sackville Street. This put me in the Riverdale Isolation Hospital for six weeks, but left me with no after effects that I know of.

When my brother and I were small boys my mother took us to the East End Day Nursery on lower River Street, where she paid a dime-a-day for our workday supervision. I remember it particularly for the old wagons and sleighs of The New Method Laundry next door, which offered us a natural jungle gymn on, over, and under which we would play. I remember too my favorite lunch there was a hamburger stew and mashed potatoes, that I enjoyed very much. The old girls who were doing their sociological thing in running the day nursery were a pretty decent lot, I suppose. The only thing about it that I hated was my after-lunch nap on a mattress on the floor. How long I went there I don't remember, but it may have been years. I know that I was a regular pupil (patient, inmate?) there all the time we

6

lived in Cabbagetown and while I attended Park School. The Day Nursery was replaced after World War Two by an Ontario Brewers Retail store, a much truer projection of the social character of the neighborhood.

One thing that always hands me a cynical laugh is the statement by somebody who, while weeping crocodile tears over poor kids, says something about them never having seen a cow. Who the hell has ever gone through life suffering a trauma from not having seen a cow? Believe me there are much worse things about living in a downtown slum than the deprivation of not having seen a cow. Among the worst are the aforementioned bedbugs, endemic illnesses and hospital clinic medication, the complete lack of privacy at home, the lack of decent bathrooms and toilet facilities or the forced sharing of them with other families. There are too much social regimentation, education, and leisure-time supervision by representatives of charities and social agencies, and a lack of decent food and shelter. A great many of these things have been partly eliminated or alleviated today, so please understand I'm writing about the dark ages of fifty years ago.

The two biggest days of the year to me and my childhood friends were Christmas and the day of the annual Sunday school summer picnic. Christmas and Santa Claus were just as important, and the latter just as real as he was in the better neighborhoods of the city. Until the age of eight or nine I believed in a just, generous, and eminently nonpartisan Santa, who brought me 99¢ Sandy-Andys and/or a box of toy soldiers, while delivering expensive Christmas presents to the richer kids who needed them.

My mother always took my brother and me to see the Eaton's Santa Claus parade, and it was on my way back from seeing Santa's triumphant arrival at the downtown department store that I was hit by a car. It happened on the north corner of George and Queen Streets (which, honestly, has also disappeared since then, George Street today running only to Queen, then skipping a block). The car that hit me was a Star, and according to my mother I would have been killed if I hadn't clung on to the front bumper and allowed it to drag me into the intersection. I suffered only a concussion as a consequence. My mother used to say, "The driver was such a nice man. He took us both in his car to St. Michael's Hospital, where you came back to consciousness and were examined by a doctor."

Another big event at Christmas was the delivery, along every street I lived on as a child, of charity food boxes donated by the

7

Salvation Army, Rotary, Kiwanis, church groups and other organizations. If my mother was assured we were going to get a Christmas fowl, canned goods, small cake and pudding from one group she would go out of her way to cancel any supplementary gifts from other donors. This wasn't true of many of our neighbors, some of whom received four or five different boxes, allowing them to gorge themselves on chicken and plum pudding almost through January. The families that did this were the antecedents of the carbohydrate-fatty old slobs who do the same thing today. Send a middle-class newspaper reporter and photographer down to a slum, or worse still a featured "sob-sister," and invariably they'll write a heartrending and totally unrealistic piece of tearful crap about the worst, ugliest, sloppiest professional slum-dweller on the street. What this type of slum inhabitant has in great measure is gall and pushiness, and the clean decent poor families are seldom written about at all.

The annual Sunday school picnics were the big event of the summer season. In those days in Toronto an outing usually meant a trip across Lake Ontario on one of the fourteen passenger ships then working during the summer months from the city to Port Dalhousie, Wabasso Park, Niagara-on-the-Lake, and other picnic spots. The poorer or more tight-fisted churches and sects only took their congregations to Toronto Island or in-city spots like High Park. Not being as honest as my mother I generally found out from other kids what Sunday *their* church was giving out the picnic tickets, and in turn I was everything from Presbyterian to Gospel Tabernacle, for at least one day of the year. Actually I was a soprano choirboy in the Church of England until both my voice and my illusions changed.

Middle-class liberal bleeding-hearts whose ego demands that they throw themselves into causes aimed at helping the slum kids are not only a nuisance to the kids themselves, but a complete pain in the ass to me. In my childhood years in Cabbagetown and Riverdale we kids had everything going for us except money for clothes, fruit juices, and a stomach full of food, and what we didn't have we didn't particularly miss.

Clothes were no problem for there were always charitable clothing depots, second-hand clothing and shoe stores, and after unemployment had become an epidemic that put diphtheria back into a secondary subject of conversation, the city relief department opened clothing depots of its own. While I'm on the subject of slum clothes I must add something to the Cabbagetown Christmas scene. This was the receipt by hundreds of children in my neighborhood of "Star Boxes," which were small

8

boxes about the length of a shoe box but a little wider, containing Christmas goodies from the *Toronto Star*. There were boxes for both boys and girls, and though I've forgotten what the girls' boxes contained I remember what was in the boys' boxes to this day. There was a small toy of some sort, perhaps a puzzle or a baseball, a bag of over-sweet colored candies, a pair of leg-length black woollen stockings, and a knitted woollen sweater of a color I can only describe as puce.

On the day after New Year's when we charity recipients went back to school it was possible to pick us out by our uniforms. The boys' sweaters had a high roll-neck, and they seemed to have been knitted out of steel wool. We knowledgeable charity-hounds would cut a slit down the front of the itchy unwearable collar, re-making the sweater into an open-neck creation. The Star Santa Claus Fund officials never did tag to the fact that though their sweaters were warm enough to hold off an Arctic blizzard their recipients preferred freezing to itching to death. Years later, when as a member of the *Toronto Star* staff I was posted to the basement of Massey Hall to pack these boxes I noticed that they hadn't changed a bit since my childhood. I sincerely hope that since then some understanding official of the Fund has discovered that putting such an article of clothing on a boy is like putting burrs under a horse's collar, and has switched the order for sweaters to ones knitted out of sheep's wool rather than made from barbed-wire discards.

When everyone dresses poor, and there are greater urges than being in style or dressing better than another, clothes return to their original place in the scheme of things, as protection from the weather and nothing more. Strangely, it was not until the mid and late sixties that the hippie generation brought back a sensible viewpoint on clothes, though for the wrong reasons.

We Cabbagetown children were gifted with innumerable places to play, from back lanes with board slab fences to lines of freight cars, from clean sandy beaches at Cherry Beach to the city's most exciting wide river valley, the Valley of the Don. We could swim in the Don River or in nearby Lake Ontario, we could dive off the concrete piers around the ship turning basin and ship canal or off the wooden pilings into Toronto Bay. We could skate on public rinks in Riverdale Park, Regent Park or on the hockey cushions in every schoolyard. We could go up the Don and see small animals, dozens of varieties of birds, and every kind of flora indigenous to Southern Ontario. We could visit the odorous old Toronto Zoo, a five-minute walk away from anywhere in Cabbagetown, and see an elephant, bears, lions, tigers, mountain goats, monkeys (especially an exhibitionist masturbating Chacma baboon who always played with himself when he smelled females in his audience). We received a free schoolkid ticket for the Canadian National Exhibition on Children's Day each year, and a quarter or half-dollar if our parents could afford it. When we'd squandered our pittance on the Midway we could pick up shopping bags full of free samples and sales brochures, and after that we could, and did, go into the Horse Palace or the Coliseum building and see horses by the dozen and cows too innumerable to count. "Poor kid, he's never yet seen a cow!" Madame, excuse me, but you're full of a by-product of the cattle business.

Riverdale Park, before it was bisected by the Don Valley Parkway and the Bayview Extension, was the playground of the children and young people from both sides of the Don River. During childhood it was a wide natural wilderness in which to play, in later years a place for hikes, corn roasts, and weiner roasts, and after puberty the most popular spot—with the possible exception of the sandy wooded savannah that led down to Simcoe Beach—for youthful experimental sex education in Toronto's East End. Somehow, sex has never seemed the same to me since I stopped arriving home from a date with grass-stains on the knees of my trousers.

During my schooldays the Toronto Street Railway, which later became the Toronto Transit Commission, ran daily free streetcars all summer to various swimming spots in Toronto. The kids in the West End were taken to Sunnyside Beach. We East Enders were given a free ride on an old car from the streetcar loop at the Woodbine race track at Kingston Road, west along Queen Street and then along King Street, ending up at the old fruit market where the O'Keefe Centre now stands. The Danforth Avenue toffs picked up their free car on the Danforth, which took them to the Bloor Street viaduct, where they rushed down the hill to the Don Valley to swim naked at the old Red Bridge over the Don, south of the Don Valley claypits and brickyards and what is now known as Pottery Road. We Cabbagetowners and Riverdaleites didn't need a streetcar; we hiked up the Don Valley to the Red Bridge.

But to get back to the Queen Street free car. We underprivileged kids, who felt nothing but pity for the Rosedale private schoolboys who had to wear bathing suits, used to disembark from the free car after a slow, song-filled ride. We serenaded every policeman we passed with an ear-splitting rendition of "Brass-button, bluecoat, couldn't catch a nannygoat!" and

10

jumped off and raced across the street to the fruit market like a raid of ancient Goths.

We'd swipe any stray fruit we could on our marauding way through the ancient wooden market, but the main prize was potatoes. Whenever we could avoid the gesticulating Italian fruit vendors, and this was most of the time, we'd fill our pockets with spuds. Then out and across the wide level crossing of the railroad tracks, which emerged from Union Station in those days, down to the ferry wharf, and aboard our private yacht, also free, the old *S.S. Luella*.

When the last staggering fruit-and-vegetable thief had boarded the boat, the old captain (whom we probably sent to an earlier death than he'd looked forward to) would pull the whistle lanyard, and away we'd go, across Toronto Bay to Hanlan's Point. We'd rush across the isthmus that had been separated from downtown by the Western ship channel, or gap, and end up shucking our clothes on the lakeside shore of the island where the Toronto Island Airport is now located. This sandy paradise, known affectionately to all as "bare-ass beach," was patrolled by a couple of life-guards. After our swim and general horsing around we'd gather driftwood and dry bush and build fires in the sand in which we'd bake our stolen potatoes. When the old *Luella* signalled us back to the bayside wharf with her asthmatic ship's whistle we'd don our clothes again and amble back across the island. Our less-noisy return trip by the free car to our stops through Moss Park, Cabbagetown and Riverdale was a tired, sunburned return from paradise. Who wanted to be rich?

Every poor kid of my childhood and early youth had his own hang-ups; my particular *bête noire* happened to be summer camps. On several occasions I was conned, or my mother was, into either volunteering or being sent to such summer camps as Bolton Camp, run by the *Toronto Star's* Fresh Air Fund or the Salvation Army Children's Camp at Jackson's Point on Lake Simcoe. I used to hate every minute of it: the regimentation of certain hours for games, for baseball, for swimming, for camp-fire singsongs, the insane mock-jolly attitudes of the camp counsellors, who, like my cruise ship "activities people" of later years, always seemed to want me to play volleyball (shuffle-board) when what I really wanted to do was read (sit at the bar) instead.

I became homesick my first day at camp, but not for our crummy house or flat but for the city activities of the summer, and stayed homesick until I was rescued by bus or train from

11

forced fresh air, "wholesome food," and in the case of the Sally Ann, from their evangelical proselytizing. I didn't want to be rescued from the hot humid city, and I certainly didn't want to be saved from sin. One summer I toughed-out the Salvation Army camp for two weeks, and on the day of my release was informed that my mother had requested they keep me for another session. No convict lifer, finding that his parole had been withdrawn, felt worse than I did at that moment. I even sought refuge at the next evening's bible session by going forward to the mercy bench and confessing to an indifferent deity that from then on I would forego the pleasures of sin and become as dour and nutty as my keepers. As my sins at the time consisted of smoking a very occasional Honeysuckle cigarette, lying, going to movies, an irresolute lusting after the sins of the flesh, and other things that would have had the devil laughing himself to death, I deliberately rushed from the straight-and-narrow on the day after my release from camp, and went to a Saturday matinée at the old Teck Theatre at the corner of Broadview Avenue and Queen Street. Say what you will about sin, like sex and smoking it's great to get back to it!

Recently, some old Cabbagetown wino, in a so-called sociological study of one of my old neighborhoods, now called Trefann Court (which, incidentally, should have been burned down as a health hazard fifty years ago), told a naive young journalist that I'd modelled a criminal character in my novel *Cabbagetown* after a guy, whom he named, that had gone to school with me. I told the journalist and his publisher that the old man's accusation, and the journalist's implication, that my books were *romans à clef*, with characters modelled after real people, was literary slander. As a matter of fact none of my boyhood or youthful friends became criminals.

Until my on-the-road days years later, my only brush with the law came one winter day when we lived at 42 Lewis Street in lower Riverdale. A small gang of us used to go down to the empty lots north of the ship channel and play touch football in the sand. (On one occasion we went down there on Easter Sunday and made a raft which we paddled around in a pond beside a tar factory. I fell in and ruined a brand-new $18 grey Easter suit my mother had made the down payment on at Morrison's Credit Clothiers.) Anyhow, on this particular day we tired of playing in the sand, and decided to board one of the tied-up lake boats which were wintered along the ship channel. These ships were usually guarded by a watchman who made his quarters on one of them for the winter. Whether the watch-

12

man was around or not that day I don't remember, but we broke into the galley and crews' mess and proceeded to have a throwing fight with the ship's chinaware, ending up by spraying the ship's interior, and ourselves, with fire extinguishers.

A few days later a special constable, who combed the East End beaches on a never-ending safari against fornicators, vagrants, rubbydubs, and, especially, youthful depredators, knocked on our door and handed me a summons inviting me to Juvenile Court to face a charge of malicious damage to property. The special constable, whom we called "Detective French," promoting him before his superiors did, gave me his sternest stare and warned me of the dire consequences of not going to court.

A couple of days later, along with four or five other members of the gang, my teeth brushed, hair combed, and wearing my best Sunday clothes, I stood in the dock and faced Juvenile Court Judge Mott. Because I was the oldest of the group by a couple of months, I bore the brunt of Judge Mott's wrath. I remember that at one stage of the proceedings he threatened to place me in the Working Boys' Home for a couple of months, "to straighten you out and give you a realization of the seriousness of the charge you face." I was the only boy not accompanied by his mother, for my mother couldn't afford to take a day off from work. We were each fined $10 and costs, and my fine (which I later repaid) was taken care of by one of the boys' mothers, Mrs. Reitberg, Alex Reitberg's mother, from Empire Avenue.

From then on I suppose I had a record as a juvenile delinquent and I became the natural prey of another type of "social worker," the gentlemen of the Big Brother Movement. One day, when I was still fifteen, I was visited on lower Logan Avenue where we then lived, by one of these guys. He told me he was going to get me a season ticket to the Broadview YMCA (which he did), and then he pulled me on to his knee and kissed me on the cheek. I was having no part of that caper and I broke away. I guess I'd been aware of homosexuals since my preteens, and if anyone *was* one, he was. I used him as my model for Mr. Gurney in *Cabbagetown*.

Today, and ever since the day of the Big Brother's pass at me, I've had no use for *that* organization. I recognize that my attitude is an unfair one, and that by and large most members of the Big Brother Movement are decent, helpful heterosexuals. Nevertheless I wouldn't give a dime to see them form the Honor Guard at the Second Coming of Christ.

Though my mother was to live until I was 55 and I had a

13

couple of grandchildren of my own, I'd like to tell the rest of her story now.

Because of her pride, stubbornness, shame or whatnot my mother turned down many invitations from other members of her family to return to England. I guess the last time she saw my father—the last time I saw him anyway—was in a Toronto court, where my mother had taken him on a charge of non-support of his two sons. She never did get any support from him, as far as I know, and she brought up my brother and me, and two younger half-sisters who were born of a disastrous common-law union later, in the best way she could as a working woman. She held many unskilled little jobs, and when these failed her she worked by the day scrubbing floors and cleaning house for sloppy broads too lazy to do it themselves; pay: two bucks and carfare on the days she could get the jobs.

For a period of some years she worked as a counter woman in the T. Eaton Company's employees' cafeteria on downtown Hayter Street. In those long-gone spring days Toronto was more militarily British than Manchester or Glasgow, and boasted the largest regular and militia garrison in North America. Every Toronto school had a cadet corps. On the day of the annual public and secondary schools cadet parade down University Avenue, in my red tunic and blue serge knickers, I would take a chum or two to the cafeteria where my mother worked, and she would sneak us a meat pie apiece and a glass of milk. With our dummy wooden rifles under our arms we would stroll home along the downtown streets munching the meat pies and other things she would place in a bag for us.

From the day she took my father to court she dismissed him from her life and refused from then until her death ever to talk about him to me. During the war I paid a visit to my birthplace, and though I asked my mother's younger brother John, her younger sister Nellie, and even my father's sister about him, none of them knew what had happened to him.

Only towards the end of her middle age, while my brother and I were away to the war, did my mother get the kind of job that suited her, one she should have had years before. She became a member of the night office-cleaning staff of the Lever Bros. soap company and began buying a small cottage in the city's nearby East End. She wrote to me all through the war, telling me about winning medals for her blood donations, and how she had walked home from work during the big blizzard of 1944 in snow up to her waist. She was only a little bit of a woman, but

14

as tough and dauntless as they come. I don't think she ever weighed as much as a hundred pounds until she was over fifty.

She worked at Lever's until after the war, when she was old enough to draw the old age pension. My sister Marg married a young man when he returned from overseas, and my sister June married a man who remained in the R.C.A.F. Today Marg, who is a grandmother several times, lives in a small community north of Toronto, where her husband works for the township. June and her husband live in Ottawa.

My brother, who is a painter with the Toronto Board of Education, lived with my mother in the cottage, which he finished paying for, until the old lady became senile and we had to put her in a nursing home. She died of pneumonia at the age of 79.

I guess what I remember most about my mother is not her youthful beauty, though she had been a beautiful young woman, but her strength, intractability, and self-reliance, which I for better or worse have inherited. Among my good memories of her are the many times during periods of unemployment in the Depression years when she gave me her last dime to buy myself a package of tobacco and papers. Perhaps the mental picture of her I will never lose, and the one that sums up for me the kind of woman she was, is of lying awake long after midnight and hearing her in the kitchen, after a long day of working for someone else and having to get up early in the morning to work again, scrubbing our laundry on a scrubbing board or ironing it on the kitchen table.

I suppose that the professional sociologists and psychologists could find a great many errors in my mother's life-style and in the way she brought her children up. Her conduct at times, out of sheer ignorance of the consequences and what it might do to the psyches of her children, especially to me who was the oldest, was lamentable and injurious. Nevertheless she was a good, clean, hard-working mother to us all, and a credit to the working class.

I didn't cry for her when she was buried, for crying wouldn't have been enough.

School was always a breeze to me, and I wrote my high school entrance examinations at 13, failing them by 6 marks in grammar. This didn't bother me particularly, but because my marks in all other subjects were quite high my teacher should have either given me a second examination in grammar, or given me the benefit of the doubt. He didn't, and I stubbornly refused to continue school all summer in order to do the examinations again in August. Besides I had to work during the summer months.

I'll admit that grammar wasn't my strongest subject, and still isn't. Mathematics was one of my weaker ones too, but I managed an 87 in that subject. Anyhow, because of my failure I was banished to a technical high school where the dodo and dingbat types of teachers we had in those days thought that anything was good enough for the scruffy working-class kids who were destined to be graduated as printer's devils, sign-painters, milliners' assistants, sewing-machine or turret lathe operators, or better still to drop out of school at fourteen and spend the rest of their days on shipping floors, parcelling desks, or as waitresses and elevator operators.

I remained in the technical school for almost three years, and as God is my judge the only things I learned there (and have now happily forgotten) was to become an excellent draftsman and in printing class the layout of the printing compositor's California case.

My technical school days were far from happy, for not only did I recognize that we were being conned by a stupid educational system and even more stupid teachers and instructors, but I was barred from all after-school activities by having to work as a bicycle delivery boy for a Danforth Avenue fruit store from 3.30 to 6 p.m. every schoolday, and from 9 a.m. to midnight on Saturdays, for $3 a week.

I was too small to make any of the school athletic teams, but I was an excellent long-distance runner, coming in third out of fifty-four starters in a six-mile cross-country race through the farmlands, flying fields, and river valleys that are now East York, Don Mills, and the former town of Leaside, interior suburbs of present-day Toronto. The school magazine, the *Tech Tatler*, called me "The sweetheart of the race" because at 13 I was the youngest finisher I guess.

One of the after-school activities I missed was taking part in the various shows put on in the auditorium, especially one musical show I particularly admired. I became thoroughly stage-struck and fell in love with every girl in the show, through attending all of their noon-hour rehearsals. Not that I'd have ever been invited into the school's showbiz clique of course, no more than I was ever invited into the group of literary figures who put together the high school paper.

I often submitted short pieces of horrible verse to both the printing class paper and the *Tech Tatler*, but that's as far as it went. It gives me great satisfaction today to realize that all the school *literati* probably ended up as hairdressers and drivers of moving vans.

With the exception of a couple of effeminate pseudo-jocks who liked to coach athletic teams or supervise the nude swimming in the school pool after four p.m. the teachers were an underpaid, undereducated, and supercilious bunch of suburban twits, who looked forward all day to returning to their bungalows in the O'Connor Drive district to tend their petunias.

If they didn't know enough or care enough to teach us anything, I didn't give a damn about learning anything, so I didn't. I failed my first year, Grade Nine, exams for psychological reasons that were beyond their comprehension. At the end of my second year in Grade Nine I stood first in the class, just to show them I could when I wanted to.

I remember only three guys from my technical school days: Jim Christie, from my class, who became a junior hockey executive, "Sleepy" Boukydis of the Diana Sweets restaurants family, and a character called "Huck" Finn whose specialty was urinating from the balcony during affairs in the auditorium.

My drafting portfolio took second prize in the school's annual exhibition, the first prize being suspiciously given to a student whose father was an engineer, and who submitted a pictorial blueprint of a Pacific-type railroad steam locomotive. On performance I should have specialized in drafting in Grade Ten, but I just didn't have the three or four dollars to buy a T-square and a case of drafting instruments. I opted for the printing course instead, knowing that a school as stupid as mine wouldn't insist that I buy my own printing press before starting the course. Apart from learning the layout of the compositor's California case—which with a dime will get anybody a phone call —I learned that "upper case" meant capital letters and "lower case" means small-letter type.

Oh yes, I also became a member of the school tumbling team. I was a lousy tumbler, but because of my size I sat pretty at the top of the tumblers' pyramids.

Such subjects to me as physics, chemistry and geometry were just so many magician's tricks. It was nice to know that a needle will float on water due to water's surface tension, that a liquid always finds its own level, and that an isosceles triangle is one with two equal sides running at right angles (or is it?). I wondered what use I could ever make of the chemical symbols for hydrogen, nickel, and carborundum, and I was right: I've never made use of them during my life.

The only woman teacher we had, a very pretty one, used to give us geography lessons, or what came under the heading of "geography" in those days. One afternoon she informed us that if it weren't for the laws of gravitation everything on earth would be drawn and held to its centre. In my stupidity over the whole time-killing exercise I told her she was wrong. I suppose she'd never been challenged before in her whole young pretty life, and if she had taught that the moon was formed of Roquefort cheese most of her male students, who probably used her as a masturbatory fantasy, would have agreed.

"How am I wrong, *Mister* Garner?" she asked.

"Because if you were right everything on earth would flow to the equator."

Without a word she skittered down the aisle, picked up a large atlas on the way, and slammed me with it over the side of the head.

Perhaps I was wrong earlier: I probably learned more than I thought I was learning in technical school. I was wrong of course in mistaking the centre line of the earth's surface as the earth's centre, but I learned more from the young teacher's anger than I did from the lesson. From then on I never challenged a pretty girl's intellectual theorems, secondhand or not; if they were pretentious or screwy I just blamed them on something I'd said the day before, or on the time of the month.

I became a steady smoker in high school, and found that the most filling lunch for a dime was a Danforth Avenue cake shop's meat turnovers.

Forgetting my schooldays, which is one of the easiest periods of my life to forget, I left the technical school on my sixteenth birthday, February 22, 1929, and the next day began work as a copy boy on the *Toronto Daily Star*.

I remained a copy boy at the *Star* through the collapse of the New York stockmarket, and quit over my refusal to guide a party of giggling teenagers through the newspaper's new building the following November, just in time to meet the Great Depression head on and jobless. On second thought I didn't quit but was fired, having stubbornly refused to accept the alternative. This was a preview of the subsequent pattern of my life.

At the *Star* I ran copy from the old Toronto City Hall down Bay Street to the newspaper building on King Street, ran copy from the High Courts at Osgoode Hall, and from the County Courts on Adelaide Street East, picked up photographs of newly-demised celebrities and unknown accident victims, and learned to use a typewriter. I was always sending in little squibs about a horse dying on the street, a trolly running off its tracks, and other less-than-epochal stories of downtown Toronto. I would type them on a piece of editorial copy paper in the newsroom with "Garner" in the upper right-hand corner, and take them in and place them on the desk of the managing editor, H. C. Hindmarsh. One day Mr. Hindmarsh asked somebody who "Garner" was, and when he was told it was a copy boy he put through a two-dollar raise for me. I was now receiving $8 a week.

Returning to the city hall one afternoon by the side door on James Street I noticed an argument going on between a young man in a car and a policeman, who wouldn't allow him to park. The young man shouted, "Take it in yourself then!" and threw a test tube on to the city hall lawn. When the policeman picked it up and entered the building I went with him, up the elevator to the top floor, which then housed the city health department. I discovered that the test tube held a diphtheria smear sent in for analysis by a doctor, and carried down to the health department by the doctor's son, whom I'd seen throw it on the grass.

I sat down at a typewriter in the press room, typed "Garner" on a sheet of copy paper, and wrote a paragraph covering the incident, delivering it to the managing editor's office on my next trip to King Street. Within a few minutes a cyclone struck the *Star* editorial department. Mr. Hindmarsh came out into the newsroom, called Tim Reid, the city editor, gave orders to Fred Davis one of the paper's crack photographers (who was later to take all the pictures of the Dionne Quints), and sent Fred Griffin, the *Star*'s top reporter, to City Hall. Across my short submission Mr. Hindmarsh had written in thick black pencil, "This is important! What is being done about it?" I wish now that I'd retrieved my copy from a wastebasket, much as many

19

ex-*Star* men probably wish they had retrieved Ernest Hemingway's famous Toronto zoo story a few years earlier from what might have been the same basket. The story was printed on the front page, with pictures.

I was called into the managing editor's office, congratulated by Mr. Hindmarsh, given another two dollar raise (which gave me $10 a week, equal to the head copy boy's salary) and personally conducted around the third, fourth, and fifth floors of the building and introduced to Mr. Joseph Atkinson the president and paper's founder, Biddy Barr the chief librarian, the composing room foreman, the business manager, and other department heads by the awesome H.C.H. himself. Mr. Atkinson gave his secretary, Mr. Palmer, instructions to teach me shorthand to boot, every Thursday afternoon. I stopped the shorthand lessons when we reached Circle S, and was fired from the paper shortly afterwards. For a long time I regretted being fired from the *Star,* but looking back on it it may have been the best thing that ever happened to me.

Working at the *Star* not only taught me to type, but by watching the reporters, and once or twice even taking down their copy over headphones and writing it for the city desk—at 16!—I learned how to write sharp condensed prose. Through months of sitting in the city hall press bureau I also absorbed a great many things from such *Star* reporters as Gordon Sinclair (the press room cribbage champ), Athol Gow, the *Star* head police reporter, and many other reporters from the, then, four Toronto papers. I also learned that what a writer needs, more than mere formal education, which he doesn't really need at all, is a shallow knowledge of a great many things; things he can only learn outside of school.

The week after I was fired by the *Toronto Star* I got a job delivering telegrams for Canadian National Telegraphs. Working in a telegraph office might offer more preparation for writing than working on a newspaper, strange as it might seem. Two famous alumni of telegraph offices have been William Saroyan and Henry Miller.

I have been accused, since becoming a writer, of getting my inspiration from various other writers: Somerset Maugham, Ernest Hemingway, Theodore Dreiser, John Steinbeck and even James T. Farrell (who once reviewed a book of mine for the *Toronto Telegram* with what I can best describe as a patronizing attitude). My actual literary mentors were John Dos Passos, who taught me how realistic fiction should be written, and J. B. Priestley, who has written better about young romantic love than any author I have ever read.

Besides those two I have learned from and been influenced by countless other writers, while trying to imitate none. I have learned to write dialogue from John O'Hara, short stories from Hemingway and many other writers, the flashback and interior monologue from James Joyce, and from John Steinbeck I learned how to write with affectionate compassion for the poor and downtrodden. As a matter of fact I was as poor as anyone I have ever written about, for a great part of my life. I don't think though that I was ever downtrodden, for it was never my nature to let myself be. Even when we were on home relief during the Depression I always fought for my rights, and I remember leading a strike of handbill-deliverers against a shoe store owner in the Flatbush neighborhood of Brooklyn who was paying us 25¢ an hour, when I thought we should get 30¢. That got me kicked out of the Bowery YMCA, as other flare-ups of recalcitrance have got me kicked out of dozens of places since.

I think that the years I spent on the bum, as well as the years of my childhood when I had to live on charitable handouts, forged the abrasive personality I still wear today. The years on the bum coincided with the years when I was growing into manhood, and because of this, and their effect on my writing, they deserve mention here. Much that happened to me during those years has been long forgotten, but as a shorthand picture I can't do better than to write what I can recall.

One summer day in 1933 my friend Howard "Skinny" Moore and I set out for the United States with a package of makin's, a dime in cash, and a bag of my mother's cucumber sandwiches. We slept the first night on somebody's lawn in Oakville, Ontario, and made it to Niagara Falls the following day, hitching rides. We split the dime between us to cross one of the bridges to Niagara Falls, New York; I made it past the US Immigration, Skinny didn't. I went on to New York and Washington and ended up in California. And that's how it was done.

We were two of the many boys and young men who became bums, hoboes, migrant workers, or temporary tramps, call us what you will, who were part of the phenomenon of the Great Depression. During the years between 1930 and 1939 I travelled across Canada from Montreal to Vancouver and from Massachusetts to Mexico, with shorter serendipity trips here and there through the Canadian West, the US South, and the damndest places you ever heard of in search of work—"They're taking on tomato pickers in Santa Barbara"—in search of change, for adventure, or just for the fun of it. . . .

I rode the Rock Island when Johnny Cash was still a school-boy, from Tucumcari, New Mexico to Kansas City, Kansas. I rode freights on a score of railroads, but never made it on the Blue Streak of the Cotton Belt, the fastest freight train in the United States, one of the smaller regrets of my life.

I've ridden a transcontinental transport truck across the Arizona high desert, with the jackrabbits jumping in the headlight beams like Saskatchewan grasshoppers, and a way freight from Calgary to Revelstoke, British Columbia, through the Connaught and spiral tunnels of the CPR, breathing coal smoke and exhilaration. . . .

I lived one summer in New York on 60¢ a day, and stooked wheat along the Soo Line and Assiniboine Line in southern Saskatchewan for a buck a day and board, which was the going wage that year. When I'm asked why I rode the freights and beat my way through much of Canada and the United States instead of working at the terrible little jobs I had in Toronto between trips, my best answer is that when I was home I was poor, but when I was on the road I was merely broke. And there's a lot of difference between the two.

I wrote a short story about travelling through West Virginia, called "Another Time, Another Place, Another Me," but here is another incident that happened on the same trip. I was picked up and sentenced to seven days in the county jail on a vagrancy charge, in Keyser, West Virginia. The long term prisoners, a bunch of Appalachian hillbillies without the Southerner's courtesy or the Yankee's sense, put me through a kangaroo court on the charge of breaking into jail. They humiliated me, taunted me, and gave me all the joe jobs to do. On the morning of my discharge the turnkey's wife, who was also the jail cook, asked me to take the prisoners' breakfast out to the cell blocks. I carried a large tin platter of fried eggs and a pot of coffee into the jail yard, shouted the breakfast call to the prisoners, and— while they watched me in impotent rage and horror—I dumped the eggs on the ground, poured the coffee over them, and did a victorious war dance on the mess. Then despite the din I shouted a soldier's goodbye to the prisoners, walked back through the turnkey's house to the street, and hurriedly caught a coal truck out of town.

There was a kid riding a flatcar on a CPR train out of Broadview, Saskatchewan, who got his foot caught in a coupling, and had to ride like that until the train hit the top of a grade and we could release his foot. I'll never forget his ashen face and the blood seeping out of his boot. . . .

In Kamloops, British Columbia, I worked for a time in a relief camp for 20¢ a day, and another year I helped build a generator building or something at the RCAF station in Trenton, Ontario, for the same money. Driving past it one time when my children were small I told them I'd built the place for $5 a month, but I don't think they believed me.

In Lordsburg, New Mexico, I slept in the same cell in the town lockup once occupied by Billy The Kid. I don't think the motel proprietor there believed me either when I drove through the town last year. He made a second perusal of my American Express card.

Along with a few thousand Canadian and American boys, I came off the road long enough to fight in the Spanish Civil War, and Skinny Moore is buried, I suppose, in a mass bulldozed grave somewhere near Teruel, in Spain. Generally speaking the guys on the road were not political at all, although in the American Northwest the older hoboes still carried the old red Wobbly card of the I.W.W. (Industrial Workers of the World) anarcho-syndicalist movement. The Communists tried to organize the hoboes with very little success. Here in Canada we had the Regina riots, when the Mounties tried to stop several hundred hoboes from riding the freights to Ottawa. The American government under Franklin D. Roosevelt was much smarter than its Canadian counterpart, and it set up several administrations such as the Works Projects Administration and the Civilian Conservation Corps, which gave jobs to thousands of young men.

The worst railroad bulls in North America were Texas Slim in Longview, Texas, and Step-'n-a-Half in Marshall, Texas—both on the Texas Pacific Railroad; Denver Bob on the Denver, Rio Grande Western; and in Canada, Capreol Red of the CNR at Capreol. The only one I failed to meet was Denver Bob.

Sex on the road has become part of the hobo legend but it was largely imaginary. A lot of guys used to brag that some woman whose house they hit for a lump (a food handout at the door) invited them in to help move a bed, but it was mostly in their minds. We were generally as ascetic as monks. There was some homosexuality on the road with a few old pederasts travelling with their younger "punk," but we were generally sexually frustrated heterosexuals. There were always prostitutes in the cities, and sometimes a round-heeled girl would wander into a hobo jungle. Most of us were too broke to buy it, and too dirty and lousy most of the time to attract it. . . .

I spent plenty of time in jail cells as an overnight guest, from Baltimore to Yuma, Arizona and from Windsor to Vancouver, although I also stayed at a great many YMCA's and hit the missions from Montreal's Municipal, "The Muni," to a place on Vancouver's Pender Street. I also spent a little time in the "vag tank" of Los Angeles' Lincoln Heights Jail. I was run out of several towns, and in Windsor, where I'd failed in a try to cross the border to Detroit, I was transported one morning to the county line in a police car and put on the highway. That was a lucky break for me, for I was picked up by a young Italian in a car with Illinois plates and given a 600-mile hitch to Troy, New York, the longest single ride I ever picked up on the highway.

In Coteau Junction, west of Montreal, several of us were pulled off a CNR train and treated pretty badly by a sadistic CNR police sergeant and his men. It was during an Empire Economic Conference in Ottawa, and they were stopping all vagrants from going there. This CNR bull stood us up alongside the train where we were frisked. None of us had any money but a foreign-born guy who had about $12; he was made to spend it on a train ticket to somewhere. The rest of us were then ordered out of the yards and on to the highway.

I always liked being on the road better in the United States than in Canada. The CNR and CPR police set up block points— the CNR's at Transcona, east of Winnipeg, and the CPR's at Nipigon on the north shore of Lake Superior. It took a lot of ingenuity to get past the train searches, but somehow most of us made it.

Things got so hungry riding through the northern Ontario bush country that the government had to set up a relief station at Nakina, where the hoboes were given a meal ticket to a Chinese restaurant. One time I signed on as a drover in charge of a couple of carloads of cattle coming east from Winnipeg on the CPR; that time I "rode the cushions" as we called it, and came through the bush in an old passenger coach attached to the freight train. My only duties were to see that the cattle were fed and watered in such feeding points as White River, Ontario.

Railroad employees could be about equally divided between good and bad, and most of the time there were so many of us riding the freights that even the bad ones were afraid to be anything but good. I'll always remember a dining car steward on the CPR who used to throw bundles of food down from his train as it came off the bridge over the Red River from Winnipeg to St. Boniface . . . St. Boniface had one of the biggest hobo jungles in Canada. . . .

After I came home from Spain I went legitimate for a while and became, of all things, the manager of a cooperative grocery store in Port Credit, Ontario. I finally gave this up in 1939 and went down to Southwestern Ontario to work the tobacco harvest. I arrived too early, and picked apples and strawberries while sleeping in an empty boxcar on a siding of the old Michigan Central Railroad. When the harvest began I hired out as a primer, that is the guy who strips the prime leaves from the plants in the fields. One Sunday morning we listened to the radio as Canada declared war on Germany, and I had the farmer pay me off, and returned to Toronto and joined the army.

Young people today are either indifferent to the Great Depression or have an exaggerated view of it. It was tough, but it wasn't all hunger and sadness. There were picnics, corn roasts, and cheap dances. People still hadn't been divided one from the other by status and the family car, and we did things communally. Young people fell in love and married. After all, a married relief cheque was better than two single people getting nothing at all. People learned to cope with constant unemployment and penury, and many of them rose to heights of bravery and unselfishness they never would have reached in normal times. Babies were born, whether their fathers were employed or not, and their young mothers made do with handmade or hand-me-down layettes. A wicker laundry basket is just as good a bassinet as a store-bought one.

Do you want to know something? I don't think I'd have wanted to miss the Great Depression for the world.

To go back a few years, I must relate an incident that has had a great bearing on my choice of books ever since. At the age of 12 I joined the newly-opened Ashdale & Gerrard Street Toronto Public Library, children's section. In those days librarians were not the educated specialists they are today, and I think most of them were actually the old maid mistresses of retired city aldermen. As soon as I received my library card I asked the harpy at the desk if she could recommend an adventure book suitable for me. She walked a few steps to a rack and came back with R. D. Blackmore's *Lorna Doone*. I took it home, but found I couldn't read it. In fact the only person I have ever met who *has* read it was an old sportswriter friend who has also read Dickens' *Bleak House*. Nothing short of ten years in solitary could make me read the book even today.

Lorna Doone prevented me from reading many pre-twentieth century classics, I am sure, just as watching *Kismet,* starring DeWolfe Hopper, at the old Broadview Theatre prevented me forever from watching costume movies. Despite my belief that much seventeenth, eighteenth and nineteenth century literature is dull and uninspiring, my reading has been catholic in the extreme, and I have dutifully read some Shakespeare, pruriently read Chaucer and Boccaccio, and partly read some of the Russian, French, Spanish and German classics. George Bernard Shaw, in his *The Intelligent Woman's Guide To Socialism And Capitalism* turned me into a social radical, something neither Marx, Engels, nor Proudhon could do. Hilaire Belloc almost reconverted me again, and his friend G. K. Chesterton, while entertaining me immensely, gave my radicalism a tinge of cynicism for which I am eternally grateful.

The only novel I have ever read five times is James Joyce's *Ulysses*, though I have read some other favorites more than once. The funniest book I have ever read, bar none, is Joseph Heller's *Catch-22*, and the best novel I have read during the past ten years is Ken Kesey's *One Flew Over The Cuckoo's Nest*. Over the years I have read practically all the good contemporary novelists and short story writers, English, Irish and American, though my tastes run to American fiction. For years following Word War Two, I collected books by my favorite authors, a bibliophile who built up a fiction library of 1500 titles. One day, just before moving from one apartment house to another, I decided to get rid of them and gave them as the basis of a library to a Salvation Army Alcoholic Clinic. I thought that seeing as how alcohol had done so much for me, I should return the favour.

In 1933, at the age of 19, I beat my way by highway and freight train to California, first to New York, then down the Atlantic coast to Washington, west to Cincinnati, south to Jackson, Mississippi, and west again across Louisiana, Texas, New Mexico, and Arizona to Los Angeles. For a couple of months I settled down in various missions around Los Angeles' Fifth and Main streets, and spent almost every afternoon in the public library, where I began by reading the books on abnormal psychology, including Krafft-Ebing, moved on to Freud, Jung, and Adler, and from the psychologists to the philosophers, Spinoza, William James, Schopenhauer, Descartes, and Nietzsche.

The first hint I received that I might someday become a writer came one evening in New York, probably in 1935, when I was bucking the extra board as a bus boy, usually working lunches for 65¢ and one free meal, for Stewart's or the Exchange Buffet chains of cafeterias. Having to live at the time on 65¢ a day I rented a cell covered over with chicken wire in a Bowery flophouse called The Majestic Hotel at the corner of Houston Street. One of my fellow denizens of this two-bits-a-night luxurious hostelry was a young man named Slats Fisher, who had recently been sprung from the Nevada State Penitentiary after serving time for safe-cracking. Some evenings Slats and I would walk up to Union Square to listen to and argue with the political orators, mainly Communists.

This was in the days before paperback books, and the bins on the sidewalks in front of the second-hand bookstores on lower Fourth Avenue were filled with old magazines. My eye was caught by some copies of *Story* magazine, then edited by Whit Burnett and Martha Foley. I glanced through one of them, read the first paragraph of a story called "The Happiest Man On Earth" by Albert Maltz, and bought the magazine for a nickel. That night I read the whole magazine while lying on my bunk in the flophouse. The Albert Maltz story was about a desperate jobless father who, to feed his kids, gratefully accepted a job driving a truck carrying nitro-glycerine. The projected life span for such drivers was a mere month or two, but the pay was so

27

fantastic during the Depression that he took the job. Another short story I remember, which may have been written by Alvah Bessie, in *Story*, was about an old derelict who made a precarious living fishing through open sidewalk gratings for dropped coins. Two young punks happened by, saw that the old man was fishing for a lost half-dollar, stuck a wad of gum on the end of a stick they were carrying, and fished up the coin themselves. They left the old man in tears, cheated out of what would probably have been his biggest coup of the day.

These two stories, and subsequent ones I read in second-hand literary magazines, were the first utterly fascinating pieces of short realistic fiction I had ever read. Suddenly I wanted to become a short story writer and write stories such as these, about ordinary people, living ordinary lives, happy or sad about the everyday things of life. The unrealistic pap I had been fed up to then by the big consumer magazines was junk, as I had somehow always felt it was.

Later on I was taken on by Stewart's as a regular swingshift bus boy, sometimes working days in the Bronx or Queens, evenings in Times Square, and nights in Brooklyn or Greenwich Village. I met thousands of people, the Jews in the Seventh Avenue garment district, the stock brokers' clerks down near Wall Street and The Battery, and the homosexuals and lesbians in the Village (where we had a policeman standing between the doors to the Men's and Women's washrooms, allowing only one person to enter each washroom at a time) and the cold and hungry derelicts in other parts of the city who dropped in, bought a cup of coffee with their last nickel, then sat at their table to get warm, sometimes falling asleep.

After reading some old issues of *Story*, and some of the college quarterlies, I bought myself a pad of notepaper and a pencil and tried to write short stories in my flophouse room. Nothing came of my efforts but badly spelled, poorly punctuated, and unorganized pieces of beginner's fiction which relied heavily on the symbolism of birds taking flight or other mock-romantic, amateur notions of what a short story was. To become a short story writer was too difficult a job, and after a few more efforts I gave it up.

By this time I'd worked my way up from pearl-diving in the kitchen of the One Park Restaurant (in the basement of No. 1 Park Avenue) to head bus boy, and this was followed by a job as a door-to-door salesman on Long Island selling soap and cleaning products that had been recovered from warehouse fires, probably set by the bankrupt owners. I became a pretty good salesman, and from my 7¢ commission on each 25¢ package I sold I made about $3 a day. I even moved from the Bowery to a rooming house run by a landlady called Mrs. Bull, right on the corner of Sixth Avenue and 52nd Street, where the elevated trains threatened to crash through my window.

That winter I returned to Toronto, filled with an urge to write short stories but still unable to write them. Occasionally I would make a half-hearted stab at it, only to give it up when it proved too difficult.

Up to now I had told nobody that I wanted to become a writer, for I believed then, and I still believe, that a beginning writer should keep his anonymity to protect himself from the amateur criticism of family, friends and others. Some people who rush to show their early attempts at writing are so hurt and shamed by the criticism they receive that they quit there and then. A writer has to learn his own trade by himself, writing for himself and to himself, until he knows he has become skilful enough to submit a manuscript to a publisher or editor.

One day in the fall of 1936 I sat down and printed with pen and ink (even now I don't write in longhand but "print" with a pen) a short piece I titled "Cabbagetown," which I mailed to *Canadian Forum*. To my delighted amazement the magazine accepted and published it. I had suddenly become a published writer.

My old Bowery flophouse friend Slats Fisher and George Bernard Shaw, the most unlikely combination I can think of, had made me a socialist. I read all the socialist, communist, and anarchist literature I could get from the Gerrard & Broadview Toronto Public Library. Slats Fisher had become a political mentor of mine one evening as we walked along 14th Street when he said, "Those Commies are a bunch of nuts, but communism or socialism is the only thing for the working man." This coming from an unregenerated confessed criminal was an eye-opening revelation to me.

I joined a C.C.F. (Cooperative Commonwealth Federation) group which met in a vacant-store clubroom at the corner of Logan and Gerrard Streets in Toronto's East End, and in a few months I was voted president. Those were happy days, for I was a rabid young radical neophyte, living in a rooming house on Langley Avenue, just outside the gates of Riverdale Park, from which I could hustle girls to my room. Ted Joliffe, later to become leader of the C.C.F. opposition in the Ontario Legislature, came down to our club almost every week and showed us how to run it, not in any supercilious way but as a dedicated friend. At the time I was working as a clerk in a haberdashery, a Style Cravat Shop, on Danforth Avenue. During one of the years when I was a ranting, dedicated socialist I took a freight train to Ottawa, as a CCF delegate to the first Canadian Youth Congress. My Ottawa "hotel" on that occasion was a cell cot in a downtown police station, where I'd asked the desk sergeant for a bed for the night.

The proclaimed leader of the socialist faction at the Congress was a man who is now very high in the heirarchy of the United Steel Workers. To me he was a doctrinaire socialist functionary, whom I disliked on sight, whether he deserved it or not, just as I was to dislike so many doctrinaire Communist functionaries later on. We were a cross section of Canadian Depression youth, from the fascist followers of Adrien Arcand, through Conservatives, Liberals CCFers, Communists, Trotskyites, and even Fieldites, and Lovestoneites, and I wonder what ever happened to the last two I have named.

We held public meetings in what I remember as a large theatre or opera house, interminable party caucus meetings, visits to the visitors' gallery in the Parliament Buildings, and we CCFers were introduced to a caucus of the handful of CCF sitting members of Parliament. I was much impressed by the courtesy shown us by Mr. Woodsworth, the CCF Party leader at the time, and the deputy leader, Mr. Coldwell. I was completely turned off however by Mr. Tommy Douglas, the Saskatchewan ex-Baptist minister, who gave us what I considered to be a supercilious brush-off. I have never liked the man since.

I made one insane, inane call to revolutionary arms at a public meeting—much as I read about young radicals doing the same thing today—and have been ashamed of my naive exhortation ever since. The Toronto *Daily Star* gave me a three-column head for that piece of ill-timed rhetoric, which I wish they hadn't.

When the Congress was over I returned to Toronto in the same way I had gone to Ottawa, by freight train.

Interviewers and people who write about me seem to be intrigued by the various crazy jobs I've had, especially the one where I soldered cemetery flower holders in a Toronto tinsmith shop. To me this was one of my saner jobs, along with buffing doll's legs in a toy factory, learning to chew snuff (called "snoose") while running a shavings blower in a small plant that made 12-inch wooden rulers, running a button-patterning machine until I carved the pattern in the back of my left index finger, and packing Lux soap flakes.

Believe me, I had crazier jobs than those. In 1928, when I was fifteen, a friend of mine named Chuck Sanderson and I were the first two people to enter the gates of the Canadian National Exhibition, after sleeping outside since early the evening before. Today the kids who perform this zany feat are given watches, passes to the Midway rides, and other things, but all Chuck and I got was our pictures in the Toronto papers.

I suppose it must have been the year before this that I went down to the Exhibition grounds early and found myself a job on the Midway, in a show called Bill Rice's Water Circus, where I became a diving show property boy. Among such duties as pumping air with a bicycle pump to Father Neptune who kept his head in a small air bucket under the water of the tank until it was time to make his appearance on the surface with the ballyhoo chorus mermaids, I also used to cover the surface of the small tank with gasoline and set it afire just before one of our high-divers made his dive. Many years later I wrote a short story about this, called "Captain Rafferty," which first appeared in *The Yellow Sweater And Other Stories*.

As I've probably already mentioned, besides my being the most indefatigable job-hustler I ever knew, my mind ever since I was a kid has been the receptacle of more trivia than I'll ever be able to use. This store of mostly useless information not only got me one of the craziest jobs I had during the Depression, but also won me my first tailored-to-measure suit.

I forget what year it was, but I attended the Danforth Avenue Businessmen's annual picnic in East Toronto's Withrow Park one evening just as a Master-of-Ceremonies was asking contestants for a quiz contest to step up on the stage. My only previous stage appearance had been in my very early teens, when I won first prize in a Charleston dancing contest in a Parliament Street movie house, long torn down to make room to build the Regent Park Housing Project. Anyhow, at the businessmen's picnic I and several older male contestants mounted the stage for the quiz show.

One by one they were eliminated, unable to answer questions like: "Name the German general who helped Wellington defeat Napolean at Waterloo?" "What are both cross-threads of a piece of fabric called?" "Who invented the cotton gin?" and other such esoteric trivia that was right up my alley. I answered them easily: General von Blücher, the warp and woof, Eli Whitney. Finally I was the last contestant on the stage, and I could see that the M.C. wasn't happy that the shabby kid standing alone in front of him had eliminated all the local Danforth Avenue dudes, some of whom may have been his friends. He searched through his question cards for the one final question I had to answer to win, hoping, I suppose, it would be the one that would eliminate me too. The prize was a Tip Top Tailor custom-made suit, and I not only needed a suit, custom-made or not, but I wasn't going to allow any Danforth businessman scissorbill to beat me out of the prize.

He'd probably have beaten me on a question demanding job expertise or dealing in physics or chemistry, none of which were my strong points, but out of his own stupidity he picked not the toughest question but the one that needed the longest answer. I can see him leering down at me yet, probably either an undertaker or a florist, who seem to have been our perennial aldermen and controllers in the city government from what was then Toronto's Ward One.

He gave the crowd a supercilious aldermanic grin, turned to me and spat out "Name the forty-eight states of the United States!"

I had him! American geography has always been my forte.

I stepped up to the microphone and began: "Main, New Hampshire, Vermont, Massachusetts, Rhode Island, Connecticut, New York. . . ." I almost missed Delaware, but put it in after Virginia rather than ahead of it. I could see him ticking them off on his answer card, as the crowd was as silent as the crowd that watched David slingshot Goliath.

". . . Montana, Wyoming, Colorado, New Mexico, Arizona, Utah, Idaho. . . ."

There were a few titters from the crowd, and the M.C.'s face began to purple with embarrassed apoplexy.

I finished going south to north along the Pacific coast, "California, Oregon and Washington."

The Master-of-Ceremonies cried triumphantly, "You missed Maryland!"

I said into the microphone, "I did like hell!"

Some of the crowd laughed, and others began to boo. One big guy from down on Empire Avenue stepped to the platform steps. I knew him as a man who worked at the Eastern Avenue gasworks and also played amateur softball in a small field at the foot of Logan Avenue. He shouted up into the purple face of the M.C., who stepped back a couple of paces, "I know the kid said Maryland, because I play the horses at Laurel, and I was waiting for him to name the state. He's won fair and square."

The crowd began shouting, "Sure he did! Give him the prize, you phony bastard!" and a few other south-end-of-the-ward compliments.

The Master-of-Ceremonies, seeing not only his Rotary honesty but a hundred future votes slipping away from him, handed me a voucher for a suit from Tip Top Tailors, and I read it, stuffed it into my pocket, and jumped down into the crowd where several members of our Riverdale Park gang were waiting. Later in the evening somebody unknown to me let the air out of the tires of the M.C.'s car that was parked on Carlaw Avenue. I have no doubt it was somebody from my south end neighborhood. I don't think any of my neighbors ever liked any of our aldermen, especially those who were undertakers or florists.

The next day I took my voucher to the Tip Top store on Danforth between Carlaw and Pape and they measured me up for a grey double-breasted suit. I wore it for years, until I became a clerk in the Style Cravat Shop. There I bought myself a pepper-and-salt Irish twist, thirty percent off, from Warren K. Cooke, whose line we handled. *That* suit I wore to the Spanish Civil War.

There was a strange sequel to winning the Danforth Businessmen's quiz. I was given a job by an amateur vaudeville producer, who used to send me around to various Toronto and suburbs movie houses, where I became a professional quiz contestant. The pay was two bucks a night, and a chance to watch the picture for free. I remember playing the Pape Theatre, a couple in the city's west end, and one in the town of New Toronto. My theatrical life was a brief one, and it ended one night at the Beaches Theatre when the impresario ran out on me with my two bucks. It was fun while it lasted though, but that's showbiz.

The funniest part about it is that this is the first time I ever mentioned it as one of the crazy jobs I held in the Depression.

When the Spanish Civil War broke out I became involved in it, both idealogically and personally. Through a combination of my life up to then—through class, intellect and political idealogy—I was an anti-fascist, and still am. When I discovered that foreigners, the forerunners of what were to become the International Brigades, were fighting with the Spanish Loyalists in University City and Casa de Campo on the outskirts of Madrid I knew I had to join them. I paid for a small classified ad in the personal column of the *Toronto Star* asking for financial support to get me to Spain. The *Star* sent a reporter to interview me, and the subsequent paragraph about the Canadian nut who wanted to go fight in a foreign war may have eventually helped me to get there.

I finally did go, through the tremendously efficient organization set up by the international Comintern of the U.S.S.R., leaving Toronto in early February, 1937, at the age of twenty-three. Though the International Brigades (there were five of them) were made up of a social, professional and leftist cross section of the world's manhood, I'm very sure I was one of the few who crossed the Pyrenees into Spain wearing a homburg and spats.

Some of my letters home from Spain were published in the Toronto papers, but I made no notes nor did any writing about the war while I was there. On my return from Spain I tried my hand once again at writing short stories, but they were all rejected by U.S. and Canadian magazines, and I tore them all up. I wrote another small essay titled "Christmas Eve In Cabbagetown," which the *Canadian Forum* accepted and printed in their December 1938 issue. My writing apprenticeship was still haphazard, and I had no real intention of becoming a writer.

One evening during the spring of 1939 I was walking across Toronto's Bloor Street Viaduct when I turned to the girl who was walking with me and said, "War is going to break out in September." "You're crazy!" she exclaimed angrily, though I knew her anger had been caused by much more than my war prognostication. Though this young lady, like a great many other people, did not believe World War Two was imminent, I somehow knew it was. And because I knew it I was dead set against getting involved with a girl. Also, I hadn't tried to write anything for months.

In July I hitchhiked down to Southwestern Ontario, where I harvested apples and picked berries, waiting for the tobacco harvest to begin. I was too early, and I went hungry much of the time, sleeping either in a small park in the town of Simcoe or on a sidetracked boxcar on a Michigan Central branch line. When the tobacco harvest began I hired out from the slave market in Simcoe as a "primer" at $3 a day. My first boss was an ignorant South Carolina redneck who ate with his fingers and thought *The Wabash Cannonball* the greatest piece of music ever written. Later I worked for a Canadian family on a farm about ten miles west of Simcoe. From my apple and berry-picking jobs plus a stint on a haying crew, I picked up the theme of a short story I wasn't to write until the following year, "The Conversion Of Willie Heaps." From my jobs on the two tobacco farms I gained the knowledge to write the short story "Hunky" many years later.

One Sunday we heard over the radio that Germany had invaded Poland, after signing a non-aggression pact and a treaty to split Poland in two with the Soviet Union. Great Britain declared war on Germany and my forecast was proved correct. A week later the radio told us that Canada had also declared war on Germany, and that afternoon I told my boss's wife that I was returning to Toronto to join the army. "What about Benny?" she asked, mentioning another member of the priming crew who had been big-mouthing at every meal how he had been trained on the new Bren gun in a Brantford militia unit and was just dying to join up. "I don't know about him," I said. "You know what I think?" Mrs. Smith asked me. "I think he's just a bullshooter. I sorta knew though that you'd want to go." She gave me what money was coming to me, kissed me, told me to be sure and write to them, and she'd send me cigarettes and things, told her daughter to drive me in the Model T to Simcoe and the bus depot, and I went.

The Smiths, if that was their name, were kind, hard-up farmers who had gone into tobacco a couple of years before when their sandy farm was found to be excellent for growing tobacco but nothing else. I used the South Carolina farmer as my model for the Belgian farmer in "Hunky," but only the shed I slept in, some of the technical things, and the flies that swarmed around our outdoors table, from the Smith farm.

I said goodbye to the Smith daughter at the Simcoe bus depot, placed my paper-wrapped bindle in a storage locker, and walked across the street, where I bought a pint of rye. I wasn't much of a drinker in those days, and I was thoroughly looped by the time I boarded the bus for Hamilton. Somewhere on the journey the driver threatened to throw me off if I didn't stop singing, but I made it to Hamilton and changed buses to Toronto. The next day, September 11, 1939—which was a Sunday if I remember right—I went down to the University Avenue Armories and joined the 23rd Medium Battery, Royal Canadian Artillery. We received a living allowance for the next few weeks until our barracks in the Government Building in the Canadian National Exhibition Grounds was readied, then we moved down there.

My unit went overseas in either December or January, but I was left behind as a Communist suspect for having fought in Spain. In March I had myself paraded before the colonel of the No. 2 District Depot and told him I wanted a discharge or I'd go over the hill; I hadn't joined the army to stay in Toronto. I was given a "Services No Longer Required" discharge and found a job putting up wooden hangars at Malton Airport.

After a month or so of this I quit the job, just as I'd quit every job I'd had before it, and hung around in a flat my mother rented in Toronto's East End, sleeping on the kitchen floor. One day I had an inspiration for a short story, which I titled "The Conversion Of Willie Heaps." It turned out to be a good story, without the phony symbolism and imaginative imagery I'd used in my previous attempts at short story writing. I wrote it at one sitting at the kitchen table using my hand-printed longhand. Though I felt it was my first real short story, I also knew that it was flawed by something, though I didn't know what at the time.

36

In late May I hitchhiked to Halifax, with the romantic idea of working my passage to England and joining the King's Own Yorkshire Light Infantry, the *Koylies,* from the county I had been born in. I failed to get a berth on a ship, but by a fortuitous accident I was passing the north gate of the naval dockyard one day when they were accepting recruits. I'd never been a sailor yet, so I joined the navy. Apparently they didn't care about the Spanish Civil War or Communism, for nothing was said about these things. I served in the navy from June 1940 to October, 1945. But more about that later.

The only writing I attempted during the war was in 1944, after being drafted to a shore depot in Quebec City. I was living in a rooming house above a restaurant and some stores on the Rue St. Jean, and one evening the old urge to write—which I'd been successful in quenching, mainly with beer and rum, for the past four years—hit me again. I began writing a novel about the war at sea which I titled *Convoy,* but this effort was torpedoed and sunk without trace after I'd written five or six pages. I wasn't willing yet to give the time and effort necessary to become a novelist.

In 1940 I'd been drafted to Quebec City to pick up one of the new corvettes being built there, but my ship wasn't ready before the ice formed in the river. In the meantime I was taken on strength of a small patrol boat, *H.M.C.S. Eileen,* and later on an armed yacht called the *Ambler.* I also met a girl there in Quebec City, an Acadian from the Gaspé Coast named Alice Gallant, and the following summer when I was serving on a corvette named *H.M.C.S. Arvida,* she came down to Halifax and we were married there, in St. Mark's Anglican Church on July 5, 1941. By the time I tried to write my novel *Convoy,* I was the father of a daughter and son.

In August 1945 I was one of the earliest dischargees, and was returned to Canada from Newfoundland on a destroyer. In Toronto I was given 90 days accumulative leave. I went down to the Gaspé, and brought back my wife and children. My mother was then renting a small cottage, but with her, my two half-sisters, and *my* family it was like living in a phone booth. When my brother returned from the army in Europe conditions became intolerable. My wife wanted to go back home until I found a place for us to live, so before Christmas I put her and the kids on a train for her parents' family farm. If I'd known what I was to know later, I'd have bought my wife a commuter's ticket.

Just before New Year's, 1946 I rented a room in a rooming house on Toronto's St. Joseph Street, and bought myself notepaper, a fountain pen (there were no ballpoints then), and a pencil. I didn't buy myself the most necessary tool of all, an eraser, nor did I own either a dictionary or a *Roget's Thesaurus*. I also signed up with the Department of Veterans Affairs for a three-month course in Co-operative Management. The course would give both myself and my wife a small income during the winter, would give me the time on evenings and weekends to write a novel, and it seemed right up my alley after managing a co-operative grocery store seven years before.

On New Year's Day, 1946, I printed with my fountain pen the title, *Cabbagetown* at the head of a blank sheet of notepaper, and under it, "By Hugh Garner." The book I began to write that day was to become a veritable monkey on my back for the next four years.

I decided to write a partially autobiographical novel, in the third person, using as my protagonist a boy and young man my own age, and beginning it the day he left the East End technical high school on his sixteenth birthday. Though I hadn't been living in Cabbagetown myself while attending high school, but in the Riverdale district across the Don River, I had remained quite close to the people of Cabbagetown, having prewar male friends who lived there, and going out with Cabbagetown girls. Our gang during the years 1936 to 1939 had hung around in Riverdale Park, which straddles the Don River and separates Cabbagetown and the district north of it from Riverdale to the East, and half the gang lived on Cabbagetown and Moss Park streets while the other half, including myself, lived in Riverdale.

I sensed too that "Cabbagetown" was a more colorful name for a neighborhood than Riverdale; it was still a collection of slum streets as it had been during my childhood when I *did* live in it, and was much the better title for a novel.

I did two things during the next three months: I wrote an eight hundred page hand-printed novel, and took off forty pounds of fat I'd acquired in the navy and in drinking up my ninety days' leave pay and my war service gratuities after being discharged from the navy the previous October. During the three months while I wrote the book I did no drinking at all, for I never do when I'm writing. I wrote a chapter every evening in pencil after deciding to make my chapters fifteen pages long, and on weekends I corrected the previous week's work in ink. I decided some time after I began the novel to divide it into three parts: Genesis, covering the period from March, 1929 to June, 1932; Transition, covering the period from June, 1932 to October, 1933; and Exodus, covering the period from October, 1933 to February, 1937.

My protagonist, Ken Tilling, lived on a street I lived on as a small boy, Wascana Avenue. He shared some of the jobs I had held at his age, took some of the boxcar trips to Western Canada that I had taken, hung around with a gang in Riverdale Park, and finally went off to fight in Spain in 1937. I made him about my size, gave him my personality, but that was all. Other than that he is a fictional figure. His alcoholic mother is completely fictional (my own mother never took a drink in her whole life), his girl friend Myrla Patson is also completely fictional, as are all the other characters in the novel. Incidentally, and to answer once and for all a question about Myrla I am sometimes asked, I never knew a girl from Cabbagetown who became a prostitute, though no doubt there were some, as there are girls who go into prostitution from all city neighborhoods and not only slums.

Ernest Hemingway once said that the best parts of his books were the parts he had made up himself, and not the true parts. I believe this is true, and though "truth may be stranger than fiction" it's not half as interesting.

Cabbagetown and the Co-operative Management course both came to an end in late March, 1946. I read an ad in the Employment Wanted column of a newspaper placed there by a North Toronto housewife who wanted to take on typing jobs at home. I called her up, told her I had a book manuscript which needed typing, and she and her husband came down to see me. We came to an agreement on fee, $65, which was a good bit of money in those days.

The thirty-odd students in the Co-operative Management class, mostly but not all war veterans, voted me class valedictorian. With my novel finished (I thought) and safely away at the typist's, I began drinking beer during the evenings. A day or two before I was to give my valediction, we students were taken on a tour of the Canada Packers plant, where I exchanged smiles and waves with an old gunner friend from the 23rd Battery who was killing steers with a sledge-hammer.

At various times during the winter we had been taken on trips to visit various producer co-operatives in towns adjacent to Toronto, and this was our final inspection, a meat-packing plant to which, presumably, some of us who finally became managers of producer co-ops would ship our cattle or other products.

Everything went fine at Canada Packers until we reached the hog-killing room. There a middle-aged immigrant stood beneath a rail which ran through a doorway leading from the pens, dipped towards a tank of boiling water, then ran through an inside door into the butchering room. Every few feet along the track a pig was hung by a chain fastened around one hind leg. The screaming of the pigs, especially as they came through the swinging doors and were able to see what was happening, was ear-splitting and to me heart-rending. Zoologists and animal trainers claim that the domestic pig is one of the most intelligent of animals, and I believe it. Some of them struggled so hard that I feel sure many of them break their legs in the chain that strings them up to the moving track. They screamed and struggled as they came closer and closer to the killer, who stood there wearing rubber boots and a neck-to-foot rubber apron, a long sharp knife in his hand. Behind him on an oil-cloth-covered table lay several other knives. Using his left hand to hold the pig steady he plunged the knife with his right into either the lower neck or upper breast of each pig, immediately releasing a thick stream of blood when the knife was drawn from the wound. They continued to scream and kick until their bodies were immersed in the boiling water, which I supposed allowed their bristles to be more easily removed. Their blood ran in rivers into a drain-hole in the floor.

The sight, sound and smell of that killing room will remain with me always, and the casual attitude of the workman seemed to me similar to the attitude of the S.S. executioners in the Nazi death camps which came to light when the war was over. My sorrow for and sympathy with these poor screaming animals was mixed with a sorrowful hatred for the man who killed them. I tried to rationalize my feelings against him by telling myself that to him it was a job, probably the only one he was able to get which gave him the wherewithal to feed, clothe and house his family. I also knew that when he left it there would be other men clamoring to take his place. My attempts at rationalization did no good.

That day in the pig-sticking room will remain in my memory forever, along with the time I saw a wounded Moorish kid, shot in the head and one knee, at the ambulance lines and clearing station during the battle of Brunete in the summer of 1937. Some of the rear-echelon Loyalist Spaniards, the kind who wangle jobs far enough behind the lines to avoid being killed but are able to claim they were in the battle—and it's the same in every army—were taunting the wounded enemy prisoner, shouting "Moro! Moro!" and denouncing him for fighting for the Fascists as if he'd had any choice. Finally they heaved him on to the back of a mule and led him around a bend in the road, from which I heard the single revolver shot as they killed him. I thought of the soldiers who had captured him, Internationals or Spanish troops it didn't matter, who despite the fact that he had been trying to kill them and might have killed some of their comrades, had treated him as a human being, having his wounds bound up by a battalion doctor who then sent him back to the safety of the clearing station along with our own wounded. I compared the brave men in the front lines with the bastards six kilometres back. Both the captured Moor and the slaughtered pigs had made me suddenly sick for all mankind.

I got drunk on the night following our visit to the packing plant, and the next day when I was supposed to give my valedictory address, I told the teacher he and the whole co-operative movement could go to hell. I was immediately expelled, and I walked the few yards along Bloor Street to the King Cole Room of the Park Plaza Hotel where I got drunk all over again.

When I sobered up I realized I was now what William Saroyan had once called himself, "an author, still unpublished." A week later when my hired typist brought me back the typescript of *Cabbagetown* I was horrified to find that she had typed it on onionskin paper, so that anyone reading it would find they were also reading words typed five sheets down. I said nothing to the lady for it was my own fault for not telling her to type it on white bond paper. I decided then and there to type my own scripts and I've always done so.

In the spring of 1946 I rented a house from the Department of Veterans Affairs in the western suburb of Etobicoke, in a veteran's housing project open to those who qualified by having overseas service and at least two children. A couple of weeks before this I'd also found a job as a clerk with War Assets Corporation, a crown company set up to wind up war contracts and retrieve buildings, machinery and any material or manufactured items that were now surplus due to the ending of the war. I got the job through an old next door neighbor of mine, Bill Bolton, who had given me a job the fall before when I was still drawing navy pay. He'd been an employee of the federal employment office then, after war service as an air force pilot; now he was an inspector with War Assets.

As soon as I settled into my brand-new five room house (situated at the farthest end of the street on a corner lot) I brought my family back from Quebec. I furnished the house with second-hand furniture I bought with my re-establishment credits. The living room didn't look too bad, the bedrooms were fully furnished, but I could only buy a small table with which to furnish the dining room. My job only paid $32.50 a week, and my rent was $34 a month, so as yet I couldn't afford a stove. My wife cooked on a two-burner hotplate. As soon as things became fairly shipshape I went to work with a typewriter I rented for $5 a month to re-type *Cabbagetown* on white bond paper.

The re-typing took a couple of months to do, for I could only type in the evenings and on weekends. In the meantime I typed up my short story which had lain in an old suitcase at my mother's house throughout the war, and though I knew there was something wrong with "The Conversion Of Willie Heaps," I didn't know what it was and none of the editors who read it would tell me.

When the new typescript of *Cabbagetown* was finished I took it to the Macmillan Company of Canada, partly because its name was more familiar to me than any other publisher's and because its offices were downtown and I could reach them easily from the War Assets office.

The person in charge of Macmillan's at the time was an elderly lady who never condescended to meet me. An assistant editor on the Macmillan staff, Peggy Blackstock, did see me however, and she was very courteous and understanding to this unknown author who had walked through her door. Miss Blackstock was the first person even remotely connected with editing or publishing who read my novel, and only the second person in a publishing house I'd ever met.

While I was attending the co-op school, and *Cabbagetown* was still being written, I had entered the offices of J. M. Dent & Co. a few doors away from the school on Bloor Street. I asked the receptionist if I could see an editor, and she took me to a desk in the corner and introduced me to Mr. C. J. Eustace, who later became president of the firm but was then the senior editor I suppose. He asked me what he could do for me, and like an unmarried girl seeking an abortion I said, "I have a friend, sir, who is writing a novel, and he wants to know how it should be typed and presented."

Mr. Eustace didn't even crack a smile as he answered, "Tell your friend to drop his manuscript in here when it's finished.

Have him type the novel, double spaced, on one side of white bond sheets, 8½" by 11", number each page, place his name and address on the title page, and place the typescript in a cardboard box, with the pages loose but in numerical order. The best kind of box to use is the one the typewriter paper came in."

That was the only editorial advice I ever asked for until I became a professional writer, and I haven't asked for much advice from anyone since. The best advice I ever got about writing short stories came from a *Saturday Evening Post* writer named Arthur Mayse, a Canadian who later wrote a newspaper column for a Victoria, British Columbia newspaper. It was at my first literary cocktail party in 1949. Mayse told me, "Always write short stories seventeen pages long."

About a month after submitting my 800-page manuscript of *Cabbagetown* I got it back in the mail from Peggy Blackstock. She told me there were some things in it she liked very much, but it was far too long and should be cut in half. It was like being asked to cut off a leg.

Back to the old table in the dining room again, crossing out paragraphs and sometimes whole chapters, then beginning the boring pick-and-shovel work of re-typing the book. During recent years when I have been an instructor in writers' workshops, I have been amazed and disgusted by young writers who have been too lazy to re-type a six-page short story, but have submitted it with inked-in changes, crossed-out lines, and sometimes with unnumbered pages. When I'm handed a manuscript like this I know the writer will never have the guts to become a professional, even if he or she might have a modicum of talent.

After a couple of months of cutting, changing and re-typing I once again took *Cabbagetown* into Peggy Blackstock at Macmillan's. After a few weeks she called me, and asked me to come down and see her. I went down to her office, and she told me that the book was now of manageable size, but there were still many changes to be made. She was unspecific about the required changes—for instance, she didn't tell me that throughout the book I had left out the comma in sentences such as, "Where are you going, George?" and "Eddie, I don't know what you mean." I asked her if the editor had read the book, and she nodded, and rightly or wrongly I decided that this person was against it, and me, whom she had still never met. I took the manuscript home again and made more changes in it. By this time I was sick to death of the story, fed up with having to make changes in the script, and sick with the thought of having to spend all my evenings and at least parts of my weekends re-typing it.

I submitted it again.

Though by now I hated the book I also loved it. I knew that I was one of the generation of new authors who were attempting to change the Canadian literary scene by writing realistic urban-setting fiction. We weren't the first; Morley Callaghan had done it during the thirties, and Frederick Philip Grove had written realistically during the 1920s of prairie life. The only novel I remember from my English classes at the technical school is *Settlers Of The Marsh* by Grove, which I thought was a very good book, but unfortunately didn't reflect the lives of city-dwellers. I thought then, and I *know* now, that *Cabbage-town* was the best Canadian novel written up to that time about the effects of the Depression on the Canadian urban poor.

Somehow I found out my mistake with the leaving out of commas, and by myself I discovered how to write short stories, quite a few of which I wrote during this period of my life. I also discovered on my own what was wrong with "The Conversion Of Willie Heaps," and I re-wrote it. I had made the mistake of not starting the story at its real beginning, "I could see Willie coming along the road from his place, . . ." but had cluttered up the beginning of the story with geographical and sociological descriptions of the locale of the story. This is a mistake made by many beginning short story writers, and was a mistake made by Frederick Philip Grove in every story except one, "Snow," which is the only good short story he ever wrote.

Since I had first submitted *Cabbagetown* to Macmillan's two years went by. My daughter had started school, we were all eating regularly if not expensively, I had never missed a rent day, and I had bought a new electric stove about a year before, on time, and had thrown out the old two-burner hotplate. Most furnaces in those days were fueled with coal, and every fall I would go down to the town of New Toronto and borrow $150 or $200 from a Household Finance office with which to buy my winter's coal. I called Household Finance "my bank," with the laughs not completely hidden in the wry.

The urge to become a writer could no longer be ignored, and I would wite short journalistic pieces at the breakfast table and short stories whenever I could think of a title, theme or plot. Not knowing anybody in the newspaper or magazine business all of my stabs at journalism were torn up, but I kept sending out the short stories to Canadian and U.S. magazines. I collected a thick sheaf of rejection slips, and I once said to my wife, not altogether jokingly, "I'm going to paper the bathroom with them." Every rejection slip just made me more determined than ever to sell my first story.

There were evenings when I'd dismount from the bus at the corner of my street after work and be almost afraid to pick up our mail at the small branch post office we used before house-to-house mail deliveries were introduced in the neighborhood. When the postmistress handed me a large manuscript-sized envelope from a magazine I would carry it home, afraid to open it until after supper, knowing it was another rejection.

Fifteen years later, after I won the 1963 Governor General's Award for Fiction with *Hugh Garner's Best Stories*, William French, the literary editor of the Toronto *Globe & Mail* mentioned in a piece he wrote about me that I had always seemed to have a stubborn determination to succeed, and he was absolutely correct. Writing or becoming a writer is not only the honing of learned talents and acquired skill, but is also an ego-inspired will to succeed. The way this will-to-succeed is carried through the early years of neglect and failure in the eyes of others depends entirely on the writer's determination, and as Bill French said, I had that stubborn, perhaps poor-born York-shire streak.

Some of the stories I wrote in the house in Etobicoke were not good, but a few of them were very good, and I realized they were, despite anything editors said. I had to wait a few more years however to prove it.

One Sunday afternoon, during a period when Macmillan's had the manuscript of *Cabbagetown*, I took the bus and street-car to downtown Toronto and began walking the streets in the same haphazard fashion I often do to this day. I remember crossing the Bathurst Street bridge across the railroad yards and a serendipity thing happened, I found the titles and themes of three short stories. I turned around and hurried as fast as public transportation would let me to my dining-room table. The short story titles and themes were: "One, Two, Three Little Indians," "Our Neighbors The Nuns," and "The Yellow Sweater." Instead of typing the Indian story on my rented machine I took a pad of paper into the living room and sat down on the sofa and wrote it in longhand. I finished it before supper, and typed it that evening and the following one, finding I had to make no changes at all. The nuns' story was written during the next few days, as was "The Yellow Sweater." These stories began their rounds of the magazine story editors, and were returned to me, from all of them, with rejection slips attached.

During the fall of 1948 War Assets Corporation came to an end, and with it my job. I also received back my manuscript of *Cabbagetown* from Peggy Blackstock. This time she had typed a two or three-page criticism of it, and made the suggestion that I should submit it to William Collins Sons, who occupied a floor in the Macmillan building on Bond Street. A few days later I took the manuscript in to Collins.

I had received a month's severance pay from War Assets, and I used the next month to polish my short stories and begin the writing of a novel dealing with a Canadian corvette on convoy escort across the North Atlantic. I had no title for the book, but its theme was the story of a ship's company of about seventy officers and men during an ordinary boring crossing of the ocean, with a minimum of action. The book's sub-theme was the effect of a young sailor's death on the rest of the ship's company, and on the dead boy's young buddy in particular, because of the captain's decision not to bury him at sea but to take the body to Newfoundland for burial. As my free month came to an end, and I had to find another job, I had taken *H.M.C.S. Riverford* across the Atlantic to the harbour entrance of St. John's. I left my corvette sitting outside the harbour for months.

I was unable to find a job through the government employment office, but one day when the Garner finances were down to less than a dollar I happened to be passing the Massey-Harris farm implement company as I walked west on King Street carrying only my suburban bus fare. I entered their employment office. A sign on the wall listed the openings in several job categories, one of them being "Inspectors." Having watched the so-called inspectors at War Assets Corporation I knew that the job was an unskilled one, a phony undefined no-talent trade that needed only a slight native intelligence and the ability to read a blueprint. I had learned how to read blueprints years before in my drafting course in technical school, and I'd retained a cursory knowledge of machines and machine shop procedure both from technical school and the War Assets Corporation. I wrote on an employment form that I was applying for an inspector's job, and also claimed to have been an inspector with War Assets. I was hired, and a young man led me through the factory into a cavernous hellhole in which the punch press department and the forge were combined.

I worked for several months as a punch press department inspector, and hated every minute of it. We worked swing shifts, a week from 8 a.m. to 4 p.m., the next week from 4 p.m. to midnight, and the next from midnight to 8 a.m. My foremen

46

and fellow inspectors were good working-class guys, and being one of them myself we got along fine. I also got along fine with the punch press operators, who had one of the most boring and dangerous jobs in the plant. Having a different shift every week did not allow me to become accustomed to the constant changes in eating and sleeping habits, and I'm still haunted by the memory of my wife waking me up on the living room couch and saying, "Hugh, it's half past ten; time to get ready for work." The job was a dirty-overall job, which in itself didn't bother me, and my pay cheques were bigger than those from War Assets, so I suppose one thing cancelled the other out. Besides, I'd finally found some use for something I learned at the technical high school. After I'd worked there six weeks I was eligible to join my first trade union, the United Automobile Workers, which I promptly did.

My writing suffered, of course, from the shift work, and I found myself unable to continue with the three-quarters-finished manuscript of the corvette book. My short stories went out and were returned with the old monotonous regularity. I didn't go looking for a shoulder to cry on, primarily because I'm tremendously independent and a loner by upbringing, and secondly because I knew now that I could write very good short stories such as "The Conversion Of Willie Heaps," "One, Two, Three Little Indians," "The Yellow Sweater", and "Our Neighbors The Nuns."

A peculiar thing happened to me; I found myself unable to read the book review pages of the newspapers or magazines I bought. To me they were filled with praise for books and stories that I knew, even then, were far less worthy of it than my own, which I was unable to sell to anyone. The one memorable line I read, about that time, on a book page was written by William Arthur Deacon, the book editor of the *Globe & Mail*. He wrote, "There is no such thing as good writing, only good re-writing." By that criterion, for I was constantly re-writing and polishing my stories and *Cabbagetown*, I should have been about ready for the Nobel Prize.

My novel manuscript came back from William Collins Sons, and Charles Sweeny asked me to add some humour to it. I thought his request was crazy but I complied, adding the street dance chapter to the book. I sent it back again.

One day my wife and I discussed my failure to get anything published, the lousy job I had at Massey-Harris, and whether or not she and the kids should return to her father's farm until I finally proved I could become a professional writer. My wife

Alice has always been a timid little French-Canadian farm girl but a strong determined woman too when she had to be. She has always been quietly understanding, and though she has never tried to unduly influence whatever quirky paths I have decided to take she has always been aware of my moodiness and my loner's life as a writer. She agreed to take the children back to Quebec again, while I would quit the job in the punch press department so that I could concentrate on my writing.

I quit Massey-Harris, gave notice to the management that I was leaving the house in the veterans' project, and began selling the furniture, most of which was secondhand anyway, except the kitchen stove, washing machine, lawn mower and a few other items. I had to sell the furniture in order to get enough money for train fare for my family back to the Gaspé coast. Anyhow I sold everything, except some kitchenware and a large box of tools I had acquired, which I sent down to my father-in-law's farm by railway express.

My next-door neighbor, an ex-R.C.A.F. pilot and prisoner-of-war named Stan Barnes, said to me, "You're selling out, Hughie! Don't you know you're breaking up your life?" I had to agree with him, and I didn't know whether I was separating myself from my family temporarily or permanently right then. All I knew was that I wouldn't be any good to either my family or myself unless I became a professional writer.

There came the day when I, my wife and children, set out from the house in a taxi, headed for the Toronto Union Station. I guess it was a wrench to both Alice and me, leaving our first house, with the future looking so bleak and unpromising. I put them on the train, and returned to my emptying little suburban house until my month's rent ran out.

After shipping the kitchenware and tools to Quebec, and selling off the furniture to neighbors and a secondhand dealer, I was left with less than a hundred dollars, a veterans' insurance policy for $1,000 with which to bury me, and a suitcase full of clothes. I was out of work once again, with no home or family, nobody who believed or knew I was a writer—or cared for that matter—unable to sell any of my stories; I'd reached the nadir of my life. I called up the typewriter rental company and told them to pick up their machine; now I'd even got rid of the tool of my trade.

On my final day in the housing project I bid goodbye to my neighbors and friends—there'd already been some family break-ups on our street and the wives didn't think much of me for sending Alice and the kids back home—and took a taxi downtown. When the cab-driver asked me where I wanted to go I told him to take me to the Walsingham Hotel on Jarvis Street, a comfortable hostelry owned by an old friend, Mr. Freeman, in which I'd lived for a couple of happy carefree months nine years before when I'd first joined the artillery, and for a time after returning from the war. I stayed at the Walsingham for a week or two, and then for reasons which now escape me, but were no doubt connected with my lack of money, I moved down the street to the corner of Jarvis and Dundas, and checked into the Warwick Hotel.

During the week or so I lived at the Warwick I entered a short story contest run by *Maclean's* magazine, entering "One, Two, Three Little Indians." The stories had to be sent in under a pseudonym, so I combined the names of the hotel and the street, using the pen-name "Jarvis Warwick." It was a pseudonym I was to use many times in later years, when more than one of my articles and stories appeared together in a magazine, and I also used it as the author's name of a novel I wrote a couple of years later, *Waste No Tears*.

"One, Two, Three Little Indians" did not win a prize in the *Maclean's* contest, though ironically I'll bet that it has been reprinted, broadcast and telecast, translated and everything else more than the total of *Maclean's* short story winners in the history of the magazine. To this moment the story has been revived thirty-six times, on radio, television, in anthologies and textbooks, and translated into several foreign languages. It is in high school textbooks in Canada, the United States, Great Britain and West and East Germany.

When the contest results were announced and I found I had not won a prize, I went over to *Maclean's* where I met W. O. Mitchell, then the fiction editor. We had never met before, but when I told him I was the author of the Indian story he sat me down in his office and said, "I don't know what the hell was wrong with the judges, but in my estimation it was one of the best stories we received. Even after the prizes were announced I tried to get it printed in the magazine anyhow, but the editor turned thumbs down." The editor of *Maclean's* at the time was Arthur Irwin, who afterwards accepted a sinecure in the Canadian diplomatic service in, I think, Australia and Mexico.

Bill Mitchell showed me a chit attached to the manuscript of the Indian story which he had circulated among the other editors, including Pierre Berton, John Clare and others, and they all had scribbled favorable comments about the story and agreed with Bill that the magazine should print it. Though

Mitchell did his best to get the magazine to publish it, he finally had to mail it back to me.

I moved from the Warwick Hotel to a rooming house at the corner of Bay and Grosvenor streets, now long torn down and replaced by an Ontario government building. I found a job as a shipping clerk with Shulton Limited, the manufacturers of men's after-shave lotions and male cosmetics, rented another typewriter, and began writing again. I refused even to look at the partially completed manuscript of my naval corvette novel.

One day Robin Ross-Taylor and Charles Sweeny of William Collins invited me to lunch at a Yonge Street bistro, and brought with them a charming, exuberant and volatile lady named Doris Hedges, whom I found out was connected with the Benson & Hedges tobacco family. Doris was trying to set herself up as a Canadian literary agent, and I gave her several of my short stories. I think but I can't be sure that Taylor and Sweeny also gave me back *Cabbagetown* at this time. My manuscript had gone back and forth between myself and publishing houses so often by now that I'd lost count. I've certainly lost it by now. A couple of weeks later I received a note on monogrammed colored paper from Mrs. Hedges exclaiming about my stories, especially one of them (which one I no longer remember), "I'll eat my hat if I can't sell this story soon!" I hope she didn't mean the gorgeous but inedible creation she was wearing on our first and only meeting, or if she did I hope she enjoyed it. Of course she didn't sell any of the stories, and finally gave up her attempts at opening a Canadian literary agency in Montreal.

I quit the job at Shulton's—it seems there is a short length of work time past which I can't stand *any* job—and began working in the shipping room of the T. Eaton Company's mail-order department. I managed to save up my return fare to the Gaspé Coast from the overtime I worked during the Christmas rush, and took a trip to see my wife and family over the Christmas holidays.

The job at Eaton's was strangely fascinating to me, for a time. An older man and I were stationed at the foot of a large chute that sent parcels down from seven or eight floors of the mail-order building. We would bend down, pick up the parcels, and throw them into bins for postage, express, freight or other delivery. It was a wonderful job for the weight and figure, and I was in tip-top shape. When I left the mail-order shipping manager offered me a permanent job but I turned it down.

When I returned to Toronto I was once more out of work, and my landlady had rented my room to somebody else during my absence. It had been a good room overlooking a convent garden on Wellesley Street. She gave me a narrow room next door to a group of male Irish immigrants who kept me awake nights with their drunken arguments.

My next job was as a "chief file clerk" with the British-American Oil Company. My job consisted of having two girls file away the blueprints from the drafting department. My usual routine which relieved the monotony was to report to the office in the morning, then take off for a movie, a shower at the YMCA (my rooming house bathroom led all of North America in unnatural pollution), going for downtown walks, and reporting back to the office at lunch time and again at 4:30 p.m. The girls were well able to handle the blueprints, both having worked there longer than I, and indeed the job of "chief file clerk" was dropped when I was fired.

I was still playing catch with William Collins, my *Cabbagetown* manuscript being the ball, and writing the odd short story now and again. I missed having my family with me, and once, when I was suffering the regrets and remorse of alcoholic withdrawal, I sent my wife the fare to Toronto, and she came up for a couple of days.

One day at the office I received a phone call from Charles Sweeny, who told me he was sorry but they were turning down *Cabbagetown* once more. His words had a finality about them, and I knew William Collins had no desire to see the manuscript again. And what a typescript it was by this time! One chapter would be done in an elite typeface and the next in pica, a reminder of my succession of rented typewriters and the many changes I'd made in the script. I told Charles I understood, and just to send me back the book. He and Robin Ross-Taylor had both been naval officers during the war, and he said, "Have you ever thought of writing a book about the navy?" I answered, "I started one a year or so ago but wrote only two-thirds of it." "All right, how about finishing it and bringing it in?" Without much enthusiasm I said I would.

That evening I re-read the corvette book, found it much better than I'd expected, and on the following Saturday morning began writing again, letting *H.M.C.S. Riverford* enter the harbour of St. John's Newfoundland.

I wrote all day Saturday, all day Sunday, and on Monday morning I finished the book, which I titled, *Landlubber Lying Down Below,* from the words in a song we used to sing in various Toronto public schools. I took the manuscript to the office on Tuesday morning and after signing in, walked with it

51

under my arm through downtown Toronto and presented it to Charles Sweeny at William Collins Sons, then located on Avenue Road north of Bloor Street. I expected the same thing to happen to it as had happened to *Cabbagetown.*

Late Thursday afternoon I received another phone call from William Collins, and both Charles Sweeny and Robin Ross-Taylor congratulated me on the book. One of them told me they were very anxious to publish it, and they would like me to go up to their offices and sign the contract on Monday morning. They would pay me a $500 advance on royalties. I told them, as nonchalantly as possible, I'd be there.

I almost wasn't however, for Thursday happened to be our payday at British-American. The selling of a novel in two days should have meant more to me than it did, I suppose, but I was not too much surprised, even though nothing else I had written since the war had found a taker at all. I was insanely happy though that I had finally cracked the editorial shell. That evening a draftsman named Walter, to whom I confided my good fortune, and I went on a monumental pub-crawl. I don't know where or when *I* ended up, but Walter ended up in a police cell in a downtown precinct. I stayed drunk throughout the weekend, even giving drinks to the Irish bog-trotters who lived in the room next to mine.

On Monday morning I signed the contract with William Collins Sons, and Robin Taylor and Charles Sweeny took me to lunch in the rooftop restaurant of the Park Plaza Hotel. Sweeny told me they didn't like the book's title and asked me if I'd mind if they changed it to *Storm Below?* Feeling the cheque for $500 in my pocket, and realizing I'd jumped my first and most important hurdle in the writing business, I didn't care what title they gave the book.

When I'd started writing *Storm Below* my mind was made up to write about a normal, stormy, sometimes-foggy crossing of the North Atlantic, without derring-do and with a minimum of anti-submarine action. That's how most convoy actions were. I decided to keep the action within the ship and the ship's company, trying to show the camaraderie of the ship's company, the relationship between the officers and the men, and the conflicts that often arose between several dozen young Canadian males when confined to a very small space for long periods of time. The book, though based on an amalgam of many convoy escort groups I served in, with the ever-present stress of sudden death as part of everyone's life, was a sociological study of a small warship's crew rather than a study of the Battle of the Atlantic and its relationship to the crew of a small Canadian corvette.

Altogether I served on eight small Royal Canadian Navy ships, working my way up through the ratings in the supply branch until I was discharged as a chief petty officer. Being a supply rating was not the most romantic job in the navy, and most supply people held shore jobs, in stores and victualling depots, some of them throughout the entire length of the war. Due to a constant and abrasive attitude towards bureaucrats of every sort, in armies and a navy as well as in civvy street, I was earmarked from the beginning as a guy to be gotten rid of, consisting in this case of "Give the bastard a sea draft."

This was fine with me, for I was happiest aboard a ship, where to all intents and purposes I worked as my own boss, with only a lackadasical supervision by the senior officers and some poor lieutenant who among his other duties had been ticked off as "supply officer."

During the early years of the war the Royal Canadian Navy corvettes, small shallow-draft escort ships copied from fishing trawlers, were Great Britain's assembly-line answer to the need for escorts for the convoys that were literally the United Kingdom's lifeline to North and South America, Africa and the Far East, especially those convoys that were plying the North

Atlantic sea-lanes from the United States and Canada to Great Britain, where the German U-boats were concentrated.

The corvette, with somewhere about 1,000 tons displacement, drawing only 9 feet of water forward and 14 feet aft, was outfitted with museum-piece 4-inch guns, .5 twin Browning machine-guns port and starboard on a stern gun-platform, and four depth-charge throwers, two starboard and two port. A pair of depth-charge rails from which were rolled as many as ten charges at a time could be built in hundreds of small shipyards at a fraction of the time of a destroyer, and indeed were.

The Royal Navy, which introduced the corvette, or re-introduced the name of a former fighting ship of hundreds of years before, named its corvettes after British wild flowers, giving the ships the name of Flower Class corvettes. The British, who have a long history of military naval romanticism, called these little ships H.M.S. Rose, Thistle, Candytuft, Hepatica, Trillium, and so on. For a very short time I served on *H.M.S. Fennel,* built in Canada for the Royal Navy, but then later turned over to Canada, where it and perhaps nine other Flower Class corvettes kept their original horticultural names.

When Canada received the plans for the corvette many shipyards were put to work building them, in Lunenburg, Levis, Quebec, Sorel, Montreal, Toronto, Collingwood and Port Arthur in the east, and in west coast shipyards as well. The plans called for the same open-decked corvettes as the Flower Class, but the Royal Canadian Navy named theirs after Canadian towns, just as their Fleet Class destroyers were named after Canadian rivers and Canadian Indian tribes, and the old four-stacker destroyers we received from the United States after rivers indigenous to both countries, such as Columbia, Hamilton and Niagara.

Besides *H.M.S. Fennel* I served on *H.M.C.S. Collingwood, Lunenburg, Arvida* and *Battleford,* plus two armed yachts early in the war, *Moose* and *Ambler,* and a small ex-R.C.M.P. patrol craft, *H.M.C.S. Eileen.* After serving three years at sea, and by this time a petty officer, I could no longer, under the supply branch's rules, be drafted to sea unless I volunteered. I served instead in charge of "mess traps," the navy name for mess and galley equipment, in Halifax, and later in the supply depot in Quebec City, ending the war in Newfoundland.

I have some small regrets in not taking drafts that were offered me to *H.M.C.S. Sioux,* a new Canadian Tribal Class destroyer being built in England, and to *H.M.S. Uganda,* a cruiser turned over to the Royal Canadian Navy, which took part in the Battle of Iwo Jima in the Pacific and made a round-the-world cruise. These regrets however are outnumbered by my malicious joy in knowing that every sea-draft I turned down had to be filled by some officious petty officer Uriah Heep who had hoped to spend all of his navy time dishing out victuals, stores and clothing in Toronto, Winnipeg or Edmonton, where you could make a lead-pipe wager of a thousand-to-one he'd never be torpedoed. As "Popeye" Chambers, Chief Torpedo Gunner's Mate, and President of the St. John's, Newfoundland, Chiefs and P.O.'s drinking society "The Gag And Vomit Club," used to say, "I got a fiendish delight out of it."

I have many warm memories of the navy, both afloat and ashore. It started me drinking in earnest, made me hundreds of temporary friends from shipmates to wet canteen drinking companions, showed me parts of the world I otherwise wouldn't have seen, and let me take part with millions of my generation in a war that despite today's anti-war sentiment happened to be a good one.

This autobiography is not a war book, so I'll confine my memories of it to a few random things that have stuck in my mind over the years.

There was the time when the *Lunenburg* escorted the troop-ship the *C.N.S. Lady Drake* from Quebec City to Lake Melville in Labrador. The *Drake* was filled with American workmen going to begin the building of Goose Bay Airport, and both ships lay at anchor in this wonderful inlet from the open sea for about a week. I remember trading hundred-pound bags of sugar to the Indian and Eskimo fishermen for hundred-pound bags of beautiful lake trout, and the friendliness of the sleigh dogs belonging to the fishermen. One of our telegraphists from Hamilton bought an Eskimo dog puppy and took it home with him on his next leave.

I remember one morning when the corvette I was on at the time was steaming from Halifax to Newfoundland and we made a circled inspection of a three-masted square-rigged ship out of another age. This lovely ship against the early morning sun was one of the most beautiful sights I've ever seen. We had to inspect her as best we could, and signal her presence to shore, for she might have been a U-boat supply ship on station to supply the submarines then working the Gulf and the St. Lawrence River.

I remember the sight of the light from Cape Farewell at the southern tip of Greenland as we passed with a convoy, and how supercilious we felt when after lying at anchor all night off Martha's Vineyard, early in 1942, we steamed into Newport

Rhode Island to the U.S. naval base to take on fuel and supplies. The U.S. navy "boots" or new recruits came down to the jetty and stared in awe at a real Atlantic convoy escort force; dirty, camouflaged, un-shipshape, four Canadian corvettes and the lend-lease four-stacker Norwegian destroyer *Lincoln,* our escort leader.

I remember winter ice-ups on the Grand Banks, searching through the Bras D'or Lakes for a reported submarine, the sudden upward surge of temperature as we crossed the Gulf Stream in the middle of the Atlantic. I remember the bum-boats putting out from the Donegal side of the River Foyle on our way up to Londonderry, and offering us Irish linen and embroidered table cloths in exchange for food, and I remember flogging casks of tea in Derry, a pound of tea for a pound in cash, and then throwing my ill-gotten wealth away in Cassidy's Railway Bar on the Derry dockside, guzzling large glasses of Guiness' stout.

I remember my first sight of the Clyde, the North African shoreline, Gibraltar, and the street fights I enjoyed with an American sailor in Boston and an Englishman in Belfast. I remember the ferry between Larne, Northern Ireland and Stranraer, Scotland, and of losing my travel warrant and ration cards in Dumfries. I remember too, giving away a kit-bag full of apples, oranges and other fruit I was taking to my Aunt Nellie, while passing through Preston, Lancashire, where the NAAFI tea was free to the troops and I had to change trains for Leeds.

I remember ten-day North Atlantic convoys and one that took us twenty-six days, so that we dubbed our ship the *Santa Maria,* after that of Christopher Columbus. I remember a Norwegian whaling factory that had been torpedoed in one of our convoys south of Iceland, and how we were sent back to sink her with our 4-inch gun so she wouldn't be a menace to navigation. I remember a drunken Irish stoker on the *Battleford,* a Royal Navy replacement we'd picked up in Greenock, stripping himself naked in drunken bonhomie and sitting on the ship's yardarm when we were tied up at Gibraltar's North Mole. He had to be coaxed down like a monkey from a pole.

I remember the night-and-day "payday stakes" poker games in the seamen's mess on convoys, that needed more skill at bookkeeping and exchanging I.O.U.'s than it did in playing the game. I remember passing through fishing fleets in Cape Race fogs, and, once, reporting a fog-buoy trailed by a merchantman as a periscope, so that a pair of coders, painting a bulkhead, came running on deck covered from head to foot with red lead.

I remember the sight of a fully-lighted Spanish ocean liner off the Portuguese coast, the first lighted ship we had seen in years. St. John's, Newfoundland was blacked out during the war years, but Gibraltar (flanked by such well-lit Spanish towns as Algeciras and La Linea) wore all its lights night and day. U-Boats sank a number of ships in the St. Lawrence River, mined the approaches to Halifax harbour, and one of them, which we were sent out to search for, sent a spray of torpedoes into the harbour entrance of St. John's, most exploding on the rocks beneath Signal Hill.

Among my drunken capers was one in which I was chased by a maddened Spanish baker wielding a long bread-cutting knife in Gib (all seaport towns were called by their slang names, "Gib" for Gibraltar, Portsmouth, England "Pompey," Halifax "Slackers," and so on). I'd called the baker a "Fascist bastard."

My craziest caper took place at Jetty Five in the Halifax Naval dockyard, when my ship the *Lunenburg* was waiting for me to arrive with a load of potatoes before sailing. I'd lost the civilian driver of a small two-wheeled cart which carried supplies from the Victualling Depot to the ships, and with my cap turned backwards and playing a drunken Ben Hur I'd galloped the old horse and cart through the dockyard, scattering pedestrians, including Admiral "Jetty" Jones, into the lawns and ditches.

When I reached the ship's side (we happened to be tied up dockside for once rather than third or fourth ship out) the captain, Lieut. W. E. "Bucky" Harrison, R.C.N.R., was standing on the bridge with the officer-of-the-watch and the navigating officer, ready to put out to sea. The quartermaster piped the duty watch to help me load the potatoes aboard, but I had a prior duty. I unhitched the old nag from the cart and drove him up the gangplank to the boat deck where he got stuck between the port boat and the forrard davit. The seamen who were to cast off the lines were ordered to "Get that fucking thing ashore!" by the bos'n.

The captain turned, blinked, and asked, "What the hell are you doing, Garner?"

"Bringing our mascot aboard, sir," I answered, giving him a snappy salute.

He turned away, whether to laugh or cry I don't know.

I received a token stoppage of leave sentence, but there was nowhere to go anyway except into the drink.

And of course I remember one of the times in my life when I was suddenly overcome with pride at being an Englishman.

An escort force my ship was in at the time, and I now forget what ship it was, had left a mid-ocean convoy and was proceeding through a hurricane with thirty and forty-foot waves to Halifax. Our escort destroyers were two old Royal Navy V-and-W destroyers *H.M.S. Witch* and *H.M.S. Wanderer*. The whole escort force was suddenly ordered to turn away from Halifax and proceed as fast as the hurricane winds and waves would allow to Sable Island where a large U.S. tanker, the *S.S. Independence Hall*, was breaking up on a sandbar, and perhaps some other ships as well. Our telegraphists and coders passed the word to the rest of the ship's company as they always did.

Riding a corvette in a hurricane is like riding a rodeo broncho up and down the dips of a roller-coaster. The cooks would have been fried by their own galley stove or boiled to death in their stew, so it was every man for himself as far as food went, and we hooked our arms around a convenient stanchion and ate ship's biscuits and bully beef out of its can. The waves were so high that what should have been my fear of the ship foundering turned to a fear of heights as we crested a wave and could see down into the next trough far below.

We eventually emerged from the storm and took up positions in the lee of Sable Island's sand dunes and sand bars where the water was relatively calm. A mile away we could see the broken-off stern of the *Independence Hall* tilting at a crazy angle from a sand bar. Lining the stern rails were the survivors of the crew, including a woman. The closest-in ships put out a boat apiece, but the waves just dashed them against the ships' sides and they had to be pulled up again. One of the English destroyers got a boat away but it was swamped, necessitating a rescue of its crew. It was then that the "Limeys" of the second destroyer showed us what British seamanship was all about. It lowered a whaler and boat's crew, but instead of them trying to approach the singing stern of the tanker by oar or inboard engine they rigged a mast and sail. And with their sail, and accompanied by the cheers from the other escort ships, they manoeuvered through the still-high waves, brought the boat to the side of the stricken tanker like a yachtsman bringing his skiff into a yacht-basin jetty, and caught the lines thrown to them by the terrified crewmen of the tanker.

One by one the crew of the tanker were lowered into the destroyer's boat and taken back to its ship, tacking now against the wind. It must have taken much longer to do than I remember, but what I do remember is the professional pride all of us felt in this magnificent and imaginative feat of seamanship, and the pride I personally felt in also being an Englishman.

With the survivors aboard the destroyer and at a signal from the escort force leader we put about and headed for Halifax.

Another memory I have of my navy days, and one that is shared I'm sure by thousands of Allied veterans of World War Two and other wars, is of one of my drunken capers that went wrong. This one occurred in Sydney, Nova Scotia in the summer of 1942 when I received a telegram from my wife announcing that I was now the father of my first child, a daughter named Barbara Ann, born at the Hôtel Dieu Hospital in Campbellton, New Brunswick.

I was on the corvette *Lunenburg* at the time and our escort force was working with five-knot convoys that were then assembled in Sydney.

It was a practice on most of the corvettes I served on to collect all the tots of rum in a mess when it was one of the hand's birthdays and give them to him. The guys in my mess, signalmen, telegraphists, coders, cooks, officers' stewards, the sick bay attendant and myself, presented me with a large jug of rum to celebrate my daughter's birth. Giving *me* collected tots was an appreciated gesture, but as I was the ship's supply rating and therefore the purchaser, keeper and disher-out of the ship's rum (under the careless supervision of the Officer of the Day of course) I had worked out years before my own subterfuges to steal rum from the spirit locker.

Anyhow, it has never been a habit of mine to look an alcoholic gift in the mouth so I shared by new fatherhood with my messmates not wisely, which would have been impossible for me in those days, but too well. Later in the day, not being able to hear thunder or see lightning by this time, I ignored all naval protocol such as reporting to the officer of the watch, the ship's quartermaster, jetty sentry or anyone else, and nipped ashore through the naval dockyard, sans exit pass, and went downtown. There I bought a pair of white baby shoes for my new-born daughter (which she wouldn't have been able to wear for months yet), had them gift-wrapped and parcelled, and mailed them to my wife.

From then on I have no idea what I did, but whatever it was it was joyful. I *do* remember weaving my way back to the dockyard in the darkness, having an altercation with the dockyard officer of the guard, calling him a string of obscenities, and being taken under guard back to my ship. I seem to remember, though, I can't substantiate it, I was nabbed climbing over the dockyard fence.

The next morning I was paraded before the *Lunenburg*'s first lieutenant, or second-in-command, and informed that I was to be weighed-off as we called it by the Naval Officer-in-Charge of the Sydney Naval Station, a Royal Navy Captain or Commodore if I can remember *that*. I was marched under escort to an office building (I'd had a couple of morning tots to straighten me out or at least make me presentable) and there I faced the elderly commanding officer.

I was charged with being drunk aboard, breaking ship, breaking into ship and using offensive language to the officer of the guard, to which I pleaded guilty. The elderly commander, who had probably weighed-off thousands of drunken sailors in his day, looked at me with eyes that had pierced a million horizons and asked me if I had anything to say in my defence. I told him that I'd been drunk as charged but that it had been a special occasion brought on by my celebration at becoming a father for the first time. I'd gone ashore and had bought a pair of baby shoes for my new daughter.

"What happened to the shoes?" he asked the convicting officer of the guard, who told him he'd never seen them.

"What did you do with these, er, baby shoes?" the commanding officer asked me.

"I mailed them home, sir."

"Through the fleet mail office?"

My God, I hadn't even thought of what a heinous crime it was to send uncensored mail from outside a navy ship or dockyard! "No, sir. I mailed them from the post office."

He stared at me, weighing my words before weighing me off and I thought I caught a twinkle in his eye, or hoped I did. He looked at my assessment papers that followed a sailor throughout his naval service then back at me. I forget what wording he used now, but his sentence was loss of a good conduct badge and fourteen days detention. Thank the lord he was a gentleman who hadn't taken away my single hook or killick, the small anchor on a sailor's arm that denotes the rank of leading hand equal to that of a corporal in the other services.

"On caps! Right turn! Prisoner, quick march!"

I was marched with a shore patrol escort back to my ship where I hastily shoved all my gear into my seabag, tied up my hammock, slung my gas-mask, and had a couple of farewell drinks with the boys. I rejoined my escort, which had managed to scrounge a tot or rum or two themselves, waved goodbye to the *Lunenburg* and my friends aboard her (she sailed with a slow convoy to Iceland a couple of days later), and entered the shore patrol paddy-waggon for my ride to Point Edward Detention Barracks, a few miles out of Sydney.

Point Edward was a small detention centre, "glass House," "stockade" as the Americans call them, prison camp or whatever, containing only about eighteen cells. It was set in a sandy, hillocky piece of moose pasture that some local politician no doubt had fobbed off on the Department of National Defence for ten times its actual value. Surrounding it was a high chain-link fence topped by a roll of barbed wire. The barracks complex itself was set away from, I think, an old frame farmhouse that contained the offices of the prison commandant, a "meat-head" major of the Provost Corps, his flunkeys and sycophants.

I was released at the wire gates by the navy, turned over formally to the army for rations and discipline—both rotten— and immediately ordered in even worse language than I'd used to the naval guard lieutenant the night before to double-time my way about a hundred yards to the major's office.

Unless you've ever run, wearing a complete navy square-rig uniform, half Wellington boots, Burberry raincoat, carying a gas-mask slung over one shoulder, a large navy seabag clutched under one arm and a navy hammock, mattress and blankets on the other shoulder, you won't know what I mean when I say it was rough. It was made doubly rough by a lance-corporal guard who trotted a few feet behind me urging me on with every vile imprecation he either learned down on his farm near Yarmouth, Nova Scotia or picked up at the prison.

I was paraded, completely winded, before the major, a mousey little son of a bitch who probably ran a Yarmouth haberdashery or refused people of the district jobs from the local employment office. He was a perfect prototype, along with his German opposite numbers in Dachau or Buchenwald, of the meek, frightened, masturbating, little sado-masochist suddenly plummeted into a position of authority over his betters. (It was later that I learned that the camp staff had been recruited in Yarmouth and vicinity.)

This twirp gave me a lecture on how "they'd soon straighten me out," and how I was now in the Canadian armed forces engaged in a vicious war against the enemy, and a lot more crap along the same line. If I'd been one tot drunker than I was I'd have told him that I'd already served two years at sea, and no fucking idiot in the Provost Corps was going to tell *me* about the war. Luckily I was just not-enough-drunk to keep my mouth shut, which saved me from beginning my fourteen days with a gang-beating and a diet of bread-and-water.

I don't want to ;o into things at Point Edward in too much detail, for it was just an incident in my life. I was young, in perfect physical condition, and there was nothing those hillbillies could do to me that I couldn't take.

One of the lance-corporal guards (we had to address them always as "Sir") made me double over to the cellblock where I was shoved into a cell, told to unpack my things and lay them out in prescribed order on the bare wooden slat bunk, and sit on the edge of it until I was told I could get up. As the prison was run by the army the regulations covering the precise laying-out of all gear and toilet goods was based on army kit. Navy and Air Force prisoners had to figure out a different way to abide by regulations.

An army detention barracks, in the Canadian army at least, has never been described by a writer, or if it has I've never come across it. U.S. army or marine stockades have been written about rather widely, and also the British Imperial Army glass-houses, a story about one of them in North Africa being made into an excellent movie, *The Hill.* Anyhow all service prisons, their commanders and staff, are cut from the same mold which is pressed into the odorous ooze at the bottom of a latrine.

Everything in a detention barracks, officially ordered and condoned by the top brass of all three services, is meant to punish physically and insult, humiliate, and psychologically "break the spirits of" the prisoners inside them. There is no nice-nelly pretence at rehabilitation or constructive discipline. The only "discipline" the cretinous guards know is the ability to keep themselves in uniform without doing any of a war's fighting, be obsequious to their superiors, moronically nasty to the better men they are guarding, and go to town in groups in case they should meet up with a former prisoner on the street. Oh yes, they also learn or improve on their nascent sadism to the point that they actually *enjoy* it. It is not their victims, or few of them, who come out of detention crippled, but the guards themselves.

It's daily mail delivery through the peepholes of the cell doors. I hear the guard delivering the mail. "Here's a letter, you asshole, from that whore of a wife of yours in Winnipeg!" Or, "Stand up, cunt, your regular fuck has wrote to ya!" I hope God killed them all with cancer.

On my first afternoon in the joint, sitting at attention on the edge of my bunk (I'd already received the usual first-day visits from the resident cretins, who pussyfooted up the corridor in their sneakers, slammed aside the cover to the peephole in the

62

door and shouted "Stand to attention, you cocksucker!" whether you *had* done or not) I heard the sounds of somebody being literally thrown into the cell next to mine. The wooden cell walls ended about eight feet up where they were replaced by fine wire grillwork, for ventilation purposes I suppose. Later on I heard my next-door neighbor being ordered out to fill a wash-tub with cold water, then heard him, with much cursing from the guards, being brought back with his heavy tub. There was a silence for a couple of minutes, then came the unmistakeable sound of him scrubbing clothing on a washboard. I learned over the next few days, from snatches of conversation we had through the grillwork of our common wall and whispers in the chow line or at morning ablutions, that he was a deserter from a Nova Scotia regiment who had been ordered to wash his heavy battle dress uniform in cold water and without soap. He must have scrubbed at it constantly, except for our work and pack-drill periods, for three or four days.

The things you surrender at the guard-house on your admit-tance to a detention prison (I refuse to use such euphemisms as "camp," "centre," or "barracks"), along with your dignity as a human being, are your wallet, all letters and private papers and all smoking equipment. I'm no longer sure but I believe that the soldiers also had to leave behind their Brasso, so that buttons, slop pail, and metal buckles and clasps had to be pol-ished to a high sheen with sand.

I only had fourteen days to do, unlike some of the other prisoners who had sentences of 60 and 90 days and even six months, so for me things were a kind of lark. I found I could do without cigarettes, I didn't let the childish defilements of the guards get under my skin, I jumped to attention when spoken to or hollered at, and always answered "Sir!" out loud. For relaxa-tion I read the Bible, a copy of which, according to King's Regu-lations and Orders, was placed in every cell occupied by a Protestant prisoner; the Roman Catholics were given a racy bit of literature called *Faith Of Our Fathers*.

A young ex-shipmate of mine, a signaller called Jimmy, was finishing up a 60-day stretch by working in the kitchen. This was the usual routine to fatten up long-term prisoners before their release, so that their skin-and-bones wouldn't bring about a government investigation which would uncover the fact that the major had been stealing much of the rations and selling them on the black market. Anyhow, young Jimmy sneaked me some tobacco and matches one day, along with my plate of boiled dog. That evening, after I'd spent my usual two hours washing down the cell, including the bottoms of the cracks in the floor, I rolled a couple of cigarettes out of the "so-and-so begat so-and-so" pages of the Bible and wafting the smoke through my high window with my towel enjoyed a smoke. Enjoyed is not the right word, for I no longer needed a smoke, the risk I was taking was foolish, and I only did it as a gesture of defiance and contempt against my idiot keepers.

Though I saw two young seamen, who had been scrubbing the cell corridor, taken into an empty cell by three guards (because one had spoken back to an obscene order to hurry up) and there beaten up with billies and army boots, I found that there was even humour of a sort in a place like that.

Each morning, after we had sand-scrubbed our slop-buckets to a mirror-like shine with handfuls of sand, and if you think this was easy try it sometime with an ordinary galvanized iron pail, we would double to the washroom, mark time while we shaved ourselves with laundry soap and a communal safety razor, mark time while we brushed our teeth, mark time while we washed or showered ourselves, and even keep marking time while we defecated in an outdoor privy containing three seatless toilet bowls. Unless you reported on sick parade, which was a hazardous thing to do, you were forced to evacuate yourself at that specific time each day, and do it while moving your feet "at the double." Not only that but you had only a certain time on the toilet bowl, and had to get out when the guard shouted, "You three bastards next!"

After that, and after making sure that everything on your bunk from your toothbrush to your rolled-up blanket was not even one millimetre out of the prescribed line, all the door locks would buzz from a central switch and you would hurry to the door, throw it wide open, and take one step forward into the corridor, making sure you dressed to the right with a precision worthy of the peacetime Brigade of Guards. There you would stand at strict attention until the major, followed by an N.C.O. flunkey, deigned to pass by on his daily inspection.

It was my luck from the point of view of humour and my bad luck from the point of view of possible consequences to find myself each morning standing face-to-face about two feet apart from my fellow prisoner from across the corridor, a Private Macdonald of the North Nova Scotia Highlanders.

As soon as Macdonald's eyes caught mine we would both have to stifle an insane urge to giggle. Somehow, and I don't know how to this day, I managed to pull a straight face until the major and his entourage had passed. Macdonald however was caught twice vainly trying to stifle his laughter. The first time he received a dressing down and extraordinary pack-drill, and the second time the little twirp of a major, who had never dared strike anyone but his mother in civilian life, slapped him hard across the face.

"Any complaints?"

Eighteen voices: "No, Sir."

"Carry on back to your cells."

About turn, one, two, three steps, shut but don't bang the door, sit down on the edge of your bunk and await the order for pack-drill.

The packs, which were standard army haversacks, were placed at each doorway while we sat waiting in our cells. All except two contained a block of heavy hardwood, while the others were filled with really heavy blocks of concrete. For his first laughter episode Macdonald got one of the concrete packs and for his second, besides the slap across the face, he again received "extraordinary pack-drill," meaning the concrete block, which he continued to get every morning until I left detention. After the second time Macdonald was caught we avoided each other's eyes, but just having to do so always brought me to the edge of loud laughter.

We marched back and forth across the drill field in the loose sand, wheeling, turning, halting, forming columns, sometimes quick marching and at other times doubling through the orders. I didn't mind it except my stylish half-Wellington boots, though good for drunken strolls down the main streets of various ports, were not made for close-order drill. I developed dime-sized blisters on my heels, which I soaked each night in cold water in my slop bucket. Nothing short of gangrene would have made me report to sick parade, for that would have meant sitting on the edge of my bunk all day soaking my feet, and in plain cold water at that.

Every afternoon we formed a work detail, which consisted of shovelling sand into a truck, moving it from one place to another, and shovelling it out of the truck. Not only was it the ultimate in stupidity but along with the morning's pack drill it gave us appetites that made us recognize that one single solitary baked bean on our plate was a food object not to be despised.

Jimmy, my kitchen contact, not only sneaked me a half-dozen extra beans whenever he could, but one day sneaked me a comic book. This was discovered rolled up in my blanket during a cell tear-down they called a "routine accoutrements inspection" or some such para-military phrase. Jimmy had already spread the word around the prison that I was a veteran of the Spanish Civil War, which gave me a modicum of notoriety among the other prisoners and a begrudged stature among the meathead guards. It must have been this that saved me from punishment over the possession of the comic book. Anyhow, I heard nothing more about it.

I hadn't wanted the comic book to begin with, for I was quite content in reading all the dirty stories in the Bible. I can readily vouch for the fact that if anyone wishes they can get a good fortnight's pornographic reading from the Old Testament alone. I received my discharge before I reached the Christian New Testament, and anyhow I don't suppose the pickings are too good there. Incidentally, thin biblical pages make excellent papers for hand-rolled cigarettes, and because they've been blessed, both by the giver and the receiver, there isn't a cough or lung cancer from Genesis to Malachi. I don't remember now what chapter contained all the "begats," but I don't think any of my cell successors ever missed them.

When I reported back to the naval dockyard I found there was a draft waiting for me, this time to the corvette *Battleford* in St. John's, Newfoundland. I was sent by navy truck to North Sydney and there I boarded one of the ferries to Port-Aux-Basques, Newfoundland, and from there took the C.N.R.'s "Newfie Bullet," a passenger train of infinite exoticism, to St. John's where I made a pierhead jump to the waist of His Majesty's Canadian Ship *Battleford*. The next day we pulled out to pick up a convoy headed for Britain, our own destination being Londonderry and Joe Cassidy's bar.

We had had our share of attacks by U-boats but I was in only two big convoy battles. The first was during the fall of 1942 (the worst year of any on the North Atlantic) when my ship was part of an escort force guarding a North African convoy. It happened as we were crossing the Bay of Biscay, and we were attacked simultaneously by German Junkers 88's, that flew out from France, and submarines that were waiting for us.

The four-inch gun crew of the *Battleford* were magnificent gunners, and from my own action station on a pair of twin Browning .5 machine-guns on the stern "bandstand" I watched them as they threw H.E. shells with pinpoint accuracy at a Junkers who was about to make a pass over us. Their shells were exploding, it seemed from my angle of sight, almost in the Junkers' cockpit. The pilot hurriedly turned and flew away.

66

I don't think we were attacked by any U-boats that day, nor do I remember us dropping any depth-charges, though other ships of the escort and the guns on the merchant ships were busy on that beautiful warm millpond-sea afternoon. A little later on as we watched the bombs and torpedoes sending geysers of water up around the merchantmen I got my first chance in the war to fire on a German plane.

My guns were on the starboard side, and suddenly I saw a big German bomber coming out of the west to pass directly over the *Battleford.* I opened up on him, my guns at their highest elevation, hose-piping my tracers at him as we'd been taught to do in the anti-aircraft "dome" in Londonderry. He was far too high for me to hit him with machine-gun fire and all I did was satisfy myself that I'd shot at a plane and startled hell out of the depth-charge thrower crews who manned the four deck throwers and the stern depth-charge rails.

The second big battle, I think, was the worst defeat a Canadian convoy ever took on the North Atlantic. We fought for almost a week, from Christmas Day, 1942 to New Year's Eve. We lost in all 14 ships, one of them a rescue ship loaded with survivors from other sinkings, one of the first ships sunk being our oiler, which carried a deckload of extra depth-charges.

But I'll let Joseph Schull tell his version of it, from his excellent naval history, *The Far Distant Ships.*

> December brought still grimmer experiences. Convoy ON-154 westbound, entered the western fringes of the 'black pit' area about Christmas day. The convoy consisted of forty-four merchantmen, a rescue ship, and a British special service ship, *Fidelity,* which carried a plane. Several U-boats were spread out in lines of patrol across the vulnerable zone and one of the pack sighted the merchant ships.

[I'm pretty sure we were spotted first by a German four-engine Focke-Wulf, which circled the horizon until dark on Christmas Eve, and gave our position to the U-boats.]

> She began to shadow, and during the next day six or eight more U-boats closed in with her. Meanwhile a furious gale was adding to the convoy's difficulties. Ships were being damaged and driven apart from the main body; and as warning signals and sighting reports began to pour in, the escort, consisting of the destroyer *St. Laurent,* with five corvettes, *Kenogami, Battleford, Chilliwack,*

67

Shediac, and *Napanee,* made desperate efforts to round up vessels scattered over miles of sea.

At two o'clock on the morning of the 27th two ships were torpedoed. By four o'clock two others had gone down. The U-boat pack had not completely gathered; the tentative assault was not fully pressed home and ceased with dawn; but there was no abatement of the gale. The corvettes which had steamed hundreds of extra miles in attempts to screen defenceless stragglers, began to run low on fuel. As darkness fell on the evening of the 28th, *Chilliwack* was forced to drop astern of the convoy and attempt the new experiment of fueling at sea from the tanker *Scottish Heather.* The difficult operation had not progressed very far when *Scottish Heather* was torpedoed; and with her went the escorts' hope of fuel.

Throughout a tense night the full-scale attack still failed to develop. The U-boats nosed about in a leisurely way probing for weak points in the screen and apparently waiting for still more reinforcement. The situation, in spite of its apparent quiet, was worsening steadily as more U-boats gathered and the escorts' oil stock fell lower. During the following afternoon *St. Laurent* ordered *Fidelity* to fly off her plane in an attempt to drive some of the shadowing U-boats under. The take-off, in the midst of a half-abated gale, brought new disaster. The plane ran along the water, crashed into a twelve-foot wave and all its landing lights flared with the shock of impact. For a moment watchers in *St. Laurent* saw plane and occupants tossing in the midst of a great, lighted dome of water. Then the aircraft disappeared, and although the pilot and observer were recovered there was no further hope of air support.

[We on the *Battleford* also watched the plane being shot off from its catpult, and fall like a paper dart into the sea. "Tough shit, Mac" somebody said, as we went back to our jobs on the ship.]

That night the U-boats, with their dispositions made, came in for the kill. *Battleford,* on the starboard beam, got the first radar contact and fired starshell.

[Mr. Schull made a slight mistake there; we were at action stations every night, from just after supper until breakfast, and the sun hadn't quite gone down when the subs approached us. Our lovely gun-crew fired high explosive at them, not starshell, for we could see them with the naked eye. We watched them submerge.]

In the wavering light four U-boats were discovered; steering straight for the convoy in regular line ahead formation, separated by intervals of about a mile. Signal lamps flashed along the German line as *Battleford* opened fire; and the boats turned and made an orderly retreat, drawing the corvette after them. Meanwhile *Kenogami* had reported another contact. *Napanee* spotted a conning tower a moment later; and then attacks broke out from all directions simultaneously. U-boats bored directly in among the columns, firing salvoes of torpedoes from all their tubes. Streams of tracer fire from merchantmen criss-crossed in the night to indicate the many sightings, snow-flake flared above torpedoed vessels, and behind the convoy, as it struggled on, the sea was dotted with the wrecks of blazing ships and the multiplying lights of rafts and life-boats.

Within two hours nine ships had gone down. 'At one stage of the attack,' reported *Shediac's* commanding officer, 'Torpedoes were so numerous in the convoy . . . that the officer of the watch remarked, "there goes ours now, sir," . . . as if next week's groceries were being delivered. The entire space between the columns seemed filled with the white tracers of the U-boats and the pink tracers of the merchantmen.'

As dawn came the attackers drew off to the horizon. Little more than a breathing spell seemed indicated; a pause to rest their men, signal their triumphant battle reports, replenish their tubes. The convoy was still far from air cover or relief; and absolute disaster threatened. *Battleford* had actually to take *Shediac* in tow. With only four escort ships remaining about the convoy there was no possibility of effective defence. The senior officer ordered that vessels of the convoy should make their escape independently if they judged that they had the opportunity to do so.

In fact what made the U-boats call off the attack were several big Royal Navy "Fleet" destroyers that had steamed out from Gibraltar to our aid. When we saw them coming over the horizon, as we left the convoy with the *Shediac* in tow, we knew it was the submarines' turn to take a shellacking.

To resort to a cliché, every cloud has a silver lining, and ours showed up when we towed the *Shediac* into the oiling jetty of Ponta Delgada on the island of São Miguel in the Azores, on the afternoon of New Year's Eve.

First of all, Red Strachan, the *Battleford's* Coxwain, or chief seaman on a corvette, conned the captain or the first lieutenant or somebody that we should "splice the mainbrace—doubled." That meant that every man aboard received two tots of navy rum, which meant four ounces of a drink powerful enough to derail the C.N.R.'s International Limited on a straight track. To keep our double tots from burning gaping holes through our gullets, we had to top them off with Cokes from the cupboard-sized canteen just forward of the ship's waist.

The ship's officers, and the officers from the *Shediac*, were invited by the island's governor or the British consul to attend the New Year's Eve ball at government house, I guess it was. As soon as every officer left the ship, dressed in their No. 1 uniforms—except one poor sub-lieutenant who was left aboard as officer-of-the-watch—the festivities got under way. The assistant cook hadn't been able to bake bread since we'd picked up the convoy off the mouth of the Clyde, what with the gales and his action station on a depth-charge thrower, so we broke out tin-lined boxes of ship's biscuits which we spread with jam or bully beef for our supper. Both cooks were too looped to cook anything, and the rest of us were too looped to care.

One of the officers' stewards, a young guy from Windsor, Ontario, decided drunkenly also to attend the governor's bash. Later on he told us that he'd been dancing with the belle of the ball when he passed our captain and first lieutenant on the dance floor. "What did they say?" somebody asked him. "Nothing. They were too surprised to say anything, I guess" he replied. The Captain of *H.M.C.S. Battleford* was Freddie Beck, now a Toronto lawyer, and our First Lieutenant, or second-in-command, was another Torontonian named Pete Spragge. They are both very nice guys, whom I meet on rare occasions when I'm downtown.

The next morning we oiled up—at an oiling station also used by German U-boats somebody said, for at the time Portugal was a neutral country, more neutral towards Germany than to us I would think. Then we eased our hangovers with single tots of rum on the pipe "Up Spirits."

I went ashore and through the British consulate ordered everything exotic to us but indigenous to the islands such as pineapples, bananas, and pomegranates, along with fresh meat, fish, eggs, and especially bread. When we were finished oiling, the payday stakes poker games began again and the drunks began buying the saved-up rum from the day before that was being hoarded by the non-drinkers aboard. I always thought that any sailor who would take a lousy six-cents-a-day temperance pay in lieu of two ounces of navy rum was off his perch, but on every ship I was on we had all kinds. We even had a couple of guys who didn't swear.

There was an announcement over the intercom that all non-watchkeepers would be allowed a couple of hours ashore after thirteen hundred hours, so everybody who had no duties aboard changed from work shirts, softball sweaters, pajama tops, wind-breakers, or leather vests they'd received in ditty bags from the I.O.D.E., Navy League ladies, and others—which were our usual sea-going gear—and changed into uniform. The seamen, stokers, signalmen, and others who wore what we called "round rig," even put on their clean, ironed "salty" blue collars, that they used to fade to a very light blue with Javex and other products to make them look old and long-worn. I put on my No. Ones, a civilian-tailored uniform I'd bought when I picked up my P.O.'s rating, at the Fifty Shilling Tailors in beautiful downtown Londonderry. It was the only uniform I owned at the time.

When the liberty party were mustered along the port side, I spotted some young Ponta Delgadians standing on the jetty, wearing tattered bits of clothing and with bare feet. I ran to my forward stores and came back with an armful of canned goods, fruit, pork-and-beans, bully beef, and even some cans of smoked pilchards, that the crew cursed me for every time I put them on the breakfast menu. I used to tell them I was under orders to carry twenty wooden cases of them to shore up bulkheads if we were ever torpedoed. "Then what the hell are you feeding them to us for?" some guy would always ask. It was a question I never did find a suitable answer to.

Feeling like a Sally Ann mission stiff handing out Christmas candy, I gave a couple of cans to every young civvy on the oil-ing dock. They thanked me profusely and began trading cans with each other, like kids at home traded baseball or hockey cards.

"*Olé, Chico!*" I said to one of them, "*Tu hablar español?*"

"*Si, Señor. Un poco.*"

"*Donde esta la casas de puta?*"

The liberty party were staring at me open-mouthed. They

thought the young man and I were talking Portuguese, when we were really talking broken Spanish. Suddenly I'd become the ship's linguist.

The young man on the dock motioned with his arm, and said, "*Venir, Señor.*"

"*Una momento, por favor.*"

The bo'sun who was mustering the liberty party, shouted, "Garner, get back in line! Just because you're a P.O. now doesn't give you any privileges."

"Up you with a squeegee!" I muttered as I stepped back with the libertymen.

As we filed down the gangplank the guy behind me asked, "Hughie, what did you ask that guy?"

"I asked him where were the whorehouses."

The word spread back along the line faster than a grassfire.

When we reached the jetty about twenty-five of the ship's company clustered around our new-found guide and me. I was just drunk enough to tell them "Don't worry, boys, it's all on me." I was rubbing my lucky sixpenny bit in my pocket as I said it. It was the only money I had.

There were some dissenters and deserters of course; guys who only visited gift shops and cathedrals. I'll bet there's living room sofas in Canada today that still sport cushion covers with views of the Derry Guildhall, Labrador white fox pelts, and phony hand-painted views of Gibraltar with the rock-side gun emplacements painted out. I remember an Engine Room Artificer on a former corvette I served on who had a thing about cathedrals. He'd search for the cathedral in Las Vegas. He was a reformed drunk who should have been a medieval monk, except he'd joined a Calgary gospel tabernacle.

I said to our guide, "*Un grande casa?*"

"*Si. Mucho grande.*"

"*Bueno. Cuántos chicas?*"

"*Muchos, Señor.*"

Our broken Spanish would have horrified a taco parlor waiter, but it sure impressed the guys from the *Battleford*.

The civvy guy held up all ten fingers and shoved them forward twice.

"What'd he say, Hughie?"

"It's a big house, and there's about twenty dames in it."

"Let's go! . . . Lay on, McDuff! . . . Let's get there before those salts from the *Shediac* beat us to it!"

Our guide led us down some side streets lined with white adobe-looking houses on it; all the girls ran indoors when they saw us coming and peeked at us through the front room curtains. Our radar mechanic, a Royal Navy Englishman who cut the Blondie comic strip out of the Canadian papers and sent it regularly to his bride in Folkestone, said, "I'm just going to get a drink and watch you blokes."

"Okay, Dagwood, nobody's forcing you to do nuthin else."

We finally came to a large house with a front courtyard behind wrought iron gates.

"*Esta casa,*" our guide said, pointing.

"Give the guy a quarter, Fletcher," I said.

Two stokers handed the guide a quarter apiece. We stormed through the gates and I knocked at the front door. I used to be an expert at finding bordellos, a skill that I lost with marriage. A short time before this two Norwegians from a lend-lease destroyer re-named the *Lincoln,* which had been our escort leader for a trip or two, had asked me, in Belfast, where they could get some girls. I stopped a young spalpeen in the blackout and interpreted their question to him, handing him a thrupenny bit. He led us to a big house where he said there were more girls than in any other place in the city. There were, but not the kind the Norwegians were looking for. Under a small blue light when the door's blackout curtains were parted I found myself facing a coiffed nun. I apologized profusely, and the nun broke into a laugh when she saw we were sailors and guessed what we were looking for. This time the door was opened by a middle-aged *senhora,* who smiled with her gold teeth. This was the real thing; madams look the same in any language. She led us into a large front room, where we sat down around a long oval table.

"*Vino, Senhora,*" I ordered imperiously. "*Todos vinos.*" She thought I was an officer because of my brass buttons and gold badges. I'd even had the good conduct badge restored, I'd lost for my earlier caper while serving on the corvette *Lunenburg.*

Several of the "girls" brought in a couple of dozen bottles of wine, of every color and shape, just as *they* were. To be honest most of them were crows. "Rejects from the Roxy Burlesque chorus," as one of our E.R.A.'s put it.

"What's this stuff, Garner?" a Vancouver telegraphist asked me.

"How the hell do I know? Maybe it's Catawba."

"It looks like California muscatel."

"Who cares what it is?" asked a guy from Cape Breton, pulling one of the skinny trade-ins on to his knee. Soon everybody was into the goof, whooping it up, singing, copping pinches and feels from the girls, pulling them on to their knees. Even Dagwood, the radar mechanic, seemed to be making up his mind whether to remain a voyeur or go for broke with his marriage vows with a little girl wearing a brassiere and skirt, who was ruffling his carefully waved blond hair.

It was one of the greatest afternoons of our lives.

The table half emptied several times as the *Battleford* crazies left it to be led upstairs by the ladies of their choice. We were nearly all half drunk to begin with but soon we were completely boiled. The signal bo'sun shouted, "Spud [not his right nickname] here is still a virgin. Garner, get him a broad." He pointed to a young signalman.

"I'll get him two!" I shouted down the table with a munificence that would have put Diamond Jim Brady to shame. And I did just that. Poor Spud, too scared to go upstairs but too drunk to resist, was led from the room. Several of us followed him and his pair of afternoon *inamoratas,* climbed up the wall of the adjoining crib and cheered Spud and his lady friends on.

It finally soaked into my alcoholic consciousness that this caper had to end soon, and that my sixpence-with-the-hole-in-it wouldn't even pay for the short drive back to the oiling dock. When the madam left the room to get more wine I tried the French windows behind me and found them to be open. I jumped up on the window sill and shouted, "Hey, you guys, I'm leaving before the cops arrive. I'm broke."

There was a quick scramble from the table, with girls and women being spilled from knees with loutish informality. I jumped into the courtyard, pulled open the front gate and ran faster than I've ever run in my life in the direction of the ship. When I looked behind me there was a small mob of sailors on my heels, with others spilling out of the front gate, some with their shoes and jumpers in their hands. Those in the rear were each carrying an appendage on their backs, an angry *puta* who was scratching any part of their bare skin she could get her fingernails into. I began to laugh, but quit when I realized I was being overtaken and passed by those who had once been well in the rear of the *Battleford* harriers.

None of us could afford to stop until we rushed up the ship's gangplank.

"What the hell's going on?" the bewidered jetty sentry asked.

"Nothing" somebody told him. "Just make sure your sidearm is loaded."

It was the only time in my life I ever commandeered a whorehouse. That evening whenever I had to go up top I made sure I stayed on the side of the ship that was offshore from the jetty.

The sick berth attendant was busy for a while swabbing scratches with iodine and picking gravel out of poor Spud's soles, for he'd been forced to run back to the ship in his bare feet.

I fully expected we'd have to fight off the whole Ponta Delgada police force, but nothing happened that night. Nor did the officers seem to be aware that anything was wrong or if they did they kept it to themselves. They must have known *something* had happened for the assistant officers' steward had more adhesive tape on his face and neck than an Egyptian mummy.

The next morning as we were casting off our lines to follow the *Shediac* out to the open sea I went up on deck to take a last look at the town. The madam was standing with two of her girls on the jetty, and when she saw me she shouted a string of Portuguese curses in my direction and made a closed-fist gesture with her right arm aimed upwards and her left fist clenched in the bend of her right elbow. I knew what it meant, and to placate her I shouted, "*La consul de la Inglaterra! Much dinero. Bajar la consul a Inglaterra!*" My terrible mixture of poor Spanish and worse Portuguese only got me another string of curses, this time from all three of the women.

Whether the *senhora* ever placed a claim with the British consul or not, I don't know. Sometimes I get the feeling that somewhere in a musty British Admiralty file is a claim for uncountable bottles of wine and for favors received from the proprietress of a bawdy house in Ponta Delgada, São Miguel, Azores, levelled at the ship's company of His Majesty's Canadian Ship *Battleford*.

The *Shediac* and our ship made our way without further incident to the harbour of St. John's Newfoundland. I stayed drunk for the first couple of days out of the Azores, giving pineapples to anybody who had enough strength left to wash my face and neck now and again. "Who'll dhobi Hughie for a pineapple?" was my pitiful cry.

The rumour had got about St. John's that the *Shediac* and *Battleford* had been sunk. When it was mentioned to me at the naval stores I told my questioner that none of the escort force had been torpedoed, but the ship's company of the *Battleford* had taken an awful beating from some of the ladies in the Azores. I refused to explain what I meant, for nobody would have believed my story anyhow.

So much for the battle of the Atlantic.

Sometime during the years that *Cabbagetown* had been on its rounds of publishing houses, I'd sent it to J. M. Dent and Company. Apparently Mr. C. J. Eustace had considered publishing it but sent it back to me after holding it for about eight months. One person who had read the manuscript for William Collins was Professor Macdonald of the University of Toronto's School of Social Work. When the book was first published as a paperback in 1950 the U. of T. sociology department placed it on their required reading list.

From my $500 advance on *Storm Below* I sent my wife a money order and dropped into the Underwood Typewriter showrooms where I bought an Underwood Noiseless portable machine for $128. I am still using it twenty-four years later, almost to the day. It's still a good typewriter but its "noiselessness" has gone forever.

I never did return to my job at the British-American Oil Co., and they were probably as relieved as I was at giving up my pretence at being a "chief file clerk." The week following my abandonement of the oil business I received a notice of dismissal, my unemployment insurance book, and whatever pay I still had coming to me.

From the day I signed my first book contract with William Collins I became a professional writer, though only a couple of people knew it up to then. My publishers sent me to Ashley & Crippen, among the best and most expensive portrait photographers in Toronto, and a young man there took my photograph for the dust jacket of *Storm Below*.

No matter what was to happen to me in the future, and being broke and having my heart broken was to happen many more times, I was now the author of a to-be-published book.

I have a poor memory for placing events that happened many years ago in their correct chronological order, especially the crazy little jobs I took to keep me alive and writing. I have also erased from my memory most non-essentials such as past names and dates, in order to concentrate on the job at hand, whether it be a short story, magazine article, television drama or novel. Because, as I have already written, a writer has a shallow knowledge of a great many things but seldom an in-depth knowledge of one, my mind is always filled with trivia. This trivia might be used by me at any time, next year or never, but I keep collecting it, almost subconsciously.

Almost constantly I am forced to refer to things I have written to find the names of characters, who to me are dead as soon as I have used them in a book or story. This has caused me certain embarrassments at times, and I remember once compiling one of my books of short stories and finding that too many of my protagonists bore the Christian name "Edward." On another occasion, while talking with a group of English Lit. students at Queen's University, I found some of them referring to a "Mrs. Evans." Finally I asked, "Who in hell is Mrs. Evans?" and the group laughed. Someone told me she was my protagonist in a short story called "Waiting For Charley" collected in *Men And Women.*

Among many things left out when dealing with the early post-war years is the fact that during the writing and re-writing of *Cabbagetown* I had added some pieces first written as short stories to the manuscript. I have done this since with short stories, which may have been unsaleable due to their theme or dialogue in the early, more puritan days of Canadian publishing. This has prevented my having a backlog of unpublished stories and has meant that I have used, and sold, nearly everything I've written. I've never been able to afford to write things I couldn't sell.

Once, in the middle of a night when I was finishing the writing of *Storm Below,* one of the Irishmen knocked on the wall separating our rooms, letting me know my typewriter was keeping him awake. Remembering the countless times those *lumpen* idiots had kept *me* awake, I yelled to him through the wall, telling him to go perform an impossible sexual act. That shut him up.

When the first draft of "Some Are So Lucky" was written and re-typed I took it down to *Canadian Home Journal* and handed it across the desk to Miss Macpherson (actually Mrs. Herbert McManus, wife of a friend with whom I was to work some time later in the editorial department of *Saturday Night*). A week or so afterwards Miss Macpherson phoned my rooming house and asked me to drop in and see her. She told me that she and her assistant editors had read the story and had liked it and that she would be willing to publish it if I'd make some changes in the script. I asked her what they were and she told me she didn't like my overuse of the first person singular. She also didn't like the story's title, and as a matter of fact neither did I. I re-wrote the story the next day, titled it "Some Are So Lucky," and took it back to *Canadian Home Journal.* I received a cheque some days later for a sum it would have taken me a month to earn in the crummy little jobs I'd been working at up to then. The story was published in the issue of August, 1949.

I've always been thankful that I didn't have to start out writing for low-paying periodicals and trade magazines as many writers have been forced to do. Though I was forced to sell some of my stuff later on at much lower prices than I received for my first short story and magazine article, there was something about hitting the top-paying magazines first that bolstered my ego and my arrogance. Having started with top fees I was unwilling from then on to take less. There were times, of course, when I *had* to sell things cheap, and on occasion, because of its content, I *gave* a short story to one of the "little magazines" in order to get it into print.

There was a time back in my early years as a writer when I wrote quite a few allegedly humorous articles which I thought were just right for *Mayfair* magazine. All of them were returned to me with a rejection slip. The editor of *Mayfair* at the time was Stan Helleur, previously a columnist with the *Toronto Telegram.* One day I decided to go down and ask him what he didn't like about my articles. The magazine's offices were then in an office building at the corner of Toronto's Adelaide and York streets. I was told by the receptionist that Mr. Helleur wasn't in, but if I wanted I could see the managing editor.

A tall, heavy young man with glasses came over to me and introduced himself as Bob Fulford, now editor of *Saturday*

Night. I told him I'd come to see Helleur about the number of articles he was turning down. Fulford invited me downstairs to a corner coffee shop.

Fulford didn't seem interested at all in my articles, but asked me why I didn't submit one of my short stories to them. At the time I was getting between $250 and $400 for my short stories and the top price *Mayfair* could pay was around $75. I didn't say anything but I thought, "the hell with you, Mac".

Some time later Stan Helleur bought one of my funny little articles, and asked me in a note why I hadn't submitted more of them to his magazine. I didn't tell him that I couldn't get them past his managing editor. Years later I sold my second and last article to that particular magazine. All the *Mayfair* turn-downs were sold to equally low-paying publications eventually, including *The Globe Magazine,* the *Financial Post, Caravan, Royal York Magazine* and *The Canadian Broadcaster.*

During the first couple of years as a professional writer I wrote several short stories, "The Man With The Musical Tooth" and "A Painting For Paulette" being two of them. "The Man With The Musical Tooth" was returned to me by *Maclean's* with the terse note, "This is too far-fetched." A couple of years later I read in a newspaper a true story about a man who, like my protagonist, had a tooth-filling which acted as a radio receiver. I never did sell "A Painting For Paulette" to a magazine but it was broadcast twice on the radio program "John Drainie Presents."

But to return to my first magazine article sale in the winter of 1949 while I waited for my first book to be published.

One afternoon I dropped into the office of *National Home Monthly* to meet J. K. Thomas, the publisher. His editor was Joy Brown, now wife of Jock Carroll, then the Toronto editor of the *Montreal Standard* and now the book editor of Simon & Schuster Pocket Books of Canada. (I've seen generations of editors playing editorial musical chairs!) Joy told me that Mr. Thomas was busy with a visitor, Leslie Roberts, the well-known journalist and broadcaster. I said I'd wait, and sat down. I sat, and sat, and sat, until finally Joy went into the editor's office and told him I was waiting outside. When she came out again she asked me if I couldn't put my visit off until another time, as Mr. Thomas was very busy.

"Who does Mr. Thomas think he is, Jesus Christ!" I exclaimed. I told her what I had to say to him wouldn't take a minute. I suppose his curiosity was aroused by the rude, brash young nobody waiting in his outer office, for the next time his secretary returned she ushered me into the editor's office and introduced me to J. K. Thomas and Leslie Roberts. I told Jake Thomas, who was to become a good friend of mine and who literally kept my family and me eating during the following winter, that I had an idea for an article about Toronto, satirically titled "Toronto The Terrible." It would be a put-down of those Canadians in the Maritimes, Prairies, the West Coast and Montreal whose preconceived notions of Toronto were biased and untrue. I also told him I had a novel coming out in a couple of weeks.

Jake said, "Okay, write the article and I'll consider it."

I shook his hand and also the hand of his bemused visitor.

Grasping the doorknob on my way out I turned and asked, "By the way, how much do you pay for articles?"

I think he said "Two hundred dollars." I left the office.

Over the next two or three days I wrote the article, a "think piece" that needed no research, typed a fair copy, and took it in.

Jake was delighted with it and bought it right away.

When *Storm Below* was published, Leslie Roberts wrote me care of my publishers and told me he had bought the book out of curiosity, but had lain awake all night in a hotel room reading it.

The Toronto article came out in the September 1949 issue of *National Home Monthly,* and was quoted and given an accolade by Gordon Sinclair, whom I hadn't seen since running his city hall copy down Bay Street to the *Star* building twenty years before.

During 1949 I turned one of the chapters of the unsold *Cabbagetown* into a short story called "The Go-Boys," which along with two or three articles I sold to *National Home Monthly.*

Very early in my professional life I learned several important things about writing. Creative fiction is written on a different literary level from journalism, and different approaches and styles were necessary for the writing of a novel and a short story. Distortion and hyperbole are part of the journalist's craft, but are death to the serious creative writer. The judicious use of polysyllabic words is fine in a novel, but in a short story, which calls for discipline and simplicity, the short word is always better than a longer one.

A writer, especially an unknown beginner, must learn that the trade of writing is not only the talent he puts into his work but his ability to sell it once it is written. A writer can not rely on his own knowledge that a piece of writing was good; he has to sell this idea to an editor first in order to reach the public. He must trade his natural shyness and modesty for an aggressive salesmanship, renewed with every attempt to sell what he has written. Perhaps because of my background this wasn't too hard for me; if I *knew* a piece of my work was good I didn't let myself be discouraged by any Mickey Mouse editor. If he didn't buy it somebody else would.

I had to learn all the other odds and ends of my trade as I went along. Never use a story as a vehicle to show your erudition, esoteric knowledge, or ready use of a foreign language. Don't set a story that would be perfectly at home where you live in some exotic setting to impress an editor, or for that matter your readers, with what a well-travelled person you are. Learn to *imply* dialect by the use of one or two words rather than use it in every word of monologue. I also learned a very important business lesson by seeing what became of other writers who ignored it: always live up to a contract once you've signed it, and don't let a magazine editor or publisher ignore the terms *he's* signed. They are just as binding on him as they are on you.

As a writer I have been very fortunate in never having a manuscript lost, and I have no idea what would have happened to me in the early days if this had happened. It sickened me many years ago to hear that Ernest Hemingway had left a novel manuscript on a French train and that it had never been recovered. In the days before Xerox the re-typing of a long manuscript, for a person like me who could not afford a typist, was a horrible possibility.

When *Storm Below* was published in March 1949, I was pleased to find that it received feature book reviews and generous critical acclaim from coast to coast. This was due in part to the fact that it was the first Canadian novel ever about the Royal Canadian Navy, and also, I suppose, because its author was completely unknown to almost everyone else in the business. Being unknown I hadn't yet had time to make enemies of those I deplored and despised, as I would do later.

Though the sale of a short story and a couple of articles during the previous winter had helped me support myself I hadn't yet been able to cut myself off from having to accept silly little jobs. Through an old friend, Howard Rutsey, who had been on the night desk at the *Star* when I was a copy-boy there, and had joined the same artillery battery as myself in 1939, I found two jobs.

The first of these jobs had been in 1946 when I was hired by Rutsey, on a commission basis, as a housing inspector for the

Department of Veterans Affairs, visiting the houses, flats and furnished rooms of veterans who had applied for veterans' housing. I'd recommended those families I found to be living in clean and decent surroundings, even though many were forced to share accommodation with parents or live in downtown rooming houses, but I turned down all the slobs. I can be fooled by some things but not when it comes to differentiating between the deserving and undeserving poor.

Howard was later involved in a small mining tip-sheet and he introduced me to the editor, an elderly American gentleman whose name I have forgotten but who came from Olean, New York. My job was "scalping," or re-writing, mining and financial stories that I stole from the *Northern Miner,* the *Financial Post* and other legitimate papers. Though I didn't know a stope from a headframe I worked at the job for several weeks, separating the paper's ill-advised readers, mostly Americans, from their investments. In those days the phony investment rackets were flourishing in Toronto, and indeed throughout Canada, and the suckers were little widows in Palo Alto, California or retired railroaders in Reading, Pennsylvania. It hands me a laugh today to hear the wails of the Canadian nationalists, some of them the same ones who robbed Americans blind in the forties and fifties, bewailing the takeover of Canadian industry by U.S. investment.

Suddenly the owner of the tip-sheet, without prior warning, fired me. At the time my family and I were depending on his lousy $40-a-week job for rent and groceries. This owner, a crook of dubious nationality and parentage, even refused to pay me my final week's pay. Through the insistence of Howard Rutsey and the American editor I finally got my forty dollars.

It was my first hack writing job, but was not the last time I had to depend on hack writing to support my family. Many writers have had to do the same thing. Arthur Koestler wrote phony sex manuals in Berlin, William Faulkner and a generation of American novelists ground out hack movie scripts in Hollywood for instant cash, Scott Fitzgerald wrote his "Pat Hobby" stories for *Esquire,* and Ernest Hemingway wrote page-filler junk for the Toronto *Star Weekly.*

Trying to be a serious creative writer while at the same time having to grind out magazine journalism for a living was hard on me in two ways. Firstly, I had to keep switching from one writing style to another, and using various nuances of each as well, depending on what I was writing at the moment. When I was working on a novel I would have to break off my narration and accept a magazine assignment, using a different technique of writing. This isn't a cry of sorrow: I was young and versatile, and it didn't leave me with any traumas. And the Garners kept on eating regularly and I never missed a phone or electric bill, or a beer either. I never allowed myself to go into debt, though I did have monthly payments to make. I even had a credit card from my old friends at Household Finance allowing me a thousand dollar credit anytime.

The second way that my schizophrenic writer-journalist existence hurt me was that I was becoming known as a journalist while being put down as an author. My novels and short stories weren't taken as seriously by the critics who were convinced I was a popular magazine journalist, and nothing much else. Some university professor or a housewife in Salmon Arm, British Columbia, would write a nothing novel that the critics and reviewers would go ga-ga over. This bugged me, but I was unwilling to give up writing for magazines, where I could make what was then a month's average pay in a couple of days, to get a non-writing job in the daytime and write my pure, unsullied prose only on weekends. I'd already *had* that craperoo approach to literature.

Canada has always been a country of one-book authors. During my years in the business I've seen dozens of amateur novelists and one-shot short story writers shoot off like sky-rockets to the unstinting applause of the literary camp-followers, only to fall to the ground as squibs. I've also seen good writers who couldn't make it past their first book for reasons known only to themselves, and equally good prospective writers who for lack of guts, or for greed, allowed themselves to become publishers' whores or radio-TV hacks.

The public may be fickle and uncomprehending, but so are the literati, which translated does *not* mean the country's working writers but the editorial and academic hangers-on. This species of fauna used to wear tweed jackets with leather elbow patches but lately has swung to velour jackets and sideburns. The female of this sub-species used to be a failed housewife and mother but is now "liberated" to the point where she has a job on the literary periphery, in public relations, editorial-secretarial jobs, as the mistress of book editors or forgotten minor poets, and such. I think she cries a lot.

The members of this bookish "in group" exist from one literary cocktail party to another, cherishing invitations to such exotic dining establishments in Toronto as Mr. Tony's, Captain John's, the Westbury Hotel, the Inn On The Park, the Bombay

Bicycle Club, and even drunken bashes in publishers' offices. At other times I'm sure they eat TV dinners or have Sunday brunch at a Macdonald's Hamburger emporium.

The Toronto branch of the Canadian literati, which is the only one I know enough about to satirize, clutches the latest literary find to its collective dropped bosom, and if the new author is young, male and presentable he receives the usual follow-up propositions from both male and female members. If he's smart he tells his publisher to spend the publicity budget on advertising, if he's half smart he goes to the party completely stoned, and if he isn't smart at all he allows himself to be conned into things he regrets by individuals who can talk about books without reading them and about literature without knowing what it is.

On the day *Storm Below* was published William Collins Sons threw a cocktail party for me in their offices on Avenue Road. I had to arrive there before the guests, and I used up my waiting period sampling the punch. By the time the party got under way I was about a dozen drinks ahead of everyone else. There were some very nice people there (I've never been afraid to use the word "nice," which some latent homosexuals I've met deplore as feminine), including authors, literary editors, radio disc jockeys, public relations people, book-sellers and book salesmen. There were also a peculiar breed of freeloaders who somehow sneak into every literary cocktail party I've ever attended.

It was a good party, unlike many later literary parties I was to attend—there's one Toronto publishing house, for gawd's sake, that serves *tea* at its parties—and I used it as the basis for a satirical article published in the April 4, 1953 issue of *Saturday Night* magazine. This article or essay (an article is what *Maclean's* publishes; an essay is what *Maclean's* turns down and you later read in *Saturday Night*) was re-printed as an advertising brochure by the magazine, and finally died in the pages of a non-book I compiled for The Ryerson Press, titled *Author! Author!* in 1964. It was called "Cocktails And Canapés" and was run under a department heading of mine, The Literary Life. Here's how it went.

Shortly after I became what is laughingly referred to as a published author, a snobbish friend of mine said, "I sure envy you. Now you'll be able to mix with the social set." Up to then the thought had never occurred to me that writing and the social life had anything in common, and the thought occurs to me even less since meeting the literati on their home ground. But strangely enough there are many people who use a literary reputation, no matter how tenuous, to advance themselves on the social front.

The claws of these literary lions are blunted by handling tea-cups and martini glasses rather than by pounding typewriter keys, but they have learned to mouth *hors d'oeuvres* along with their inanities, and eat their cake with a fork—and the literary snobs clutch them to their flattened bosoms as they'd clutch a Gutenberg first edition.

Next to a funeral service for a pet cat there is nothing so ridiculous as a literary tea. Most legitimate authors avoid them as they would an outbreak of anthrax, and the hosts usually end up serving watered drinks to the same old matriarchs, spinsters and fruity young men who make a habit of turning up regularly at these affairs. Another group which attends these bookish *auto-da-fés* is a hard to define segment of the elderly male popualtion whose members function as literary dowsers, able to discover, through built-in divining rods, all free liquid refreshments within a ten-mile area.

Although he later learns the folly of accepting literary invitations, the beginning author is usually forced to appear at one cocktail party (his own) at the outset of his career. His publishers take this opportunity to introduce him to a few book store proprietors, librarians and critics and then leave him stranded in the middle of a group of well-padded parties who could be mistaken for ex-Floradora Girls, rooming-house keepers or superannuated madams. All of them seem to have more affinity with bookies than with books, and although they gush over this fresh addition to the literary ranks, none of them will ever read a word he writes.

The new author has been looking forward for years to meeting members of his own species, but he finds very few of them at his coming-out party. He tries to spot the successful authors by their conversations, clothes and general demeanor, but usually misses by the length of *War And Peace*.

The tall man in tweeds hovering near the bar looks the way an author should look, and so, with a deprecatory smile, our young author approaches him. He turns out to be quite affable and friendly, and our neophyte takes advantage of the moment to spin a long dissertation on current literary affairs. The other listens to him politely, nods sagely now and then in the right places, and occasionally offers a *bon mot* of his own. Finally, after the third or fourth cocktail, they introduce themselves; the tweedy individual turns out to be a chartered accountant who has his office in the publishers' building, and what's more he's never heard of our hero before.

Making sure he won't be caught like that again, our author steers clear of further hit-or-miss conversational entanglements and nods frigidly in answer to the warm smiles turned his way by a dear old lady wearing a velvet choker, and a shabby unshaven man standing by himself with a drink in one hand and a *Racing Form* in the other. The next day he discovers he has high-hatted the only two *bona fide* authors in the joint: one of the leading female novelists of the day, and a man whose short stories have been an inspiration since his high-school days.

The thing that all new and future authors should realize is that literary cocktail parties are merely excuses for old friends and enemies to meet each other over a drink, and that none of the guests has any interest whatsoever in the new author who is being introduced. The lady novelists are there primarily to price each other's clothes, the newspaper critics and male writers go there for a free drink, the librarians make an appearance in the hopes of finding a husband, the booksellers are there to get a line on their rivals' lists, and the great majority are hung-over disk-jockeys, out-of-work actors, advertising receptionists who filch their boss's party invitations, and the assistant editors of trade journals who supplement their incomes by free-loading from the canapé tray.

At my own debut my publishers pulled a novel twist, and, instead of me autographing copies of my *magnum opus*, a copy was autographed by the assembled guests and presented to me. This switch saved the publishers the price of a score of free copies of the book and gave me the strangest collection of autographs assembled on a document since the signing of the Japanese Peace Treaty. I can decipher about half of them and of these, two are literary figures. There is one signature that I used to kid myself belonged to George Bernard Shaw, but lately I've become reconciled to the idea that it is really the name of a salesman who travels in wicker furniture, and who found the party while searching for the men's room.

Although the literary reception may be deadly, the bookish *soirée* is positively necrological. These affairs are usually put on by a group of ex-Girl Guides who have given in to a strange urge to broaden their minds as well as their hips. Through a dulcet-toned doll on the entertainment committee, they manage to rope in several people who have a nodding acquaintance with the written word. The first of these affairs I attended became my last at the precise moment that an Amazon with a mustache like Marshall Budyenny's stepped to the podium to recite a piece of her own poesy called, "Light of Life—Past Enduring." I may be mistaken about the title however, for due to the mood I was in by then, and the way she stretched her a's, it sounded like "Light the light, Pa's appearing,"—which would have been an improvement, come to think of it.

We had no sooner recovered from this exposure to native culture than a mousey little man with a loose upper plate took the centre of the stage, accompanied by a wave of applause that would have gladdened the hearts of William Faulkner and H. G. Wells combined.

I was hypnotized by his clattering dentures, but I heard enough of his speech to know that he was bewailing the economic position of the author in modern society. This was a subject dear to my heart, so I applauded with the rest of the audience when he finished. Towards the end of the evening I asked a club member who the little man was. She looked at me as if I'd questioned her daughter's legitimacy and informed me icily that he was Mr. Borstad, the president's husband. Later on I discovered that he had once authored a sexy little tome called "The Stamp Lover's Encyclopaedia."

The act that followed Mr. Borstad on the program was made up of a man and woman who were the co-authors of a children's history book. In all fairness to this unhappy duo, I must admit they stretched an uninteresting subject to interminable lengths without once waking the sleepers in the last two rows of seats.

The evening dragged on and on as various other literary relics spoke about their pasts, and for the finale (s'help me!) the female Marshall Budyenny recited some of Shakespeare's sonnets, while she accompanied herself on the dulcimer.

By this time, the ex-Girl Guides' girdles were beginning to pinch, and I was getting a little seat-bound myself. When the chairwoman announced that the speeches were over and that coffee would be served, I relaxed and tried to make like a visiting celebrity. My languid pose only lasted a minute though, for I was pressed into service as a waiter. By means of skilful maneuvering, I managed to work my way to the door, grabbed my hat and coat, and emerged into the wonderful noisy, smoky, unliterary night.

Over the years authors have evolved hundreds of far-fetched excuses to protect themselves from debilitating contact with the literary set. At least one of them, to my knowledge, made an unnecessary trip to California just to escape a speaking engagement before a Women's Literary Guild, and considered the money well spent.

If you were to fire grape and canister through the assembled memberships of all the literary clubs from Digby to Dawson City, your bag would include almost every variety of literary character except working writers. Any so-called author who managed to get in the way of your fusilade would be considered fair game under most provincial conservation laws.

The literary party, whether it be a luncheon, cocktail or tea, is an anachronism that brings together authors who do not write and book lovers who do not read. And it is not always the visiting authors who get the worst of the deal.

One of the saddest sights this side of the Iron Curtain is that of fifty or a hundred innocent citizens being bored to death by a stammering stumblebum who accepts a speaking engagement and then discovers he has nothing to say. Authors who fancy themselves as orators should cultivate a vaudeville routine to amuse their audiences. The lady novelists could either give a cooking demonstration or an illustrated display of flower arrangements, while the males could entertain with sleight-of-hand tricks or by writing forgettable prose on a blackboard. Any change at all from the *status quo* would be a forward step in our cultural life, and it might even induce book lovers to read.

Absolutely the worst kind of party to dim the gleam in a tyro author's eye is what is extravagantly called the "autographing party." This is a form of ordeal by fire in which a nervous young man or woman sits at a table in a bookstore and catches peanuts in his or her teeth, tossed to them by giggling middle-aged women shoppers with tired feet. Unless the author is accompanied by a movie star wife or husband he or she would draw a bigger crowd demonstrating linoleum cleaner in the hardware department, and the questions asked would make more sense. A well-known author friend of mine was placed on exhibition this way in one of the country's biggest department stores last year. This store had been selling an average of twenty copies of his novel every day, but on the day he autographed his books the sales slid to five, two copies of his book being bought by his sister.

The mésalliance between the speaking writer and the listening reader is beyond redemption, but they continue living together in the hope that something short of death or divorce will end their unhappy union.

At a literary cocktail party some years ago my dalliance with the punch bowl was interrupted by the feminine head of the welcoming committee and her coterie of dedicated followers. She, dear old soul, slithered up to me at the bar and asked, in a voice that filled the room, "Tell me, Mr. Garner, do you write your books yourself?"

I peered at her over the rim of my glass and answered loudly but politely, "No, Ma'am. I usually get my mother to collaborate with me on the swear words!"

Since that day, for some reason or another, I have never been invited to a literary tea. Which serves me right!

Since then, of course, I've attended dozens of literary affairs. The ancient literary clique of my early years has changed to the swinging set of today; a different cast but the same old picture show. The semi-literate natives have now become Canadian nationalists, as dumb as their forebears but far more gross and rude. Where a business suit and necktie used to be *de rigeur* among authors, now the uniform has changed to a pseudo proletarian-cum-revolutionary denim jacket and dungarees. What hands me a laugh is that their wearers are neither proles nor revolutionaries but middle class dropouts playing the latest literary charade.

A year ago I was one of a panel of eight or ten poets and writers who made a presentation to a provincial committee set up to study the allotment of more funds by the provincial government to working writers and poets. The three committee members, all prominent journalists and publishers themselves, gave us what I considered to be a very patient and understanding hearing. It broke up however when five members of the panel (by pre-arrangement I'm sure) turned the hearing into a phony confrontation reminiscent of a hippie demonstration or a foot-stamping show of pique by members of the Gay Liberation Front and retreated from the stage into the audience. I don't know what the hell it did for their psyches but it did nothing at all in furthering the cause of more provincial funds to authors and poets. Not that these particular five really cared about money for writers; each of them, from the hippie grandmother journalist to the dungareed Joycean would-be novelist, are all supported by wealthy fathers or working husbands, wives and mistresses.

The laughable part of the whole contretemps was that these literary play-actors were ignored by the members of the news media, and it was some of us who may not have made much sense but were at least polite enough to remain on the stage with the committee, who received the newspaper and TV publicity that the five let's-pretend-we're-militants seemed to crave so much.

So much for the old and the new in the literary life for the moment.

One day in the spring of 1949 this new novelist, having drunk himself broke, went down to the federal employment office and flashed a guy behind a desk a book of employment stamps, some of them dating back to the days at Massey-Harris. I began drawing unemployment insurance, then the munificent sum of $17 a week for a married man. A few weeks later I left my Bay Street rooming house and took a train for the Gaspé Coast.

That summer was one of the happiest of my life. My unemployment payments were transferred to the office in Amqui, Quebec, which was about fifty miles by highway or rail from my father-in-law's farm, so that each week a $17 cheque was mailed to me. I divided it, five dollars to my mother-in-law, a unilingual French-Canadian lady and the best mother-in-law anyone ever had, put five dollars away to pay my train fare when I decided to return to Toronto, and spent the other seven dollars on myself and my family. The only expenditures I had all summer were an infrequent pint of rum, tobacco and cigarette papers, and *Time* magazine, which I believe then cost twenty cents. Every week I would walk, my unemployment cheque in my pocket, down the seven mile dirt road through the woods and past the infrequent small marginal farms of the valley, to the ferry boat which transported me across the Restigouche River to Campbellton, New Brunswick. I was always afraid of meeting a lynx, bear or bull moose, but the fourteen-mile weekly hike kept me in excellent shape.

I also kept myself in shape, and helped to pay for my family's and my board, by taking over the large family vegetable garden. All the neighbors and visitors to the house—almost all of whom were Acadians as my wife's family were—said the Peter Gallants had the best vegetable garden in the valley.

In the meantime three newspapers had bought *Storm Below,* the *Montreal Standard, Newark Evening News* and *Chicago Sun-Times,* and they all published condensed versions of the book in their Sunday supplements. William Collins Sons began to send me letters they had received on my behalf from seven or eight of the best New York literary agents. I chose one, whose name I now forget, and sent him some of my short story manuscripts.

My half-share of the money received from the newspapers augmented my $17-a-week income, and I gave most of it to my wife and her mother.

In the evenings in our bedroom, by the light of a kerosene lamp and using my wife's trunk as a desk, I wrote a couple of short stories, one of which was "Red Racer," a story of a French-Canadian farmer's fight with a forest fire that threatened his farm. I sold this the following winter and it was published first in the July issue of *National Home Monthly.*

By the time my garden's salad vegetables were big enough for the table and the root crops were thriving I took to our bedroom where I wrote a novel using the top of my wife's trunk as a desk. It was published under the title *Present Reckoning* as a William Collins "White Circle" paperback the following year. In September 1949 I bid my family goodbye again, and returned to Toronto.

This time I moved into a third-floor room in a large house on Bedford Road, in what is known as Toronto's "Annex" district. This was during the period when the old middle class families had given up their huge old houses to rooming house tenants, but before the hippie communards and so-called affluent young swingers bought them again as townhouses.

My new landlady was a tall angular woman who composed Congregationalist hymns. Though landladies are different in kind they belong to the same sociological sub-species, and I've recorded them in the following essay, called "Chatelaines And Charlatans" published a long time ago in the *Star Weekly.*

Here's how it went.

Little has been written up to now about that wheezy mem-sahib of single bliss society, the rooming house landlady. In those nostalgic free-wheeling days when I was able to skip with all my chattels shoved into a cardboard suitcase I met her in many cities, hiding behind her eccentric disguises. Now I can look back on our landlady-tenant relationship from a position safely separated by time and space.

When I recall my ex-landladies dispassionately I find they have a tendency to run together in my memory like colored clothes in a tub of boiling water. The collective "her" is embedded in my mind as a varicosed amalgam of all the landladies I ever knew. She was kind yet shrewish, open-minded but suspicious, trusting and stingy, dour yet often pleasant on rent day.

Landladies have lied for me to my boss, made me mustard

plasters, lent me money, introduced me to spinster nieces, trusted me for the rent—and had me evicted from my room by the police. They have been of all shapes and sizes, nationalities, faiths, creeds and denominations. I once occupied a back bedroom in the house of a spiritualist. I've also lived in the houses of a member of the Socialist-Labor party, a Theosophist, and an old lady in Quebec City who had a photograph of Mahatma Gandhi over the mantelpiece. I spent much of my youth and young manhood collecting landladies with all the zeal that others put into collecting stamps. The landladies I am writing about, of course, are the hard-sell professionals, not the housewives who rent out the spare bedroom to help pay off the mortgage.

Right here let me give a bit of gratuitous advice to the young hopefuls who are about to move to the city and live in a furnished room. Don't let a friend or fellow employee con you into moving in with his or her family, don't take a room in a strictly uptown residential district, and don't be the sole roomer in a private house. Get a room downtown in an establishment that has several other roomers. You'll be closer to everything, you'll have more fun, and you'll meet more zany characters in a week than you'll meet for the rest of your life in the suburbs.

If you are as lucky as I have been in my haphazard choice of landladies, you will have nothing to regret in the dull years which are bound to follow the introductory ones of rooming house domicile. For a born non-conformist I got along surprisingly well with most of my landladies, or at least it seems so now that our relationship has become one of memory rather than fact.

A few weeks ago I was cutting along a downtown Toronto side street where I used to hide out in the second-floor front room of a slightly tipsy replica of a Charles Addams haunted house. There on the starboard-leaning front porch was my old nemesis herself beating a rug on the porch rail.

I walked up to her and said, "Hello, Mrs. Darling." (Landladies tend to have whimsical names.)

"Good morning," she replied warily, searching me with her X-ray vision for a sales blank or a subpoena.

"That rug looks mighty familiar," I said. I stared at the hole made by a friend of mine with a spilled potable he had distilled in the anatomy building of the nearby university.

"Did you used to live here?" she asked, showing her new store-teeth and mentally reviewing her uncollected room rent accounts.

My ego was shattered but I managed to answer with a nod.

She stopped shaking the rug in my face and said, "I recognize you now. You're the young man who was president of the Vaughn Monroe Fan Club in 1946. The mail you used to get! The post-office was going to cut off deliveries until I gave you your notice. Why, one day—"

"No, Mrs. Darling," I interrupted. "That wasn't me. That was Lou Cheeseman in the room next to the bathroom, remember? He had a life-size cardboard cut-out of Vaughn that he used as a screen to hide his hotplate."

"Oh yes. He still owes me nine dollars."

"I lived in the second-floor front. My name is Garner."

"Oh, I remember you now!" she shouted triumphantly. "You were studying dentistry. When did you arrive back in town, and how is business in Sherbrooke?"

"Terrible," I murmured, completely crushed.

"Well, cheer up. Fluoridation will never be voted in. I'm anti-fluoridation you know."

"It figured," I said.

She took a closer look at me. "You're not a dentist!" she cried accusingly. "You're the fellow who was writing a book and living on his veteran's gratuities."

"That's right, Mrs. Darling."

"You're the one that pretty near burned the house down by building a paper fire in the fireplace!"

"It was a clear case of either lighting a fire or taking an ice-pick to bed with me," I said. "I figure that at today's prices I burned about $2,000 worth of literature before the fire trucks arrived."

"Well, Mr. Garbutt, I have no vacancies at present," she said, giving the rug a final flip in my face and disappearing through the ensuing dust into the house.

All landladies are one of two things: wrestling fans who cheer the villains, or hypochondriacs. I've never met one yet who didn't suffer from one of the more stylish psychosomatic ailments. Their diseases are never serious enough to kill but just uncomfortable enough to give them an excuse for being miserable.

Following the Saskatchewan harvest one Depression year I rented a room in east-central Vancouver for a month. My landlady was the hypochrondriac queen of the Pacific coast. One cupboard of her kitchen cabinet was filled with enough pills and nostrums to halt an epidemic, and she ate aspirins like candy and took Lydia Pinkham's for chasers. She never complained of any specific illness, but suffered from everything debilitating without fear or favor. She looked as healthy as an Amazon, but she had taken to heart the aphorism that an ounce of prevention was worth a pound of cure. She even took medicines prescribed only for male diseases.

One morning she took up a position at the foot of the stairs and caught every tenant as he left for work. When I came swooshing down to make my daily trip to the employment office (where I was September, 1931, euchre champion) she stopped me.

"Look, Mr. Garner," she said, handing me a newspaper clipping. It was incomplete but I read a paragraph dealing with the government's new bilateral trade pact with, I believe, Monrovia.

"That's very interesting, Mrs. Bottomley," I said, handing the clipping back but wondering if she hadn't finally flipped her unkempt lid.

"Silly!" she excaimed. "Look at the other side."

I turned the clipping over and there was her photograph. Beneath it was the statement, "Since taking Dr. Crump's Soothing Syrup I have not experienced one uncomfortable moment from chronic bronchitis." It was signed "Teresa Bottomley." Her testimonial was true enough, for she'd never had bronchitis in her life.

"Your picture in the papers and everything, Mrs. Bottomley! You're a celebrity!" She brushed aside my remark with a modest smile while I escaped into the street.

Mrs. Bull, who ran a rooming house situated above a row of stores and a Chinese laundy at the corner of Sixth Avenue and 52nd Street in New York 25 years ago, was as typical a landlady as I ever met. She was a large motherly woman of uncertain age and lineage who, during the Depression, took in some of the overflow from the Hartford House on 54th Street, a government-sponsored flophouse for mendicants with a college education. How I came to be living there (or at least eating there) is another story.

Anyway, there were four of us staying at Mrs. Bull's. A frustrated show business entrepreneur named Slade; a fellow called Bill who spent his days in the Museum of Natural History; a disbarred lawyer from Cleveland; and myself. We shared a comfortable corner room with cross ventilation from the Sixth Avenue elevated railway tracks and Leon and Eddie's night club a few doors east on 52nd Street. I was prepared to settle there and sit out the Depression, but two things sent me on my way: the authorities found out I'd never gone to Northwestern, and the disbarred lawyer ran amok. The evening he went berserk he was under the hallucination that Mrs. Bull was his ex-wife, and he chased her into the street with a pair of shears. She had us all thrown out, giving me my introduction to the theory of guilt by association.

I once lived for a time as a "house guest" in a boarding house off Waterloo Road in London. The place was run by an angular pince-nez'd harridan who hated her guests only slightly more than she hated her position in life. Not only did she make us rise and shine and attend breakfast to the numbered strokes of a gong, but she was as adamant as a regimental sergeant-major when she refused victuals to those unfortunates who were a minute late for morning parade.

The bathtub on my floor was fitted with a wooden cover. In order to have this cover removed and the bath filled with tepid water it was necessary to make an appointment with the land-lady through a little skivvy who sidled through the corridors like a frightened mouse. I made the mistake of asking for bath water on my first day in the establishment. My request was met with such scorn and evasion by the landlady that I went without bathing until I moved to more congenial quarters when my second week's rent was due. Via the bathroom window as a matter of fact.

For many years I have been of the opinion that most land-ladies are slightly fey, but whether this is a requirement or a result of their occupation I don't know. I do know though that their queerness in dress and behavior would drive a convention of psychiatrists into their own rubber-walled cells. I have had a landlady who bred pink parakeets, one who had the name "Ernest" tattooed" on her upper arm, one who wrote hymeneals for inter-racial marriages, another who went on Jamaica ginger binges that she called "Jake's curse," and one who tried to set fire to an unrequiting lover's bed. With some exceptions my ex-landladies ran the gamut from psycho-neurotics to psycho-naturopaths. I have had landladies who tried to make their lodgers take their shoes off in the vestibule, and others who refused to dislodge a cobweb for fear of disturbing the "homey" atmosphere of their bug-traps.

Even today I can spot a downtown landlady on the street, for her ensemble is generally made up of seized or cast-off clothing left behind by roomerettes who have left to become exotic dancers or medical missionaries in the Philippines. It's a socio-logical fact that the landlady is usually the worst-dressed person in the house. Why this is so I'm not prepared to say but it probably explains why she owns the house while her tenants pay rent for the temporary tenure of a made-over broom closet.

I wish that Margaret Mead or somebody would make an anthropological study of the love-life of landladies. Most of the ones I had were grass widows of middling to ancient vintage whose husbands had been banished from the family hearth, eaten by their mate like male black widow spiders, or had taken it on the lam with the week's rent receipts. The still-married ones had colorless spouses who were glimpsed at rare intervals carrying out the ashes, shovelling snow or performing other menial tasks. I have always believed that such husbands had been poor slobs who had fallen too far behind in their rent and were serving life sentences for their dereliction.

Every rooming house has a female guest who is referred to by the landlady as "That!" or "The woman in the third-floor back." These unhappy creatures are always painted by the landlady as being beyond redemption, and in my formative years I used to picture them romantically as sexually free alcoholics, drug addicts, fratricidal killers or pensioned kept women. Actually their only sin was that they demanded *two* clean sheets a week.

In the winter of 1934 I lived for a short time in a rooming house on Figueroa Street in downtown Los Angeles run by a spiritualist lady whose name I have forgotten. Three times a week she held seances in her living room with an old man called Charley as her assistant. Charley's roommate was a normally quiet old fellow who worked as a cleaner at the city hall and used to tiptoe into his room about two in the morning.

One night there was a horrible scream from the upstairs hallway, and we all ran to our doors to see who was being murdered. The city hall cleaner was backed against the wall in the hallway. He managed to blurt out, "There's a ghost in my room!"

One of the braver roomers—not me—looked in and beat a hasty retreat. "It's a hand, a ghostly hand, moving around the room by itself!" he said.

By this time the landlady was hurtling up the stairs, followed by her husband and two girls who roomed on the first floor and worked in the five-and-ten.

"What is it? What is it?" the landlady was shouting as she came.

"There's a ghost in my room!" the cleaner cried.

"Nonsense! There's no such thing as ghosts," she answered, which was a funny statement for *her* to make I thought.

96

She went to the doorway of the ghostly room and cried, "Charley, come out this minute!"

Her assistant came to the doorway and stared about him. "The light bulb burned out is all," he said.

"I thought I told you to wash your hand after the meeting," the landlady scolded him.

"I forgot."

He went into his darkened room to get his soap and towel, and one of his hands shone luminously in the darkness, seemingly moving about by itself. The next day poor old Charley, ectoplastic hand and all, got his flitting papers, both from the house and, I suppose, from the spiritualist movement.

In many rooming houses I lived in the landlady rented all the rooms and moved herself and her shabby mementos into the cellar, from which she emerged at odd times of the day or night looking like a lightly ash-dusted dryad. I have the feeling that the modern basement apartment or recreation room started this way.

My frequent run-ins with female keepers-of-the-gate were usually caused by a clash of wills. I refused to bow to their dictatorial whimsies and I carried on a vendetta for months with a landlady who had an insane compulsion to paper the halls and bathroom with cautionary signs. My fellow inmates and I were cautioned against bathing more than twice a week (a completely unnecessary warning to most by the way), turning on the hall lights, keeping guests after 10 p.m., walking too heavily after lights out, not paying rent on the day it was due, not scrubbing out the bath after use, and a dozen other prohibitions that have happily slipped my mind.

As soon as a new sign would go up I would scribble in an appropriate comment or tear the sign down. I avoided detection for a long time, but finally the landlady's suspicions centred on me. Though she couldn't prove anything she got back at me in other ways. She held on to my mail for days at a time, left my bed unmade, and one night when I was reading a book she pulled the main switch and plunged the house in darkness. I ran into the hall and shouted that I was going to make a bonfire of the furniture to read by. This caused a minor panic, during which the police were called. After smelling my breath and listening to my explanation the officers warned me to keep the peace, and told the landlady that shutting off the house lights was a breach of the law. I moved the following day, by request.

I can only mention in passing the meek little chatelaine of a Montreal rooming house where I once lived, who was discovered sheltering one of Canada's most wanted criminals in her basement den. Or the landlady who thought I was a fit subject to proselytize into membership in the Mormon Church. She used to read me "uplifting" sermons she wrote herself, and these illiterate confections, despite the promise of a plurality of wives, kept me from ever becoming a Latter Day Saint.

Then there was the little old Toronto landlady, one of my all-time favorite people, who after getting plastered on wine every Saturday night gave all the roomers their notice, only to retract it shakily on Sunday morning. Her name was Mrs. Leicester or Lyveden or one of those names that remind me of King Arthur's round table.

Before I forget, I must give a short paragraph or two to the landlady of a Morris Street rooming house in Halifax, who made the mistake of renting a room to me and two naval buddies while we were taking a course early in the war. One of these guys is now an executive of the New Brunswick Telephone Company and the other is a Manitoba real estate salesman. One morning a woman roomer opened her door to pick up her newspaper but instead found the future executive passed out on her threshold. She ran out of the house in her nightgown screaming that there was a dead man lying in the hallway. The landlady, a 200-pound Irishwoman, rushed up from her basement retreat and planted a strategic kick to my roommate. He let out a yell that set every gull to flight from Bedford Basin to Chebucto Head.

"I knew it would be one of you drunken bums!" the landlady screamed. "From now on I'm renting no more rooms to sailors! I hope we win the war but in the Battle of the Atlantic I'm on the side of the Germans!"

With that bit of patriotic sagacity off her ample chest she went back to her basement lair, where she was probably happily engaged in counterfeiting ration coupons or perhaps just dismembering a corpse.

I'd just like to say to landladies everywhere—past, present and those undergoing their novitiate—thanks for a million laughs at the time I needed them the most. I hope all your tenants remain sober, sensible and solvent, and that every deadbeat you ever trusted sends you a cheque in tomorrow's mail.

Much later I was to write a novel titled *Silence On The Shore,* about a fictional rooming house in Toronto's Annex district and my fictional landlady, Mrs. Grace Hill, was to become a composite of some of the real landladies you've just been reading about.

After moving from the Gaspé back to Toronto I wrote several magazine articles which were bought by various Canadian magazines. One of them, a revelatory sociological piece about Toronto's Jarvis Street, was on an assignment from *Maclean's*. The managing editor of *Maclean's* at that time was Pierre Berton who knew a hell of a lot less about Jarvis Street or any street in Toronto for that matter, than I did, and who had just come down from Vancouver. Berton had been conditioned by the *Maclean's* editors to think that a magazine article had to be researched to death. Though an excellent non-fiction writer and assiduous researcher himself, he, like all of the literary Lochinvars who had invaded Toronto from the West, knew nothing of the city at that time. Twenty years ago Jarvis Street was a synonym to Torontonians for prostitution, but except for a few B-girls who hung out in its barrooms most of the whores had long before begun to ply their trade on Dundas and other neighborhood streets.

A short time before being given this assignment Gordon Sinclair had written a piece about prostitution in Windsor, Ontario and had been assigned to do a follow-up piece about Toronto. He had a more pressing story to write and told the editors of the *Toronto Star* to get me to show a reporter around the Jarvis-Dundas neighborhood.

The *Star* phoned me, and I agreed to do the job. I took in tow a young reporter (one who later became an editorial writer on the paper), spent the paper's money recklessly on Henessy Three-Star brandies, introduced the reporter to bar-girls, street-walkers and chippies, and drunkenly earned my fee for the evening. The reporter got a story, including a vignette about a young married woman whose husband had just beaten her up, and who offered to sleep with both of us for the sake of a bed for the night. Early in the morning I bid my companion goodbye and ended up drinking wine in a Church Street bootlegging joint at four a.m.

Anyhow, I wrote the Jarvis Street piece, beginning at its upper end at Bloor Street, where it faced the façade of a chronic-case hospital cruelly named The Home For Incurable Children, and continued south on the street, past the Anglican

Church headquarters building and some remaining large respectable family houses. There was the one in which the Masseys had lived, the same Massey family that owned the Massey-Harris Company in which I'd worked, and including Vincent Massey, a former Governor General of Canada, Raymond Massey the actor, and the rest. I described Jarvis Collegiate, the CBC buildings, and so on, getting lower each block both in altitude and social position. I described the Walsingham Hotel in which I'd lived, and below Dundas Street the rooming house where I'd been a roomer before the war. I continued my description of the street, which changed so dramatically from north to south, past the Crippled Civilians retail store and workshop, the lower Jarvis pubs, the St. Lawrence Market, to where the street ended at a soft-drink bottling plant. I described its denizens also: the rich, not-so-rich, poverty-stricken, the whores, junkies and criminals who had made Jarvis and Dundas streets *their* corner.

When I handed the piece to Pierre Berton he told me to go back and interview the unfortunates in the Crippled Civilians workshop. It was embarrassing to me and to them but I did it. Not that it mattered a goddam to the story, but it seemed to matter to Berton and the other *Maclean's* editors at the time who were beginning to seem like nuts to me.

There was a block of cheap rooming houses situated where the Moss Park armouries now stands, which I described from a viewpoint on the opposite sidewalk after nightfall. I saw a young man in one of the upper rooms practicing his violin and a girl ironing some clothing on a dresser top. Berton, who had a blind, prejudiced eye for a semi-fictional vignette in a factual article, asked me, "What was the violinist's name?" Christ, that was the last straw! I said, "I didn't find out his name, but it sure as hell wasn't Jascha Heifetz!" Berton rewrote the piece himself, something like me writing about Vancouver's Stanley Park, and it became a piece of *Maclean's* pap called "The Stately Street of Sin" over the magazine's by-line "Gratton Gray." I didn't write anything more for *Maclean's* for five years. Instead of my $300 fee I received only $150. I suppose the other $150 went to the fictitious "Gratton Gray."

As a footnote, let me add that many magazine journalists were constantly being put off by the insane desire on the part of the editors of *Maclean's* to write only the truth, the whole truth, and nothing but the truth, as if they were bloody court reporters. I once met Trent Frayne on Yonge Street, and he was quite distraught, having just had an article turned down by the magazine after spending a month on it. Mackenzie Porter, for years one of the stable salaried *Maclean's* writers, once had six or seven articles turned down in a row.

One thing I'd learned at the outset of my freelancing days was not to put my faith in one group of editors or all my talents into one sales market. I had seen what it had done to others, forced to depend on and genuflect to editors or script buyers at the CBC, *Maclean's* or any other single market upon which they became dependent.

In the fall of 1949 I borrowed three hundred dollars from my mother and bought a house trailer that looked like a chicken coop on wheels. It was a single-room rectangular structure with a bed at either end, a table, a pot-bellied stove called a "Quebec heater" in those days, a couple of kitchen chairs, and a tapless sink. The man I bought it from had it towed to an empty lot in Scarborough, an eastern suburb of Toronto, where it was parked alongside two other much better trailers owned by their occupants. I think I paid five dollars a month ground rental, which included the privilege of drawing water from a tap at an old farm house on the lot, inhabited by some sort of hill-billy family, and also the use of a communal outdoor privy. My family returned to Toronto and we lived in this chicken coop all that winter, quite a severe one. My daughter attended a new public school across the street, at the corner of Danforth and Birchmount Roads.

The trailer was heated by coke I bought in small heavy paper bags at a nearby country store, my wife did the washing in the small sink, and the children used a chamber pot for a toilet. I was kept alive, as I've already mentioned, mainly by the articles bought by Jake Thomas for *National Home Monthly*. One of the ironic things about life in the "trailer" was that my wife's raccoon coat, which she'd bought during the war, was worth more than all our other possessions at the time put together. The cold and damp even ruined the fur coat.

Though *Storm Below* sold 1,400 copies in hard covers, and was printed as a Collins paperback, selling another 20,200, I made only $461 from it in 1949. Collins bought *Present Reckoning* as a White Circle paperback, giving me a $200 advance during the winter of 1950. My total income from my writing in 1949 was about a thousand dollars.

One day during the winter of 1950 I was down at the CBC, trying in vain to sell one of my short stories for radio broadcast, when I ran into an old friend from my Spanish Civil War Days, Ted Allen, who was later to become a playwright in England. Ted told me that an outfit called Export Publishing located in

102

the town of New Toronto was looking for paperback manuscripts (which they then sold throughout the United States and
Canada), for which they paid $400 cash. I went down and saw
them, and they told me to write them a book. I went back to
my mobile chicken coop, sat down at the table near the pot-
bellied coal stove, and wrote a 250-300 page quickie novel called
Waste No Tears. After writing it once, and correcting it in
pen-and-ink, I typed a fair copy and took it in to the publishing
house. Altogether the writing, correcting and rewriting had taken
me ten days, a speed record even for me, driven by the incipient
starvation of my family. I used as my author's *nom de plume*
the same one I had used in the *Maclean's* short story contest,
"Jarvis Warwick".

I waited and waited for Export Publishing to pay me my four
hundred dollars but they kept putting me off. Finally I went
downtown to the only lawyer I was acquainted with, D'arcy
Kingsmill, who had been one of my officers in the artillery at the
outbreak of war, and showed him my contract with Export
Publishing. He wrote them a letter which they couldn't ignore,
for Mr. Kingsmill was not only a paid-up member of the *real*
Toronto Establishment but his law firm was one of the most
prestigious in the city. I received my $400 cheque and Mr.
Kingsmill charged me a token fee of only $10.

By this time it was spring, and I paid my mother back the
$300 I'd borrowed from her, sent my family back to Quebec,
and abandoned the chicken coop where it stood. I moved downtown again into another rooming house.

William Collins Sons offered to publish *Cabbagetown* in a
White Circle paperback edition, and by now, sick to death of
even thinking of the book, I gave it to them for an advance on
royalties of $200. They brought it out in 1950, halved in length,
and to their surprise (but not to mine) it was a best-seller,
selling more than 45,000 copies. In those days, and for a great
many years later, I tore up my manuscripts as soon as a book
was published, but in the case of *Cabbagetown* I kept one of the
full-length manuscripts.

Now I was the published author of three novels, one in hard
covers and two paperbacks, but was poorer than I'd been while
working as a shipping clerk or punch-press inspector. I kept
myself alive, paid the rent, and drank a lot of beer on the fees
I received from magazines for pieces of journalism. Jake
Thomas bought articles on the Jehovah's Witnesses, a lonely
hearts' column interview, and others; Jock Carroll had me interview a Toronto Indian magistrate called Martin, and this ap-

peared in the *Montreal Standard.* Mary-Etta Macpherson of *Canadian Home Journal* bought a piece called "Do Canadian Schools Educate?"

"One, Two, Three Little Indians," the story Bill Mitchell had tried so hard to buy for *Maclean's,* had now gone the rounds of almost every magazine in North America with no takers. I finally sold it to *Liberty,* as the first short story they bought from me, after Jack Kent Cooke, the magazine's publisher, read it and liked it. The irony of the whole thing, looking back on it, was that at the same time I sold *Liberty* the short story I also sold them a silly little article titled "Dear Mr. Hollywood." I received $100 for the Hollywood piece but only $50 for "One, Two, Three Little Indians," which was published in the December, 1950 issue.

During the late months of 1950 I sent "The Conversion Of Willie Heaps" to John Sutherland, the editor of *Northern Review,* one of the first of the Canadian "little" magazines. Sutherland took it right away, and when it was published in 1951 it shared a prize of $150 given to the best short story published in the magazine that year. My co-winner was a woman then living in Philadelphia, the niece or granddaughter of Charles G. D. Roberts.

The next year "The Conversion Of Willie Heaps" was reprinted by Martha Foley in her annual *Best American Short Stories, 1952.* Along with it three more of my short stories published in 1951 were listed in the anthology's Roll of Honor, more than any other North American that year. They were "The Yellow Sweater" from *Chatelaine,* "A Couple of Quiet Young Guys" from *Canadian Forum,* and "Our Neighbors The Nuns," also published in *Northern Review.*

In 1950, besides "One, Two, Three Little Indians," the only short stories I sold were "Coming Out Party" to *Chatelaine,* and "Red Racer" and "The Go-Boys" to *National Home Monthly.* "The Go-Boys" was the shortened chapter from *Cabbagetown* in which Bob McIsaacs and Sam Spilluk are pursued by the police following a hold-up. In 1951 I sold a total of seventeen short stories to Canadian magazines, a figure I have never since equalled.

Short stories are not only hard to write and sell, but they are a very hard literary commodity to pre-judge for popularity. Sometimes a story that its author thinks will become popular doesn't, and another, that he may have written quickly and without any thought to its future, takes off and sells over and over again year after year. I have already mentioned "One, Two, Three

Little Indians" but another one titled "A Trip For Mrs. Taylor," a close runner-up, was published first in *Chatelaine* in 1951.

"One, Two, Three Little Indians" had almost as hard a time seeing print as did Ernest Hemingway's "Twenty Grand" which was turned down by fourteen American magazines before being published in the *Atlantic Monthly*. On the other hand "A Trip For Mrs. Taylor" was accepted by the first magazine I sent it to, and was bought in two days. Perhaps I can use it to answer the question "How do you dream up a short story?"

During the years 1951-1953 my family and I lived in three furnished flats on Centre Island, one of a ring of Islands in Toronto Bay, a mile from downtown. In those days the Island population consisted of an all-year citizenry of about 5,000 hardy Bohemians (as they were then known), social misfits, old middle-class families who had used their houses as summer cottages in the pre-war years, gouging landlords who divided their rickety shacks into "apartments," altogether the damndest gang of non-conformists ever gathered together.

During the summer of 1951 I drank myself broke, and my $75 monthly rent day was less than a week away. I had to write a saleable story fast, and at eight o'clock one evening after the children had been put to bed, I dreamed up a story about a little old lady, an old-age pensioner who was determined to take a summertime trip on a train. I used my mother as my protagonist, thinking hard on what she would pack in her old suitcase if she were Mrs. Taylor. By three the next morning the story was written, and after a few hours sleep I typed a corrected copy of it.

When I began the story I hadn't the slightest idea how I was going to resolve it, or what adventures (plot) Mrs. Taylor would go through before I'd stated my theme. The theme of the story is that anyone with determination and an unquenchable urge to do something can do it, and that the anticipation of a trip and the getting ready for it can be just as exciting for an old lady like Mrs. Taylor as the actual trip itself. Also that the memory of the trip is something she would cherish for the rest of her few remaining days.

I invariably write short stories and novels with only a preconceived idea or theme in mind, letting the plot develop as I go along. Luckily I possess something I can only call "story sense," which allows me to let my characters develop naturally as the story unfolds.

That afternoon I took the story up to *Chatelaine* and into the office of Almeda Glassey, the fiction editor. Almeda told me that the magazine was looking for stories interesting to young marrieds, and when I told her my story was about a 75-year-old woman she didn't seem too hopeful that *Chatelaine* could use it. I told her I'd written it for the rent money and that I'd be very grateful if she would read it right away and give me a quick refusal or acceptance. She phoned the next day and told me that both she and Byrne Hope Sanders, the editor, had read it, that both liked it, and they wanted to buy it. They bought it and printed it in their October, 1951 issue and repeated it in July, 1958.

The day after my phone call from Almeda I went up to the Maclean-Hunter accounting department and picked up the cheque. Nearly all the magazines were good to me in this way over the years, and it helps to explain why I didn't send more new stories to the United States instead of to Canadian magazines which as a rule had their offices in Toronto. When I needed money I needed it *right then,* and I couldn't wait for some guy in New York, Boston or Philadelphia to make up his mind whether or not to buy my stuff. In those days I knew almost as many accountants as I did editors.

Magazine editors have always belonged to two categories: those who liked an editor's job as some people like being ledger-keepers or life insurance underwriters, and failed writers who take editing jobs to stay as close to the writing business as they can while drawing a regular weekly or monthly salary. The latter type make bad editors, and if I were to ever become the owner of a publication none of my editors would be failed or would-be writers.

The best editors, both on magazines and those who put in time in publishers' offices, are the main cogs in the editorial machinery, of which more later on. Right now let me say that my favorite magazine editors have been people like Robert Weaver of CBC Radio, Mary-Etta MacPherson of *Canadian Home Journal* (who became a published writer herself *after* she left the magazine business), J. K. Thomas of *National Home Monthly,* Keith Knowlton when he edited *Liberty,* and Ray Gardner of the *Star Weekly.* Only the laws of libel and slander prevent me from naming the idiotic editors it has been my misfortune to write for in the past. Their lack of understanding and intelligence, their lack of proficiency in English composition, and their disregard for writers still maddens me.

Though by now I was recognized as a good short story writer by Canadian editors and also by American anthologists and literary agents, I was totally ignored by the judging committee of the University of Western Ontario's President's Medal Awards, or whatever the hell it's called. I'd complied with their regulations, sending them tearsheets of "One, Two, Three Little Indians," "A Trip For Mrs. Taylor," "The Conversion Of Willie Heaps," "The Yellow Sweater" and others of my better stories during 1950 and 1951, but when I failed to win a short story prize for any of my 1951 stories I gave up. If I'm not mistaken, that year *no* short story won the short story prize, but instead it was given to Farley Mowat for a chapter from a book of his about Eskimos.

I had no quarrel with Farley winning the prize, he's always been a good friend whom I admire both professionally and as a person. As for the literary academic grandmas of Western, I tender them the same advice I gave to my next-door neighbor who knocked on the wall when I was typing the final chapters of *Storm Below.* I believe, with a mixture of sincerity and choler, that too many of our past literary judging panels, including the one at Western and also the literary loonies of the Canadian Authors Association (who, God help us all! used to give out the Governor General's Awards) were motivated not by critical judgement but by snobbery and sycophancy. To them there was only one magazine in the country, *Maclean's,* while others were beneath their contempt.

If critical acclaim had been the measurement by which a novel was judged by the senile amateur writers and poetasters of the Canadian Authors Association, my first published book, *Storm Below,* would have won the fiction prize for 1949. Instead it was given to Philip Child, a respectable academic member of the C.A.A. for a piece of fluff called *Mr. Ames Against Time.* I may occasionally forget the continuity of my writing years, writing as I am from memory and without notes, but believe me I don't forget, nor will I ever, the little stupid bastards who made my beginning years as a writer even harder than they would have normally been. A pox on all of them.

It was sometime in late 1949 or early 1950 when I first contacted a man who since then has done me so many favors and saved me from so many disasters that I shall always be in his debt. He is Robert Weaver, now Head, Radio Arts Programming, at the CBC. I forget what Weaver's title was in those days, but I remember that despite a few tries I'd never been able to sell anything to the CBC. One afternoon I got up from my favorite table in a Toronto Bay Street pub and walked to the telephone in the lobby. I called Weaver at the CBC and asked him if he was buying "Our Neighbors The Nuns" for one of his programs.

107

I forget exactly what I said—I was so stoned I didn't even remember the following day, never mind twenty-two years later —but I'm sure my language was obscene, scatalogical and very un-nunlike. Anyway, despite my rude polemic and not because of it, Bob Weaver bought the story and broadcast it on March 31st, 1950. It was the beginning of a friendship that has lasted to this day.

Because *Cabbagetown* was such an unexpected success when it was published, William Collins Sons agreed to bring out a book containing nineteen of my short stories in hard covers in October, 1952, called *The Yellow Sweater And Other Stories.*

Recently Robert Fulford, editor of *Saturday Night,* in a review of my fourth collection of short stories in *The Toronto Star,* said that my best collection was my first, *The Yellow Sweater.* It certainly contained some memorable stories, but my choice for my best collection would have to be *Hugh Garner's Best Stories,* for not only did this book contain the twelve best from *The Yellow Sweater,* but also some good new stories.

By the end of 1952 I was writing only the occasional short story, a condition that was to continue for the next ten years. By then I was the author of five books, and I decided more by accident than intent to become a magazine journalist. The money was good, the markets in Canada wide and flourishing, and the writing of magazine articles much easier than the writing of short stories. But more about that later in this book, and more also about *Hugh Garner's Best Stories* when I get to it.

I think the main thing I learned during my first three years as a professional writer was that an author has to be able to afford to write a novel, something every would-be novelist should consider. I also learned that the printing of a novel is the best way for a short story writer to get his short stories into print, strange as it may seem.

When *The Yellow Sweater* was published I received a very encouraging letter from Morley Callaghan about the stories, and I remain grateful to him for this. I applied for a Guggenheim Fellowship around this time, but was turned down. Morley Callaghan had consented to write a reference for me, which he did, but unfortunately the Guggenheim Fellowship Committee didn't think I deserved an award. Looking back on it over the distance of twenty years I think that with a small fellowship grant I may have written a good novel or two in the early fifties, instead of writing magazine journalism. In those days the ideas came easier and my writing was fast and facile; unfortunately I was unable to afford the time that novel-writing needs.

Though I was getting to know a few writers by this time I made no effort to socialize with them, in the same way and for the same reasons that I've never made an effort to become socially friendly with editors or publishers. With the exception of a night spent at Charles Sweeny's house in a small town north of Toronto, and a party at Robin Ross-Taylor's apartment, my only social contact with editors and publishers was the occasional luncheon or talking to them across their office desk.

I started out as a loner and, at the expense of sometimes having to insult people who were unaware of this personality trait and became importunate in their invitations, I managed to remain one.

It was Bennett Cerf I think who, speaking of the New York literary establishment, said something like this: "The publishing trade is overrun with a gang of Ivy League bums hustling to save their asses, people who are losers with no place else to go. The general ineptitude which cloaks the profession provides the mantle under which such clucks can succeed in concealing themselves from discovery—and get some pretty sharp French food while doing it."

Well said.

Books of short stories have always been notoriously hard to sell, both by an author to a publisher and by a publishing house to the public. William Collins Sons made me no offer to publish *The Yellow Sweater* as a White Circle paperback, and as a consequence the book failed to earn enough to cover the advance on royalties they had paid me. However, from my point of view my books of short stories have been a lifetime source of income. My short stories usually follow this pattern: they are first sold to a magazine or to the CBC for radio reading or adaptation to TV dramas, then collected in a book, and after the book is published, the individual stories are sold to textbook and anthology publishers or in foreign translation. I did my own adaptations for TV in the 1950s-1960s, a job I'm about to return to since some of my scripts have been ruined by bearded weirdo adapters lately.

As a journalist from 1952 to let's say 1960, I was able to squander my talents on hundreds of magazine articles, enjoy a lifestyle that allowed me to drink with my male friends in downtown beer parlours for days at a time, yet earn enough money in a few days of hardworking sobriety to keep my family for a month. One year, during the 50s, I was surprised to find that my income was much higher than the median income of most other Canadians; that's when I should have sunk my money into Xerox and Polaroid stock instead of into Molson's Export Ale.

I've often sensed when being interviewed by representatives of "the media" that they want to ask, "How do you manage to be so prolific as a writer and still drink as much as you do?" The answer is, simply, I don't drink as much today as people think I do, and as a matter of fact I never did. Except for the nineteen-fifties when I spent a lot of my time in beer parlours I've always been a binge drinker. This has meant that though my intake of alcohol over a year has probably been less than that of most social drinkers, I've drunk it all on three or four occasions. And I've always been a public drunk. In order to write I must be perfectly sober, and if you ask me so does almost every other writer in the world.

During my early years as a freelance writer, 1949 to 1952, my income had been quite modest, to put it euphemistically. In 1949 I sold two magazine articles, in 1950 five, and in 1951 eleven. The rest of my income came from my short stories and books. From 1952 until the very early sixties almost all my income came from magazine articles and essays, while from 1956 on I earned some from my television plays.

As I've already said, my family and I lived from 1950 to 1953 on Toronto Island, and sometime during those years I found myself not only running out of money (I'd always lived from hand to mouth anyway, so this wasn't as traumatic as it seems), but out of ready markets for my magazine journalism, or thought I was, which is the same thing. I became a little panicky and went to see Keith Knowlton, the editor of *Liberty*.

On my first visit to *Liberty*, back in 1947, I'd been given a polite brush-off by Knowlton's predecessor, a New Zealander named Wallace Reyburn. Reyburn had moved to England, from where he sent newspaper columns to the *Toronto Telegram* for some time. He may be dead now, I don't know; so many freelance journalists have disappeared into the anonymous ooze.

Anyhow I went in to see Keith Knowlton, who had been a friendly managing editor of the magazine on my first visit. Keith was a good, discriminating editor but was a little timid in asserting himself, especially to the owner of the magazine, Jack Kent Cooke.

After moving the editorial offices from Simcoe Street the magazine had set up shop in a suite of offices on Bloor Street near Avenue Road. Jack Kent Cooke, however, along with the business offices of the Cooke enterprises (radio station CKEY, Ottawa radio station CKOY, the Toronto Baseball Club, *Liberty*, Broadcast Sales, and a couple more things) had settled into the top floor of a four or five-story office building above a restaurant near the corner of King and Yonge Streets.

I told Keith that I was getting a little panicky about the freelancing dodge, and that I couldn't bail myself out every month by writing a sure-seller like "A Trip For Mrs. Taylor." Keith, who has always been a nice guy, said he'd tell Jack Cooke and see if Cooke could give me a job. The following day I received a call from Jack, whom I'd met when I sold him "One, Two, Three Little Indians," and he told me to drop in and see him the following morning.

The next morning, wearing a made-to-measure sports jacket and Daks slacks, I was ushered into Cooke's large rectangular office where he sat at the end of a long conference table, his back to the wind ws on King Street. The office had been professionally decorated, and when I went in a lady interior decorator was talking to Jack about a pair of oversize lamps he wanted to decorate each end of a semicircular couch along the inside wall of the office. Jack motioned to me to come in, and said to the decorator, "What the hell do I look like, a millionaire?" Then he laughed.

I walked up to the head of the conference table and said, "It's good of you to see me, Mr. Cooke."

"It's good to see you, Hugh. Don't call me Mr. Cooke, that's my father's name."

"Okay, Jack."

"Keith Knowlton tells me you're looking for a job?"

"Right."

"What can you do?"

"I can write."

"I know that; I've read some of your stuff. Can you sell?"

"I have to sell everything I write."

"Yeah, that's true. Would you like to be a salesman?"

"No, I'd sooner be a writer."

"Do you want to work for *Liberty*?"

"Not particularly, though I'm in no position to turn down any job."

As if it had just occurred to him, though later I was to learn that he studied things very carefully before coming to a decision, he said, "How would you like to do public relations for me—for the ball park, the radio station, *Liberty*, and so on?"

"Great."

"What salary would you want?"

I thought for a minute and answered, "I can get by on eighty dollars a week."

"All right, Hugh," he said. "Come down here tomorrow morning. I guess you'll need a secretary?"

"I suppose so."

"All right, I'll get so-and-so up at the radio station to hire you one." He stood up and we walked to the door. I was introduced to Neil Watt, and to Jack's beautiful secretary, Beverley. "What do you want to be called?" he asked me. "I have publicity people at the ball park, CKEY, and *Liberty*, and you'll be over them."

I said, "How about Public Relations Director? That's as phony as any other."

"Okay, Hugh," he said, laughing. "I'll have them move a desk into the back corner of the main office for you. Do you want a typewriter?"

112

"Yes, please."

"Okay, when you come in at nine tomorrow morning it'll be all set up."

I took the ferry boat back to Centre Island, feeling a great burden had been lifted from me. I'd liked Jack Cooke the first time I'd met him, I'd liked the way he'd hired me, and I was to like him from then on, more than anyone I ever worked for in my life.

By the time I reached the Island I was just in time to make the co-ed beer parlor of the Manitou Hotel on "The Drag" as we natives called the main business street. Luckily for me I wasn't barred from it at the time, and I went in and joined some of the regulars at one of the tables. Bill Sutherland, the proprietor of the Manitou until his death, often barred me for short periods of time, or cut me off. Once he told me and a friend of mine, Rags Johnston, that he was going to take down two of the pictures of Indian chiefs which decorated the walls of the beer parlor and replace them with our photographs. "You two guys cause more commotion in here than any Indian who ever lived," Bill said.

The next morning I began work as the public relations director of Jack Kent Cooke's enterprises. I also joined the Toronto Men's Press Club.

I had hard luck with secretaries. The first one was a shy little girl who fell off a horse one Sunday and broke her arm. She was replaced by a tall, dark, statuesque, grass-widow who lived in the old Metropole Hotel and was always going broke before payday. One day an announcer from CKEY was talking to me at my desk, and being piqued by something my secretary had done or failed to do I asked him the rhetorical question, "What would you do if she was *your* secretary?"

"I'd rape her," he said.

I had two more secretaries before the summer was out but both of them, like the grass widow before them, quit to get higher paying jobs. They were all nice girls, and I gave them each long, lying, flowery recommendations when they left. The truth was I didn't need a secretary at all, and I'd often tell them to take the afternoon off just to get rid of them. By this time I also had a combination commercial artist-sign painter working under me, who did all the signs and artistic displays for the various companies. I fired the publicity man at CKEY and replaced him with a friend from the Island who was out of work. He worked at the radio station for some time until he quit to go to Maple Leaf Gardens doing publicity. I replaced him with my last secretary, who worked as public relations girl for the radio station until she quit to get married.

The publicity man at the ball park was a little Jewish guy whom Cooke had taken out of the soft drink and hamburger concession for the job. During the off-season the job consisted mainly of selling seats to season ticket holders. Cooke knew that a large percentage of the Toronto ball fans were Jewish and his move made sense. One day Jack and I were talking about this man and Cooke said, "Sometimes I think some of my employees are sent here just to try me. Do you know what so-and-so was calling baseball until I found out about it?" I shook my head. "He was calling it hardball," Jack said, breaking into a laugh.

I made quite a few boo-boos myself. One of my jobs was to lay out the advertising copy for the ball park, and one day through a slip of my pen I gave any woman who attended the following evening's game a free seat. Jack just smiled, rather wryly. I guess that was the day he added me to his list of those employees sent to try him.

The first couple of months on King Street slipped by, and I'd now found another place to be cut-off in or thrown out of, the Toronto Men's Press Club. From my wet-canteen-drinker's point of view the *men's* press club should have been just that, a place where a member could relax, blaspheme and use obscenities, and generally conduct himself as the men I'd known in armies and a navy had done. Unfortunately the Toronto Men's Press Club, then situated on Yonge Street north of King, had attracted to its membership people who had previously worked on newspapers or for various facets of the "news media," and were now in advertising, public relations—as I was myself—or such other nine-to-five jobs. Many of these people, plus some legitimate newspapermen, had the rules changed so that women could be admitted to the club at lunch time. These wives, mistresses, secretaries, or what, would sit in the lounge where they could overhear everything from the bar. I often got into loud, swearing arguments or told drunken stories, and my gravelly voice could be heard all over the club. Consequently I was always being cut off.

One evening I went up to the third floor (furnished with long soft divans and couches, to which I would retreat when I was noontime-sober for a nap) and fell asleep. The next thing I knew the club was shut for the night, so I called my wife, told her I was locked in the press club, and would be home in the morning. I then went back to sleep.

I woke up early in the morning (my usual getting up time

even now is between 5 and 6 a.m.) and went down to the bar, terribly shaky and disjointed, and tried to figure out how to get a drink. The shelves and cupboards behind the bar were padlocked but I noticed that the bartenders had left a bottle of Martini & Rossi vermouth standing in its slot. It was like a man dying of thirst on the Sahara finding an oasis. I spent a pleasant hour or so emptying the vermouth bottle, a drink I usually detest, even in a martini. Suddenly the door was opened and the steward came in to work, He was a new man and was surprised to find me sitting at a table gulping long shots of vermouth on the rocks. He reported me to the committee and I was given a suspension.

Some time later, probably months later because it was shortly before Christmas, I attended the club's Children's Santa Claus Party, taking my two small children. I got drunk fairly early, of course, and then sat in the lounge with the other parents and children singing Christmas carols. I recognized Santa Claus as a man named Warren Tooze I had known for years, in whose militia bugle band I had once played. When the party was over and the children had received their presents, I took them home. The next time I tried to enter the club I found I'd been summarily barred pending a meeting of the membership committee.

I couldn't figure out why I was barred but seemed to remember putting dirty words into the lyrics of the Christmas carols. The club committee barred me forever from the club, "forever and ever and a day" as one wit put it later. Two other members were also barred or suspended at the same meeting, an old friend, a non-practicing lawyer from the Island, and an out-of-work club member whom I'd got to know at the bar. The first was accused of using suggestive language to the bride of a sportswriter with whom he was dancing, the other was accused of borrowing money, which he didn't repay, from the bartenders, and I was accused of something or other, which I didn't bother to check. We were all given a chance to appear before the club president and the committee the following week to deny our guilt or offer our apologies. I was unable to deny my guilt for a breach of regulations of which I was unaware, and I sure as hell wasn't going to apologize for anything to any committee. Consequently my permanent ouster has continued to this day.

About a year later I bumped into Don Goudy, presently the "Star Probe" columnist for the *Daily Star*, who had been the press club president at the time I was barred. I asked Don just what the charge was against me, was it for putting dirty words in the Christmas carols? "No, Hughie," he said. "It was for giving away, at the top of your voice, the identity of Santa Claus." That was one piece of myth-destruction I didn't get away with.

While I was a member of the press club I probably did Jack Cooke more good, in the sense of promotion and public relations, than could have been done by anyone else. I tried to destroy the attitude then prevalent among members of the press (as well as among the business community and the Toronto Establishment) that Cooke was a ruthless parvenu who paid low wages to his employees, fired them on whim, and a person who flaunted his new-found wealth everywhere he went.

Actually Jack Kent Cooke was a tough, intelligent, intuitive, perspicacious man who, having begun with nothing and made a fortune the hard way through his natural ability and salesmanship (he was probably the best salesman in Canada), was envied by those who were unwilling or unable to do the same. He also had a great sense of style and impeccable taste in clothing, furniture, office and home decoration, and other such things. I learned a lot from him about millionaires, style and taste, and how the Establishment (of which he was never accepted as a member) lived and acted. I used a lot of this to describe the character "Alex Hurd" in *A Nice Place To Visit,* a novel I wrote fifteen years after last seeing Jack Cooke.

He once collared me in his office—he and I were both high school dropouts and the same age—and showed me a book he was studying on "taste," asking me which of four illustrations in the book was the most tasteful. I pointed one out, and he congratulated me and told me it was the same one he had chosen. On another occasion he asked me how to pronounce the word "dour" and I pronounced it "dower." "So did I, Hugh, until I just found out it's pronounced 'dooer.'" He used to buy his clothes at Brooks Bros. in New York, we were both in our late thirties and early forties at the time, and I stuck to Daks English clothes. One day I went to the office wearing a loud large-checked sport jacket, a real coat-of-many-colors. Jack said "Where in hell did you buy that goddam Mackinaw, fer chrissakes!" He was wearing a Brooks Bros. American tweed sport jacket that looked like something he picked up in a department store bargain basement, though for once I kept my mouth shut.

Through Cooke I met all the prominent local politicians, accompanied him to a dinner at a synagogue where he was awarded a "Brotherhood Award," and drank with him and Toronto's then-mayor after five in his office. I also met Mr.

Clifford Sifton, the kindly, gentlemanly scion of a *real* Toronto Establishment family, who took me to lunch at his club, and asked me to write a book about Queen's University. I forget whether I turned it down or Mr. Sifton gave up on me or what, but the book was never written by me.

Since then I have been to luncheon in private clubs with some members of the Establishment, the last time being with Gavin Clark, of the Rolph-Clark-Stone Clarks, the lithographers. These infrequent luncheons with members of the real *bourgeoisie* have brought back the conversation between Scott Fitzgerald and Ernest Hemingway. Fitzgerald said, "The very rich are different from you and me." Hemingway replied, "Yes, they have more money." I tend to agree with Fitzgerald; the very rich *are* different from most of us of the lower orders. Canada's *haute bourgeoisie* is the closest thing we have to an aristocracy, and I, the professional proletarian, have always got along well with them.

During the first summer I worked for Cooke, three or four months after going to work for him, he called me into his office at quitting time, and when I was seated next to him at the conference table he asked "How much am I paying you, Hugh?" though he knew very well. "Eighty dollars a week." "All right," he said, "dating back to April 30th your salary will be a hundred dollars a week." Some time later he gave me another raise, so that I was earning (well, maybe not *earning*) $6,000 a year, which was a very good salary in the early fifties. The public relations director for one of the chartered banks at the time told me *he* only received $4,500 a year.

Cooke signed notes for bank loans for many of his employees, sent the family of one of his CKEY announcers to Arizona to live because one of the children suffered from a severe asthmatic condition, and did many anonymous acts of kindness. He kept notorious drunks on his payroll (including me) despite many phone calls he received from people with whom I'd probably been drinking, and what's worse probably been buying drinks for, who reported my drunkenness. He always told me about the calls, and laughed as he mentioned them.

During the year I was Cooke's public relations man I did little writing of my own, though two of my stories, "One Mile Of Ice" and "One, Two, Three Little Indians" were brought out in an anthology, *Canadian Short Stories*, edited by Robert Weaver and Helen James.

One noontime Jack Cooke came to the door of his office and shouted, "Hugh, have you had lunch yet?" I nodded. He waved to me to come to his office and I went. He was bubbling over with a great secret he wanted to get off his chest. Though sometimes moody and often secretly hurt, Cooke was a man who *enjoyed* being a millionaire and what it bought him. He would have people up to his house on Bayview Avenue, where his pretty and charming wife Jean (née Carnegie from Port Perry, northeast of Toronto) would make late-night toast and fry sausages. Sometimes they would sit out on their patio listening to records of the big swing bands of the nineteen-thirties. "The patio opens up from the back of the house, from the lower floor," he once told me, after I had turned down an invitation to visit with them for the weekend. "From the basement?" I asked. He laughed. "Yeah, from the *cellar!*" I was one of the few employees he ever invited to his house, and probably the only one who turned him down.

On the particular day I'm writing about we ran down the stairs to the street and walked west along King to Bay Street. "Guess what I bought today, Hugh?" "*The Toronto Star?*" I asked, for the *Star* was then reputedly up for sale, and I knew he'd made a bid to buy the *Globe & Mail* when it was sold. "Fer chrissakes, use your head!" "Well, you asked me and I made a guess." "I just bought Consolidated Press," he said, unable to contain the news any longer. Consolidated Press then consisted of the *Canadian Home Journal, Saturday Night, Farmers Magazine* and a few small trade papers, if I remember right.

We went to lunch at the National Club, and Cooke, who had to constantly watch his weight, ordered a bowl of soup and coffee. I had a coffee too. Jack bought himself an expensive cigar (the only time I ever saw him smoke anything but a cigarette), and he told me we were going to move up to the Consolidated Press building the next morning.

"I'm going to move *Liberty* down there too," he told me.

"What am I going to do, handle public relations?"

"No, I'd sooner have you on the staff of *Saturday Night*." I sensed this was the real reason he had been keeping me in mothballs, so to speak, as his public relations man. "You're a writer, not a publicity flack."

The next morning I presented myself at the offices of *Saturday Night* and spoke to Bob Farquarson, a former editor of the *Globe & Mail,* who then was editing the magazine, which still clung to its old newspaper format of newspaper-sized pages that folded in the middle. I'd met Bob earlier, both at the *Globe & Mail* and once when he'd bought an article from me for *Saturday Night.* He was pleasant to me, but apprehensive about the change in ownership. B. K. Sandwell, a charming gentleman who had been connected with the magazine for years, was then Editor Emeritus. He pointedly stayed away from the magazine after Cooke bought it.

I met the managing editor, Jack Yocum, now in charge of public relations for Gulf Oil. He took me around and introduced me to the other members of the staff. There was John Irwin, who later went to *The Financial Post,* Herb McManus, who was in charge of the book pages, Margaret Ness, the women's editor, who now does a weekly travel column for the *Toronto Star.* The financial editor quit, and was replaced by Bill Snead, who had been a financial writer for the *Globe & Mail* and introduced me to Willson Woodside, the foreign editor. I asked Jack Yocum what his title was. "Associate Editor" Jack told me. "Good. That's what I'll call myself too," I said.

Bob Farquarson soon quit to become a member of the Canadian diplomatic corps in Washington, his secretary Marjorie quit to get married, and the financial editor left to go where financial editors go. I was given an office next to Woodside's, a title on the masthead as Associate Editor, and began writing a weekly article on anything I wished, being given carte blanche as to subject matter. Later I added a small feature titled "The Backward Glance" to my duties.

Jack Cooke tried to hire a new editor and approached Hugh MacLennan, Morley Callaghan, Robertson Davies, Ed Copps, then an editor in the New York offices of *Time,* and Anthony West, the son of Rebecca West, who was then writing for the *New Yorker.* He finally hired Gwyn Kinsey, then the virtually unknown editor of the Woodstock *Sentinel-Review,* a Thomson newspaper. Cooke had met him when Gwyn worked on the Timmins paper. Later, after opening a Thomson radio station in Stratford, Ontario, Cooke borrowed some money from a Timmins bank and bought a radio station of his own in Val D'Or, Quebec, later selling it, after making it highly successful, for a lot more than he paid for it. He took his profits from this, borrowed more money from several Toronto mining millionaires and entrepreneurs, and bought the Toronto radio station that he re-named CKEY. Under Jack Cooke it became one of the biggest money-makers in Canadian radio.

Gwyn Kinsey, as editor of one of Canada's most prestigious magazines, was expected to go to cocktail bashes, college dinners and speak before this and that group all over the province and the country. Gwyn Kinsey couldn't do this, and he remained in his office bringing out the weekly magazine as if it were a daily paper. He was probably a very good newspaper editor, but unfortunately he didn't acquire what can be called "magazine savvy." When he left the magazine, after I had been turfed out, he was replaced by Arnold Edinborough who was his complete opposite—an academic with a great platform presence, who made a second career of public speaking.

My office on the floor occupied by *Saturday Night* (the third floor of a building at the corner of Richmond and Sheppard Streets then called The Graphic Arts Building) overlooked Richmond Street. It also gave me a catty-cornered view of a government liquor store, which was not only well situated for a guy like me but let me watch my hungover friends as they tried to sneak back to their offices and other places of work after the witching hour of ten a.m. Most of them would be making their shaky way, a pint of liquor hidden in an inside pocket of their coat or jacket, and I would startle them out of their morning-after wits with a raucous cry of "Hey, Smitty, what you got hidden in your pocket, a mickey of rye?" They would look around, unable to tell where my voice was coming from, and then hurry out of sight.

Each week I wrote a byline article for the magazine (we were a weekly in those days as were most consumer magazines), and this usually happened on Friday morning. The magazine was put to bed late on Friday afternoon, and I'd spent the first four days of the week, the afternoons at least, drinking with my cronies in the Savarin Hotel. I had also introduced a second feature that I wrote called "The Backward Glance," which was an allegedly humorous-satirical recapitulation of old issues of the periodical. These one-page features were written from a collection of bound copies of the magazine kept in the office, and sometimes from those issues that were missing but could be read in the Reference Branch of the Toronto Public Library. I did these in batches of seven or eight which I then doled out weekly to the make-up editor. I still can't believe it, but I only missed one weekly deadline while I was writing for the sheet, through incurable drunkenness of course. I learned in those days that a known lush can't afford to suffer such normal indispositions as the flu or a heavy cold. I *had* to report for work each day even though my hangovers were much more debilitating than any species of flu ever suffered by man.

I varied my carte blanche weekly contributions under such department headings as "The Literary Life," "Television" and so on, and I was one of the first television critics in the country, along with Gordon Sinclair at the *Toronto Star*, to receive a laminated press card from the Columbia Broadcasting System that allowed me entrance to any of their TV operations. The only time I tried to use it, at CBS headquarters in New York to interview Bill Paley (who was then president or something), I was sloughed off. So I went over to *Variety* and got a wonderful put-down of the network from its editor.

During my time on *Saturday Night* I varied my contributions with the occasional short story. Three of them were stories of the Spanish Civil War: "The Expatriates," "The Tired Radical," and "How I Became An Englishman." Mary Lowry Ross, former crack *Toronto Star* reporter and good friend of Ernest Hemingway but then a contributing editor to the magazine, thought the "Englishman" story was one of my best. I also wrote such short stories for the magazine as "No More Songs About The Swanee," "Ivan McGeery And The Rhode Island Red," and "The Sand House," the title of which I later changed to "Another Time, Another Place, Another Me."

After living for three years on Toronto Island in its heyday (there are really several islands, the three main ones being Centre, Hanlan's Point and Ward's, but all of them usually referred to in the singular) we moved to an East Toronto apartment house where we lived for the next eleven years. People on the Island were always asking me to write a piece about it so after I'd moved I wrote "Bohemia On The Bay" for *Saturday Night*.

Situated south of Canada proper, on a sawed-up peninsula jutting out into Lake Ontario from the industrial and business heart of Toronto, lie four miles of foreign territory known as Toronto Island. Like most other things about it its name is a misnomer for it is not one island but eighteen, and they are only islands by virtue of several man-made canals or lagoons and of a nineteenth-century storm which plowed a gap through the neck of a peninsula.

The first natives were Indians who set up housekeeping in the Island's pine woods and used the sap of the balm-of-Gilead trees to heal their wounds. Later on their health resort was usurped by white fishermen and the wives of the British officers who picnicked there while Fort York was burning. The present-day natives are those who have lived there more than ten years, and the conquerors are a transient population who rent beaverboard "apartments" upstairs, downstairs, and along the boarded-up verandas of the natives' houses. This is the only known island conquest in history where the natives have emerged as the landed gentry.

Like New York's Fire Island the summer population is much larger than the winter one, numbering around 15,000 in comparison to the 3,000 or so hardy souls who live there all year round. The population, both winter and summer, is a polyglot one that contains some of the zaniest citizens allowed to run around without a leash. One of the older inhabitants has described the Island as "the only unfenced insane asylum in the world."

Although living conditions and life-styles are Bohemian in the extreme, very few writers or painters make their homes there for long; they can't stand the social pace and there are too many diversions popping up between themselves and their Muse. Many of the inhabitants belong to a half-world that includes chronic alcoholics, wife and husband deserters, beachcombers, deadbeats and spinsters-on-the-make. The majority of these live on Centre Island, the biggest of the chain, and one given over to a peculiar type of Edwardian architecture that is a hodge-podge of widows' walks, wings, cupolas and closed-in porches added to the houses as if thrown at them by a demented tent-maker. The normal fringe of the population is in a minority on Centre Island, as it is on Hanlan's Point, while Algonquin Island is settled by a peculiar stuffy type of water-borne suburbanite who tries to pretend that the less-inhibited Centre Islanders do not exist.

The Islanders have their own kind of snobbery and are prone to think they own the islands by right of tenure. In reality the land is classed as a city park and their lots are only leased to them by the City of Toronto. The hordes of picknickers who flock there in the summer by ferry from the mainland, especially the tens of thousands who crowd the streets and beaches on Sundays, are known locally as "Lower Slobbovians." What these people think of the shorts-clad bicycle-riding Islanders has never been revealed.

In the early days the islands, or the peninsula as it was then, was covered with a forest of pine trees. These were cut down during the nineteenth century and today the islands are planted with willow and poplar trees. Bears and deer were once hunted there but today the four-footed fauna consists of a few muskrat, raccoons and common household rodents. A few years ago however a deer was found wandering around the place. Where it came from nobody knows, but when someone first reported seeing it the Toronto Humane Society ignored the information, thinking naturally that the frantic telephone calls were the result of mass alcoholic hallucinations.

Several years ago one of the natives who was returning to Centre Island from the city in a canoe thought he was being pursued by a sea-serpent, and he crossed Toronto Bay in the fastest time on record since Ned Hanlan, the world's rowing champion, lived there. The "sea-serpent" kept pace with him and followed him right to the back door of his house, breathing down his neck. After a generous libation of sea-serpent cure the Islander shakily parted the kitchen curtains and found himself face to face with a steer that had escaped from the stockyards the day before. Why it had chosen to take a midnight dip is no more of a mystery than why other escapees of various kinds have chosen Centre Island to hide out on.

Despite the pollution and the generations of commercial and amateur fishermen who have fished the bay, lake and lagoons, the islands are still an easily accessible fishing spot for many indigent Toronto fishermen. These patient souls are rewarded with catches of pike, perch, carp, catfish and several species of bass. A couple of years ago when Lake Ontario rose to its highest level in history and threatened to wash the islands free of their polyglot habitations it was common for the natives to kill pike and perch with clothes props and broomsticks from their verandas.

The islands are also a natural habitat for both sea and land birds, which include 25 species of duck, blue herons, loons, rail, bittern, coots, mud hens and ring-necked pheasants, to say nothing of many kinds of song birds. The islands play host all year round to field naturalists and bird-watchers who stalk the beaches and thickets armed with copies of *A Field Guide To The Birds,* cameras and binoculars, which they are careful to keep trained on the more orthodox members of the bird family rather than on some of the more exotic types to be found on Centre Island.

The Island police force is a pretty tolerant organization, known locally as "The Keystone Cops." There are no motor vehices allowed there during the summer and only service trucks in the winter months; hence there is no traffic problem except that caused by the hundreds of bicycles that share the sidewalks with the pedestrian population. The only motor accident in years was caused by the police cruiser banging head-on into a large balm-of-Gilead tree that has stood in the middle of Lakeshore Avenue since Confederation. The Toronto Fire Department has a station on the Island, equipped with a small pumper and a jeep fire-engine, plus a fireboat. The fire department is the most efficient thing on the islands and fire losses are negligible.

During the winter months a bus service runs between the various islands carrying city-bound passengers to tug boats which transport them to the mainland. The buses run on fairly regular schedules, except on the rare occasions when celebrating passengers have persuaded drivers to join them. The tug boats work on the nautical notion that once away from the dock they operate only under the laws of the sea. As soon as they pass the three-yard limit the passengers unscrew the tops from their liquor jugs and engage in wassail all the way across the mile-wide bay.

The islands have several club-houses, two yacht clubs, a Canadian Legion hall, a movie theatre and two hotels (one open all year round). This latter hotel, the Manitou, is an institution run by the biggest-hearted hotel proprietor in Canada. It has the only beer parlour in Ontario where the patrons have to watch out for kids on tricycles riding around the tables. William Sutherland, the hotel owner, placed the following ad in the Island newspaper last summer, and it is indicative of the nonconformist traditions of his establishment: "We have been in business since 1922. We've been pleasing and displeasing the public ever since. We have been cussed and discussed, boycotted, talked about, lied to, hung up, held up, robbed, etc. The only reason we are staying in business is to see what the hell is going to happen next! *The Manitou Hotel.*"

Nobody ever knows what is going to happen next on the Island, and that is part of its charm. Early in the Island's history the young bloods from Toronto used to go over there to engage in turkey shoots, shooting a chained bear with a candle, and other "sports" of the times. One historian said "In the 1850's the hundreds of Toronto grog shops and taverns supplied no end of hard liquor, and among other sinks of iniquity where gambling, drinking and fighting were rampant was the Island. Especially on Sundays and holidays." Nobody shoots bears with candles any more, but the Island is still the most uninhibited spot around Toronto.

During a somewhat lengthy period of devastating sobriety I decided to write another novel, remaining in my office after working hours to write it. I stuck with it for some weeks, giving it the title "The Legs Of The Lame" from a verse in Ecclesiastes. The theme of it was that a young carnival roustabout and game-of-chance concessionaire struck a town stiff in a carnival "Hey, Rube!," and thinking he had killed him hid in the marquee tent of an itinerant revivalist and faith-healer. He remained with the faith-healer all summer as the religious tent show travelled Ontario. Near the end of the book I was going to have the faith-healer cure a truly crippled child and thus convert the carny hand into a believer. At the end the carny hand would discover that he hadn't killed the town stiff, would discover that the faith-healer was nothing but a fake, and would go back to the carnival. I guess it was to be escape from sin, redemption, and finally escape from redemption.

I finished the book at home, but was bothered by the fact that I'd allowed the faith-healer to give the carny hand (my protagonist) a phony name to hide behind from the police. This became very confusing to me. On the other hand I read the book over a couple of years later, having been too lazy to change it in the meantime, and found the writing to be quite good. Ten years after writing it I tore it up and now wish I hadn't.

One day Jack Cooke called me down to his main floor office and said, "Hugh, there isn't a goddam office in the world that could hold you. How'd you like to take one of several alternatives to coming here every day?"

"What are they?"

"You can stay here as you're doing now, writing for *Saturday Night*; you can still use your office and write occasional pieces for *Liberty, Canadian Home Journal* and *Saturday Night*; you can do your *Saturday Night* pieces at home and bring them in; or you can write for the three magazines at home."

"I'll take the last choice," I said.

"Your salary will go on the same as now, and you'll receive your cheque through the mail."

"Great!" I said, thinking it would be a cinch to earn my salary from writing for three magazines.

Cooke and I set up a schedule of payments for each of the magazines, and the first mistake I made was in pricing myself too low. Jack tried to help me, saying, "Now, Hugh, do you think that is enough money from *Liberty*? Are you sure that's all you want from the *Home Journal*?" and so on. I assured him it was enough. I began writing once again from my apartment.

125

Not only had I priced my articles and short stories too low, but I'd failed to take into consideration the attitudes of the editors who could now pick and choose what they wanted to print and buy from me. I worked on this basis for a year, being frustrated by having stories and articles turned down by Mary-Etta Macpherson at *Canadian Home Journal,* by Keith Knowlton at *Liberty,* and especially by Kinsey at *Saturday Night.* The consequence was I ended the year $2,500 in debt to Jack Cooke on the salary he had paid me. He wrote me a letter explaining this, and telling me there'd be no more salary cheques. Having no money put aside, I had to start hustling right away.

I told Cooke that I'd pay him back the $2,500 by allowing his accounts department to skim 20 percent off each fee I received from his magazines, and he agreed. Of course now that I was no longer on the payroll of Consolidated Press I could sell stuff anywhere I wanted to.

A couple of years earlier when I had drunk myself broke and had bills coming due I made up a list of my debts and went down to Jack's office and began to read them out to him. "Don't bother reading them" he'd told me. "How much do you want?"

"A thousand dollars."

He got up from his desk, went outside, typed a company cheque himself on his secretary's typewriter, and brought it back to me. I'd paid him that back long before.

Jack Cooke had once asked me if I would take over the international news from a guy who had been inordinately proud of the fact that Igor Gouzenko, the Soviet clerk who had defected to Canada revealing the Soviet spy ring, often visited him in his office, and once the little Russian was pointed out to me by somebody in the magazine. A couple of months later I was walking through Simpson's department store when I saw Gouzenko standing at a counter. He was no longer accompanied by his RCMP bodyguards as he had been at the beginning, and I walked up behind him and in a conversational tone said, "Hello, Igor." I was afraid he was going to jump out of his shoes.

But to get back to Hugh Garner, once again a freelance writer.

From the day my salary cheques were cut off I stopped drinking and began writing articles and short stories for most of the country's magazines. What I couldn't sell to Cooke's magazines to reduce my debt I sold somewhere else. I think it was around this time that Tommy Munns, the managing editor of the *Globe & Mail,* gave me an oral contract to write some guest columns for the *Globe Magazine.* I also wrote several weekly columns for the *Financial Post.*

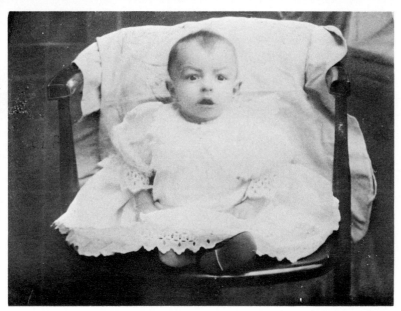

The author at the age of six months (1913)

His father, Matthew Garner

(upper left) Mrs. Annie Garner with _____ald and Hugh, at right

_____ author aged five

(upper right) The author as a choir-_____ of St. Monica's Anglican _____urch, aged ten

(below) Backview of Lewis Street, _____erdale, in 1938. From the City _____ Toronto Archives.

*ft) Taylor Street in Cabbage-
1949. From the City of Tor-
rchives.*

*t) The author's sisters, Marg
ne*

*ght) The author in the uni-
the Abraham Lincoln Bat-
1937*

rt photo, 1937, at age 23

(Below) *The Abraham Lincoln Battalion, Spring, 1937*

*p left) The author in the uni-
n of the 23rd Medium Battery,
al Canadian Artillery, 1939*

H.M.C.S. Arvida, *1941*

*p right) No. 8 St. Joseph Street,
onto.* Cabbagetown *was written
a room on the second floor*

(Above left) Hugh Garner in 1949, aged 36

(Right) Hugh and Alice, 1969

(Below) In 1968

Jack Cooke probably didn't expect me to ever repay him the $2,500 overpayment I'd received but within six months I paid it off. This was a relief to me, for I have always had a phobia against dependency on anyone.

The day I made my last sale to one of Cooke's magazines with the deletion of the twenty percent payment to Jack, I first saw the accounting department, then went and told Cooke that we were even. We had a long conversation in his office.

I don't believe I ever allowed myself to fall into debt again, and this was due not only to good luck and productivity but also to the excellent health my family and I enjoyed. We also lived within our means. For instance, I had bought a car immediately after the war, but had sold it again within a few days. During the early fifties when I was drinking a lot I didn't drive a car at all, and another rule of my life that I still follow religiously is never to drive when I'm drinking.

Jack Cooke was too smart to offer me another job. I'd given the man enough headaches as it was with my drunken capers when I'd worked for him. We remained good friends however until he moved to the States.

Around this time I wrote the stories, "The Magnet," for *Liberty,* "Not That I Care" and "Don't Ever Leave Me" for *Chatelaine,* and "Compromise" for *Canadian Home Journal.* One day Mary-Etta Macpherson said to me "I'm so fed up with nice little stories, Hugh, I'd love to get one about a bitch." So I wrote "Lucy" which she bought. I also sold a three-part novella, "Murder In The Suburbs," to *Liberty.* And still the greater part of my income was from magazine articles which were printed first in Canadian and later reprinted in English, Australian and South African magazines. Articles or extracts from them also appeared in *Reader's Digest, Magazine Digest,* and *Everybody's Digest.*

Between the day in 1949 when Jake Thomas of *National Home Monthly* bought "Toronto The Terrible" and the day in 1961 when *Liberty* bought "Lament For Canada's Dying Train Travel" I published 400 magazine articles and essays. I'd written them for almost every English-language periodical in Canada under my own name, "Jarvis Warwick," *Maclean's* "Gratton Gray," and other pen names I've now mercifully forgotten. I'd also written company brochures for the John B. Smith Lumber Co., British-American Oil, and Ed Provan, the custom tailor.

I'd been asked to submit five entries for the *Encyclopedia Canadiana,* and did those on burial grounds, cremation, undertaking, embalming, and the Toronto Stock Exchange. The last one was an after-thought by the editors, but the first four were the result of a series of articles I had written for *Saturday Night* on undertakers, called "The Sweetest Racket This Side Of Heaven." This made me an expert on the subject.

For years I was "Dr. E. Jackson Francis" who spilled out advice on marriage problems for *Liberty,* and also the guy who wrote under a score of pseudonyms the face-to-face *Liberty* pieces under such titles as "My Wife Is Frigid" and "My Husband Is Impotent." I was reprinted in periodicals as diverse as South Africa's *Milady* and Australia's *Pix.*

In the mid-fifties Jack Cooke brought Frank Rasky, a Toronto-born New York freelancer, up to *Liberty* magazine. Rasky took over a desk alongside that of Keith Knowlton. For a couple of weeks I wasn't sure which of them was the editor. Cooke hadn't fired Knowlton, but was anxious to put Rasky in the editor's job; I thought the way he did it was pretty dirty pool. Keith and I talked about it, and I told him that as long as Cooke was still paying his salary to sit it out, let Rasky do the work, and wait for a formal dismissal. I would have sat there until Doomsday, but poor Keith was not like me. After a month or so he quit *Liberty* and went to *Chatelaine* as managing editor. Later on he became copy editor of *Maclean's.* I met Jack Yocum on the street one day and asked him what had become of Keith. He told me Knowlton was now with the *Financial Post,* and that John Irwin had been pensioned off by that magazine. I phoned Keith and we talked about the old days, and he gave me the name of his predecessor at *Liberty,* which I'd forgotten.

Jack Cooke finally sold all his Canadian holdings, and through a special act of the U.S. Congress became an American citizen. Some time ago Andrew Bell, a former executive assistant of Cooke's told me he had parlayed the $7 or $8 million he was worth before leaving Canada up to something like $80 million.

A couple of years ago my wife and I drove along Hollywood Boulevard, and I was tempted to go out to Bel Air and look up the Cookes. I'm sure Jack would have greeted us with all his old exuberance, but I didn't go. Perhaps our association belongs among my friendly memories, and I prefer to leave it at that.

In 1955 I was involved in a couple of happenings that bear mention in this biographical saga. That year the Rockefeller Foundation supplied the funds to bring Canada's novelists, poets, short story writers, playwrights, editors and publishers together for the first time in a four-day summer Canadian Writers' Conference at Queen's University, Kingston, Ontario. Being comparatively unknown at the time I travelled to Kingston by train, alone, and I wouldn't have recognized most of the authors and poets if they had been sitting in the seat opposite mine. On arrival at Queen's I registered and was given a name tag, that I immediately placed in my pocket. The housing committee sent me to an off-campus, out-of-the-way frat house where a room awaited me. There I ran into a Vancouver lawyer-writer, William McConnell, an excellent short story writer one of whose stories, "Totem," had been included in Weaver and James' anthology *Canadian Short Stories*. He being a wartime ex-army sergeant and I an ex-navy chief petty officer, we proceeded to get roaring drunk on a jug that McConnell had been sensible enough to bring along.

Bill was happy with his bed in the frat house but I wanted to get closer to the centre of things and staggered over to the campus later in the afternoon. I went to the registration desk and had my sleeping quarters changed to an on-campus sorority house. As always I was travelling light, so all I had with me were the clothes I was wearing, the current copy of *Time* magazine, my shaving gear in a pocket of my suit, and an extra shirt, shorts and socks in a paper bag.

I sat down in the living room of the sorority house where the Montreal lawyer and poet Frank Scott was talking to a pair of academic types. Finally one of them approached me, asked me who I was, and took me over to introduce me to Scott. It was my only meeting with him, but he was quite friendly and made me feel at home. I excused myself and went and sat on the front steps, where I talked for some time with a small group of *Maclean's* writers.

The *Maclean's* magazine gang, like the writers from McClel-

129

land & Stewart, and nowadays from The House of Anansi, seem to travel in packs like timid coyotes or predatory night animals. I don't know why this is but it's an observation I've made at dozens of conferences, soirees, delegationary affairs and other socio-literary happenings. In earlier days the lady poets wore tweed skirts and saddle shoes while the males were halfway Bohemian in their lack of neckties or the wearing of Ascots. Today the younger literati, male and female, carry their gear in old World War Two gas containers and dress in his-and-hers artificially patched Levis and denim jackets.

When I went upstairs to lay claim to my bed I found I was sharing a room with Desmond Pacey and Fred Cogswell, two professors from the University of New Brunswick—the former of whom is an inveterate anthologist and literary biographer and the other a poet. They were both quiet academic literary types, and I don't know what the effect was when I staggered into their room, said "Hi!" flopped on my bed, and flaked out.

I have only done business a couple of times since with Pacey, once when he included "One, Two, Three Little Indians" in his perennial anthology *A Book Of Canadian Stories* and once when I turned down a request from him for a story for the little magazine *Fiddlehead Review.*

That evening while leaving a beer parlour I ran into Morley Callaghan, Ralph Allen, and Jack McNaught (who wrote and broadcast under the nom de plume of James Bannerman) and who became a casual friend of mine later on. They were all suffering no pain and invited me to accompany them to a party at the bungalow of Queen's University professor, Malcolm Ross. Professors were poor in those days—I was once invited to lunch at the Park Plaza Hotel by a Toronto University English professor and found it was Dutch treat—and if I'm not mistaken Professor Ross had only a case of twenty-four bottles of beer to share with the multitude. It was like the parable of the loaves and fishes, but without the Lord Jesus to spread them around. Besides, Ross looked upon me as an interloper, while I in turn looked upon him as the guy who had turned down some of my best stories as the editor of *Queen's Quarterly.*

I must have found something else to drink somewhere, for the last thing I remember very clearly in the morning was walking with Morley Callaghan, Ralph Allen and James Bannerman past the university stadium and arguing at the top of our voices, Callaghan and Garner versus Allen and Bannerman, that "writing" and "writers" meant those engaged in creative writing, while non-fiction was merely "journalism" and its practitioners "journalists." I found my way back to my room where I stripped

130

to my shorts and crawled into bed, no doubt waking my academic room-mates in the process.

I managed to attend all of the seminars that took place before the beer parlours opened, and heard A. J. M. Smith on poetry, Morley Callaghan on the novel, John Gray on book publishing, Ralph Allen on magazines, and Robert Weaver on broadcasting.

One evening I attended a party at Arnold Edinborough's, then the editor of the *Kingston Whig-Standard*, who had more liquor than Ross. Other things I remember are a garden party at the home of the Queen's principal, getting drunk in the hotel room of a *Maclean's* writer from Ottawa named Phillips, and spewing on his rug, and in general managing to conduct myself in my usual fashion at such goings-on. The thing I most remember about the Writers' Conference was that almost all the lady poets and authors looked as I'd expected them to look, but Miriam Waddington turned out to be a beautiful woman. The last thing I remember after the conference ended was sharing Earle Birney's bottle of Mexican tequila on the train returning to Toronto.

During the conference I received a note from an inmate of Kingston Penitentiary, through the Pen's schoolteacher, asking me to go there and speak to the journalism class. I went there at the appointed time, was taken on a tour of the dome and the ranges, and finally ushered into the schoolroom, where I spoke briefly and answered inmates' questions on writing. Many of them had read the paperback edition of *Cabbagetown*, and we spoke about that. The thirty or forty men who attended our informal seminar proved to be the best audience I'd ever had. Subsequent audiences of prison inmates have bolstered my belief that such groups are the best ones I've ever spoken with.

Later, when they were sprung from prison, several of the prisoners I'd met in the penitentiary visited my wife and me in our apartment and turned out to be the most courteous and best-behaved guests we've ever entertained. Some of them were heroin addicts, and one of them was a young man freed on a ticket of leave from a mandatory life sentence. He later became a writer and wrote a book about prison life.

I didn't meet the women inmates of the penitentiary, who were locked up in another building across the road, but after visiting with the men, and telling them I'd help them to get anything published they cared to send me, I received a wonderful poem from a woman prisoner. I took it in to John Clare, who was then the editor of *Chatelaine*.

John printed it, and I presume paid the lady inmate poet the usual fee. After the magazine had published it I received a phone call from John who said, "Listen, Garner, don't give me any more stuff from your jailbird friends! That poem was stolen holus-bolus from *Ladies Home Journal* and they're threatening to sue!" Somehow or another things were straightened out between the two magazines, and I heard nothing else about the plagiarized piece of poetry.

Years later when I told this story to a writing group in Joyceville Prison they all laughed. They were pleased that one of them had put something over on the square johns outside.

Among the many boons to Canadian writers since I became a professional are the widespread use of the Xerox machine, the belated but slow appreciation of Canadian literature by Canadians, the removal of the administration of the Governor General's Awards from the amateur clutches of the Canadian Authors Association, and the existence of The Canada Council. The Council's decisions and its disbursement of funds to every kind of artistic and cultural endeavor, and to all the arts and practitioners of them, has come under a great deal of criticism by press and public—nearly all of it undeserved. Without Council grants there would be far fewer Canadian books and little new literature at all.

In 1958 I applied to the Canada Council for a Senior Arts Fellowship, then worth $4,500. I needed the money to finance the writing of a novel I had been planning for some time. Recommendations were supplied by Jack McClelland, the publisher, Ralph Allen, editor of *Maclean's,* and Robert Weaver, the CBC executive mentioned before, who had broadcast so many of my stories. In the spring of 1959 I received notice that I had been awarded the fellowship, which would be credited to my bank account in three $1,500 drafts.

I finished whatever magazine journalism I was working on and began writing the book which I titled *The Silence On The Shore* from a poem of Lord Byron's. I had originally planned the book's length to run between 300-350 pages, but having so many different though interlocked plots to follow I ran far over the projected length. I worked on it for two months during the spring, then put it aside until the fall. It was being written to be offered first to McClelland & Stewart, for not only had Jack McClelland been one of my "referees," as they are called by the Canada Council, but he had called me up several times over the years to ask me if I was working on anything he could see with a view to publication. I don't remember now whether or not I sent him *The Legs Of The Lame,* but I probably did.

During the fall of 1959 I worked for three more months on the book, refusing all offers of work from magazines during this time. Five months for me was an inordinately long time to work on a novel, for I usually had written them fast, taking at the longest two months. Interviewers often ask me how long it takes me to write a novel, and I usually answer flippantly, "It takes six weeks to write a good novel, and a year to write a bad one." Ernest Hemingway took six weeks to write what I consider to be his finest novel *The Sun Also Rises*.

My novel was finished in late October or early November, 1959, and it had rambled on to the ridiculous length of over 800 pages. I took it in to McClelland & Stewart, and Jack McClelland picked up the heavy manuscript and handed it to one of his editors, whom he had summoned to his office. The editor's name was Jack Rackcliffe, a native of Prince Edward Island, who had lived most of his life in Boston where he had been a professor or lecturer at Harvard. My meeting with him that day was my first but I was to meet him quite a number of times in the future. He was the finest book editor I'd met up to then.

A month or so later, of course, the overlong manuscript was returned to me with a letter from Rackcliffe asking me if I would please chop out all the overmatter the manuscript contained and bring it down to a readable length. He told me, good-naturedly, that I was suffering from what is called in psychiatry, logorrhea, or abnormal volubility.

At that time, as I've said before, Ralph Allen was the editor of *Maclean's* magazine. Ralph, who was a friend of mine from my press club days, had written some good books of his own and had instituted a project in his magazine which consisted of publishing edited extracts from contemporary Canadian novels, for which the magazine paid the author $5,000 for first serial rights. Some of the novels first published in *Maclean's* were excellent, and were published later in book form, but others have still to see the light of day as a book. I weighed one fact against another, whether to submit my novel manuscript after I'd shortened it to *Maclean's*, or to re-submit it to McClelland & Stewart. I put everything off when one morning I received a phone call from John Clare at the *Star Weekly*.

John Clare had assigned me quite a few articles to write, so by then we knew each other pretty well. Another editor at the *Star Weekly* at the time was Ray Gardner. I never did discover their position on the staff hierarchy, but figured that Harry Hindmarsh, the son of H. C. Hindmarsh who had been so kind to me when I was a copy boy on his paper thirty years before, was the top editor, with John and Ray somewhere below him.

When I sat down at John's desk he said to me "How'd you like to go back to Spain?"

Not knowing whether it was a rib or what I said, "I don't know."

"How would you like to do a three-part story for us on Spain today, something about a guy from the International Brigades re-visiting the towns and battlefields he knew more than twenty years ago?"

"Okay," I said, reluctant to turn down a free trip to Europe, and especially to Spain, but a little bit apprehensive about the welcome I could expect.

Before I left the *Star Weekly* offices we came to an agreement on my expenses and fee, and I said I'd get a Spanish visa, if they'd issue me one, and a new passport. I told Clare I'd be ready to leave later in the month, but instead of flying over I'd like to make the west-east trip across the Atlantic on the *Queen Elizabeth*, the largest liner afloat and a change from the corvette crossings I'd made during the war.

I flew to New York, booked tourist class on the Lizzie, and disembarked in Cherbourg on November 23, 1959. From there I followed the route we had taken on our way to the Spanish Civil War, to Paris, down to Perpignan, crossed to Spain at Port Bou, on to Barcelona, Valencia and Madrid by train, and visited the old battlefields in the cars of my driver-interpreters. After about three weeks in Spain I went by train from Madrid to Lisbon, and from there flew back to New York.

Not being sure of my political status in Spain, or whether or not I might be thrown into prison as an enemy of the state, I kept myself well oiled for any eventuality: on the *Queen Elizabeth* with Gordon's gin and Whitworth's ale, in France by any kind of cognac that came to hand, and through Spain and Portugal with Dom Pedro brandy.

On my return I phoned John Clare, who asked me when the *Star Weekly* could expect the three-part story. I told him I'd work on it after Christmas, which I did. It was a fun piece to write, for it all had to come out of my head, not having been able to make notes over there in fear of the secret police. On January 8th, 1960 John phoned again, afraid I suppose that I was still drinking and hadn't written a word. I told him I'd just completed typing the corrected copies and would bring them in the next day. The following chapter is a transcript of what I wrote with added notes.

A LOYALIST SOLDIER RETURNS TO SPAIN

Part One

I don't know what you were doing on July 5, 1937, but I was walking in the sun down a Spanish hill near El Escorial, to the northwest of Madrid. It was a beautiful warm morning of a day that would become stifling hot by afternoon. Behind and above us, at the side of the highway where the tourist buses now pass, the ambulances and tank carriers were parked, and the doctors were setting up a dressing station.

Beneath us in the valley sheep were grazing, and the fields were yellow with the new stubble of the wheat harvest. In the small village that could be seen from the top of the hill the whitewashed houses seemed anchored to the earth with age, and the steeple of the small red church reached into the high clear sky of the Spanish morning.

Duncan was beefing as usual about having to carry two boxes of ammunition, and Herman Katz was having trouble with the wheeled carriage of our Russian Maxim machine-gun. Colin Cox was carrying my rifle as well as his own, for I was weighed down with the machine-gun itself, about the size and weight of a Vickers. I was also weighed down by two crossed belts of rifle ammunition, which I wore à la Pancho Villa. My French tin helmet was wet against my forehead, my khaki shirt was stiff with dried sweat and my corduroy pants were heavy in the heat. I was 24 years old and it was to be one of the most memorable days of my life.

Herman Katz was a department-store stock-boy from New York, Greg Duncan was a longshoreman from Philadelphia, Colin Cox had been one of the Dublin unemployed and his chief claim to fame was that he had upset Irish fascist General O'Duffy's car on O'Connell Street, and I had last worked as a haberdashery clerk on Toronto's Danforth Avenue. We formed a heavy machine-gun section of the 17th (Abraham Lincoln) Battalion of the 15th Brigade of the Spanish Republican army —one of the five International Brigades.

Along with some Spanish brigades our outfit was launching an attack down into the wide valley that stretches south from the foot of the Guadarrama mountains. Our objective was the

135

town of Brunete, and the strategic purpose was to outflank the guns that General Franco had set up in University City on the outskirts of Madrid and which were pounding the city itself.

On my recent visit to Spain to report for *The Star Weekly* on how the country now appears to a man who fought there against the present regime 23 years ago, I found great changes. These changes were not wholly in Spain or in the Spanish people, but in myself as well. It was a rewarding experience, for there are not many of us who get the opportunity to go back in time, place and emotion to our youth and young manhood. Every sight, sound and smell momentarily peeled off 50 pounds of weight and removed the veil of prosperous complacency from eye, mind and heart. I became once again, for a moment or two, the foolish young idealist who believed that all the word's problems were painted in black and white and could be solved by a political panacea. I no longer believe this, but I would no more deny my youthful beliefs than I would deny my birthright.

The fighting had begun with the dawn. To our left the El Campesino Brigade was flushing a unit of Fascist Moorish troops from an old cemetery. Farther down the hill and in a sector to our right, the Enrique Lister Brigade was engaged with Franco's Spanish Foreign Legion, who were entrenched along the highway. The Listers and El Campesinos were both crack Spanish Communist units, named after the *noms de guerres* of their generals, which would later be expanded into divisions.

Ahead of us, the English Battalion of our own brigade had just made an attack across a flat open field against entrenched Moors and Falangists who had cut them down like weeds. Up to now there had been no artillery support at all, and the boys from London, Glasgow, Cardiff and the Tyneside had deployed across the field and gone to their deaths with the grace and dignity of very brave men. But those who had lived had gone on to take the Fascist positions.

As we kept walking down the hill along a narrow gully that formed a dry stream bed, our infantry companies skirmished to the left and right, firing occasionally at isolated pockets of Fascist troops who had been left behind and isolated by the main advance.

At times, when we had to cross heights of ground, the Moors would use us for clay pigeons, firing at us from their trenches and hedgerows in the middle distance. We would run across the hillocks in single file, spaced a few yards apart. At such times

136

I would get a fit of the giggles; a nervous reaction I'm sure, for I am not a brave man. Even yet I can still recall the taste of fear against my tongue, as if I were sucking a copper coin.

About ten a.m. the Franco-Belge Battalion from our brigade went over against a strong enemy position. The little men from Paris, Lyons and Antwerp, careless, carefree, wine-sodden and wonderful, took the position after suffering terrible casualties through the lack of artillery support and natural cover.

The rest of the day seems to have been dominated by noise: the crump of mortar bombs, the sharp crack and rattle of rifle and machine-gun fire, the whine and burst of heavy shells. Once during the morning we had to get out of the way of a troop of Loyalist cavalry. They came trotting down the gully, then headed up its steep side, the horses slipping and slithering, and then, with loud shouts and sabres glistening in the sun, they charged across the fields.

They had already set up the stretcher relay stations, and the wounded were starting to move past us on their way up the hill. Our battalion set up its first-aid post in a culvert, and we placed our guns on the bank of a sunken road farther to the east. The road has been paved since then, but otherwise everything is the same. We were not firing towards the village, but against a strong Nationalist position to the east and north of it. Early in the afternoon our gun was put out of commission, and we were ordered out into the fields with the infantry companies.

The fear left my tongue and centred in my stomach like a cold ball of plasticine. Nothing was important now but my safety. I no longer thought idealistically of socialism, anti-fascism or the brotherhood of man. I no longer really cared who won the war, but only hoped it would end in the next ten minutes. I was just one big ego trying to press myself down into the wheat stubble out of sight.

In front of us, a few hundred metres away, was the village I had learned was named Villaneuva de la Cañada, which means "New Village of the Canebrakes" or something equally crazy. Its name however is no more crazy than that afternoon. I lay behind a sheaf of wheat and took occasional glances up and ahead to the church tower, from which two Moors in white turbans were firing a machine-gun, pinning us down in the field. To my frightened and fevered mind the belfry looked like the hose tower of a firehall, and I have thought of it as such ever since, though common sense has told me otherwise. There was a long unbroken line of whitewashed row-houses facing us, and from the flat roofs and every window poured volleys of rifle fire. None of us were close enough to throw grenades, and we had no mortars to call on for aid.

Later in the day the English Battalion, our Slav battalion, called the Dimitroffs, and the Franco-Belges, outflanked the village, and the little Frenchmen went in with the bayonet. . . . I didn't visit the village again for twenty-two years.

One day this winter my driver-interpreter, a member of the Falange and an erstwhile hater of *Rojos*, or Reds, called for me early in the morning at my hotel on the Gran Via in Madrid. (The Gran Via, like many of Madrid's main streets, has been renamed after fascist heroes. It is now called the Avenida de Jose Antonio, after the founder of the Falangist movement, who was executed by the Loyalists in Alicante.)

"Where do you wish to go, sir?" Carlos asked.

"First of all let's go out to the Valley of the Fallen," I said.

This was fine with him, for all the Fascists (I should really call them the "Nationalists" but during the war all members of the enemy were "Fascists" to us, and the habit is hard to break) are proud of the gigantic mausoleum that Franco has had carved within a mountain. Ostensibly it is a place in which to bury some of the dead of both sides who fell in the civil war. As far as I know there are no Loyalist dead buried there.

We drove west along the Gran Via, with its gaudy billboards, its smartly dressed office girls and the young men wearing their coats over their shoulders like capes. Though I had searched the fronts of the buildings the day before for signs of repair from the damage they had suffered during the war, I had failed to find any. The fascist government is skilful at fixing the damage its own guns and planes had inflicted on the city.

We passed the nightclubs, the milk bars and the ornate movie houses with the blown-up cutouts of Gregory Peck and Debbie Reynolds. The street today is a long way from the shuttered drabness of the war years, when the black-clad housewives would queue up before dawn to draw their ration of bread, and the crowds would run for the Metro stations when the shells came over. The bomb craters and the piles of rubble have gone, as have the paving-block barricades at the bottom of the hill.

I had a sense of unreality, a feeling that my former visits to Madrid had been an hallucination. This wasn't the city I had seen before; where I'd stood in my windowless room at the King Alfonso hotel and listened to Franco's shells tearing their paper trails above the roof. And where at times they had burst and torn at the telephone building down the street, and some-

138

times on my hotel itself so that I'd run down the stairs into the basement, around the shell-destroyed elevator shaft, to sit out the bombardment.

This couldn't be the city that was saved by the French, anti-Nazi German and Polish members of the first International column, who had rushed to it in November of 1936, and along with the Spanish Peoples' Militia, stopped the Nationalist columns in their tracks in the suburbs of Cuatro Caminos and Casa de Campo. It was the empty braggart boast of Fascist General Mola who said, "I have four columns advancing on Madrid and a fifth column of supporters inside the city." Though the phrase "fifth column" became an integral part of every language, Madrid stood off the Nationalists for thirty-three months. The city didn't surrender until after Barcelona had given up without a shot, and the war was over. By that time the people were reduced to a ration of two ounces of food a day, and they'd long before eaten all the animals in the zoo. It is a city with guts and heart, and I'm proud I fought for it.

The Gran Via or the Calle de la Pricesa couldn't be the same streets where one spring day, on a trip from the Jarama Front, I'd stopped to chat with Canadian playwright Ted Allen and American novelist Josephine Herbst, who were sitting at a table of a tatty sidewalk cafe.

Allen, who had travelled to Spain with the same group I had from Paris, had asked me, "Hugh, what do you do in the trenches during a barrage?"

I had answered truthfully, "I pray."

They and I had laughed, for it was a strange thing for a member of a communist brigade to say. As the Americans discovered a few years later, there are no atheists in foxholes.

I was remembering these things as we drove through the city, and remembering too that nobody in Madrid had worn a necktie during the civil war. On the leftist side of a class war the first thing to disappear is the male necktie.

Carlos and I drove through University City, now almost completely rebuilt, its red-brick buildings one of the municipal prides of the *Madrilenos*. It wasn't always an object of pride, but of hate, for from there the Nationalist artillery sent its shells into the city and into the homes of friend and foe alike. As I looked from the car window at what had then been the enemy's lines it was like seeing the other side of the moon.

We drove on through the Casa de Campo, which had seen some of the most desperate fighting of the war, and where some of the walls are still scarred with bullet pits. There are a lot of new houses there now, and they looked bright and clean in the winter morning sun. Here and there little boys and girls skipped along the roads on their way to school, and I thought, there are two universal and unchangeable things among mankind: children and women. The little girls had their hair in braids or pony tails, and the little boys in their knee-length pants were teasing them by tugging at their schoolbags. I must have only dreamed I was here before, I thought.

Then once again in memory I heard the strange bubble of rifle fire that used to start somewhere to the southwest of the city at night and work its way north along the front lines until it almost surrounded Madrid with a curtain of muted sound. It always happened when it rained, as it used to do on the Jarama.

"Some fool got into a panic," Duncan would say. "Now everybody in the lines has panicked with him." And we would lie on our luxurious bed in our windowless room of the hotel, drying our shirts and socks on the windowsill, and listen to the noise of the people scurrying home in the blackout. As suddenly as it had begun the rifle fire would fade out from north to south, and all would be quiet again except for the occasional sound of an artillery shell or the chatter of an automatic weapon.

Carlos increased the car's speed as we reached the open highway that leads west to El Escorial and Avila. There is not much civilian motor traffic in Spain, and on this late November day there were no tourists on the road. We passed the homes of the *nouveaux riches,* the motels, and roadhouses. Once in a while we met up with an ancient two-wheeled cart pulled by a furry-coated mule and led by a little jackass. The drivers hadn't changed, or shaved either I thought, during the past twenty years, and they cracked their whips and habitually shouted, *"Mula!"*

Late in June, 1937 our brigade had been drawn together from several small villages to the east of Madrid, where we had rested after we came off the Jarama Front. In trucks, hopefully disguised with the leafy branches of trees, the five battalions had been driven to Alcala de Henares, where we were billeted in the cathedral. Cox and some of the other Irishmen from the battalion had spread their blanket rolls on the altar, and a wit had drawn a sign which he had hung beneath them, reading, "Ireland's Gift to the Gods."

The next day we rode in the trucks to Madrid, and that night, skirting the enemy lines, we began the march along this very road. We marched for several nights through the darkness, hiding in the woods during the day from the Italian and German reconnaissance planes. With nightfall we would continue on, the brigade strung out along the highway, singing our songs, griping, arguing whose turn it was to carry what, moving to the ditches to let the tank carriers and ammunition trucks go through.

Katz was sure we were going to attack Segovia, but Duncan said he was crazy. Even *our* generals weren't nutty enough for that.

"We've got seventy thousand men in this offensive," Cox said, letting the mere size of the figure lighten the burden of the machine-gun it was his turn to carry. "They're strung out along this road for miles," he went on, unwilling to let go of his belief. "Look at the tanks and guns going up."

After a while Wallingford, our company runner, came alongside. He had been a schoolteacher in Kansas City and he still had the sarcasm of a schoolroom martinet.

"What's the news, Wally?" Duncan asked him.

"I don't know for sure. General Copic hasn't told me a thing, but I'm sure we go into action in the morning, comrades."

"Why?" asked Katz.

"Why, he asks! Didn't we get a ration of Dutch cheese and Swiss chocolate last night? Doesn't that always mean action the next morning? Up on the Jarama we never missed after getting chocolate and cheese along with our boiled dog, did we?"

Suddenly we all knew he was right. We didn't know where it was going to be, but it sure wasn't over the mountains into Segovia.

Our field kitchen truck came by, and Jack Shirei waved at us from the tailgate. Jack was our Japanese cook, who had served with the Japanese army in Manchuria, and had then been a houseboy in Beverly Hills.

"Hey, comrade, give us a lift!" Cox shouted.

"He hasn't any room in there," Wallingford said. "The truck is filled with mule carcasses and a ton of chick peas."

We stopped for a rest period and the English Battalion marched past us along the road. They were singing their marching song to the tune of *Holy, Holy, Holy,* only the words had been changed to "Hiking, hiking, hiking . . ." I recognized the voice of Taffy Owens, who had come down from Paris with our group months before. There were all the other Britishers I'd met on the Jarama Front when I'd sometimes drop over to their lines to bum a cup of tea. (They were the only outfit in the whole civil war that drank tea.)

141

There was the Romney boy, a nephew of Winston Churchill, who had been in charge of the small-arms ammunition dump on the Jarama; Ralph Fox, the English poet; the Sikh student from Oxford who always wore his sky blue turban; Scotty Robertson, who had been one of the Royal Navy mutineers at the revolt of the fleet at Invergordon; and a guy I'd met who had edited a Labour Party newspaper. As they marched past a Cockney voice shouted, "Come on, you bloody Yanks. Don't hold up the bloody war!"

I laughed aloud at the memory of it, and Carlos, my driver, asked, "What's the matter, sir?"

His voice pulled me back to the present, and I remembered this was twenty-two years later. This time I was a guest in Madrid's Rex Hotel, and was being driven in a hired car by a hired driver-interpreter along a road I had once marched along as a younger, slimmer, better man.

"I once marched along this road carrying a machine-gun," I said.

"You did?" he asked, only half-believing me.

"Yes. I was a *Rojo*. I was one of your hated Reds of the International Brigades."

He was so startled he almost drove off the road. I could see him giving me frightened glances through the corner of his eye. His fat, well-dressed, middle-aged passenger was not his preconceived idea of what a Red should look like.

As the car rounded a bend in the highway and started down a slight incline, the most beautiful panorama I have ever seen came into view. A few kilometres ahead of us lay El Escorial, snuggled on the side of a mountain, multi-colored against the gray of the hills, the big yellow monastery shimmering in the morning sun. Behind the village before it the Guadarrama Mountains reached into the scudding clouds, their snow-topped peaks showing momentarily through the scud. Beneath the town the gently undulating fields of the plain were soft green in the winter air. From the sierras a bitter wind blew down across the plain and caused the car to veer and waver with each searching gust. It was in those mountains that the band of partisans in Ernest Hemingway's *For Whom The Bell Tolls* had made their camp.

"It's beautiful," I said to Carlos. "Just beautiful."

He smiled his gratitude. "Thank you, sir," he said. "Spain is beautiful, is it not?"

"It's as beautiful as heaven," I assured him.

I think this was the first time he'd ever liked a Red.

We drove almost to the outskirts of the village of El Escorial before swinging northeast along a road that climbed into the foothills of the sierra. It grew colder the higher we got, and here and there were snow patches in the fields. The peasants whom we met trudging down the roads or driving their mule carts were incongruously bundled up against the chilly but certainly not freezing weather. We passed one wearing a soldier's woollen balaclava helmet pulled over his cheeks and chin. I wondered if it had been his souvenir of the civil war.

As we wound through the hills, the old gray trees of the valley gave way to sparse forests of young pines, aromatic in the wind. We took a bend in the road and drove along the edge of a precipitous cliff, where far below an angry stream bubbled around its rocks and tore at the tree roots along its banks. Ahead of us rose the imposing façade of the gigantic cave that is known as the Valley of the Fallen.

It is a fitting spot for a memorial to the war dead, but I'm afraid it will remain a tomb for Franco himself and such fascist saints as Jose Antonio. One *Madrileno* called it "Franco's Folly," but others were not so kind in their appraisal of this twenty-million-dollar monument to futility and fatuity.

The advertised idea behind it is a good one: a burial place for the heroic dead of both sides without fear or favor. The rub is that very few Loyalist families (and they still comprise the majority of Spaniards) would allow their dead husbands, fathers and sons to be buried there, even if the Fascists would allow it. And most relatives of dead Nationalists will not allow *their* dead to be disinterred and buried again. Then there are the hundreds of thousands of dead who were buried in common, and now unknown, graves. And what about the Moors, the Italians, the German and Russian airplane pilots, the Portuguese fascists, and the many thousands of dead of the International Brigades and of Franco's Spanish Foreign Legion?

We parked the car in a large parking space. (Like many other religious shrines I've visited as a journalist a large parking lot always adds that necessary tinge of commercialism to them.) We paid our entrance fees to a member of the Guardia Civil and climbed the broad flight of carved stone steps to a terrace that fronts the entrance.

Inside, I found myself in a gigantic room, carved out of the solid granite of the mountain. There were uniformed guides, and a few visitors were staring up at the tapestries, paintings and sculpture that lined the walls. Carlos wanted me to take my time, but I told him I hadn't come to Spain to examine

143

fascist shrines. I strode down the great length of the room and was admitted to a second one by a uniformed attendant. It was just as big and ostentatious as the first, and at its far end were a pair of huge carved wooden doors like the others we had come through. We were admitted to a room just as high and wide, but not quite as long as the first two. At the far end of it was an altar with several priests conducting a ritual before it. Between the doorway and the altar was a crypt covered with banked flowers. Carlos told me, with a certain awe and reverence, that this was the burial place of Jose Antonio. After staring at it for what I thought was a polite length of time, I turned and left the place.

In the second room, cave, basilica, whatever they call it, I said to Carlos, "Ask one of the guides where the Reds are buried."

With a great deal of reluctance and a lot of explanatory pointing at me, he asked something of one of the uniformed attendants. The guide gave me the same sort of look a hostess gives a guest who asks the price of her silverware. Carlos came back to me and said, "There are none buried here, of course." Then he said hurriedly, "We'd better get out of here, Mr. Garner," eyeing the civil guards who were standing about. So we went.

When we reached his car he asked, "Where do you want to go now, sir?"

"I want to go to a place where some of *my* friends are buried," I said. "Take the road to Brunete. Then stop somewhere where I can buy a drink."

I was quiet as we drove down the mountain roads to the plain. Far away to the east I could see the transmitting towers of Radio Madrid near Carabanchel. I remembered seeing them from that other time, when they had seemed to be beckoning us from just out of reach. We had foolishly hoped our Brunete offensive would clear the enemy out of Casa de Campo and University City, or at least cut them off, and free Madrid from their shellfire. The members of an army have to hope such things, whether their generals do or not. We took Brunete, then lost it again, and had to retreat to the spot from which we had started. That was the story of almost every Loyalist battle that year.

We swung down the last hill to the plain, and I said to Carlos, "There's a little village called Villanueva around here."

"It's not on my map."

144

"It, along with a couple of others, have been on my mind's map for more than twenty-two years. Just drive on."

We were almost into it before we passed the road sign that read "Villanueva de la Cañada."

"See, I told you so," I said to him.

We drove over a wide culvert that had a little stream flowing beneath it. It had been a dry stream bed on that hot July day so long ago, and our battalion doctor, a man named Pike from St. Louis, and his assistants, had done the preliminary work on the wounded in its relative shelter. The village itself was only a couple of hundred metres farther along the road, and we made it in less than a minute in the car. A lot of the boys from the Lincoln Battalion never did make it to the village, and never will.

We pulled the car off the street between a small new white plaster church and the row of joined-together houses from which the Nationalists had mowed us down in the wheat stubble. The house nearest to us had been converted into a small store and cantina fronted with a loosely-hanging Pepsi-Cola sign.

As we entered the tiny, one-room hovel I looked around me at some ancient cans of beans and boxes of soap-flakes on the shelves, fronted by a small bar. A little man was trying to light a small tin stove, and the room was full of smoke. His wife, a frowzy-looking young woman wearing a torn and dirty sweater-coat, was tending a baby who was sitting in a home-made wooden walker in the middle of the floor, surrounded by about twenty squatting skinny hens.

"Order us each a brandy, Carlos," I said. "I'll try to get this stove going."

The little man went behind the bar to pour us the drinks, and I fixed the broken stovepipe. Then I stirred the wood and paper inside the stove with a poker, and fanned the bottom draft door with a rolled-up magazine. The fire burst into flames, and the young woman smiled her thanks.

We had our drinks, which tasted like gasoline though I wasn't kicking, and Carlos interpreted for me as I asked the little man what he knew about the first battle for the village in 1937. I remembered the sight of the church, with its belfry and its Moorish machine-gunners, burning during the night after we'd captured the town, and I asked the proprietor to take me out to where it had been. He hurried into his coat and led the way outside and across the road to a lane between two rows of houses. Behind the houses were the ruins of the church and presbytery.

I walked out into the fields, against the tearing wind, and turned around and looked at the village from the place where we had been held down during that long hot July afternoon. What I had then visualized as a high wall was now revealed as the rear of two rows of houses with small high windows built into each; it was a natural fortress.

Through Carlos I asked our host where the dead were buried, and he shrugged and swept his arm over the fields.

"They were all thrown into holes and covered up," Carlos said. "Nobody knows just where they are now."

I thought of the guys killed that afternoon; Jack Shirei, our Japanese cook; Oliver Law, the black commander of the machine-gun company; another black, and the most popular man in the battalion, Doug Roach; a Jewish guy from New York who had hypnotized some fellows one quiet evening on the Jarama Front. . . . hell, there had been plenty of battalion dead that day. "Let's have another shot of derail," I said to Carlos, then had to translate "derail" into the awful brandy before he understood what I meant.

When we got back to the cantina I was introduced to a middle-aged farmer wearing a peaked cap and a long blue-denim smock. He was the uncle of the storekeeper and he had fought in Villanueva against us on that July day. Through Carlos he told me he'd been a member of the Sixth Bandera of the Falange, recruited from around Seville. We had captured him on July 6, 1937. It was odd meeting a man I had fought against so long ago.

"Give him a brandy," I said to the man's nephew, as I shook my former enemy's hand. "No, make it a double. Doubles all round."

The storekeeper told me that he had been a little boy at the time of the battle, and that he and his family had stayed in the cellar of the house until the shooting was over. Carlos was reluctant to translate this, and kept asking the former Falangist prisoner if we'd tortured him. The uncle told him that he'd been taken back to a prison camp, and treated as well as could be expected until the war was over.

My interpreter was confused. Ever since finding out I'd been a Red he'd been forced to give up, one by one, all the propaganda he'd heard since he was a kid. He hadn't believed we'd fought both Moors and Spanish Foreign Legionnaires in that battle, until the other two men agreed that both kinds of troops had been stationed there. Carlos' trouble was that most of the foreign clients he'd had before I came along had only asked him for explanations about the El Grecos in the Prado, and how to find a discreet little whorehouse near the Puerta Del Sol.

I picked the baby up from her walker. She was eight months old and pretty, and she had a winning smile and a running nose, and she was wet. Carlos was horrified. "We shouldn't have come to a place like this," he whined.

"You're a snob, Carlos," I said. "You're one of those snobs who got that way from giving service to richer snobs, and believe me that's the worst kind there is."

"What's the baby's name?" I asked her mother.

"Isabella," the mother answered shyly.

The name of Spanish queens.

"Isabella, you're *muy guappa*," I said. "You're very pretty. I wonder what *you'll* be doing twenty-two years from now?"

When Carlos and I left the tiny cantina they all came to the door to bid us good-bye, in the wonderfully gracious manner of the Spanish people.

"I want to go and see the priest," I said to Carlos. He stared at me open-mouthed, and I told him, "I'm not going to cut his throat."

We found a twenty-four-year-old priest in his plain functional little white plaster church. Through Carlos I told him I was a *Rojo* who had once fought there during the civil war, and had come back for a journalistic visit. He smiled at me and we shook hands. He apologized as he showed me through the church; it needed a lot more work done on it, and he was doing the interior work himself.

I said to Carlos, "Tell him I want him to say some special prayers for the dead *Internationales* who are buried around here. There's plenty of people praying openly for the dead Nationalists, and plenty praying secretly for dead Spanish Loyalists, but there's nobody praying for my old buddies. They have no flower-covered shrines like the dead Falange leader, so we'll do the next best thing. Tell him I'll buy a mass."

"Are you a Roman Catholic?" the priest asked me.

"No, *padre*, I'm a Protestant, and a poor one at that." I gave him a 500-peseta note. "This will help you finish building your church. After all, my brigade burned down the old one."

The young priest swiftly hid the money in his soutane, shook my hand, and wished me God-speed and a pleasant visit to Spain.

147

In the car we drove back the way we'd come, I looked back, and the village was fading into the plain once more, tied to the earth by the affinity of time.

I was thinking of all the guys who were buried somewhere under the grey-green grass of the winter fields, and of how every one of the International's dead is *our* Unknown Soldier. I thought of Wallingford and Taffy Owens and Jack Shirei, and the new Toronto kid who'd just arrived with the battalion and had died on the stretcher with the bullet in his lung, and of the short story I'd once written around him. I thought of all the young men whose names I'd forgotten or had never known . . . The Canadians, Americans, Frenchmen, Slavs, Spaniards, Irishmen, Cubans, Englishmen and Belgians from our brigade. I thought too of Ralph Fox, who is also buried there, and of how they said he was as great a poet as Auden or Spender . . . It should have been the generals who were shot.

"This must be a great day for you," Carlos said.

"Yeah. Just great."

We didn't speak again until we were once more entering Madrid. Then I began asking silly questions about the historical buildings we passed. Not that I gave a damn about them, but I wanted Carlos to think he'd made the day worth while when he handed me my bill.

A LOYALIST SOLDIER RETURNS TO SPAIN

Part Two

It's funny how some inconsequential names will remain in your memory for years, while others which you should have remembered will be forgotten. For instance, I have remembered the names of two stamp collectors from St. Paul, Minnesota, Jones and Peabody, since crossing the Atlantic on the liner *Berengaria* in February, 1937, when I was on my way to the Spanish Civil War. Unfortunately I have completely forgotten the names of the eight other Spanish volunteers who accompanied me on the ship. I do remember that two of them, new Canadians, were from Sudbury, Ontario, while the other six were from Detroit, five of them undergraduates of Wayne (now Wayne State) University.

The sixth one, the leader of our group, was a young Russian Communist named Dan. He was a fine young man who became a section leader in our machine-gun company. The last time I saw him was when he left the lines during the Brunete offensive with a bullet hole through his hand.

We volunteers carried identical suitcases containing a World War One U.S. army uniform, a khaki sheepskin coat, a first-aid kit, boots, socks and underwear. We had been outfitted with these at an army surplus store in New York the day we boarded the ship. Dan instructed us to tell any questioners that we were a hockey team on our way to Europe. The bags may have fooled some people, but I'm afraid we didn't look too much like a hockey team.

At that time, the volunteers for the International Brigades were pouring through the induction centre in Paris by the hundreds every day. The Europeans travelled by train, bus and on foot, those from the British Isles by channel steamer, and those of us from North and South America by liners, freighters and any other ship accomodation that was available. The French liner *Ile-de-France* was one day behind us carrying 30 Americans from New York, and behind it was a ship of the Holland-American line with a passenger list that included more than a hundred volunteers. The only ships that didn't carry Spanish Loyalist volunteers were those of Italy, Germany and Portugal, who were our enemies.

Though none of us were romantics, or even gave it much thought, we were probably volunteer members of the last Crusade.

I recently returned to Spain for *The Star Weekly* to write a few of my experiences there as a member of the Loyalist Republican Army twenty-two years ago, and also to record some brief impressions of what Spain looks like, to me, today. The *Berengaria* has long been scrapped, and this time I crossed the Atlantic on that swift-moving Grand Hotel, the *Queen Elizabeth*. The two crossings were as different as chalk from cheese, but I'll remember the first one long after I've forgotten the second.

All railway passengers from Paris to Barcelona have to change trains at Cerbere-Port Bou on the French-Spanish border, which is actually in the middle of a tunnel on the Mediterranean. This is because the railway tracks in Spain and Portugal are of wider gauge than they are in the rest of Europe outside the Soviet Union. This, I was told by a Spanish friend, was done to protect Spain from invasion by other European nations under the crazy assumption that, if an invader couldn't get his trains across the border, he couldn't bring in his army. This Quixotic logic is one of the bafflements of the Spanish character.

149

On the way from the French border to Barcelona on my recent visit I had breakfast on the train with a young Frenchman who was in the orange export business in Valencia. He had a lot of luggage and a parcel about a foot square, wrapped in heavy paper and tied with string. When we detrained at Barcelona I helped him with his bags, then offered to carry his parcel.

We walked up the platform until we found a porter with a hand-truck, and I placed my own bag on it and also my friend's parcel. He loaded his other bags on the truck and we started towards the exit to get our taxis. Immediately, a young soldier wearing a German-type coal-scuttle helmet rushed over and stopped the porter. He was joined by another young soldier, and I'm sure that if they'd been carrying rifles and bayonets they'd have held us at bayonet point. The first soldier called to someone behind me, and our group was joined by a secret policeman wearing a trench-coat and trying to look like Robert Taylor. The soldier pointed at the parcel, then at me, and everybody glared in my direction.

The secret policeman gingerly picked up the parcel, held it to his ear, then slowly shook it back and forth. Its owner, the Frenchman, ran over to him and presumably asked him what was the idea. After a lengthy palaver in French, Spanish and Catalan the policeman placed the parcel back on the hand-truck, curtly dismissed the soldiers, and we went out to the taxi stand.

"Imagine those guys thinking I'd carry a bomb into the country like that," the Frenchman said. "That's a police state for you."

But to return to 1937.

When we Loyalist volunteers arrived in Paris from Cherbourg on the boat train we were taken to the International Brigades' induction centre, located appropriately enough in the Place de Combat in the Belleville neighborhood of the city. I remember it as though it were yesterday, yet when I went there recently to find the spot, it had disappeared. And so had the Hotel Minerva on the Rue Louis Blanc, where I'd lived for six weeks after coming out of Spain. Time seems to have a habit of rubbing out old landmarks, or moving them from one place to another. After twenty-two years everything seemed to have been shifted, in Spain as well as in Paris.

At the induction centre we were given a cursory medical examination and, if you could see lightning and hear thunder, you were judged fit enough to serve as cannon fodder for the Red Army generals and Communist satraps who sent us against the enemy in suicidal daylight attacks in order to make the com-

150

muniqués to *L'Humanité* and *Pravda*. Of course none of us dreamed of such things at that time.

I was shown immediately to a room, situated on the ground floor of a two-story building surrounding a dirt courtyard. I undressed and threw myself into the biggest, most luxurious bed I'd ever seen. The French may be primitive in their plumbing arrangements, but they have us beaten by the thickness of two feather ticks when it comes to beds. I had just fallen asleep when the door was thrown open, the light switched on, and two men wearing alpine costumes and carrying skis entered the room. I sat up as if shot by springs. By now I'd begun to expect anything, but this was ridiculous.

They smiled at me, and I gave them a sickly grin in return. The older one, a man in early middle-age, said something to me in German and I indicated I didn't understand.

"Do you speak English?" I asked.

The younger of the two, a boy of about twenty, said, "A little."

"Are you going to Spain?"

"Yes, of course." They both smiled again.

"*Kameraden*," I said, and where I picked *that* up I'll never know.

We shook hands, and I told them that we could all sleep in the bed by sleeping sideways. They nodded, and began to shuck themselves of their heavy clothing and ski boots.

Their story, which I pieced together from what my two bedmates told me and what I learned the following day from some of their comrades, was an epic one.

The older of my roommates was an Austrian Alpine guide, and the seven other young men in their party were university students from Vienna, members of the underground Social-Democratic movement in Austria. Following the assassination of Premier Dolfuss in 1934, the country had become a quasi-fascist state under a corporative constitution. They had decided to go to Spain where at least the people were fighting fascism instead of just knuckling under.

Ten young men and a girl student had started out, ostensibly on a skiing party into the Alps. They had made arrangements with a guide (my older roommate) to lead them across the mountains into Switzerland. It was a hazardous undertaking, not only because it was the dead of winter but because of the border guards. Just as they were crossing the final pass into Switzerland they met an Austrian border patrol, which opened fire on them. Three of the young men and the girl had been shot, and the others, joined by their guide who could not go back, had kept on to Switzerland and freedom. They had no passports, so they had crossed Switzerland by train and then had to ski across the Alps again into France.

The following summer, in Madrid, I met the lone survivor of the group. He told me that they had all served in the Ernst Thaelmann Battalion, a German unit of one of the International Brigades, and all but he had been killed. The Thaelmanns had been part of the Loyalist forces that had decimated two Italian regular army Blackshirt Divisions in March, 1937, at the Battle of Guadalajara, northeast of Madrid.

These young Austrians were wonderful men—tall, handsome, intelligent, polite. I thought of them in particular when my Fascist driver-interpreter in Barcelona (a lying old son of a bitch, and the only person I met in Spain whom I truly disliked) told me that the International Brigades had been formed of the scum of Europe's slums. Some scum!

The evening after my arrival in Paris some hundreds of us boarded a special train at the Gare d'Austerlitz for the trip to the Spanish border. We were a widely and wildly assorted group: Frenchmen going to join the 14th Brigade, Swedes, Swiss, Danes, Poles, German anti-Nazi refugees, Cuban Negroes, Romanians, Oxford undergraduates, a deserter from the Royal Italian Navy, a Boston actor who was as gaunt and thespian-looking as John Carradine (and who was killed on the Jarama Front), three Polish nurses, a group of Irishmen who were going to the American battalion because they wouldn't serve with the English, two "Geordie" coal-miners (both of whom were killed near Brunete), the Austrian boys, ex-members of the French Foreign Legion, men who had fought for the Moroccan rebel leader Abd-el-Krim against the Legion, about thirty New York Jewish boys who were undergrads at City College, Ted Allen, the Montreal playwright but then a communist newspaper correspondent, and Colin Cox from Dublin, both of whom I wrote about in Part One of this series.

That was about the most exhilarating train ride I ever took. For the first and I suppose last time in the lives of most of us we had the feeling that we belonged to a world-wide group of brothers, a group that ignored national boundaries and language, race, and in many cases, even politics. Many of us were not communists; some were socialists, some ardent trade unionists or followers of the co-operative movement, and some merely believed that fascism had to be destroyed. Some had no politics at all. Some were Roman Catholics and others were pious Jews, members of Protestant denominations or atheists. Our common bond was that of the *esprit de corps* of men going to fight together in a war.

A great many of the young men at that time had the fanaticism of the Communist Party card-carrier, but some were idealists and others adventurers. Some, I suspect, had joined to escape a nagging wife or the boredom of chronic unemployment. It didn't really matter; a bullet doesn't ask your politics, and the adventurers died just as bravely as the arrogant political fanatics.

On the train we divided ourselves mainly along lines of language. Before we reached Orleans we could hear the Frenchmen singing in the coach ahead, and before we reached Limoges the Irishmen were drunk and were fighting the 1916 "throubles" all over again. An American Jewish boy, with ,hick glasses, led a group in a long repetitious song that sounded like *Schnitzelbaum*. From a compartment down the corridor came a beautiful melodic voice. When we went to investigate, we found it belonged to a big Welshman whose name I found out later was Taffy Owens.

By the time we reached Toulouse, we were half drunk from the wine that had been purchased at every stop. Cox had related for the fourth time his exploit in upsetting General O'Duffy's car, and there were instantaneous friendships between drunken Croats, Dutchmen and Poles. The train grew relatively quiet in the early morning hours as most of us grabbed some sleep. The train rushed on through the wine country, the small stations brightening up the compartment momentarily as their platform lights ran up and down the window. From up ahead came the peevish scream of the locomotive whistle as we hurtled south and east in the direction of the Spanish frontier.

It was still early in the morning, with the workers trudging out into the fields and vineyards, when we detrained at Perpignan and marched along the streets carrying our coats and suitcases under the bored glances of the impassive populace. To us, who had come so far, it seemed unbelievable that these men, who lived so near, should not have crossed the border into Spain to fight. In our idealism we believed it was the duty of all free men to help the Spanish people. A great many of us lost our idealism later, but at that time it was a warm and wonderful thing.

We were led into a large Moorish courtyard where we threw ourselves to the wind-scored ground under the small dusty trees. From beneath an arch a couple of men were doling out tin mugs of black, sugarless coffee and large chunks of hard dry Spanish

153

bread. We queued up for our first taste of Spanish army fare, and some of the dyed-in-the-wool communists ("Red Rotarians" as we would call them later) pretended it was better than bacon and eggs. At lunch time, or *comida,* as a hasty linguist or two had learned to call it, we were given tin plates full of chick peas and chunks of meat. At that time the meat was beef, but later on we would learn to eat horse meat, mule meat and even jackass meat which, while doing double duty as food and dental floss, is not something you'd find on a hotel menu.

In the afternoon we piled into buses and rode up into a pass through the Pyrenees. When we reached the border the sight of the Spanish soldiers drew cheers from the men in the buses, but we were met with sullen stares. We weren't aware then that these soldiers were members of Anarchist brigades or the P.O.U.M. (*Partido Obrero de Unificación Marxistá*), the Trotskyite political group for which George Orwell fought, and which hated to see so many potential Stalinist enemies entering their country. They passed us through however, and we crossed the divide and crept down the steep Spanish slopes to a gigantic stone fortress at Figueras, where we were bunked down in the cold dim reaches of its underground passages.

There were some English boys there, going home. We crowded around them to ask what things were like in Madrid. One of them said, "Things are awful, comrades. You'll find out." His companions nodded their agreement.

They had no civilian clothes, so I gave one of them a brand-new suit I was wearing and my hat and coat as well. It didn't strike me as ludicrous at the time, but I had entered the war wearing a homburg hat and spats. I was one of the most stylish recruits any army ever got.

The next morning we marched through the streets of Figueras to the railway station, singing our songs, booing the POUM signs, and trying vainly to look like soldiers rather than a rabble. The people ignored us, for Figueras was a strong Trotskyite town.

A short time ago I passed through Figueras again on a train. It was a cool sunny morning, much as it had been the first time I saw the town. There are no POUM signs there now, but the grey-uniformed police lounge beneath the Falangist symbol with its crossed *fasces* of arrows above the police headquarters' door.

Down the Costa Brava, the Mediterranean coastline of Catalonia, the seaside cottages are rented for the season to British, Scandinavian and German tourists. During the civil war there were no tourists, of course, and the resort hotels were used as hospitals and convalescent homes for the wounded.

As we rolled on south, twenty-two years before, through the brown fields and vineyards, through the cork forests and woods filled with Mediterranean pines, the Catalan farmers plowed their ancient fields, their skinny horses treading daintily around the grape roots. The women in their long black shapeless dresses drove the small brown scrub cattle along the roads or pounded the washing against the stone parapets of the wide water cisterns behind the houses. Today it has not changed one bit, except for one great difference. There are no black and red anarchist flags flying from the farmhouses, and there are no signs above the small factory gates announcing that the plant is being run for the workers by the workers of the C.N.T., the large anarcho-syndicalist trade union.

I saw only one tractor in the fields all the way from the French border to Barcelona. A Spaniard in my compartment, who was returning on a visit from the United States, said, "I'll bet it's the only one for fifty miles around. Spain is one country that'll never be rich enough to supplant the horse."

Today Spain is a study in contrasts. There is terrible unemployment and poverty, but out of the midst of the city slums rise new buildings that only serve to show the shabbiness of the old ones surrounding them. While most railroad lines in France are electrified or dieselized, those in Spain, except for the extra fare *Rapido* trains, still use ancient steam locomotives. I saw one in Tarragona that bore the date 1889 on its running-board. As we ran through the railway yards entering Barcelona, an Englishman who has lived in the city for ten years pointed out some new self-propelled aluminum and stainless steel coaches of the type we call dayliners in Canada.

"They are marked with the name of a Spanish manufacturer," he said, "but I happen to know they were built in Italy. It is just one of the dodges indulged in by the present régime to pretend it is more advanced than it is. In Barcelona we have ancient trams that would have been condemned twenty years ago in Cairo, and old double-decked buses bought second-hand from the London transportation system. It takes years here to erect a building that in any other country would be put up in months."

Travelling through Barcelona, Valencia, Albacete, Alcala de Henares and Madrid, I found that the Englishman had been right. In Canada we put a temporary wooden fence around a construction project, but in Spain they build a permanent brick wall, made to remain for years. Just south of the Pyrenees in

155

Gerona province the Nationalist government has erected a large bright-yellow brick sanatorium. Like everything else it has built, it is meant primarily as a monument to the Franco government; treatment of T.B. patients is secondary. It commands a wide sweep of the valley, and is meant to be seen by every train and highway traveller.

The Englishman told me that some doctor friends in Barcelona had told him there are many new hospital buildings but few drugs or equipment. "The aspirin tablet is the most common prescription in Spain today," he said. "Franco can spend $20 million for a silly self-aggrandizing tomb like the one he has built in the Valley of the Fallen outside Madrid, but Spain has no money to equip its hospitals or modernize its transportation system."

Loyalist Spain could buy few arms or build few hospitals in 1937, but she had something modern Spain has not: human energy, a fighting spirit, and a great hope for the future. She didn't lose this hope on the fighting fronts, but in the government cabinets of the United States, Great Britain, France and the other democracies. She also lost it in the oriental wiliness and deviousness of Joseph Stalin, who gave her just enough arms and equipment to keep the war going for three years until both sides were exhausted and Spain was impoverished. Leftist politics are a dead issue in Spain today and the ex-Republicans (and I believe them to be still the majority of the people) have searched for new values on which to rebuild their lives. I came away from Spain convinced that though freedom and the vote are wonderful, there are more important things to a man who tries to bring up a family under conditions of bare subsistence.

That February morning in 1937 we pulled into the Barcelona railway station and found a train across the platform filled with refugees from Malaga, a town on the southeast coast, which had just been taken by the Nationalists. Incidentally, this was the place where the novelist Arthur Koestler was taken prisoner, to be later sentenced to death and consequently released. The frightened little refugees sat staring through the windows of the train compartments stunned by what had happened; their homes and possessions gone, their babies hungry and crying, the future a bleak unknown.

Some of the New York Jewish boys from our train jumped to the platform, ran to the station restaurant, and came back laden with milk, fruit and bread, which they proceeded to pass around among the refugees. It was entirely unselfish and spontaneous, and for the benefit of those who don't care much for

Jews, or think that all Communists are rats, I record the incident here.

Besides George Orwell, fighting with a POUM division in Catalonia and Arthur Koestler, being transferred as a prisoner from Malaga to Seville, André Malraux, the distinguished author of *Man's Hope* and other books, was leading a Loyalist Air Force fighter squadron on the Madrid Front. Elliot Paul was in the Balearics, probably thinking of writing *Life And Death In A Spanish Town,* John Dos Passos and Josephine Herbst were in Madrid, and Ernest Hemingway was making plans to come to Spain, where he would arrive a month later. It was a great war for the literati, and the Loyalist forces probably contained more distinguished novelists and poets in relation to their size than any fighting force since Caesar's.

Today, Barcelona has a façade of slightly shabby hustle and bustle. Its main business streets and boulevards, especially the Ramblas with its tree-bordered wide centre strip, are filled during the siesta and the evening hours with the young men and girls from the nearby offices, textile and chemical plants, that are Barcelona's main industries. It is Spain's biggest industrial city, and a few months ago it even had an abortive industrial strike that was quickly crushed by the government. As anachronistic as it now seems, even to me, Barcelona was governed and controlled for three years by the Anarchists and Syndicalists. It was not the fighting city Madrid was however, and it gave up without a shot, even before Madrid, which had been under siege almost since the war began.

Barcelona is now a police city, and police uniforms are obvious everywhere. When I mentioned this to a taxi-driver he winked at me and held up three fingers. "We have one army and three police forces," he said with a cynical laugh. Cynicism is the replacement of hope in modern Spain.

In the war days the city was drab, with shuttered shops and business places, and a complete blackout at night. The Ramblas and the Plaza de Cataluna, its main square, showed only shadowy figures of soldiers and their women, and of Anarchist army patrols. Today it is well lighted in the evening, the neon signs winking above the cypress and palm trees. The marquee lights of the movie houses beckon to the passers-by as they feature dubbed-in dialogue of *Solomon and Sheba* and American cowboy epics. In the daytime the streets around the Ramblas are alive with color after the flower markets open with their displays of giant 'mums and cyclamen. There is also a bird market, its open stalls surrounded by hanging cages full of song birds

157

and parakeets which symbolically fill the air with their murmured protests at their imprisonment. My guide told me that the Fascist government has closed up many of the outdoor cafes since they were hotbeds of anti-Franco intrigue and neo-revolutionary talk.

It is a beautiful train ride down the shore of the Mediterranean from Barcelona to Valencia, with the subtle change in climate much the same as that between San Francisco and Los Angeles. Valencia is the heart of the orange country, and I found that the city had hardly changed at all since I had last seen it, and used it as the locale of a short story, "The Expatriates." The ancient tandem trolley cars still circle the palm-centred main square and the lottery ticket sellers still cry out, "Lotteria! Lotteria!" in their quavering voices. Stencilled on the two pillars fronting the headquarters of the *Guardia Civil* were two anti-Franco slogans that showed signs of much scrubbing but are still legible to those who pass by. The shoeshine "boys" in Valencia are mature men, and I felt ashamed for them as I passed them on the corners. In all the cities of Spain there are too many able-bodied men in the tourist service trades, and each time I sat down to dinner in my hotels to be served by four servile waiters, I would wish it was in my power to get them men's jobs running a turret lathe or driving a transport truck. To illustrate Spain's poverty, there are also vendors who sell one cigarette at a time from an opened package in their hand.

In Madrid I asked a fellow hotel guest, a construction engineer, how much they paid their Spanish labourers, but he wouldn't tell me.

"It's against government policy to gossip about such things," he said. "I do know that the equivalent of $15 a week is a substantial wage here, and that street labourers make about a dollar a day."

The Americans accept a lot of humiliation from the Franco government, causing the ordinary Spaniard to hold them in contempt. U.S. Air Force personnel cannot appear in their uniforms off base and must wear a suit coat and necktie at all times when they are in civvies, no matter what the temperature. During the civil war the Russian pilots in the Loyalist Air Force also had to wear civvies, but you could always tell them by their snub Russian noses or Mongol cast to their features, and their brown leather windbreakers. They used to keep to themselves, and wouldn't talk to the Internationales or Spanish soldiers; maybe they knew that our enthusiasm was a waste of time.

As the extra fare *Rapido* train climbed the long slopes from Valencia to the interior plateau we passed orange groves with the fruit clustered on the trees. In the half darkness of the winter night the trees had the appearance of harbingers of Christmas. When we had gone through this country in 1937, on an old slow troop train, the peasants had come down to the railroad tracks from their farms and had poured bushel baskets of the fruit into our coaches. This had been Socialist and Communist country then and the people showed their appreciation for our coming to fight with gestures such as this. That "one for all and all for one" feeling it gave us was something I'm sure I will never experience again.

We had arrived in Albacete, the depot town of the International Brigades, on a dull cloudy evening in mid-February, a few days short of my 24th birthday. The next day the several hundred of us who had arrived together the evening before were marched to the Plaza de Toros, the bull-ring, and there lined up in three ranks.

Several Communist Party functionaries spoke to us in as many languages, giving us the pep-talks common to the type of soldier who fights a war with a briefcase under his arm. Then a multi-lingual staff officer, probably a Russian, and one of the "political commissars" we had at all levels of the army, asked us to surrender our passports, which he promised would be kept for us at the *Intendencia,* or army headquarters. (The passports of the men killed in Spain were sent to Moscow, and were used by Soviet secret agents and couriers later on.) He told us of the desperate situation in Madrid, warned us not to expect any mercy if we were captured, and told us we would be paid seven pesetas a day, which was later raised to ten.

Last fall, on a CBC panel show, I was asked by a lady panelist if I had gone to Spain to fight for money. I told her there wasn't enough money in the world to pay a fighting infantryman, and though a man may go into an army during wartime for many reasons, money wasn't one of them. I thought of this a short time ago when I airmailed a postcard from Valencia to Toronto; it cost six pesetas or ten cents.

While we stood there in the bullring in the morning sun the men who could fill certain army categories were asked to step forward from the ranks. This went on for some time, with truck drivers, clerks, telegraphists, auto mechanics, and others leaving the ranks until those of us who were left looked as if our ranks had been raked with grapeshot. I was just smart and cowardly enough to know that the remnants who were left would automatically become infantrymen. They called for those who played a musical instrument to step out to join the International Brigades band (incidentally, I never once saw or heard *that* organization play a note), those with hospital experience, cavalrymen, men with artillery training . . . our ranks were getting thinner and thinner, and I was becoming certain that I was destined for the cannon-fodder. They finally called for signalmen, and I stepped forward.

As I, along with nine or ten other erstwhile signalmen, marched out of the bullring I looked back and saw that those who were left were being divided into language groups and assigned to the various brigades then at the front.

At that time there was no infantry training whatsoever and an infantryman learned to use his weapons by firing at the enemy. By becoming a signaller I had at least postponed that possibility.

I was luckier than I knew, for the 15th Brigade, particularly the Abraham Lincoln Battalion whose officers were Communist Party amateurs, unlike some of those in the other battalions of the brigade, was thrown into a suicidal daylight attack against the Nationalist trenches on the Jarama front on February 27th, and half of the battalion was killed or wounded. The English, Franco-Belge and Georgi Dimitroff battalions refused the insane order from the brigade commander, and it was the poor naive Americans who died for a headline in the New York *Daily Worker*.

One of the wounded was my former roommate in Toronto, Henry Scott Beattie, a former Cabbagetowner, and one of the dead was a kid I'd gone to Duke of Connaught Public School with, in Toronto's East End, named Leige Clare, who had been an amateur wrestler. The American battalion never did fully recover from the stupidity of that attack, and when I finally joined it a couple of weeks later its members were depressed, frightened and apprehensive of any orders from Brigade.

We so-called signallers were taken from the bullring to our barracks, the *Caserne Posada,* a former inn, and given cots on a glass-enclosed balcony overlooking a courtyard. There we were addressed by another multilingual political commissar. Albacete was a great town for army desk-wallahs, the head of whom was the old Communist Frenchman Andre Marty, whom Hemingway reviled in *For Whom The Bell Tolls.*

Around the second night I spent in Albacete the Italian Savoia-Marchetti bombers came over for a couple of hours in waves and bombed the town. It wasn't much of a bombing compared with what other cities were to withstand during World War Two and later, but at that time it was a scary omen of what was to come. Strangely, though, I wasn't very scared at all, and after being driven out of my bed by successive waves of bombers, and once marched out in the fields, I kept going back to bed and to sleep. In the morning we wandered around through the town to see the results of the bombing, and the one thing I remember about that was a child's crib hanging up in a tree.

When I returned to Albacete a short time ago, I had no trouble finding the *Caserne Posada,* or the *Gota de Leche* (Drop of Milk) hospital, where I'd been a patient in the fall of 1937. I failed, however, to find the little basement cantina lined with wine vats, that we called "Ali Baba's." I was anxious to have another anisette there for old time's sake.

We signallers were of all nationalities, including an Italian naval deserter, two Hungarians, and an American called Reid, whom I write about at greater length later on. We were taken to a room piled high with mud-caked French army field telephones. "These have to be taken apart and scraped free of mud," one of the officers said.

"Where did this mess come from?" somebody asked.

"They have been recovered from the bottom of Barcelona harbour," the officer answered. "They were on a ship that was bombed and sunk there a couple of months ago."

Being a depot town soldier engaged in the job of cleaning mud from field telephones wasn't my idea of fighting in Spain, and besides I now began to feel like a slacker for not staying still in the bullring and being drafted into the infantry. I began to scheme how to get out of this Mickey Mouse signalling outfit, and about a week later I found myself detoured even farther from the front to the artillery school at a village called Almansa about half way back to Valencia.

Almansa was fun. We had no artillery pieces, and spent most of our days watching an officer draw artillery positions in a sand pile. We were quartered in a convent from which the nuns had been evicted when the fascists in the town had holed up in it, and the peoples' militia from the village had successfully stormed it during the early days of the revolution. Something I must add, which of course I didn't include in this piece for *The Star Weekly,* was that the village had a wonderful little five-peseta whorehouse where I spent most of my evenings. We artillerymen had some great parties with the girls, and I remember two of my fellow soldiers in particular, a Belgian opera star (whom I recreated as a character in my story "The Expatriates") and an American called Brown, who had been torpedoed on a ship between Marseilles and Spain. I found an old hand-written leather book in the convent, dating from 1489, which I carried in my pack until I lost all my possessions in the Brunete battle the following summer.

After a week or so of the good life I met a fellow Torontonian who drove a truck, and I hitched a ride with him from Almansa to where the Lincoln Battalion was in the trenches on the Jarama Front southeast of Madrid. Along with two Swedes, who went into the English Battalion, I climbed the path from the valley village of Morata de Tajuna to the American trenches in an olive grove atop a ridge, 150 metres from the Nationalist lines. The battalion was short-handed after the debacle of February 27th, and I was handed a rifle, my name was put on the pay list, and I was sent to the machine-gun company. I was happy to find that my section-leader was Danny Leppo, the young Russian who had been in charge of our small party aboard the Berengaria, the finest non-commissioned officer I have ever met in two armies and a navy. He introduced me to Herman Katz, with whom I shared a shallow dugout cut under an olive tree. I also met Duncan, the Philadelphian, and re-met Colin Cox from Dublin, who had been one of my compartment-mates on the train down from Paris. The four of us were to be together for the next few months, except when we left Danny behind in the lines, after Cox, Duncan and I had been sent from the Lincoln Battalion to a punishment unit by Oliver Law, the black Red Rotarian from Chicago who was then the machine-gun company commander. Duncan, Cox and I finally deserted from the *Corps du Geni* (if that's its spelling) and went first to Madrid and then to the El Pardo Front, where we joined an Anarchist brigade. But that's another story.

A LOYALIST SOLDIER RETURNS TO SPAIN

Part Three

The Jarama is a small river that runs north to south, a few miles east of Madrid. It curves to the west below the city and becomes a tributary of the Tagus, flowing west into Portugal and emptying into the Atlantic at Lisbon. To the east of it runs the Madrid-Valencia highway, which during the civil war, to all practical purposes, was the only means of entry to Madrid from the rest of Loyalist Spain. The holding of this highway was vital to the defence of Madrid. The Nationalists made a determined effort to cut the highway in late 1936, but were beaten back by an International Brigade—at that time French, German and Central European in nationality, but also containing the newly-formed English Battalion. From then on there was always one of the International Brigades on the Jarama Front. My Brigade, the 15th, was in the trenches there from February until June, 1937, when we were relieved by the 14th French-speaking brigade.

There isn't much to write about Jarama that wouldn't apply to trench warfare anywhere and in any war. It was a holding action and, except for the stupid and disastrous daylight attack that the Americans made on February 27th, the fighting consisted mainly of scouting parties, sniping, false night attacks when both sides opened up with everything they had, light artillery barrages and machine-gun duels. The winters on the Castilian plateau are cold and wet, and we stood in the trenches with the cold rain running down from our French tin helmets on to the sopping ponchos we wore above our variegated uniforms.

The trenches on the Jarama were west of the highway and of the small village of Morata de Tajuna, which served as our brigade supply depot, bathing and delousing station. The front lines lay along the crest of a row of hills from which the ground fell away steeply to the valley below, where the cavalry and artillery were quartered. The Lincoln Battalion's sector was in an olive grove, the shallow dugouts behind and in the rear walls of the trenches dug under the roots of the trees. On our left was a Spanish brigade and to our right, in succession, were the English Battalion (named, Communist-like, after some Hindoo Communist martyr, whose name was so unpronounceable that even the Englishmen didn't use it), the Franco-Belge Battalion, and the Georgi Dimitroff Battalion. Another Spanish brigade or division continued on from their right. The fifth battalion of our brigade, the Spanish-American 24th Battalion, was in reserve.

On my recent return visit to Spain for *The Star Weekly* I made two trips to the old Jarama front to try to recapture some of the flavor of those months during the winter and spring of 1937. I was disappointed, for I found it difficult to re-orient myself to the topography and even more difficult to recapture the feelings of that earlier time. The Madrid-Valencia highway was almost bare of traffic, where once it had throbbed day and night with the camions bringing in food and ammunition. The village of

Morata was just another old and shabby Spanish village, stinking from the open sewers along the gutters. Once it had been a reminder to us up on the hills that the world was also a place of women and children, and houses that were not observation posts but family dwellings.

One landmark I will never forget was a large ducal house, surrounded by formal gardens, that nestled against the base of the hills behind our trenches. It was used as brigade headquarters and its kitchens had been converted into the brigade cookhouses. I used to take my turn going down there to fetch back the dixies of food for our machine-gun section. There was one spot in the path that wound down through the hills that was under observation by the enemy, and they would quite often open up with a machine-gun on it as a stretcher party made its way down the hill or a battalion runner or food-fetcher came within their sights. It happened to me on a couple of occasions, and the machine-gun bullets cracked around my head. At one of these times, while I was struggling up the path with two dixies filled with lentil stew, the machine-gun opened up, and I just threw the heavy dixies aside and fell on my belly. Whether or not I retrieved the covered containers of stew or not I now forget.

Most of us in the American battalion were pretty naive about war, and we didn't know at the time that all bullets that pass quite close to the head have the sound of a sharp crack, and not the whine of far-off bullets that are heard in cowboy pictures. The communist propagandists took advantage of our naiveté and spread the word that the enemy were using explosive bullets. In turn some of us, by means of a cross made in the point of our copper-jacketed bullets, turned them into dum-dums, which would spread open in flight and make a wide tearing hole in any human body they happened to hit.

The English battalion cook was a short pimply-looking bloke whose forbears were probably cooks for Captain Blood and Henry Morgan. He was a real piratical character who wore a dish-towel wrapped around his head and stirred the mule meat and chick peas like a dishevelled Merlin mixing up a devil's brew. The Englishmen used to tell a story about him. Late in 1936, before our own battalion was even formed, the English Battalion, along with the rest of their brigade and Spanish troops, had been driven from the heights and almost down into Morata itself. The English cook had shouted to his assistants before taking off, "The Fascists are coming! Poison the rice, comrades! Poison the rice!" Luckily it hadn't been necessary, for

164

the Internationals, led by the English Battalion, had fought their way back up the slopes and established the line we were then in along the ridge.

I remember the inside of the big house very well from that winter and spring. On the walls of the upstairs hallways hung autographed photographs of bullfighters, and though most of the furniture had been stolen during the earliest days of the revolution—for people who lived in such houses were naturally on the side of Franco—it was still a magnificent home. The owner had been an ornithologist, or at least a bird-jailer, for in the garden were two large aviaries like tall cages covered with strong wire mesh. In the first heady days of the revolution, or the counter-revolution depending on your politics, the summer before, all the birds had been given their liberty by the people of the village, who like the birds themselves had been the serfs and playthings of the boss-man in the big house on the slope. Whether the aristocratic owner and his family escaped with their lives from the vengeful villagers or not I never knew.

Anyhow, the brigade used these large bird-cages as cells in which to hold the brigade drunks and recalcitrants for short periods of time. When I visited our cookhouse or passed them on my way to Morata for a bath and a change of uniform, I would often stop and talk to the prisoners, some of them from our battalion. They would be sitting on the floor of the cages, nursing their hangovers and looking for all the world like large grounded khaki parakeets. When any of the boys stopped to chat with them they would rush to the wire and beg cigarettes. We would push the loosely-rolled smokes we called "pillow cases" through the mesh one at a time, then leave them some matches and cigarette papers in which to re-roll them. Though any of us could have done short stretches in the bird-cages, the majority of prisoners there were generally French drunks, with Spanish, Irish and English making up the rest.

While I'm mentioning cigarettes I may as well say that on occasion we also received a package apiece of French Gauloises, that we called "Galowsies." Instead of matches and kerosene lighters most of us carried Spanish wick lighters, that consisted of a wheel and flint and a brass tube through which stuck a thick rope-like length of wick. These would light off the spark from the flint, and they were used by the Asturian miners, the *dynamiteros*, who used them to light their bombs and explosive devices. Some soldiers carried lighters with yards-long lengths of wick wound around their waists.

The Lincoln Battalion usually drank coffee with its meals,

and as I said the English imported their own tea. The Franco-Belge Battalion stuck to the cheap *vino rojo,* or red wine, that was the standard Spanish army beverage. We received it too, and it was brought up from the cookhouse in galvanized pails, which we dipped it from with our tin mugs. During the night watches in the trenches (usually every third man was always standing-to, and we changed watches night and day) an old Chilean tin-miner called Pancho and his young Spanish Assistant, would come through the trench carrying canteens of brandy, hot coffee, bread and French bully beef. We would each take a good slug of the brandy, make ourselves sandwiches with the bully, and wash it down with black coffee. To me it was the tastiest meal of the day.

Last December, along with Carlos, my driver-interpreter and possible secret police watchdog, I drove out east along the Calle de Alcala, past the Madrid bullring, through the suburbs, and down the highway to Morata. We parked the car in the village street while I tried to find, unsuccessfully, the place where we had bathed under the cold-water showers and had picked clean clothes from a pile in a corner. The battalion had started out more or less uniformly dressed, but when our first uniforms had become dirty and lousy, we had been forced to exchange them for the clean clothes from the corner grab-bag. That winter and spring on the Jarama I'd worn several types of uniforms and shirts that ran from army khaki woollens to greyish-green denims, and from khaki shirts to striped flannel jobs. I still had the sheepskin coat I'd brought from New York, and my favorite uniform was a khaki shirt and khaki corduroy trousers.

I asked Carlos to drive me up the road that had bisected the two lines of trenches on the ridge to the west, but he claimed he couldn't find it. Then I asked him to drive me to the big house with the gardens and aviaries, which had been our brigade headquarters. He looked at me as if I was crazy, which I probably was, and told me that the family probably wouldn't want to meet a member of the proletarian army that had made a mess of their estate. I guess he was right. We settled for a drink in one of the local cantinas.

There's more to say later about the Jarama, but first I'd like to go back in time to Albacete. I mentioned in the second part of this series that I'd met a man in the signal corps called Reid. I'd like to tell you more about him, for he was a remarkable man in a war that had many remarkable men. When I met him he was in his late forties, completely unprepossessing, and he wore an ill-fitting uniform, blue beret and steel-rimmed glasses. He had the sharp lined face of a quizzical ferret, claimed to be Irish-American, and told me he had served in World War One as a signaller with the Fourth Canadian Mounted Rifles, a Toronto cavalry regiment that had fought as infantry.

On my second morning at the signal barracks he sidled up to me and said "These Comicals are nuts."

"Comicals?" I asked.

"Sure. The Communists, so called."

At that time, to me, the Communists in Spain were above reproach, and hearing them called "Comicals" was like listening to someone blaspheme in church. I tried to draw away from him but he stuck with me.

"Are you a Commie?" he asked.

"No, but I'm a sympathizer."

"Why? You look too intelligent," he said.

I got away from him and avoided him for the rest of the day.

The following morning he cornered me again. "Why did you come to Spain?" he asked.

I gave him the usual answer about anti-fascism, the plight of the Loyalists, youthful adventurism and so on.

"Most of the comrades believe they are saving Russia by being here," he said. "They don't care about the Spanish people. Look what the Commies are doing to the people in Catalonia."

He was referring to the suppression of a revolt by the POUM there.

"They were Trotskyites," I said. "They were backed by Fascist money."

"Bah!" Reid shouted. "Don't fall for that stuff. Don't let them make you into a rubber stamp."

During the following week, despite our differences, we became good friends. He told me he had been sent to Spain by the U.S. Socialist Party as the first, and as it later turned out, the only member of a Socialist brigade to be called the Eugene Debs Column. He had been an organizer for the Industrial Workers of the World after World War One, and he still carried the Wobblies' red card. He spoke nostalgically of the Seattle general strike of 1919 and of Big Bill Haywood and other half-forgotten radicals of the twenties.

Once, when I accused him of being a Trotskyite, he fixed me with a scornful stare and said, "I hate the Trotskyites only slightly less than I hate the Orthodox Commies. I have never had any use for either Mr. Bronstein (Trotsky) or Mr. Two-gash-willy (Stalin) since they put down the Russian naval revolt at Kronstadt."

I'd heard of members of the Internationals being shot for saying far less, but this fact didn't stop Reid.

One morning in the *Caserne Posada*, after a political commissar had given a long speech in several languages, Reid shouted, "Let's hear what you have to say in English!"

An officer stepped forward and explained to him that there were only two or three English-speaking comrades in the ranks.

Reid was insistent.

In thickly-accented English the commissar repeated his pep-talk about fighting to the death against world fascism, believing in the glory of the Soviet Union, and trusting in the wisdom of Comrade Stalin. When he was finished Reid just stared at him and shook his head.

The surprised commissar asked, "Are you a member of the Party?"

"No, I'm a member of the world proletariat."

"But what party do you belong to?"

"None. I'm anti-authoritarian."

I edged away from him. Telling a communist political commissar that you were anti-authoritarian was like telling your father confessor that you didn't believe in God. The commissar was nonplussed and he decided to ignore the apostasy. He went on with his pep-talk in French.

Reid was a self-educated man, and his university had been the New York public library. His knowledge of literature was phenomenal and he could quote Dickens and Melville by the page. The night before I left for the artillery school at Almansa, he asked me if I had ever read *Jurgen*. When I admitted I hadn't he said, "James Branch Cabell is the only 20th-Century U.S. writer who will become immortal."

I saw him only one more time. Several months later near Brunete I noticed a familiar figure plodding along a ditch unreeling field telephone wire.

"Hey, Reid!" I shouted as we hurried past.

He straightened up, gave me a wave and a grin. Then he cupped his hands and shouted, "Have you read *Jurgen* yet?"

"Yes. I read the Tauchnitz edition up on the Jarama."

I have remembered Reid all these years for to me he was the epitome of the old native North American radical, fiercely independent, rebellious, not tied to any foreign political ideas, and self-assured in what he believed to be the truth.

The character Noah Masterson in *Cabbagetown* was based partly on Reid, as I remembered him.

My driver, Carlos, and I drove up a paved road near Morata on another day after my first visit, and over the heights where both lines of trenches had made up the Jarama Front. It was up this same road, early in 1937, that a truckload of Americans and Canadians had driven right into the Nationalist lines, where they had either been taken prisoner or shot. It had been up this road too that Cox, Duncan and I had carried our picks and shovels when we had ended up for a time in a punishment battalion, with the unenviable job of going out into no-man's-land and digging trenches.

It was impossible to tell, in 1959, where any of the trenches and dugouts had been in 1937, and the olive groves flourish as if they had always grown, undisturbed by man or his shells, bullets or grenades. The signs of the civil war have been eradicated from everything but memory.

Since I returned from Spain this last time people have asked me what it is like living under a fascist dictatorship. I have to tell them truthfully that, except for low wages and hard times which can be found in both fascist and communist countries, things aren't too bad, if you avoid politics. Franco's dictatorship is not as harsh as Hitler's was in Germany or Stalin's in Russia. The people of Spain seemed to me to be apathetic, cynical and, at the moment, uninterested in either further wars or revolutions. Most of them seem to have the hope that some day, perhaps after Franco's death, the country may become a democracy, but it is just a hope. When I told people in Madrid that I had been a *Rojo* who had fought there during the war, many of them seemed delighted that I had returned for a visit. When they shook my hand however they warned me not to tell anyone else.

The desk clerk in my Madrid hotel was a multi-lingual German named Walter, whom I felt sure was a former SS man hiding out for his war crimes. He was taken aback the day I told him I'd been a member of the Red International Brigades, but he winked, put his finger to his lips, and laughed along with me. I suppose it was an incongruous thing, two former enemies, in two wars, laughing together at the past. Two castaways from long-lost ideologies and long-lost wars.

During my month-long visit to Spain I was both drunkenly foolish and soberly careful in what I did. Obviously the Spanish government knew I was an ex-member of the Republican army, for I'd had to apply for a visa to the Spanish consulate in Mont-

169

real before leaving Canada, and I'm sure they have a list of all those thousands who served in the International Brigades. To protect myself as much as possible I made no notes at all, nor did I carry a camera or bring out any photographs.

I made certain to report my whereabouts to Canadian or British consulates in Barcelona, Valencia and Madrid, and mailed many postcards from different places to John Clare at *The Star Weekly*. I presume that I was more or less always under surveillance by Franco's secret police, through my interpreters and some hotel employees, but everyone—with the exception of my lying old interpreter in Barcelona—was always courteous and friendly.

As to the life of the average Spaniard under Franco's dictatorship, I left Spain confirmed in a belief that I have always held: that a human being is the most adaptable of animals who can adjust himself to anything, when he has to.

I had lunch one day in Madrid with a different interpreter, not Carlos. This man told me he had been a Loyalist during the war, which may have been a secret police ploy or not. He told me that most Spaniards do not hate Franco too much, believing him to be a puppet pulled this way and that by the leaders of the Falange, the industrialists, landowners and the hierarchy of the Roman Catholic Church. Unlike most of the fascists, who blame much of Spain's poverty on the fact that the country's gold reserves were spirited off to Moscow during the civil war and have never been returned, he claimed it was being bled white by absentee *hidalgos* or gentlemen of leisure, and by the graft of government members and industrialists.

The Spanish people, unlike those in some authoritarian countries, are not isolated from what is happening in the rest of the world. I was asked by a Spaniard in Valencia what difference to Toronto the St. Lawrence Seaway had made. I told him it had meant a great increase in ocean-going shipping and that the first Spanish ship to ever come to Toronto had arrived last summer. He seemed proud and pleased. It is possible to see Spanish-dubbed English and American movies in most places, and to buy French, English and American magazines and newspapers at most book stores and newspaper kiosks. I even saw a book titled *Carlos Marx* in a Madrid bookshop window.

Poverty shows up in a country in many curious ways, and in Spain it is apparent in the paper money, which is the oldest and most dilapidated, I dare say, in the Western World. The banknotes are filthy and many of them lack corners or have been repaired with scotch tape. A hotel clerk told me the government was going to issue new silver coins in 1960, which was wonderful news to him.

In the early summer on the Jarama Front there was an outbreak of dysentery in the Brigade, and especially in our battalion. Most of us had it, some much more seriously than others, and many men, who really couldn't be spared, had to be sent back to hospital. Among them was our battalion commander, Marty Hourihan, a quiet Communist dock-worker from Philadelphia. His place was taken temporarily by Oliver Law, the black machine-gun company commander, who came from Chicago.

Some of us, apparently, had rubbed him the wrong way, but his personal hatred for me stemmed from an argument we'd once had over my taking a second helping from a rice pot before he'd taken his first. He also held grudges against other members of his company, especially Duncan and Cox, for what I was never able to find out. Cox, Duncan and I, along with many more battalion soldiers, disliked Law, not for his colour but for the same reason we disliked some white officers and commissars, whom we referred to pejoritively as "Christers" and "Red Rotarians."

One afternoon, shortly after Law had become acting battalion commander, a clerk from battalion headquarters came up to the trenches and told Duncan, Cox, myself and another comrade, whom I no longer remember, to put on our helmets, packs, blanket rolls, gas masks and rifles and report to the battalion headquarters dugout. There had been rumors for several days that we were being pulled out of the line, and I told the others that it was obvious we were an advance party being sent somewhere to ready billets for the battalion when it left the line.

The battalion clerk gave Duncan a sealed envelope and told us to report to a Czechoslovakian officer at the base of the hills near the truck lines.

"See, I told you guys," I said.

I should have known better, for I've had trouble with authorities all my life, from Sunday school teachers to army and navy officers.

We picked our way down the steep pathway towards brigade headquarters and Morata de Tajuna, being extra careful crossing the spot that was under observation by the Nationalist machine-gunners. This would have been one hell of a day to be killed.

Duncan said, "I'm glad to get away from those trenches. I can't stand the sight of those lizards that run in and out of our dugouts and packs."

"Or the lice," Cox said, scratching himself.

The lizards had given me a few scares too. I didn't know what they were called, but they were beautifully coloured and about a foot and a half long, from their dragon faces to the tips of their thick tails. The hills of the Jarama Front were alive with them.

When we reached the truck lines we gave the sealed envelope to the Czech officer whose name was written on it. He read it, then said in English, "All right, comrades, pick yourselves a cave in the side of that cliff over there, and put your equipment in it. You won't be going up to the lines until it's dark."

"Going up where?" Cox asked him.

"You've been transferred to a trench-digging detail, comrades. Our job is to construct trenches at the front."

The four of us stared at him open-mouthed. We'd all seen members of this punishment outfit working outside the front lines at night, and it just wasn't our idea of a way to stay alive very long. Besides, our battalion was scheduled to leave the front lines soon. What burned us up too was the fact that none of us had been charged with anything, and it was just "Comrade" Law's way of getting even with us for real or imagined slights. We each cursed him loud and long.

The other three had been in the suicidal aborted attack of February 27th, so their disillusionment with the communist military had begun before mine had. Now I shared with them their hatred of the whole rotten Communist Party set-up; now I knew that Reid, back in the signal corps, had been right.

That night we were handed picks and shovels and, along with about twenty Frenchmen who had fortified themselves with plenty of wine, we followed each other, single file, up the paved road to the front lines. As soon as it was dark enough we climbed over the sand-bags of the forward trench in front of the English Battalion's position, took our places a few feet apart in a line stretching in the direction of the enemy trenches only a couple of hundred metres away, and began digging like mad. The drunken Frenchmen were talking and laughing, and I expected any moment to hear the chatter of a machine-gun, or not hear it but instead fall dead into the grave I was digging for myself. When there was sniper fire in our direction we would lie flat until it stopped, then begin digging again, while the drunken Frenchmen went on with their interrupted chatter.

This suicidal business went on for several nights with,

strangely enough, only two Frenchmen being wounded. By that time I was so jumpy I'd feel myself all over for wounds whenever a bullet cracked near by, and Cox and I began spending more and more time in the English Battalion's trenches.

In the early morning, after making our way down again from the lines, we would just get to sleep in our cave when a battery of French 75's would open up from a field behind the village, sending a salvo of shells low over the hills into the enemy's rear area. I would spring up in a cold sweat, and it would take me hours to fall asleep again.

One morning the four of us talked things over, and we agreed it was only a matter of time before we'd be killed. In fact that had been Law's idea when he sent us down there. We also agreed that taking off from that outfit was not like deserting from the battalion at the front, and we agreed that we'd go to Madrid. We had lots of money, for our pay came to us regularly every ten days in the line, and there was nowhere to spend it. After we'd seen Madrid, we'd go and tell our story to somebody in the International Brigade headquarters there, and demand to be sent back to the battalion.

That afternoon we left everything behind in the cave, and bummed a ride in an army truck to Madrid. We had no safe-conduct passes, but as we were going towards the front and not away from it none of the sentries at the frequent checkpoints asked us for any.

We all paid for rooms in the Hotel Alfonso on the Gran Via, which was a Communist army hotel, and began spending our money in the bars and down in the red light district. None of us were what could be called drinkers then, and apart from a little wine and anisette most of our money went for postcards home.

One afternoon I was crossing the Puerta del Sol when I ran into "Comrade" Law. He stopped me and asked me what I was doing in Madrid. I asked him what the hell he thought I was doing, and walked on. That evening as I sat in the bar of the Alfonso with Duncan and a couple of Cubans from the 24th Spanish-American Battalion, two young secret policemen came over to our table and asked me for my pay book. I handed it over, and they asked me to join them at another table. I took one of the Cubans with me as an interpreter. He was a big Negro who had played semi-professional baseball in the United States.

One of the young policemen told me I had been accused of living off the avails of a prostitute. Through my interpreter I told him that the person who had charged me with that must be crazy. I'd only been in Madrid a couple of days, and before that I'd been down on the Jarama Front. This was my first visit to Madrid, I didn't know one prostitute by name, and I had plenty of army pay in my pocket.

I knew who was trying to frame me, it was Law. This was my first and last taste of Communist smear tactics, but from then on, in Spain and later, I knew what they were.

My black interpreter told the young policemen that an officer who didn't like me for personal reasons was trying to frame me. He also told them that I and my three *Nortamericano* buddies lived right here in the hotel, that he had been with me every evening since we'd arrived, and that such a charge was ridiculous. He finally convinced them, and they shook hands with me and left.

Next morning the four of us decided we'd better get out of Madrid. One of the boys said he'd met some Anarchists whose brigade was on the El Pardo front, northwest of Madrid, and that they'd take anybody into their outfit. We hitched rides up to El Pardo and joined the Anarchist brigade.

The front there was static and the fighting consisted largely of both sides sniping and lobbing grenades at each other between the village's empty houses. We were quartered in a large three-story school building. The food was even worse than it had been in our own brigade, and before long we found that we'd cut ourselves off from our own comrades and also of any chance of receiving any mail from home. After a few days we decided to return to Madrid and give ourselves up to the International Brigades headquarters.

We separated in Madrid, and I decided on my own to go to see the chief English-speaking political commissar in Madrid, explain things to him, and ask him for a pass back to my outfit. I walked out to a residential neighborhood of the city where the political arm of the Internationals had set up shop in a big private house surrounded by a high wall.

Inside, I was told to wait until lunch was finished, and I sat down on a chair near the entrance to the dining room. When I peeked through the doorway I saw a long refectory table at which were sitting all the Communist commissars, functionaries and flunkeys eating fried eggs and steaks. We'd never even seen an egg at the front, never mind a steak. The table was being served by pretty little Spanish girls, and these stinking rear-echelon wallahs were joking and laughing together in a dozen different languages. Some guy told me to go upstairs and wait for my commissar in his office.

174

I waited there at least an hour before he made his appearance. He gave me a curt nod before sitting down at his desk. I'd found out earlier that he was a second-rate English novelist, who'd lived in Spain before the war, and had written two novels. He was one of those toadying, snivelling little communist "Red Rotarians," whom I'd never even seen at the front, probably because he'd never been there.

I told him my story, leaving nothing out, and I watched him become angrier and angrier as I went on. When I came to the part about us joining the Anarchist brigade he became livid with rage. "You're a deserter!" he shouted.

"I suppose that technically I am," I said. "But I don't call it desertion when we run away from a suicide battalion, where we shouldn't have been sent in the first place, and join a fighting unit at the front, Anarchist, Communist or what."

He began screaming at me, threatening to have me shot. I hurriedly backed out of his office, ran down the stairs, out into the street past the sentries at the gate, and just kept going.

That afternoon I met somebody from one of our brigade battalions, and he told me the Brigade had been pulled out of the line and replaced with the 14th (French-speaking) Brigade. The 15th was now billeted in several villages south of Alcala de Henares. I hitched a ride to Alcala, and from there made my way to brigade headquarters that had been set up in a large country house. I bummed some food from the cookhouse, and slept on the ground under a truck.

The next morning while I waited for a truck to take me to the village where the Lincoln Battalion was billeted I watched the female members of a gypsy flamenco troupe emerging from the big house tenanted by the brigade commander, Lieutenant-Colonel Copic, and his staff. Copic was the worst and most inept commander of an International Brigade, and even Ernest Hemingway derided him in *For Whom The Bell Tolls*. He never did make general, as far as I know, and I only hope he ended up in a Siberian salt mine. Or sank back into the mediocrity of the "novelist."

I asked a soldier if the gypsy girls lived in the big house with the officers.

"What do you think?" he asked me back.

During the past weeks I'd lost whatever illusions I'd picked up about the idealism, self-discipline and self-sacrifice of most of the Communist Party functionaries and officers I'd met. There were some, but very few, for whom I had any regard at all. One of them had been the battalion commissar of the Georgi Dimitroff Battalion, a man who went under the *nom-de-guerre* of "Chapeyev." He had been wounded seventeen times, and had lost an eye, and his men all loved him. After Oliver Law, the "novelist" and his buddies with their eggs and steaks, and now Copic and his gypsy whores, the only Communists I had any use for, and I liked and admired a great many of them, were the men in the ranks.

When I finally made the Lincoln Battalion headquarters I was taken under guard from headquarters in a small village down a hill to a small white building used as the village slaughterhouse but now being used as the battalion jail. Duncan and the other deserter whose name I've forgotten were already there, along with a Mexican comrade and a happy Irish drunk. My two friends didn't know what had happened to Cox, whom they'd last seen in Madrid.

The village threw a fiesta that evening for the battalion, and about seven o'clock two young girls came down the hill to the slaughterhouse and handed in two pails of wine. They told us the village people didn't think it was right that we prisoners should be shut away from all the festivities. Bringing the wine to us was a gracious act typical of the Spanish people.

The next morning Cox arrived back, and the four of us were charged with desertion before Marty Hourihan, who had by then returned to the battalion from the hospital. Our advocate was an Englishman, an ex-Indian Army cavalryman who had transferred to our battalion from the Loyalist cavalry, and was now second-in-comand of the Lincolns. He spoke so eloquently on our behalf that the charge was reduced to being A.W.O.L., and the time we had spent in the slaughterhouse was our only sentence. This ex-British officer hated most of the Communists anyway, and in a couple of talks I had with him later I found he'd been an officer in the Bengal Lancers. I lost track of him during the advance on Brunete, but I hope he survived.

After a pleasant week in the village, sleeping on our blankets in the plaza in front of the church, we got our marching orders once again. We climbed aboard the tree-camouflaged trucks on the road below the village while the villagers waved us goodbye from the top of the cliff.

That night we were billeted in the huge cathedral in Alcala de Henares, the town which is the birthplace of Cervantes. On this last trip to Spain I had Carlos drive me there, ostensibly to see Cervantes' birthplace. Actually I wanted to see the cathedral, for on the morning after our arrival there I met the most famous Canadian who served in the Spanish Civil War, Dr. Norman Bethune.

176

As I came out of the cathedral into the morning sunlight that day in 1937 I saw a small panel truck marked "Canadian Blood Transfusion Unit" or some such in both English and Spanish. There was a slight man standing beside the van wearing "Canada" flashes on the shoulders of his gray coveralls. I told him I was a Canadian, and he introduced himself to me as Dr. Bethune of Montreal. He also introduced me to a tall young assistant of his named Hazen Sise, whom I learned later was the son of the president of Bell Telephone of Canada. Dr. Bethune later died while serving with the communist forces in China. I don't know or care whether Dr. Bethune was a Communist himself or not, but I count it a privilege to have met him.

On the evening of the day I met Dr. Bethune, we set out in a truck convoy for Madrid, before we began our night marches to the jumping-off place of what was to develop into the Battle of Brunete. The end of that trip is where I started this series, and where I'll finish it now.

A million people lost their lives in the Spanish Civil War. It was a bitter, cruel and wasteful war that dragged on from 1936 to 1939. Some cynics in Spain today, and indeed all over the world, believe it would have been better not to have opposed Spanish fascism at all. I do not agree. Though my own part in it was a very insignificant one, going there to fight was one of the few things I am proud of having done. It is always better to fight for what you believe in. To a proud and brave people like the Spaniards that is a wonderful thing.

I took the three parts of "A Loyalist Soldier Returns To Spain" down to John Clare at *The Star Weekly* sometime late in January, 1960, and they were published in the issues of April 9th, April 16th, and April 23rd. The editors were pleased with them, and so was I. Having had to write them from memory was quite a feat in itself, considering the fact that I'd been consistently drunk throughout the whole of the trip. Several months later Clare phoned me and told me *The Star Weekly* was entering them in the non-fiction category of the President's Medals Awards at the University of Western Ontario. "Good luck!" I told him, having no expectations whatever of *that* committee ever awarding me anything. Of course my expectations were realized; the series didn't even receive a thank you, as far as I know.

There were other things happened to me in Spain, and on my return trip. I'll mention a couple of them now, just for the record.

Howard "Skinny" Moore, whom I've mentioned earlier as my companion on a hitch-hiking trip to the U.S., where he was turned back at the border, went to Spain after I did, and was posted to the Canadian Mackenzie-Papineau Battalion of the International Brigades. During the fall of 1937, Skinny and two other Canadian guys visited me at the *Gota de Leche* hospital in Albacete. Their battalion was in training near a village outside Albacete, and did not go into action until the late fall of 1937, though some Canadian replacements had come up to the Lincoln Battalion on the eve of the Battle of Brunete. A second American battalion, the George Washington, had taken part with us in the Brunete offensive and retreat. Both the Abraham Lincoln and the George Washington battalions had been so decimated after that fiasco that they were amalgamated, and along with the Mackenzie-Papineau and, I believe, the English Battalion, were formed into an English-speaking brigade named the Abraham Lincoln Brigade.

Along with Skinny, when he visited me, and incidentally brought me some toothpaste and a toothbrush which were almost impossible to buy in Spain at the time, was a young man named Black, who had been a masseur at Toronto's Ford Hotel. I heard from a veteran of the Mac-Paps long after the war that Black had been a medic with the battalion. During the Loyalist retreat across the Ebro River later in the war, when it became a rout and was every man for himself, Black had elected to remain behind with the wounded, and had either been captured or killed. As far as I know he never returned home.

After World War Two, when my family and I were staying at my mother's place, I received a visit one evening from Skinny's mother. From what she could tell me about the date of his last letters home I figured that he had been killed in either the first or second Battle of Teruel. I went with Mrs. Moore, whom I had known since I was a young teenager, to her lawyer's office, where I told the lawyer that I thought Skinny must have been killed at Teruel. Mrs. Moore, not having heard from her son, or from the Spanish government or the International Brigades, for over seven years, was trying to get his life insurance. She was a widow by then, and her second son had been killed in the Royal Canadian Air Force in World War Two. I don't suppose she ever did get her insurance money.

I just thought I'd mention Howard Moore, a longtime friend, and Black, who were two of the thousands of young men who died incognito, unhonoured and unsung, fighting in the International Brigades in the Spanish Civil War. That's the best I can do, comrades.

On my return visit to Spain I was travelling first class—not really, for I had tourist accomodation on the *Queen Elizabeth*, though due to the season I had a cabin all to myself—but at least it was first class as far I was concerned, after my years of travelling with a pack on my back or my razor in my pocket.

In Paris I checked into the Hotel Scribe, adjacent to the American Express office, the Café de la Paix, and not too far from Harry's American Bar on the Rue Danou. I was only there one night, for my room had been reserved by Tennessee Williams, or so the desk clerk told me. No sweat. I moved across the street into the Grand Hotel, where they gave me a small room looking out into an air shaft. Anyhow, I was kicked out of Harry's Bar, with its autographed photos of celebrities, for throwing-up on the floor. Before leaving Paris I managed to buy my wife and daughter a blouse and skirt apiece, thanks to my travellers' cheques and *The Star Weekly*, and had them mailed home. I didn't really like living in L'Opéra district of Paris, and twice since when I've gone to the city my wife and

I have lived in Montmartre and St. Germain des Prés, which are much more to my taste.

When I arrived in Madrid during that December of 1959 I reported to the Canadian Ministry there, just to make sure my government knew where I was. One of the attachés I spoke to took me in and introduced me to the Canadian Minister to Spain. He asked me which newspaper I represented, and I told him *The Star Weekly,* which apparently he'd never heard of, although it had more than a million circulation at the time. I told him it was owned by the *Toronto Star,* Canada's biggest circulation daily newspaper. He argued with me that *La Presse* of Montreal, Canada's largest French-language paper, was the biggest.

Our argument was friendly enough, and he invited me to his house for dinner. I accepted the invitation, and had the valet service at the Hotel Rex clean and press my brown tweed suit for the occasion. Not being used to diplomatic protocol, or being invited to mansions for dinner as far as that goes, I didn't realize that I should have worn a dinner jacket. I could have rented one for the occasion on my Diner's Club card.

I arrived by cab at the diplomat's beautiful big house, and was admitted by a young Spanish butler, who showed me into an ante-room. He disappeared, to announce I suppose that there was a scruffy-looking Canadian journalist who had arrived for dinner wearing tweeds. When he returned he asked me if I'd have a drink, and I told him a brandy would be fine. He set a bottle of the best Spanish brandy in front of me, and I asked *him* to join me in a drink. He did so, and the two of us sat there for a long time, talking about the Spanish Civil War and drinking brandy-and-sodas. Finally the Canadian Minister entered the room, and told me he was pleased I'd accepted his invitation, and that there was a cab outside that would take me back to my hotel. He was an excellent diplomat, and had a very friendly butler, but I never did get to his dinner table. After that I confined my social life in Madrid to drinking the *Star Weekly's* brandies and wine in the hotel's night club, where they had some excellent flamenco acts.

When I left Madrid to return to Canada I bid goodbye to my German, presumably SS, desk clerk, tipped the chambermaid, bought a bottle of Dom Pedro to carry in my pocket, and took a train for Lisbon. Never having been to Portugal I thought this would be as good a time as ever to visit it.

I travelled during the night through what had been Nationalist territory during the civil war, through large cork forests and across the wide savannahs of Estramadura. I crossed the frontier at Valencia de Alcantara, according to an old passport I still have, but I don't remember it at all. Nor do I remember passing the Portuguese customs and immigration. Anyhow I ended up, my bottle of Dom Pedro sadly depleted, in the Hotel Eduardo VII in Lisbon. Crossing a frontier between two countries that were under fascist dictatorships without remembering it was bad enough, but doing so when I was a suspicious and public anti-fascist drunk who had not only fought against Generalissimo Franco but also against Portuguese troops in the Spanish Civil War, was something else. I thoroughly believe there is a god that protects fools and drunks.

During the next few days in Lisbon and environs I was under close scrutiny by the secret police, who weren't that secret that I didn't learn to recognize, and greet now and again, the little rat of a secret policeman who used to sit in the lobby of the Eduardo VII and report on my actions to his office.

I visited the Canadian legation to Portugal, and reported that I was in the country. This time I conducted all my business with the press attaché, and the minister or whatever he was didn't make the mistake of inviting me to dinner.

My first Lisbon driver-interpreter was a narrow-moustached young pimp, who was always trying to set me up with a call-girl. I remember him once telling me that he liked women with heavy hair on their legs, a bizarre taste that I had never come across before, nor since. With him at the wheel of his small Italian car I visited the town of Estoril, the home of dethroned kings, dictators-on-the-lam and various other species of decrepit international fauna. We also drove out to Cabo Da Roca, a rocky point that he told me was the farthest westerly piece of land in Europe.

In my hotel I met a Cuban who claimed to be an ex-member of the International Brigades and also a bodyguard of the ex-Cuban dictator Fulgencio Batista. He almost begged me to go out and interview Batista, who needed all the good publicity he could get. I declined with thanks.

It may seem strange that a veteran of the Spanish Loyalist forces ended up as a bodyguard to a rightist dictator, but it didn't surprise me. I'd heard from Cubans here and there that many former Cuban Communists and sympathizers had joined Batista's entourage, just as many German Communists had ended up in Hitler's Brownshirts.

No matter where I've been in foreign countries I'm always running into veterans of the Spanish International Brigades, the last time being a couple of years before this was written when I met a waiter in Paris who'd been in a French brigade in Spain.

My next driver-interpreter, after I got rid of the pimp with the kinky sexual taste for hairy-legged women, was a middle-aged man who had once jumped a ship in New York and had become a labourer and gardener in New York's Westchester County. He was a fine man, who pointed out the Lisbon jails where President Salazar's prisoners were left to rot. One of them was a grass-covered hill, really a fortress, with small slits here and there in its sides, that my driver told me were the slitted windows to individual solitary cells.

This second interpreter had finally been deported from the United States, but the time he'd spent there had taught him English, so that he was able to set himself up in business as a tourist driver. One evening he took me home with him for the evening meal. He lived on what I presume to be a middle-class Lisbon street, in a small ground-floor flat. His wife, who was very plump and gracious but who spoke no English, laid out a very sparse meal, but which I realized was the best they could afford. They had only one egg, which the lady placed on my plate. I in turn gave it to their only child, a schoolgirl of eleven or twelve. If life was so hard for a family like that I shuddered to think what it was like for a labourer's family.

I left Portugal convinced that Salazar's dictatorship was much worse than that of Franco's, and this has been corroborated by many people I've spoken to since, who have spent any time at all in both Spain and Portugal.

The night I left Lisbon for home was one of those crazy times I've experienced often in my life. In the first place I'd finally run out of travellers' cheques, and I'd cabled *The Star Weekly* that I was stranded penniless in Portugal. John Clare, who knew better than to send me any money, sent me a return flight on a CP Air plane back to Montreal.

True to my habit of never travelling anywhere sober when I can be drunk, I was completely blotto when I checked out of the Eduardo VII to go to the airport. Not realizing that my Diner's Club card was any good at the hotel, there was a bit of an argument between me and the desk clerk. I straightened it out by asking them to give me the unpaid bill, which I would get my paper to pay as soon as I got back to Canada.

I had some Portuguese money in my pocket, and carrying my old Gladstone bag, which had lost its handle in Barcelona weeks before and which I'd had a hotel porter there in the Hotel

Colon tie up with rope, I crossed the lobby to the street to hail a cab. It was raining, and there was only one taxi outside. I was followed out by my secret police tail, who looked more ratty than ever in the pouring rain. I jumped into the cab, said, "Aeroporto" or something I hoped was Portuguese for airport, and then, feeling sorry for my stranded policeman, invited him to ride out with me.

A few minutes later, as I sat in the departure lounge at the airport, two plainclothes policemen came up to me, mumbled something that sounded like "Policia," and led me and my rope-tied suitcase upstairs to a large office. At a desk sat a fierce-looking uniformed inspector of police, and around the walls lounged six or seven policemen in plain clothes. I figured I was in for a good working-over, if not for a crime then just on general principles. When the inspector, through one of the policemen who spoke English, asked me for my passport, I handed it to him. Then I sat on a corner of his desk, and he shoved me off, cursing me I suppose in Portuguese.

Through his interpreter he gave me a lengthy questioning, and I told him I'd been to Spain doing a series of articles for a Canadian weekly paper. He asked me what kind of articles, and I told him I was a veteran of the Spanish Civil War and had been back there on a nostalgic visit. He became redder and redder, and I became more saucy each minute. I remember telling him that I'd have the British fleet come up the Tagus and shell Lisbon unless he gave me back my passport, among other things. He tried to insist I was a Communist agent, and I told him not to be silly, that I worked for a capitalist newspaper. Finally I told him he could check me through the Canadian legation.

After one particularly irate tirade on his part and an equally insolent series of answers on mine he threw up his hands, threw me my passport, and gave an order to two of his men. They escorted me down to the airport tarmac, and one of them told me I'd been ordered aboard the first plane flying to America. I had sense enough not to argue that my ticket called for a flight by CP Air to Montreal. They led me to a gangplank, both smiled and shook my hand as if glad that I'd put down their uniformed boss, and I went aboard the plane. It turned out to be a Spanish Iberian Air Lines propeller job that made one stop in the Azores, then went on to New York.

In the Azores I had a few drinks at the airport bar while the plane was refueling, and arrived at Idlewild (now Kennedy) Airport the next morning, broke but intact, and still in possession of my roped-up Gladstone bag. It was so disreputable-looking I didn't need to fear it might be stolen. Even the U.S. Customs man refused to undo the ropes to check its contents.

I spied the change wicket at the airport and searched my pockets of all loose money, French, Spanish and Portuguese. When I handed it in I was happy to find it came to twenty-four American dollars. I waited in the bar until my flight to Toronto was ready. On the Air Canada flight to Toronto I was flying on my own without engines or wings, and I still had a bottle of Dom Pedro in the pocket of my jacket. I was seated beside a gentleman from Newmarket, Ontario who bred standard poodles. Immediately I became an expert on dogs in general and poodles in particular. I must have bored the poor man to death before we arrived at Toronto International Airport.

You didn't need the gifts of prophecy or foresight by 1956 to know that a great number of North American magazines were about to fold up. Of those that were still in operation fewer and fewer were publishing short stories or fiction of any kind. The publishers and editors of these magazines blamed the public, whom they claimed preferred factual articles rather than fiction. The truth was, in Canada at least, that it was the fault of a new breed of semi-literate magazine editors, graduates of schools of journalism who didn't know a short story from a sonnet. When your livelihood depends on the sale of your writing you just can't cry in your beer about changing trends and lost markets; you have to write for the markets that are still available. A new market that had recently opened up was television drama, marked in the United States by such TV drama series as "Playhouse 90," "Studio One," and others. These television short stories, which ran from a half-hour length to ninety minutes as a rule were called "anthology drama series." In Canada the CBC, under the overall direction of an excellent executive producer, Sydney Newman, began producing memorable TV dramas in such series as "General Motors Presents" and "On Camera."

Sydney had as director-producers a number of young men born to and trained in the medium, a different breed of cat from the equally good producer-directors from radio, who saw their plays from the audio point of view rather than from the visual. The CBC was eating up dramatic scripts at the rate of three or four a week, and they were in the market for new scripts by new television playwrights. That's where the action was, so that's where I went.

One afternoon I went to the Toronto Public Library's reference branch and asked for a book on television playwriting. I read parts of it and made notes on how to set up a page of a television play. The next day I adapted one of my stories "Some Are So Lucky," to a half-hour TV script, and the next day after typing a fair copy of it, took it down to the CBC-TV drama department, where George Salverson was the script editor. He bought it for the series, "On Camera." The following week I adapted "A Trip For Mrs. Taylor" and Salverson bought that. Then I sat back to wait for them to be produced.

I waited almost a year.

Finally, I was told later, a young director named Ted Kotcheff saw the script of "Some Are So Lucky" by sheer accident, read it, and wanted to produce it. It was filmed live and on kinescope, starring Anna Cameron in the female lead and James Doohan in the male lead. Ted Kotcheff invited me down to one of the CBC's rehearsal studios where I watched the cast rehearse the play. Ted kept asking me if I was satisfied with what I was seeing, and I had to tell him I was not only satisfied but enthralled. Kotcheff and the cast did an excellent job, and it was shown over the CBC-TV network on December 17th, 1956. It received excellent reviews in the press, and on January 12th, 1957, less than a month later, was shown over the BBC network, where it also received excellent reviews in the English press, getting startling accolades in such periodicals as *The Observer* and even in *Punch*.

The CBC hurriedly produced my other TV adaption "A Trip For Mrs. Taylor" staring Katherine Proctor (an elderly Broadway actress though a native Torontonian) in the leading role. It was shown on June 3rd, 1957 on the program "On Camera" on July 12th over the BBC, and in October over the Australian TV network.

I sold outlines of four of my short stories to the CBC, for TV adaptation: "A Couple Of Quiet Young Guys," "Father's Day," "The Old Man's Laughter," and "Tea At Miss Mayberry's." "A Couple of Quiet Young Guys" was shown on the program "On Camera" and another adapted short story, "The Father," starring Joe Austin, appeared on CBC-TV on February 10th, 1958 and on the BBC on May 5th of that year.

The late Nathan Cohen was then the script editor for "General Motors Presents," and he bought a script of mine, an original this time, titled "Aftermath." It was also bought by Associated Television in England and was one of four picked up by the ABC Network in the United States. One afternoon I received a phone call from Ron Poulton of the *Toronto Telegram* who opened up the conversation with the remark, "Well, Hugh, you just blew two thousand dollars, I understand." I asked him what he meant. He told me of the sale of the play to ABC, then its withdrawal by a new-to-the-job CBC-TV executive producer, Esse Ljungh, who had been given Sydney Newman's job after Sydney had gone to England. I went down to Ljungh's office and asked him how come. I forget what lame excuse he gave me, but I knew it was not true. What was true was that I was unknown to him as a dramatist, unlike the members of the radio-writing clique who had made CBC radio drama so outstanding during the late Depression years, the war years, and until radio drama had been pushed aside by television.

Ljungh tried to mollify me by buying the television script of "Aftermath" for CBC radio, paying me less than a third of what I would have received from the ABC network for it as a TV script. I was angry at Esse Ljungh for some time but later we became quite friendly and he bought many of my stories and novels for radio adaptation and to be dramatized on the CBC network.

In 1960 the CBC bought a half-hour drama script of one of my stories, "The Magnet," and produced it on a program called "First Person" on June 15th of that year. The producer was to my mind "arty" but not artistic, a failing belonging to a lot of TV types at the time, and one which has now transferred itself to movie-making. The female lead was played by Charmion King, an excellent actress who had played Ethel Walton, under the direction of David Gardner in the second re-casting and shooting of "Some Are So Lucky." The male lead, an equally important role, was sadly miscast and was given to an actor who hoked it up and blew the whole play.

Over the few years I had been connected with television drama-writing there had been many changes in the CBC television staff. Nathan Cohen left to become the drama critic of the *Toronto Star*, George Salverson left to freelance, Esse Ljungh went back to his old job of Supervising Producer, CBC Radio Drama, and many producer-directors had left the country or had switched to stage and movie producing.

The CBC Television Drama Department moved from its haunts in a Front street loft building into quarters over a restaurant on Yonge Street. Ron Weyman became supervising producer, if that was his title, of the longer dramatic presentations, with a young woman as script editor. For the shorter dramatic shows the CBC hired an ex-Columbia Broadcasting System employee, Ed Moser, as supervising producer. Les Mc-

186

Farlane became script editor under Moser, only to be replaced later by Dave Peddie.

Les McFarlane, an older man, was kind and courteous and bought some scripts from me, including one titled "The Lost Cause" for a half-hour drama show called "Playdate." As far as I know this play was never produced. McFarlane also had me adapt an American short story "The Guardeen Angel" by F. H. Brennan for a program called "First Person." It was telecast on November 9th, 1960.

Since becoming tangled up in the CBC TV drama bureaucracy I'd had my stuff edited ("read" would be the correct word here) by George Salverson, Nathan Cohen, Les McFarlane, and Dave Peddie. Now two new faces appeared on the scene. I had no idea what the new men's backgrounds were. The CBC has always moved its script editors around like chessmen, and if it is confusing reading about the changes in the drama department cast, it was twice as confusing trying to keep up with them as a contributor.

Les McFarlane had been a short story writer for years and had a good dramatic and story sense, more than I can say for most of the others. I have no more idea how people become drama editors than I have how their book and magazine counterparts are hired. I think they just walk in off the street, or are hired from the employment office.

The new editors bought two or three scripts from me for a show called "The Serial." They dawdled around with one of these, scribbling all over it. I told them the CBC would pay for it or I'd take it to the union grievance committee. They paid me for my story and TV treatment, for they had no choice. I was by then a longtime member of ACTRA, the Canadian television and radio union.

My novel, *Silence On The Shore*, was adapted by me for "The Serial," and though I received payment for all the various steps in the contract the script was never used. This had also happened to me years before with a TV adaptation of "A Couple Of Quiet Young Guys" that the CBC had bought for a program called "Eye-Opener." My adaptation of *Silence On The Shore* was the last television drama writing I ever did. Working with people like the CBC editors I met would have given ulcers to the most phlegmatic dramatist in the world, and I wasn't him.

Early in 1970 I received a phone call from Keith Gill, the assistant to Duncan Sandison, contracts officer of the CBC. Keith told me that Ron Weyman and Dave Peddie wanted to buy some short stories of mine for a new television drama series to be shot on movie film, for TV viewing and possible sale as movies. I asked him which stories, and he told me, "Some Are So Lucky," "One, Two, Three Little Indians," and "E Equals MC Squared." I asked him what they would pay me for each story. When he quoted a sum, I told him I'd received more than that fourteen years before for "Some Are So Lucky" and others. He doubled the fee. Later, Dave Peddie phoned me and bought the same rights for another story, "The Happiest Man In The World." They were to be adapted by others, for I'd given up *that* particular form of masochism years before.

The luckiest short story I ever wrote was "Some Are So Lucky," my first story sale to a magazine back in 1949, and the first produced on TV in 1956. Up to the present, besides its appearance on BBC television, it has been shown on the programs "On Camera," "First Person," "Summer Circuit," "Studio Pacific," and "To See Ourselves." It has also been broadcast many times on radio. On television I have also been very lucky in the actresses who played the leading role: Anna Cameron, Charmion King, and Jackie Burroughs, who were all outstanding. This play holds the record for the number of times produced and shown on Canadian TV.

Robert Weaver has been using my short stories and novels on various radio dramatic shows and in readings on the CBC radio network since he bought "Our Neighbors The Nuns" in 1949 or early 1950. At last count they have been presented more than a hundred times.

If a radio or television treatment of a story bombs, the writer does not have only himself to blame as he does when it is printed. He can blame the adapter, the producer, the actors, the casting director, or even the whole production crew for its failure. And he usually does. Most of my radio short stories have been read over the air rather than being dramatized, and I have been fortunate indeed in having them read by many leading actors. Over the past few years the man who has read most of my stories over the CBC has been a very fine actor, Murray Westgate. Murray's voice is less gravelly than mine yet hoarse enough to be a surrogate for my own. And while I'm handing out kudos rather than criticism I must mention the fine radio adaptations done for me by Len Peterson.

There is an old saying that a lawyer who represents himself in court has a fool for a client, and I think the same thing applies to a writer who reads his own stories on the air. I have never been conceited enough to think I could read mine, or too cheap to split my fee with the actor who has read them. This is

188

not due to big-heartedness but to pure selfishness. The professional way in which they have been put across on the air has resulted in their being re-broadcast time and again.

Five of my novels have been dramatized for radio: *Silence On The Shore*, on CBC "Radio Stage," 1966 and on "Theatre Ten-Thirty" in 1967. *The Sin Sniper* was broadcast and repeated on the same shows in 1970 and 1971; *Storm Below* dramatized on "Radio Stage" in 1968 and repeated on the same program in 1970; *Cabbagetown* on "Radio Stage" in 1969; and *A Nice Place To Visit* on the same program in 1970. Eight short stories have also been broadcast on "Radio Stage" between the late fifties and 1971.

Now that my television and radio life has been brought up to date let's go back to early 1960 and my overlong novel *Silence On The Shore*.

During the spring of 1960 I sat down with my 800-page manuscript and began cutting it, crossing out page after page of extraneous wordage, shortening descriptions, and cutting out the bits of personal philosophy that authors quite often insert into their books. When I thought I had cut it in half, checking now and again, re-inserting some bits I had crossed out and writing the proofreaders' *stet* in the margin, I was forced to look forward to the long, dreary job of retyping the novel again.

When a novel is being *written*, that is, when the author is engaged in practicing his trade, creative writing, the hours often fly by, and sometimes he only leaves his typewriter for the sake of performing his natural functions and eating. I have never worked to a schedule nor written a certain number of words or pages per day. The only habits I have adhered to over the years are, bathing, shaving, and brushing my teeth before beginning work (and these I have sometimes ignored), dressing myself rather than sitting down at the typewriter in a bathrobe, and beginning my writing immediately after breakfast. I have gone for days, and occasionally weeks, without touching my typewriter at all, and at other times I have stuck with it for fourteen hours or more at a stretch. To me "inspiration" is the key word, despite the writers manqués who write in such "how to succeed" publications as *Writer's Digest* that "Inspiration is the placing of the seat of the trousers on the seat of a chair and writing!" This has never been true in my case.

Rewriting a long manuscript such as a novel is sheer bull labour, yet it is an essential part of the trade. Just recently I was talking on the telephone to a former editor of a popular magazine who bought many of my manuscripts twenty years ago, and he remarked on the fact that I always sent in remarkably clean scripts. I told him it was a habit I'd acquired at the beginning of my writing career, when I didn't want crossed out lines or penned additions to spoil my manuscripts for the editors who read them.

I began the long job of re-typing *The Silence On The Shore,* without knowing whether McClelland & Stewart would publish it or not. This was nothing new; all writers, or most of them, write on pure speculation. I've had to write everything on spec, even when I *had* to make a sale. I think that financial pressure gave me my discipline as a writer, for God knows I haven't any discipline in anything else I do. Errors still sneak through in everything I write. For instance, the words you are reading now are being written for the third time because of something I had to cut out of the original script; rather than cross out the offending paragraph I've rewritten it.

Though Jack McClelland had telephoned me several times over the years to ask me if I had any manuscripts, he hadn't shown much interest in the current book I was working on and had given me no encouragement to go ahead with the re-writing of *The Silence On The Shore.* I had read somewhere that Doubleday Canada was offering a ten thousand dollar advance on royalties on a Canadian novel, and I decided to rewrite my book with this in mind. I have completely forgotten how long the rewriting of the novel took me (for I *always* rewrite as I retype); it may have been weeks or even months. I think that my wife and I did a lot of driving that summer, fulfilling an ambition of mine to cover all the highways coloured red on the maps of Ontario, which we finally did during three summers. That may have been the year too that we drove down to New England to visit some relatives, and ended up, after our visit, in Atlantic City.

When the rewriting of my manuscript was finished, probably towards the end of 1960, or it may have been in 1961, I took it down to the young American editor at Doubleday, and handed it in. He was very courteous to me, but I received the book back later with a letter of rejection. Whether or not I took it to any other publisher after this I forget. Sometime during the summer of 1961, I believe, I received a phone call from Jack Rackcliffe at McClelland & Stewart asking me how the rewriting was coming. I told him it was finished and asked him if he wanted to read the new version. He told me he did. Well, at least someone was interested in it.

Rackcliffe had fallen or had some kind of accident, and the

next thing I heard he was in a ward of the Toronto General Hospital with a painfully injured sciatic nerve in the thigh. I phoned him there and he told me to bring the manuscript down to the hospital. I picked up a carton of cigarettes and went down to see him.

He was sitting in bed propped up with pillows in a large medical ward containing at least a dozen beds. He had obviously made friends with everyone there, and when I approached him he was speaking Italian to one of his ward mates. Around him, on the bed itself, and on his bedside table lay paperback books, boxed manuscripts, a writing pad, pens, pencils, and all the clutter that is usually found on a book editor's desk. I burst out laughing.

"What the hell are you laughing at, Garner?" he asked, seeming hurt by my laughter. "I'm in pain, you know. My thigh is aching terribly."

"It—it's just—just this!" I exclaimed, pointing to the literary debris that surrounded him. "Do you mean to say you're editing books here in the hospital?"

"Certainly."

I made as if to sit down on the edge of the bed.

"Watch out! You'll hurt my thigh!"

I removed some books from a chair, placed them on the floor, and sat down.

We talked about the novel, and I told him I'd cut it to the bone; the manuscript was now only about 350 pages long. I asked him about his accident but he was reluctant to talk about it. When I handed him the carton of cigarettes he accepted them with a disdainful smirk, which I felt was just his way of hiding his thanks and embarrassment. Before I left to go he had introduced me to a couple of Italian subway workers, an elderly Chinese, and several other of his friends. "I'll see you in a few days," I said.

"All right, I'll have my criticisms written out," he said.

I left the hospital admiring Jack Rackcliffe very much. Here was a former Harvard man, the senior book editor of one of Canada's largest publishers, quite content to lie in a bed in a public hospital ward among members of the downtown poor, and make no excuses about it whatsoever. Besides this he was carrying on his outside job as well. It gave him class.

The next time I went to see him, with another carton of cigarettes, he asked, "What are you trying to do, bribe me?"

I answered him with an appropriate expletive.

When I was leaving he handed me my manuscript in its

191

cardboard box and several pages of hand-written queries and editor's changes. If I remember rightly there were twenty-seven of them, all page-numbered and otherwise identified.

That evening I went over the manuscript, amazed that a man lying in pain in bed in a public hospital ward could have been so percipient. I returned his written notes to him along with the manuscript on my next visit; now I wish I'd typed out a copy and kept the original for my files.

He had queried many things that most book editors are too stupid to query. Somewhere in the rooming house that contains most of the action of the novel I had written, "The upstairs hallway was dimly lighted with a 15-watt bulb." Jack had written, "There are no such things, only 20-watt bulbs," or it may have been the other way around. Another editor's note I remember dealt with a young girl staring into a shoe store window and saying to her companion, "I like those black patent leather pumps there. They'd be good for Eleanor's wedding." He had written, "*No* girl would ever buy *black* shoes for a wedding!" Beside most of his queries and criticisms I'd written "changed" or "you're right" while against a few I'd scribbled an obscenity or told him to go to hell.

Before going back to the hospital I checked the sizes of light bulbs in hardware, department and grocery stores, and found he'd been a hundred percent right.

On January 9th, 1962 I signed a five-page book contract with Jack McClelland for the publication of *Silence On The Shore*, thereby paying back the Canada Council for the money they had given me which had made writing it possible. The book was printed and bound in England, and during the summer of 1962 there was a printers' strike over there. Copies of the book did not reach Canada until December, too late for Christmas sale, and I was told by someone at M & S that some of them had lain on the Montreal docks for ten days before they were picked up and sent to Toronto.

Whether or not the lengthy contract was McClelland & Stewart's usual one I don't know. What I do know is that it is much lengthier than most novel contracts in my files. Maybe he hoped I wouldn't sign it.

Before signing the contract, probably shortly after Jack Rackcliffe had left the hospital, I had told Jack McClelland that in the interim between cutting the book's length and taking it down to Rackcliffe I had submitted it to Doubleday Canada who had rejected it. I suppose this angered him, as it would have angered me, and was probably the breaking point in our friendship. McClelland asked me why I had done this and I told him truthfully that I was after the $10,000 Doubleday were offering. When I in turn asked him if he had read the book he answered me truthfully that he hadn't.

When the book came out it received the minimum of publicity, for McClelland & Stewart's promotion manager had taken a trip to England. In a later conversation with Jack McClelland I told him that *Silence On The Shore* was the last book of mine he'd ever publish. Despite my vociferous and wideopen dislike of the firm, Jack and I remained friendly for a long time afterwards, appearing together on a panel once at a Unitarian church. I was invited by him to a party one evening at his house, and I accepted. I haven't met him now for the past couple of years.

Being a strong believer in the legality of legal documents, and a book contract is certainly that, I had to break my contract with M & S as soon as I could under the circumstances. Practically all publishers' contracts contain a clause that reads somewhat as follows: "OPTION: The publisher shall have the option of publishing the author's next full-length manuscript in book form, or of rejecting it . . . etc., etc." In other words an author is legally bound to give the publisher of his last book the first option to publish his next. All I had were some hitherto unpublished stories.

The collection included, "A Manly Heart," "Tea With Miss Mayberry," "The Magnet," "E Equals MC Squared," "The Father," and "Hunky," all of which have since become TV plays, anthology and textbook pieces, or both. I submitted the above, plus several other stories, to McClelland & Stewart, who promptly turned them down. I probably tried some other publishers with them, but they too turned the stories down. Perhaps the six stories listed above were the only good ones my projected book contained. Anyhow, after a year or so had passed I spoke to Robert Weaver about the stories, and he suggested I take them down to The Ryerson Press where John Colombo, a friend of his, was an assistant editor. I did this, met John Colombo, and left the stories with him. I forget now what title I'd given the book of stories, or whether I'd given it a title or not.

The upshot was that some time later I was taken to lunch by Mr. C. H. Dickinson, the publisher, Frank Flemington, the managing editor, Earle Toppings and John Colombo. We went to a Hungarian restaurant quite close to the publishing house where we had a Romany meal cooked over a gypsy campfire. Over coffee Earle Toppings made the suggestion that Ryerson would be willing to publish the short stories, or some of them, if they could also include some of the best ones from my first collection, *The Yellow Sweater*. I told them that was fine with me, for the rights to the first book had now reverted to me. Somebody, and I think it was Earle Toppings again, suggested calling the book *Hugh Garner's Best Stories*. It was a mistake on my part to accept it for many stories written since would have to be included under a title like that, but I acquiesced. I signed the contract for the book, *Hugh Garner's Best Stories,* on June 12th, 1963.

Shortly after this I received a note from Jack McClelland, who reminded me that The Ryerson Press was really the United Church of Canada. Personally I didn't care whether Ryerson was owned by the Christadelphians or the Zen Buddhists. At least they printed their books in Canada, their cheques were good, and I'd shown McClelland & Stewart they weren't the only publishing house in the country.

The book was published in hard covers that fall, with a beautiful dust jacket designed by the Ryerson Press staff artist. It received good press notices, everywhere but in the McGill University paper. The book also sold very well for a collection of stories, but not sensationally so. One day in the early spring of 1964 I received a phone call from Frank Flemington, who, after swearing me to secrecy as if we were going to discuss the discovery of nuclear fission, told me that the book had won the Governor General's Award for Fiction for 1963.

This was great news, for though Jack McClelland had once told me that winning the award didn't sell too many books, I think that a Governor General's Award is a signal honor to a Canadian writer. Besides, there was now a cash grant along with it worth a thousand dollars.

One bright spring morning I set out for Ottawa for the presentation of the Governor General's Awards. I drove along the freeway to Kingston, then turned north up Highway 15 for Smiths Falls and Ottawa. I reached Smiths Falls at noon, and went looking for an old wartime buddy, Louis Lee, who had been in my artillery battery in 1939. I had heard he was now the co-proprietor of a hotel in the town. After going to the wrong hotel, and being steered to the right one, I found Louis. We sat down and had a couple of ginger ales apiece, talking about some of the guys we'd known. He'd read in the local paper that I was being given one of the awards, and he pleaded with me to have a shot of liquor "on the house" to celebrate the event. I had to

194

turn him down, just as I'd had to turn down his offers of free beers. We said goodbye, and I promised to drop into his hotel the next time I was in the neighborhood. I drove into the centre of town and had my lunch.

When I reached Ottawa I resisted an urge to drop in at another wartime buddy's place, a very nice motel at Bell's Corners, where my family and I had stayed once on a side trip to Ottawa when we were heading down to Eastern Quebec. One of the McDonalds who owned the motel had been a navy shipmate.

I drove to the Chateau Laurier and checked into the room that was reserved for me. The awards were to be given out the next day, so I walked out of the hotel and settled at a table in a nearby beer parlour and had a few ales. Another friend, this one dating from my early post-war years when he was a forestry student at the University of Toronto and I was a brand-new novelist, was now an executive with the federal forestry branch and lived out in one of the new middle class suburbs. Louis Nazarillo (and I hope I'm spelling his name right) had lived on the next street to me before the war, though I hadn't known him then.

He was a product, as several of my friends were, of an East Toronto street called Allen Avenue, that I don't suppose has changed much in the intervening years. It was a short street of small brick, frame, and tar-paper houses, in many architectural styles, running from just south of the Broadview Avenue YMCA to the Bolton Avenue firehall. One evening as Louis, myself and several students, artists and other beer-guzzlers were sitting around a table in a Yonge Street tavern near to where we all had rooms, he said to me, "I don't see how in hell you ever became a novelist, Hughie. Jeez, *nobody* from our old neighborhood ever became a *novelist!*"

Louis had become a member of a bomber crew and had been shot down over Germany, where he was made a prisoner of war for the duration. He'd phoned me as soon as he'd heard I'd won an award, and had given me his home address and phone number, and that evening he came downtown and picked me up at the Chateau. I went to his house where his Anglo-Saxon wife made a beautiful Italian supper (dinner in our old neighborhood was anything you ate at noontime), and we washed it down with good Italian wine. At the end of the evening Louis drove me back to my hotel.

The next morning I went out for a walk. I didn't know much about Ottawa, though I'd visited it on several occasions, once to cover the National Liberal Convention for the *Star Weekly*. When I found myself in front of the National Gallery I decided to drop in, and I spent one of the best mornings of my life touring the building and viewing the works of art.

After lunch I went back to the little beer parlour I'd found the day before and drank beer for a couple of hours before returning to my hotel room. During the afternoon there was a phone call and someone who said he was a member of the Governor General's Awards Committee asked me to meet him in a room off the hotel lobby. I went down, but the only people there were three men I didn't know talking together in a corner. I just stood around smoking a cigarette and waiting for somebody to approach me. I don't know how long I stood there but finally one of the three men walked over to me and asked me if I was Hugh Garner. I said I was, and he took me over and introduced me to the others. I believe two of them were Roy Daniells and Northrop Frye.

Before long other people began to arrive. Professor J. M. S. Careless, who had won the non-fiction award in English for *Brown Of The Globe*, Jacques Languirand, winner of the poetry and playwright awards in French for *Les Insolites* and *Les violons de l'automne*, Gatien Lapointe, the French poetry award for *Ode au St-Laurent*, and Gustave Lanctot for *Histoire du Canada*. The other people, I suppose, were members of the awards board, members of the Canada Council, and literary people of one stamp or another.

Finally we all were escorted to the front doors of the hotel and climbed into taxis. Northrop Frye was my escort and fellow taxi passenger, and we talked all the way to Rideau Hall. He seemed a very nice, courteous person, much different from how I'd expected the dean of Canadian literary critics to be.

At Government House we were led into a room where a dais had been placed holding two regal-looking chairs. The audience sat on folding chairs set in semicircular rows facing the dais, with the awards winners in the first row of chairs. I had a conversation with Professor Careless and his wife, who sat beside me.

Governor General and Madame Vanier entered, followed by his equerries, and the vice-regal couple took their seats on the chairs provided for them. An equerry or footman carried a hand-tooled leather-bound copy of a book to General Vanier and then announced the name of the recipient. I forget now whether I was the first to be presented with an autographed copy of my book, but we had been instructed to walk forward, bow to the vice-regal couple, then step up to the dais to receive our book and a few words from the Governor General.

196

When my name was announced I stepped forward, bowed to General Vanier and Madame Vanier, and the Governor General handed me a leather-bound copy of *Hugh Garner's Best Stories.* After congratulating me he said, "I've read the stories; they're very good." "Do you mean to say you've read them all, sir?" "Well . . . I've read some of them," the General replied, taken aback by my question. Madame Vanier glared at me. I don't know whether I broke protocol by questioning the Governor General or not. I backed off the dais and returned to my chair.

After the presentation we followed the vice-regal couple into a drawing room, where footmen served us glasses of champagne. General Vanier took turns sitting on a pair of sofas between the English-Canadian winners and the French-Canadians, talking to each of us in our own language. He was very charming, a perfect host, and a most diplomatic gentleman. I didn't go over so well with Madame Vanier, though she, too, spoke to me later. I ended up talking to the naval equerry, and we hit it off fine. There was a well-stocked bar, but I stuck to champagne, and sampled a few hors d'oeuvres.

When the reception came to an end we were all escorted to the front door of Rideau Hall, helped into taxis, and sped back to the Chateau Laurier. I flaked out in my room so that I'd be in shape for the private banquet later in the evening.

The banquet was held in one of the private dining rooms, and the award winners and guests, members of the awards committee, and the Canada Council were seated at a long refectory table. I found myself facing a very charming elderly couple from Montreal, Mr. and Mrs. Steinberg. We enjoyed a warm conversation, and I told them that we shopped at one of their suburban Toronto supermarkets at the Parkside Plaza.

Before the guest speaker, Northrop Frye, was to speak, I took the microphone and thanked both the awards committee for awarding me the fiction award, and the members of the Canada Council for giving me a grant four years before, and also for the granting of fellowships and grants to Canadian writers, which I thought—and still think—was the best thing that ever happened for the Canadian writer.

The next morning I checked out of the hotel, tipped the man who brought me my car from the parking lot, and with my cheque in my wallet drove back to Toronto. The leather-bound, autographed copy of my book is now in the archives of Queen's University, the cheque was spent years ago, and my name is on the list of winners of the Governor General's Awards.

This year the Oberon Press printed an anthology of Canadian

short stories titled *Fourteen Stories High*. In the brief biographies in the back of the book, which David Helwig edited, Gwendolyn MacEwan, George Bowering, and Alden Nowlan were all mentioned as winners of the Governor General's Award for Poetry. My award wasn't mentioned; I guess fiction doesn't count.

As a brief addendum, a couple of years ago I was talking to a pair of upward strivers, a man and his wife. The wife, one of those odious broads who love to put down us members of the lower classes, mentioned having dinner with one of the members of the Labatt clan, the beer people. I said, "It sounds rather jolly. Something like the time I was entertained by the Governor General and his lady at Rideau Hall." It was a put-down, but I don't think they believed me.

I've mentioned in a couple of places that a literary contract is a very important legal document, and that any writer must be careful what he signs. A few weeks before this was written I was invited up to a friend's house a few streets from me to meet a short story writer and anthologizer who has used a couple of my stories in the anthologies he edits. During the course of the evening we talked about copyrights, and I told him I had always paid particular attention to contracts for everything I'd ever written. He, unfortunately, had had a collection of his short stories published by a well-known Canadian publishing house who claimed by contract exclusive control of all subsidiary rights to the stories.

What had made him realize the error he had made in signing such a contract was that another publishing house had wanted to include one of the stories in an anthology they were bringing out. His first publisher had asked the ridiculous sum of $400 for reprint rights to the story, and the other firm had withdrawn its request. If he is not to be consulted about the sale of his stories, the author is at the mercy of his publishing house, and by the terms of some contracts will be unable to sell his own stories, even after the book is out of print, without their permission. In the meantime the publisher, by asking such ridiculous fees for reprint rights, is doing them both out of money. The publisher can afford it; the author cannot.

Publishers are not always to blame for the bad relationship between themselves and their authors, in fact it is often the author's own fault. I have heard of authors who have deliberately sabotaged their own contracts in order to free themselves of them so they could move to another publisher. Though a literary contract is a binding document, it is only binding when there is mutual satisfaction and friendship between the signees, just as in a marriage. On the one hand the publisher can bring a contract to an end almost any time by remaindering the author's book and by refusing to publish his next one. And an author can end the relationship by offering his publisher a badly-written piece of literary junk, knowing beforehand that it will be turned down. These things happen more often than the reading public realizes.

A publisher's editor once told me that the favorite ploy of his firm's dissatisfied authors was to bring in a slight volume of free verse, knowing quite well that it would be turned down, thus ending the contract but still complying with the option clause in it.

Throughout this book I have referred to both book and magazine editors in sometimes less than laudatory terms, and, from my point of view, justifiably. This does not mean however that I always take the writer's side versus the editor's or that I prefer writers to editors socially or otherwise. As a matter of fact I have always remained aloof from other writers singly or as a group. To me most writers, to put it bluntly, are a pain in the ass, as I suppose *I* am to most if not all of *them*.

Writing is the least homogeneous trade of any I know, and to throw a group of writers together at a party or in an association is the best way I know to observe the innate jealousy, pettiness and sycophancy of members of the human race. These observations are as true of me as they are of any other writer, so in order to protect both my dignity and my self-respect I have generally remained a literary loner, choosing my friends from among those outside the business and insisting that other writers remain acquaintances rather than personal friends.

It has been impossible to avoid all social contact with fellow writers, and I've already mentioned a couple of occasions when I found myself surrounded by them. The most hilariously traumatic occasion (an occasion can be both hilarious and traumatic) I can remember was away back when I first became known to the literati. William Arthur Deacon, the literary editor of the *Globe & Mail,* paid my entry fee into the Canadian Authors Association. Now this silly outfit, just as silly today as it was twenty-five years ago, was then as now a receptacle for aborted literary non-talent and writing pretentiousness. It has probably held more embryonic literary litter than the operating room waste-containers of Toronto's Women's College Hospital have the real thing. Certainly its gerontic membership, which could qualify by a four-line verse once published on the back page of a Sunday school paper, was much too old to contribute anything comparable to the contents of a women's hospital gynecological waste dish.

Anyhow, I received a note from Mr. Deacon telling me I'd been accepted for membership by the C.A.A., that he had paid my first annual dues, and that a meeting of the Toronto chapter was to be held the following week at an address on Prince Arthur Avenue. What could I do? It was kind of Bill Deacon to pay my first annual dues, and I owed him at least an appearance at the meeting.

It wasn't just as bad as I'd expected it to be, it was worse. I found myself perched on a collapsible chair on the outer perimeter of a group of chitty-chatty elderly ladies whose broadened A's, mink stoles and social pretentions matched perfectly their complete ignorance of contemporary writing. They looked to me like the offspring of Crimean War field officers and Dickensian almshouse gruel-servers, which they probably were. Their twitterings were composed largely of Can Lit name-droppings (*first* names, if you please) of writers deceased, defunct and deplored. God, how I wished I'd stashed a pint of rye in my inside pocket!

Things got under way with a welcoming speech by a sourpussed broad who probably spent her daylight hours chasing kids off her lawn, between composing prose that would turn the gut of a pterodactyl. She then introduced the "distinguished speaker of the evening," who turned out to be some old guy in a brown tweed suit from Kingston, Ontario, who would give us "an entertaining and informative talk on Service," spoken with a capital S.

I found myself becoming interested, for while I've never been a Robert W. Service fan, and can only recite a couple of lines of his poetry, at least a talk about him promised to get the meeting much closer to earth than I'd imagined it ever could get.

The speaker, to polite applause like the fluttering of fans, jumped right into his subject, and riding the thermal updrafts of his verbosity like a bespectacled hawk, soared off into an incoherence that would put to shame the poetry critics of a college quarterly. It was a masterful display of socio-literary bullshit. As a matter of fact it took me almost a quarter of an hour to realize that the Service he was talking about was not the author of *Songs of a Sourdough* but the service of such laudable petit-bourgeois organizations as the Rotary, Kiwanis and Lion's Clubs.

Following the finale, which I was only able to recognise because it ended in a full stop, the speaker was surrounded by a fluttering crowd of females in mutation mink looking like a flock of song sparrows around a suet bag. Somebody steered me to a serving table and handed me a coffee pot, and I made my sober rounds of the audience trying to look like a bus-boy from the Park Plaza Hotel around the corner. This was the least difficult part of the evening, for a bus-boy is what I looked like then.

Where was I before I was interrupted? Oh yeah, contracts. Back in the late fifties, I suppose it was, I was faced with a bad situation brought about by an oral contract. *Mayfair* magazine was then edited by Miss Jean Beattie, a young woman who had written a novel about the advertising business for The Ryerson Press. One day she phoned me and asked me if I would write them an article on the Canadian woman. At the time I'd write assigned articles on anything from naval history to mononucleosis—as a freelance journalist that was my job. Anyhow she invited me to lunch, then cancelled the invitation owing to something having come up at the office, so I went ahead and wrote the article, titling it "The Canadian Woman, 1960."

When the article was written I took it in to the *Mayfair* office, which was then situated, I believe, on Simcoe Street, north of where old *Liberty* had been located when I'd sold my first pieces to it. Miss Beattie wasn't in her office, so I left the article with one of the girls there. A few days later, not having heard anything from *Mayfair,* I phoned Miss Beattie and asked if she'd read the article. She told me she had. "How is it?" I asked. "Oh, the article is all right, Hugh, but the magazine has been sold." "So what about my payment?" "I'm afraid we can't pay you for it now."

I don't know what I said then, but though the money involved was only seventy-five dollars, as it seemed to have been during all of *Mayfair's* tightwad existence, I decided to do something about it. I certainly wasn't going to wait for the new owners to pay me, for they may not want to use the piece, and my contract was with the departing ownership and the departing editor. I went down to the magazine's editorial offices and saw the managing director, president or whatever title he'd given himself, and he gave me the same story Miss Beattie had given me. I walked out of his office and somewhere or other met Trent Frayne's wife, June Callwood. She told me that her husband had also written an article for *Mayfair,* and that it now looked as if neither one of us would be paid. I have no idea what the Fraynes did, but I went down to Division Court and swore out a summons against *Mayfair* for my seventy-five bucks. The summons was served, and *Mayfair* sent me a cheque, settling my claim out of court.

You'd have thought I'd raped Miss Beattie *and* the ex-officio boss of *Mayfair* the way the flack began to fly. I received phone calls from *Maclean's* editors, of the "these things aren't done, my boy, y'know," sort, and I told my callers, depending on my mood when I answered the phone, either to go to hell or do much worse to themselves. One or two people, not connected with any magazine at all, phoned and called me a beast for putting Miss Beattie into a state of shock and tears. Ian Sclanders, now dead but in those days *Maclean's* articles editor, gave me hell on the phone and told me I must apologize to Jean Beattie. I told him the same as I'd told the others, it wasn't *I* who had stolen seventy-five lousy dollars from *her*, but *she* who had tried to steal it from *me* for a job I'd done.

The *Mayfair* incident, for that's all it was, plus a lot of other things, made me decide to give up journalism as an almost full-time job and go back to creative writing. Though the eight years of journalism since publishing my last book had been fun in spots, and had given me an easy income, including lots of free drinking time, it had begun to play hob with my health. This had manifested itself in vague stomach troubles, and tests, X-rays, and everything else the doctors gave me, confirmed that they were psychosomatic. All right, if journalism gave me a belly ache, I'd stop being a journalist.

One illness that wasn't psychosomatic was an attack of hepatitis while we were living on Toronto Island, caused by a season of high water that overflowed the septic tanks and polluted the drinking water. Having been perfectly healthy up to then, with the exception of massive hangovers, I treated my hepatitis the way I'd treated my hangovers, with beer. One morning when I went to work in Jack Cooke's offices, somebody told me my face had turned yellow. Sure enough, when I looked at myself in the washroom mirror I *was* yellow, including my eyeballs. I recognized I had jaundice, but had no idea what could have caused it except my excessive drinking. Having no family doctor (my family hadn't needed a doctor up to then, thank God) I weakly and painfully stumbled over to lower Jarvis Street from our offices in the financial district.

I entered the door of the first house that had a physician's shingle outside, and gave the doctor my symptoms: weakness, jaundice, and an inability to keep either food or liquor down. He told me I had hepatitis, caused by drinking. He also told me that if I kept on drinking I'd be dead within a few months, for my liver was shot. I wondered how in hell he knew that for he hadn't examined me. As medicine he told me to take plenty of sugar. "Drink lots of Coca-Cola," he said, and I was to avoid fatty foods. I gave him his five-dollar fee and got out.

Only after leaving his shabby office did I realize he was used to treating skid-row winos, and was probably known in the neighborhood as a "clap doctor," one who also specialized in venereal diseases, gave physicals to prostitutes, and probably performed the odd illegal abortion.

When I got back to the office I told Jack Cooke I had hepatitis. "Jesus, Hugh, you look like hell!" he exclaimed. "Look, I'll get you an appointment with my own doctor up on St. Clair Avenue, and you go up there and let him take a look at you. That goddam quack on Jarvis Street could kill you." That afternoon I was examined by Cooke's doctor, a very personable young man, who confirmed the diagnosis of hepatitis, took my blood pressure, a blood test, felt my liver, and told me to go home and get plenty of bed rest, avoid alcohol and fatty foods, and just take things easy.

Within a week the jaundice had disappeared, and I felt great. I became bored with my forced inactivity, and at the end of the week went back to work. I reported once again to Cooke's doctor, who looked me over, said I was okay, and told me to lay off alcohol, especially beer, for a while. I did that for "a while," then went back to drinking beer with my cronies in my favorite pub, with no ill effects, though I kept glancing at my face in the mirror for the first sign of yellowing.

After leaving the Island for an apartment on Kingston Road in East Toronto I would occasionally drink myself into various states of ill-health. Twice I ended up vomiting copious amounts of blood while drinking, which scared the daylights out of my wife. The first time I was rushed by ambulance to Sunnybrook Veterans Hospital, where I complicated things by having an alcoholic seizure. The hemorrhaging was stopped by bed rest and bland foods, but the seizure was first diagnosed as an epileptic fit. They shipped me over to D-Block, the psychiatric wing, where I was given many tests including an electro-encephalogram, which, I presume, proved negative. I asked my doctor to spring me, which he did after a few days.

The second time I hemorrhaged was a couple of years later, and this time I was rushed to the Toronto East General Hospital, where I was placed in a semi-private room with an old Danforth Avenue Irishman, one of the most odious old beer-parlour stiffs it's ever been my misfortune to meet. My bleeding stopped as soon as I was removed from the booze and began eating again, but I think my quick recovery was due more to my desire to escape my cell-mate than the medical treatment. I still don't know whether the blood came from my stomach or a broken vein in my esophagus. I had the DT's in the East General, of an auditory nature mainly, in which I heard beautiful symphonic music. I would shut out the sounds of the old Irishman and his ignorant visitors and concentrate on the symphonies. I finally traced the music to the almost inaudible sound of a generator somewhere in the hospital, and as I'd had the DT's before I'd learned not to be afraid of them but to lie back and enjoy them.

I think that having had the delirium tremens, which started in my case in my apartment on Kingston Road when I held a conversation with our refrigerator, has helped me in my writing. I found I could write knowledgeably about a psychotic, as I did in a short story, "The Sound Of Hollyhocks," and about old Lightfoot's delirium tremens in *Silence On The Shore*. (The book was titled *The Silence On The Shore* in its hardcover and Ryerson paperback issues, as the printed pages in the paperback were reproduced by offset printing, in which the hard cover pages were photographed. In the Pocket Book edition in 1971 the pages were re-set, and the article "The" was dropped from the title.)

Another thing that evolved from my short stay in the Toronto East General Hospital was a decision of mine never to buy semi-private hospital coverage; from then on I wanted to stay in a ward where I'd have a choice of people to talk to.

Ever since my first novel, *Storm Below*, was published in 1949 I had been asked to appear as an interview guest or as a panelist on various radio and, later, television shows. Actually the first radio show I appeared on was before I became a published writer at all. It was sometime between 1946 and 1948, when I was living in the veterans' housing project, and how I came to be on it I have forgotten. It was a weekly show on radio station CFRB, in which Roy Ward Dixon, I believe, took on various people who would choose a word from a dictionary he handed them, and he would either spell it correctly or the program would pay the winner a sum that was somewhere around thirty-five or forty dollars.

I chose the word, *albedo*, meaning in astronomy the reflected light from the moon. Mr. Dixon, if that was his name, spelled it with a letter "i", and I won my thirty or forty dollars. It wasn't much, but in those days when my weekly wage was $33.50 it seemed quite a bit.

My first radio show, as a "personality" as you're called if you beat a murder rap, write a book or cross the country on a pogo-stick, was with a cigar-smoking gentleman who interviewed me over one of the CBC stations, CJBC. The interview took place in a cafeteria on Toronto's Adelaide Street, over coffee. This gentleman, who seemed to be quite a wheel in the radio industry at the time, was a fifth wheel as far as I was concerned. Like most of his ilk even sixth magnitude stardom went to his head, and he proved the old showbiz adage, "when you make the top the first thing you do is desert your wife and kids and then get your teeth capped." He deserted his family and went to England, where he disappeared. Whether he ever had his teeth capped I don't know.

Over the next twenty-five years I appeared on scores of radio and TV shows, which gave me and my books public exposure, was often fun, allowed me to meet a great many broadcasting personalities I never would have met otherwise, and paid me fees that bought the groceries.

In 1963 I moved from East Toronto north to an outlying corner of the suburb of Don Mills which had been put together by the Don Mills Corporation under the chairmanship of Mr. E. P. Taylor ten years before, and billed as "Canada's First Planned Community" or some such slogan. Actually it *was* the first, and it had been planned by Mr. Taylor and his associates to combine suburban housing and suburban industry plus one of the first giant shopping malls conceived up to then. The down payments on the single houses that filled the four "quadrants" surrounding the shopping plaza were low, and so were the mortgage payments and interest, the idea being that the industries would pay the major share of the development costs, leaving the householders comparatively unscathed. The home owners were not similarly protected from high taxes, for Don Mills remained part of the Borough of North York which suffered from a disproportionate amount of housing in relation to industrial development.

Anyhow, the homes I moved to, first an attached two-story maisonette and later a third floor apartment, were in the outer limits of the development. Living on the same floor of the apartment building, though we didn't know each other at the time, was Paul Rimstead, later a columnist for the *Toronto Telegram* and the *Toronto Sun*. Years later he interviewed me at home and gave me one of the best interviews I ever received.

The atmosphere of suburbia didn't help my writing, and except for some short stories I didn't do much at all during the two years I lived up there. With the exception of the two years I'd lived in the veterans' housing development I'd always been a city guy, and even the fact that we lived between two shopping plazas, a couple of blocks from either one, didn't help things. Nor did the fact that one of the plazas boasts a liquor store, with a beer warehouse across the street, help me much. I resented having to drive my car every time I wanted to go downtown, or almost anywhere else for that matter.

I've never been a joiner of anything, and I'd probably refuse to join the Knights of Columbus even if I lived in the Vatican. However, while I was living in Don Mills something came up that I felt I had to take part in.

A young married man, living down in an east-of-the-Don River district I'd once lived in myself, received a twenty-four year sentence for arson from a Toronto magistrate, F. Tupper Bigelow. The sentence was not only a long way out of proportion to the crime committed, but was actually almost double that given for manslaughter and murder. The convicted man had set a few fires in his neighborhood: to a car, a garage, in the hallway of an apartment house, and to the home of the family after whom Toronto's Ashbridge's Bay was named. The only casualty of the fires had been an old lady who along with several others had been living as paying guests in the Ashbridge house. The old lady, I believe, had died of a heart attack during the small fire at the house.

The arsonist was obviously a pyromaniac, and what he needed was psychiatric treatment rather than a harsh prison sentence. His neighbors and people in his neighborhood had contacted a well-known lawyer, who had formed a lawyers' committee to have the man's sentence appealed. There was also a public meeting called in the basement of a small Anglican church near where the man lived, and where his children went to school. When it was announced in the papers I decided to show a smidgeon of citizenship and attend the meeting.

What made it difficult for me was the fact that a few years before this I'd been a luncheon guest of Magistrate Bigelow at the Toronto Board of Trade. For some reason or another I was always being invited out by magistrates, judges and once by the Ontario attorney general, either to discuss things I'd written or for reasons that remain forever hidden from me. Magistrate

Bigelow and I had discussed a newspaper column I'd written about Sherlock Holmes. His Worship was a Holmes fan and a member of the Baker Street Irregulars (or whatever the Toronto chapter calls itself). Personally, my interest in Sherlock Holmes or Sir Arthur Conan Doyle can be described as minimal. I forget now what I'd said about Sherlock to draw the magistrate's interest.

The public meeting was well attended, and the basement Sunday school room of the church was filled with outraged citizens from all sections of Metropolitan Toronto. Besides those who presumably like me were appalled at the cruel sentence the man had received there was the usual ragtag and bobtail of those people who faithfully attend all protest meetings. It was an orderly and sensible affair however, and even the few beatnicks (as they were then called) were not the turned-on freaks they were later to become when drugs entered their culture.

There were resolutions from the dais and revolutionary motions from the floor, and the usual shouts of "Out of order!" from the incipient parliamentarians in the crowd. Each person as he stood up to speak gave his name and neighborhood. Somebody made the most fatuous proposal from the floor that I'd heard since giving up the CCF club presidency twenty-five years before. I stood up and challenged it, and it was defeated. Later on the meeting's chairman proposed the formation of a citizens' committee to work alongside that of the lawyers', which was led by Mr. Arthur Maloney, Q.C. I was elected chairman of the committee.

Most of the real work was done by the group of prominent young lawyers. Our group, among whose members were Mr. Ben Nobleman, and Miss Phyllis Griffiths of the *Toronto Telegram,* met a couple of times in another neighborhood church. My small contributions were some propaganda interviews on radio and TV, and some pieces I wrote for the *Telegram.* There was some precedent-breaking done by the lawyers' committee which involved letters between myself and Donald Fleming, then the federal attorney general. The young arsonist had his sentence reduced by half.

My landlord on Kingston Road from 1953 to 1962 had been a Jewish guy called Sam, who had been a very good friend, and who had offered to lower my rent when I gave him my notice to move. The people who owned the house in Don Mills to which I moved were also Jews, four brothers named Perkell. They are

208

excellent landlords too, and when I told them I wanted to move back to the city they asked me to wait until a house they were then building in North Toronto was finished, and move into that. I've always been a quick-decision, quick-move guy, and I couldn't wait. I moved into an apartment house on the next street to where the Perkell apartment building was being built. I made the mistake of moving into a place whose denizens were elderly church-goers and teetotalers, and some of the neighbors, with the help of their "Christian" ethics, had me turfed out for excessive drinking. The Perkell's house was then finished, and having been told I had ten days to find a new place to live, I don't know on what grounds except perhaps moral turpitude, I found an apartment in the Perkell's apartment building. The superintendent, Cecil Wannamaker and his wife Helen, had been employed in the same job up in Don Mills, so things worked out fine. On one occasion, before I fell under the un-Godly wrath of the "Christians," the Perkells had passed me the word that they'd pay my moving bill if I'd move into their new house. I paid my own way during my emergency flit, and I've lived in the house ever since.

While up in Don Mills I'd been living largely on my small capital, doing a few stories and articles, mainly for the CBC, *Liberty* and the *Star Weekly*. One day I received a phone call from Andy MacFarlane, the managing editor of the *Toronto Telegram*, asking me to contribute a column now and again for a new feature called "Dissent" on the opposite-to-editorial page of the paper. I began writing them, and the first one appeared on October 18th, 1963, and the last on October 27th, 1965. Altogether sixty-three of them appeared under my by-line, beginning with "I'm Against The United Appeal" and ending with "NCP: Memories Of Little Men." What NCP stood for I've long ago forgotten.

Also while living in Don Mills I had a call from John Clare at the *Star Weekly* asking me if I'd like to make a coast-to-coast trip to do a series on Canada's Indians. Though it was winter I said I would and flew to Vancouver to begin interviewing chiefs and members of various Indian tribes. I began my Odyssey by taking the ferry to Nanaimo and interviewing a chief and his wife on their reservation. They were very nice people, and the chief's wife told me her sister had disappeared into Vancouver's skidroad, where so many Indian women seemed to end up, alcoholic, filthy, in jail and out, chippying for enough money to buy a bottle of cheap wine.

Back in Vancouver I visited the Indian museum, where the curator was a Canadian Indian with the same surname as mine, married to a girl who was a Sioux from South Dakota. He gave me plenty of material about the West Coast Indians, and the names and addresses of several Indians who were practicing teachers and lawyers in the city. I interviewed a couple of them.

A couple of days later I took a bus to Seattle, where I visited the Indian House and talked with some very intelligent Indian women, and learned that the Indians were treated just as shabbily on one side of the border as they were on the other.

One morning in my room in the Hotel Vancouver I received a phone call from Ray Gardner of the *Star Weekly*. I suspect they were checking up to see if I was sober, which I was, but Ray asked me how the weather was out there, which happened to be his home town. "Lousy," I said. "It's drizzling rain all the time. It was snowing however on Vancouver Island." "I love that Vancouver winter drizzle," he said. "You can have it," I told him.

I happened to be in Vancouver that time just when the Doukhobors hit the city at the end of their long trek from the inland valley where they'd settled many years before. I talked with the matriarchal leader of the trek, a very smart woman, and watched them as they sat around the small square, in Ray Gardner's drizzle, outside the offices of *The Sun*. I was impressed very much by the dignified way they conducted themselves, and especially by the cleanliness of the children in their warm clothing. Any group that had trekked as far as they had, pitching camp at the side of the road each night, and still managed to keep the babies and children so well fed, clean and well clothed were far different from what the anti-Doukhobor propaganda had led me to believe.

On my previous visit to Vancouver, to be interviewed on television about my memories of the Spanish Civil War by George Woodcock, Professor of English at the University of British Columbia and editor of *Canadian Literature,* I had suffered what to some might have proved to be a humiliating experience, but to me was merely reminiscent of the treatment I'd received from the stubblejumpers of the RCMP back in the Depression days.

The CBC had flown me out to Vancouver first class, and had put me up in one of those expense-account motor hotels near English Bay. I was drunk when I left Toronto, and stayed drunk when I arrived on The Coast, but not through drinking rum or gin from the hollowed-out coconuts or pineapples that junior executives love to drink from in such joints. It was my habit to call a cab at the desk and ride up to the beer parlours on Granville Street. This habit didn't go down very well with the management of the phony South Sea flophouse in which I was a guest. Other times I sent cabs to pick me up bottles of Canadian Club, and drank them in my room.

George Woodcock phoned me the afternoon preceding the evening taping of two TV interviews we were going to do at one sitting, and drove me out to his house, where Mrs. Woodcock cooked a delightful dinner of *wiener schnitzel.* I think poor George was a little apprehensive that I might not make the taping, but being true to my constant unpredictability I made it fine. George, a philosophical anarchist and a believer in the generally useless splinter groups who formed their own paramilitary forces in the Spanish Civil War, such as the P.O.U.M.

in which his friend George Orwell had served, tried to draw out of me, as a former member of the Stalinist International Brigades, what I thought of the Communist assassinations in Barcelona and most parts of Catalonia. I told him I knew nothing about them, which I didn't; that we'd been too busy on various fronts around Madrid to know what was happening behind the lines, even if we'd cared. I think I also said that no matter what history might say about the Communist Party involvement in Spain, one thing was certain to me: the Communist armies, both Spanish and International, had done the main fighting against the fascists.

When the taping was finished I went up to Granville Street and drank until closing time with a couple of beer parlour habitués—or sons of habitués as it turned out, to use a phrase coined by Alexander Woollcott. I then suggested to my new-found friends that we take a cab back to my hotel, where I'd stashed a bottle of Canadian Club.

The night manager gave me a disapproving look when we entered the foyer, but we ignored him and took the elevator up to my room. After a few shots of rye I flaked out, and when I woke up my erstwhile friends had gone. From a habit of years, picked up in whores' bedrooms from Paris to Pittsburgh, I felt for my wallet and was relieved to find it still in my pocket.

The next morning I checked out of the hotel, after having the clerk call me a taxi to take me to the airport. The manager told me he didn't want me as a guest again, and I told him I'd sooner stay at the Vancouver or the Bayshore anyhow, and he could stuff his establishment, papier-maché palm trees, pimps, and Polynesian poi, wherever was convenient.

The taxi driver was a young Japanese kid, and we talked all the way out to the airport. When we arrived at the entrance to the administration building I took out my wallet and found it was empty of money, though I knew I'd been carrying thirty or forty dollars when I left the beer parlour the night before with the two guys I'd taken to my room. I'd been rolled, that was all, and I tried to explain it to the taxi-driver. Nothing else had been touched in my wallet, and I still had my Air Canada ticket to Toronto, my Diners' Club card, and all my identification including a Toronto Police press card. The Japanese kid refused to listen to reason. I was still a little befogged anyhow, which didn't help things, but I knew I could go to the Air Canada manager and sign a chit for the taxi fare, using my credentials as collateral for the loan.

The kid became hostile and we began trading punches there

on the administration building steps. One of those useless flunkeys who wears his war ribbons on his doorkeeper's uniform called the police. An RCMP cruiser skidded to a stop, one of the policemen jumped out, the taxi-driver shouted that I wouldn't pay him his fare (and by this time I no longer intended to), and I was hustled into the police car. They drove me to the RCMP lockup in Richmond, a town that belongs on my hate list along with Keyser, West Virginia, and I was questioned by the desk sergeant.

One of the cops, a perfect example of a Saskatchewan Ukrainian farmer's son who still had the gumbo stuck to his boots, treated me pretty roughly, making me remove my shoelaces, belt and necktie, pushing me around, and generally behaving as I'd expected he would. He also took away my pack of cigarettes. His partner didn't seem to be such a bad guy. They threw me into a cell block, made up of six empty cells and a long wide corridor in front of them, locked me in and left.

Holding up my trousers with one hand I made my way to one of the empty cells and lay down on the cot, trying to get a little rest. I was too angry to sleep. I knew that it was Saturday morning, and that I'd be unable to get a phone call through to anybody at the CBC in Toronto. I'd forgotten the television producer's name, and I was too ashamed to call George Woodcock to come out to Richmond to bail me out of jail. The fact that I was from Toronto hadn't helped either, for in the eyes of the hunky Saskatchewan cop I was one "a them damned hogtown bastards who'd tried to beat one of our poor little Jap cabdrivers outa his fare." I'd just have to make the best of it, even though I was sick enough to die, and getting sicker every minute.

I sat beside the running water tap that served as a drinking fountain and drank gallons of water, only to throw them up again. I desperately wanted a cigarette too, and the thought of being alone in that empty jailhouse until Monday morning was no consolation. Finally I had an idea. I shouted and rattled the bars on the lockup door until one of the station officers came.

"What the hell do you want?" he asked me.

"I want a doctor; I'm vomiting blood," I told him.

That scared him; I guess he thought of all the forms he'd have to fill out if I died in his lousy jailhouse.

In an hour or so a doctor came, and gave me a 10 milligram tranquilizer, which was like giving an aspirin to a terminal cancer patient. "You'll be all right," he said.

"Thanks for nothing, Doc."

I paced that cellblock all day and half the evening, between drinks of water and frequent spews in the sink. After dark I lay down on one of the empty bunks in a cell and tried to sleep, but couldn't. By then I'd have welcomed any cell-mate, a nut, a murderer, a rapist, anybody.

It was after four a.m. Sunday morning when I heard the metallic sound of a key in a lock, and the heavy steel rattle of barred doors. A mountie came to the door of the cellblock followed by a guy about my own age who was still wearing his necktie, belt and shoelaces. I knew by this he must be a local citizen, even though he was just as drunk as I'd been when they brought me in. I'd never been so happy to see a fellow human being in my life.

I told him my name, and he told me his. The cops had even left him his cigarettes, and I bummed one from him.

When I asked him what his charge was he told me a long involved story about owning a motel and motor court on the Kingsway in Burnaby, and after closing up for the night he'd had a few drinks and had decided to visit a friend a couple of miles from his place. He'd driven down the wrong street, and had knocked on the door of the wrong house. The irate tenant had answered the door, and finding himself facing an obvious drunk had threatened to murder him if he didn't leave his porch that minute.

"What happened then?" I asked, taking a long loving drag on my cigarette.

"I went down to my car—it's a Jaguar—and I couldn't start it. So I went back to the guy's house and asked him to phone a garage for me. Instead of that he phoned the police, and here I am. They're charging me with impaired driving, but I was sitting in a car that wouldn't start when they arrested me. I don't think that constitutes impaired driving at all, do you?"

"I dunno," I said. I was thinking to myself: Well, you got your wish, Garner. Your cell-mate turned out to be a nut who claims he owns a motel and drives a Jaguar. I'd heard this kind of drunken bumology from Los Angeles' Lincoln Heights Jail to an army detention prison.

"What time is it?" I asked him.

He still had his watch. "It's a quarter to five," he said.

"God! I still have more than another day in this place," I said.

"No you don't. Listen, I've got a guy coming in the morning to bail me out. I'll get him to bail you out too. What are you in for?"

"Probably drunk and disorderly. Drunk anyway."

"Your bail won't be much, pal. Don't worry, I'll get you out."

214

I didn't believe him, but he was somebody to talk to, and he shared his cigarettes with me. During the course of our conversation it turned out that he'd been a chief petty officer in the navy, as I had. From then on we got along great.

The next morning one of the mounties brought us a cup of coffee apiece, and we asked him what time the justice of the peace would give us a bail hearing.

"After he comes from church," the cop said.

I prayed the JP was a Catholic and went to early mass.

As it turned out he was a Protestant, but when we were finally ushered into the small courtroom that was part of the police station-jail-court complex I noticed a young man sitting in the courtroom. The justice of the peace read my name, then took a long stare at me over the top of his glasses. "Are you Hugh Garner the writer?"

"Yes sir."

"You're charged with being drunk in a public place, Mr. Garner, how do you plead?"

"Guilty."

"Your bail until court convenes tomorrow morning at ten will be twenty-five dollars.

"I have no money—" I began.

The young man sitting in the court, who had been whispering with my cell-mate, said, "I'll put up bail, your worship." He stepped forward and paid my bail. My new friend was also let out on bail, in his case a hundred and twenty-five dollars. The three of us left the court. In the police station I was given back my necktie, belt, shoelaces, cigarettes, wallet and watch. I opened the wallet and checked everything in it very carefully.

"It's all there, Mr. Garner," said one of the cops, smiling.

"I can check it, can't I? I've been robbed once in this town already," I said. I also opened my suitcase and checked the contents.

We went outside and sure enough there was my cell-mate's car, a Jaguar. An old one, but a Jaguar nevertheless. We got into it and his friend got into his own car and we drove out along a country dirt road where we parked. My cell-mate's friend, the young man who had furnished my bail, came back to the Jaguar carrying a bottle of gin and three ice-cold bottles of ale. I took a long gulp of gin and washed it down with a drink of ale. We killed the bottle of gin and the beer out there on the country road, then we parted from the man who had put up the bail.

"Where are you staying?" my friend asked.

215

"Nowhere. I have no money until the banks open in the morning."

"Come out and stay at my motel," he said.

This time I believed he *did* own a motel, and I was right. We sang all the obscene navy songs we could remember as we drove to it. My friend put me up in a vacant family suite, and I sat in an easy chair all that day shaking off the drunk that had brought me there. The following morning we drove in the Jaguar back to Richmond, I used my bank courtesy card to make a withdrawal from a branch of my bank, pleaded guilty to a charge of being drunk in a public place, paid my fine, paid off my ex-navy benefactor, and took the next flight home.

On my trip to Vancouver to do the Indian story I called up my old cell-mate (who had paid a fine for impaired driving that other time) and he invited me out to the motel for dinner, where I met his wife and family. Later he drove me back to the Hotel Vancouver, where we drank a few beers together in the basement pub.

My next stop was Calgary, where I intended to question some of the Plains Indians about their conditions. I flew over the mountains and checked into the Palliser Hotel in Calgary, which in those days at least had the largest bathtubs I'd ever seen outside of the Hotel Scribe in Paris. The next day was a Saturday, so I decided to take a bus south to High River where my old friend W. O. (Bill) Mitchell was living.

When I alighted from the bus in the small cowtown that is High River I went into the nearest beer parlour and had a couple of ales, then phoned Bill. He came to the beer parlour to pick me up, and we drove to his house in his station wagon, where I met his pretty wife, Myrna, whom I hadn't seen since they lived in Toronto. Bill and I went out and bought some Australian wine, and we had a very convivial dinner at the Mitchell house. Bill drove me back to the bus depot in the early evening, where I dropped a bottle of wine, which shattered on the depot floor. With this typical Garner gesture I bid him goodbye and went back to Calgary.

The next day I took a bus to the town of Gleichen, Alberta, which is on the C.P.R. mainline, on the border of a large Blackfoot Indian reservation. I talked with the Indian agent, and he drove me into the reservation to interview the chief. I added notes on my conversations with both these men to the pile I had already made in Vancouver, Nanaimo, and Seattle. The chief told me that his band's reservation was the largest in Canada, and that until a few years before they had owned one of the largest herds of horses in Alberta. The herd had dwindled now to a few dozen head, due to the young Indians selling them off for the price of liquor, and occasionally giving one away for a couple of bottles of cheap wine. The Indians didn't get along very well with the whites in Gleichen, being barred from the local pub, and even from the Canadian Legion hall for a time, though many of them were war veterans.

The chief also told me how he and his family also took part each year in the Calgary Stampede parade, and of the scale of fees given to them and to members of the Blood tribe who dressed up in feathers and buckskin regalia for the occasion. The highest fees were given to those who owned tepees, and all had to supply their own horses, pintos being the most acceptable. He showed me some of the better reservation houses, and some of the worst, where he said the tenants just brushed the dirt and refuse through a hole in the floor. The chief was a warm, articulate man, and when I left him he climbed aboard the snowplow with which he was plowing the reservation roads.

I had my supper in the small town, a place I remembered from thirty years before when I'd been kicked off the blinds of a passenger train there. I sat in the railroad station for a while, then walked north to the highway and took a westbound bus for the fifty miles back to Calgary.

My next stop was Winnipeg, where I checked into the Fort Garry Hotel. I called up an old friend, who had worked on the Toronto papers before the war, and later, while living on the Island, on the same mining sheet as me. Bob Noble, a Winnipegger, had gone back home, and had since worked for the *Winnipeg Free Press*. I'd visited him and his wife on other occasions when an assignment had taken me to Winnipeg, and he came down to the Fort Garry to see me. Another *Free Press* reporter and his girl also came to my hotel room, and interviewed me over a couple of drinks. Incidentally, Bob Noble has reviewed most of my books for the *Free Press*, always giving me a friendly review.

A couple of days after I arrived and had questioned some skidroad Indians in Main Street pubs I took the C.N.R. train to Churchill.

This train, if a little cleaner and far less boisterous than the one that runs north from Cochrane, Ontario to Moosonee on James Bay, is a friendly train. It carries Indians, Dew Line workers, both Canadian and American servicemen, Hudson's

Bay Company people, miners from Thompson and The Pas, missionaries and mounties. I spent a lot of time in the club car with the black steward, and met a couple of telephone linesmen who were going to Churchill to repair some wires burned down in a storefront fire.

I checked into the best-looking hotel in Churchill, along with the telephone men, and later hired a taxi which took me around the town to see the Indian village, the Eskimo village, the ice-covered Hudson Bay shoreline, and other points of interest. It was too late in the season to see the polar bears scavenging in the local dump, and the temperature was minus thirty-five degrees.

The next day, Sunday, somebody took me to the curling rink, where I proved to myself I was the world's worst curler. I went back to the hotel and bought a bottle of Park & Tilford whisky from the hotel manager, which I shared with my friends from the phone company. That evening I visited with the Roman Catholic Vicar General of the area, who gave me some information about the Indians under his jurisdiction. The following day I interviewed some of the Indians in the Indian village, and ended up in the evening in a wonderful mixed-company beer parlour, drinking with an R.C.A.F. corporal and an Indian woman. Before I left the beer parlour I bought two pints of bootleg whisky from the Indian woman, who told me to hide them under my coat.

The next morning I boarded a Trans-Air plane for Winnipeg, a pint of bootleg liquor in each inside pocket of my suit coat. On the way from Churchill to The Pas I innocently asked one of the stewardesses if she had any mixes. You'd have thought I was a Mau-Mau hijacker asking her for a match to light the fuse of a box of dynamite. She screamed, "You can't drink on *this* plane!" and ran forward to the cockpit. When she returned she had the first officer in tow. He confiscated the pint of liquor the stewardess had seen, told me he had a good mind to drop me off in The Pas, and went back to the cockpit. I'd always thought that the myth of Western hospitality was overplayed, but now I knew it was just plain bullshit.

I sat quietly in my seat in the DC-nothing as it lumbered its way to Winnipeg, and after the rest of the passengers had alighted and the crew came aft from the cockpit, I asked the first officer for my confiscated bottle of liquor. He handed it to me, and in a sudden burst of goodwill I told him he could keep it as a present. Then I got off.

I remember getting back to the Fort Garry, but very little else

218

after that. Somehow I reached the airport again, took a plane to Toronto, an airport limousine home, and then passed out cold. I know now that I'd been in and out of comas ever since arriving in Winnipeg from Churchill, and I stayed in a coma for several days after arriving home. My wife thought it was the result of my drinking, and if I'd have been in a condition to think at all I'd agreed with her. She noticed however that I hadn't urinated for days, and she finally called an ambulance which took me to the Toronto General Hospital.

The doctors there put a catheter in my bladder, gave me a long series of tests, but were puzzled as to what was causing my kidney stoppage. I swelled up, and the retention of fluids filled my abdominal cavity and spread into my lungs where it gave me pneumonia. In order to counteract the pneumonia I was given massive doses of penicillin, to which I hadn't been sensitive up to then. This time I was, and I broke out in a terrible rash which covered all of my body, including the inside of my mouth and even my tongue. Now I was suffering from three diseases at once, any one of which could be fatal.

I was placed in a private room and an artificial kidney machine was brought up, while I was made ready to be attached to it. One evening a doctor told my wife I'd be lucky to live through the night. I had no pain, but suffered from terrible thirsts, and kept falling into comas. At first they would only give me wet pieces of gauze to suck, but later the doctors asked me what I wanted to drink. They said I could have anything I craved, including beer. I told them what I really wanted was a bottle of commercial orangeade. The doctors and nurses kept asking me whether I had drunk cleaning fluid or a solvent. I couldn't tell them; all I knew was that it was something mixed with alcohol.

Every morning I would have an audience around my bed consisting of renal specialists, house physicians, surgeons, and the doctor who ran the artificial kidney machine.

The house doctor would come into my room each morning at the crack of dawn, and when I'd say, "Good morning, Doctor," he'd seem surprised that I was still alive. He would put his stethoscope to my chest, murmur a word of encouragement, and leave.

One day, as mysteriously as they'd stopped, my kidneys began to function again. Within the next day or two my pneumonia cleared up, my temperature dropped, my blood pressure went back to normal, my rash began to clear, and I began to enjoy my normal sleep. One morning when the house doctor came in to listen to my chest I mentioned something about another patient I had noticed in my ward. "Don't worry about him," he said. "You were the sickest patient in the whole hospital for a long time."

The next time one of the visiting specialists asked me what I thought I'd drunk which would have the effect of stopping my kidneys from functioning. I told him that all I could think of was the bottle of bootleg liquor I'd bought from the Indian woman in Churchill. He said, "It was probably that. I wonder what was mixed with the liquor?" I told him there was probably a very sick first officer from a Trans-Air airplane somewhere out in Manitoba, who had drunk the other bootleg bottle.

John Clare from the *Star Weekly* came to see me, as did Syd Brown and another official of the Metro Toronto Police Association. My landlords, the Perkells, sent me a large bouquet of flowers. It was one of the first illnesses I'd had that I could talk about. Usually my illnesses and operations are the kind you can't talk about at parties, operations for hemorrhoids and prostate trouble, illnesses brought on by drinking.

The kidney specialist introduced me to Dr. Stanley Bain of Don Mills, whom I was to see after being discharged from the hospital. He is a fine general practitioner and is still our family doctor.

After a few days I began pleading to be released from the hospital, though still very weak and groggy. The doctors told me I'd be weak for a long time, and not to overdo exercise and walking. The skin began peeling from the palms of my hands and the soles of my feet from the penicillin reaction, all the thick callouses came off and my feet remained tender for a long time after I left the hospital. I also found I couldn't walk as far as I'd been able to do before.

I told the editors at the *Star Weekly* that I wouldn't be able to continue gathering the material for the Indian series, and they released me from our agreement, paying me for the time I'd spent on it. One thing I'd discovered from my stay in the hospital—my chronic gastritis had disappeared. Since then I don't think I've chewed more than a dozen Tums.

Another promise I made to myself was that from then on I was going to do more creative writing, and as little non-fiction as I could get away with. In one year, 1957, I'd written fifty-six full length magazine articles, but during the ten years from 1962 to now I have written only thirty-six.

As I said earlier, though I had dealings with dozens of editors, I never became pally with them. I think it's a mistake to change a business relationship into a social one, and most editors I wrote for have remained business acquaintances or friends but nothing else. One editor made several overtures to me to be invited to my place. Just as I'd never wanted to be invited to his or to any other editor's house, I didn't want him coming to mine. Besides, my acquaintanceship with him had always been tenuous and based on mutual insult and grudging acceptance one for the other.

There were times when Frank Rasky of *Liberty* turned down an article of mine and made me so angry I tore up three days work and threw it across his desk. I remember once calling him a "vulgarian" and he looked up the word in his desk dictionary, turned to me and said, "That means I'm of the common people," which of course it doesn't. What the hell could you do with a guy like that? On other occasions, when I was strapped for carfare so to speak, Rasky would come across with an advance payment for an article he wanted me to write. Between the poles of our relationship we got along fine, and altogether I wrote nearly two hundred articles for his magazine. I wrote many of them under pseudonyms, for many issues of *Liberty* had two and three pieces of mine in it. One Christmas issue during the late nineteen-fifties had one of my short stories and four separate articles written by me.

Rasky wasn't the worst editor I met in the vulgarian ranks I wrote for, and there were many who could be accused of much worse things, sloth and stupidity for instance. There were the socially-acceptable editors, who pretended a gentility that was as phony as their imagined intellectualism, and those who had gotten their jobs through wiles generally associated with male whores. And there were the editorial department hacks, guys bucking for their superannuations, and plain misfits who had worked their way up in the firm from mailing boy. There were the educated nobodies too, guys who had been hired by magazine owners who had only gone to grade school, and whose college degrees had blinded the eyes of management to their innate stupidity.

On the other hand there was the odd percipient man at the editor's desk with an intellect honed to the sharpness of a razor blade, who knew what he and the magazine wanted, made immediate decisions and stuck by them, gave his writers quick readings and payments, and ended up being loved by his writers but fired by a business rather than literary-oriented boss.

With the exception of a couple of ventures into brief social contacts with Robin Ross-Taylor and Charles Sweeny of William Collins Sons, my relationship with publishers has generally remained that of a car buyer to an automobile salesman, a relationship formed of initial mutual distrust like the first meeting of a pair of dogs, but often growing into mutual respect and friendship.

Canada has been one hell of a country in which to be a writer. During my beginning days in the business the Canadian writer—much more then than he has to today—had to contend with the popularity (and I think it was a deserved one) of American and English writers. Canadian publishers and editors were not only convinced of the superiority of foreign English-language writers, but equally convinced that no Canadian, or damned few of them, could ever reach a parity with their American or English counterparts.

Most "Canadian" publishing houses (with the laudable exceptions of The Ryerson Press and McClelland & Stewart) found it far more profitable and safe to act as local book-jobbers who imported American and English titles, than to venture their capital on the development of Canadian literature. They would spend any amount of money to promote or even print a book, as long as the money was furnished by somebody else.

There has been a great change in Canadian publishing in the last few years, due mainly to the proliferation of small independent, experimental publishing houses, whose authors' fees and production costs have been largely underwritten by The Canada Council. These financially speculative publishers have been a godsend to young Canadian poets and writers, many of whom would never have been published at all by the old established publishers. As a corollary to this there has also sprung up a coast-to-coast spate of "little" magazines, that have furnished a showplace for the works of young new writers. I can never forget that I was first published by their equivalent of thirty-five years ago, *Canadian Forum*.

I am not in favor of a Canadian nationalistic bias in our

literature and publishing, for I think most of it is more anti-American xenophobia than pro-Canadian patriotism. In my own case my books have been published by William Collins Sons, a Canadian subsidiary of a British publishing house; a fly-by-night Canadian paperback venture, Export Publishing Enterprises Ltd.; McClelland & Stewart, a Canadian house; The Ryerson Press, also an old Canadian firm; and lastly by McGraw-Hill Ryerson and Simon & Schuster of Canada, subsidiaries of American firms.

My first publisher, William Collins Sons (Canada) Ltd., a subsidiary of an old Glasgow-based publishing firm that seemed to make a great deal of its income from publishing the King James' version of the Bible, brought out four of my first five books, treated me as well as I expected to be treated, paid me my royalties regularly (such as they were), and after we broke up gave me back the rights to my books, and we remained friends. One of the Canadian publishers treated my book shabbily, but was nevertheless honest with me financially, and at my request returned to me the rights to the book they had published. The second Canadian house had hit the downhill skids long before they ever heard of me, and though they published five books of mine they did a lousy job in selling them. The two American publishers, which up to this moment I'm connected with contractually, have done a much better job with my books to date, one of them publishing one book (and selling off the remainders of five books they took over when they bought out my last Canadian publisher), and the second American house publishing seven of my books in mass market paperback editions so far.

Over the years sixty-seven anthologies and textbooks have reprinted my short stories and essays and most of their publishers have had offices and plants here in Canada. I have no beefs against these, for they have always treated me correctly, even though in the past their fees were much less than the ones paid by American publishers.

One of the strange, laughable things about some Canadian publishers is that the most vociferous nationalists among them are nationalistic only for themselves, and not for their writers or the Canadian printing and bookbinding industries. During one recent month I reviewed two Canadian books for a Toronto newspaper, one published by McClelland & Stewart and the other by M. G. Hurtig (Jack McClelland and Mel Hurtig are both big wheels in the Canadian nationalism caper), and both books were printed and bound in Great Britain. My current

"American" publishers however have their books printed and bound in Canada.

So much for a worm's-eye view of the Canadian publishing scene, circa 1973.

Some time in 1963 I pasted up the tear-sheets of some allegedly humorous essays from Canadian magazines, mainly *Saturday Night,* and took this non-book down to John Colombo at The Ryerson Press. They brought out the book under the title *Author, Author!* in 1964. It bombed, though a few people I talked to later thought it a very funny book. I think I should share the blame for its lack of success with the Ryerson sales department.

In the meantime I was writing a few short stories, some newspaper columns, appearing on some CBC and CTV television and radio shows, and putting in time wondering how to get out of Don Mills. I appeared regularly as a panelist on a CTV show with a popular moderator who was to become a good friend of mine—Rick Campbell, whose show was called "Better Late." I'd made the TV scene about ten years before at the birth of Canadian TV on Nathan Cohen's "Fighting Words" over the CBC. True to the vow I'd made when I returned from the *Star Weekly* assignment with the kidney stoppage, I'd written very few magazine articles since. What began to scare me was that I was becoming a "talking" writer rather than a "writing" writer, and there were enough of *them* around.

By 1965 I found I had fourteen short stories ready for book publication. With the death of quite a number of Canadian consumer magazines the short story market had shrunk considerably and some of these stories had never been printed in a magazine at all. One of these, "Artsy-Craftsy" had been written years before, and had been turned down by a dozen magazines. A much newer story, "The Moose And The Sparrow", was another magazine reject. After both these stories came out in the book "Artsy-Craftsy" was printed in a McGraw-Hill anthology, *Temper Of The Times,* and recently "The Moose And The Sparrow" was sold to Van Nostrand Reinhold for inclusion in an anthology of theirs. Which only bolstered once again my arrogant certainty that I was more often right than the magazine editors were.

Fortunately most of the stories had been read or dramatized over the CBC, and a few had been published in *Chatelaine, Liberty, Tamarack Review, Canadian Home Journal,* the *Toronto Telegram,* and the *Imperial Oil Review.*

It had always been my practice to dedicate my books to members of my immediate family but when Ryerson accepted the book I dedicated it, "To Robert Weaver, broadcaster and editor, who has done more for the modern Canadian short story than anyone else in this country."

Nobody connected with Canadian writing has ever tried to deny this.

A nutty thing happened when it came to giving the book a title acceptable to the publisher. I forget now who was in on the discussion, but there were a couple of assistant editors, perhaps the managing editor, and maybe even Victor Seary, the general manager of Ryerson. I'd picked *Men And Women* as my title long before. Most of the stories in the book—the sole exception being "The Moose And The Sparrow"—dealt with the confrontation of a man and a woman. Besides, it was one of those ambiguous titles that might rope in the unwary bookbuyer who was furtively seeking a sex manual.

With a couple of top executives at the meeting, the younger editors tried to show they were on the ball by suggesting titles, usually the titles of stories in the collection. As for me, I was keeping my own title as my hole card.

Finally, in exasperation over the whole silly business, I said, "For Christ's sake, my last book of stories was titled *Hugh Garner's Best Stories*, which it wasn't, incidentally. Why don't we call this one *Hugh Garner's Second Best Stories* and see what happens?" We eventually settled on *Men And Women* and it was published under that title, in hard covers, in 1966.

An author should never go to a business meeting or luncheon with his editors or publishers unless he remembers the Boy Scout slogan, "Be Prepared."

Before we leave book publishing for a moment and go back to journalism for a change, I have to tell what happened to *Men And Women*.

Ryerson printed 2070 copies, and by January, 1969 they still had 970 copies sitting in their warehouse. In the meantime they had published another book of mine, but the thought of all those unsold copies of my book getting dusty on the shelves, not even being carried by the salesmen any more, used to bug me. I was forever going to Frank Flemington the managing editor and telling him to get rid of them.

Finally, one summer day, I went in to Frank and told him that if he'd remainder them I'd buy them myself at the remainder price. A couple of days later he told me they'd sell me the whole 970 copies at 30¢ apiece. I accepted.

When I told my wife that I'd bought 970 copies of *Men And Women* she almost flipped, picturing stacks of them cluttering up our clothes closets for years to come. I told her I'd stack them in our basement storage closet. When the books were delivered by the Ryerson truck I wheeled them down to the basement and piled them in the closet. Then I went out to peddle them.

The book had retailed at $3.95, which at a royalty of 10 percent would have earned me 39½¢ a copy. I was determined to sell them at a price, 70¢, which would give me my normal royalty.

My first call was at the Acquisitions Office of the Toronto Public Libraries, where I got rid of a 40-book package at 70¢ apiece. I then sold a couple of hundred at the same price to Peter Martin's "Readers' Club of Canada." That year, as for several years, I'd been acting as an instructor in creative writing for two weeks each summer at the Ryerson Polytechnical Institute (no relation to the Ryerson Press), and I took a package or two of the books with me each day to my classes, where I sold them, autographed, at a dollar apiece. The students of the Writers Workshop flocked in from the other classes, and I did a land office business as a book salesman. After my teaching stint was finished I went on a drunk and ended up in a large private sanitarium to dry out and get on my feet again. I returned to Toronto, filled the trunk of my car with books, and peddled them all, to patients, doctors, nurses, visitors, the cleaning staff, waitresses, dieticians, attendants, and everyone else. I ran out of books before I ran out of customers.

Back home once again I sold a package of forty books to a friend of mine, Eleanor Syrett, an English teacher at Leaside High School, for $1 apiece. Later in the year I sold the remainder of the books, almost two hundred I think, to Jack Jensen, the book buyer for Coles Book Stores. I told Jack when we met in his office that although I wanted to rid myself of the books I had left I wouldn't sell them for less than what I'd paid for them, 30¢. He gave me 35¢ a copy.

The way things worked out I made more money out of the book than I would have if The Ryerson Press had sold the 970 copies retail, and, of course, if I'd allowed them to remainder the books themselves my own royalties would have been nothing.

Ryerson, in 1968, brought out three of my old books as "quality paperbacks," *Storm Below* selling at $2.50, *Silence On The Shore* at $2.95, and *Hugh Garner's Best Stories* at $2.50.

The publishers didn't give any advance on royalties on their paperback reprints, so I re-wrote the clause in the contract covering subsidiary rights, which I retained for myself: "The Publisher shall pay to the Author a royalty of seven and one-half percent (7½%) on all sales."

A couple of years later when the United Church was winding down its ownership of The Ryerson Press, prior to selling it to the McGraw-Hill Company of Canada, they ran a huge book sale at Toronto's Varsity Stadium, where they got rid of the clutter from their warehouse, some books which I'm sure must have lain there since the days of Susanna Moodie and Thomas Chandler Haliburton. Among the many thousands of books they sold at cut-rate prices were several hundred copies of my three paperbacks. My wife and I were in Europe at the time, and I didn't hear of the sale until we returned home.

When I next showed up at The Ryerson Press I asked how many copies of my books they'd flogged at the sale. Nobody seemed to know. "Anyhow, what does it matter, Mr. Garner?" a flunkey asked. "They were all sold at below cost, so there are no royalties anyhow." "Like hell there aren't!" I said. "*My* contract reads that I receive a royalty of seven-and-a-half percent on *all* sales."

I finally went in and saw Gavin Clark, who was interim general manager during the pre-sale period of the publishing house. Gavin and I got along very well, due to our proletarian-Establishment polarity as I've mentioned before. I told him that his minions should have read my contract before they sold my books at the sale. He asked me why, and I told him that I was to receive 7½% of the selling price for *all* the books, even if they'd been sold for a dime apiece. He said he'd have the company comptroller look into it. He was as good as his word, and I was paid my royalties for the books that were sold.

Sometime during the mid-sixties Bill Drylie, a freelance columnist for the *Toronto Telegram* died of a heart attack. I'd only met him once, at a cocktail party at the Park Plaza Hotel, when I'd seemed to anger him by mentioning that I'd run copy for his father in 1929, a dour old *Star* reporter who covered the high courts at Osgoode Hall. Soon after his death I received a phone call from Andy MacFarlane, the managing editor of the *Telegram,* asking me to drop in and see him.

Andy asked me if I wanted to take over the dead man's column, and I said I wouldn't mind, if the money was right.

MacFarlane told me that my deceased predecessor had been working as news editor for the Toronto radio station CHUM, and writing the column on the side. It was a short column set right in the middle of the editorial page, and I would be given carte blanche as to content, subject of course to the laws of decency and the newspaper's point-of-view.

Something told me that Andy wasn't sure he wanted me to write the column, and I guessed that my name had come from somebody else on the paper. There are newspapermen who have worked a lifetime on a paper and never get closer to writing their own column than a chair on the rim of the city desk. I surmised that Andy, and some of the other editors, thought the job should be given to a deserving longtime employee.

MacFarlane called in another editor to look me over, Arnold Agnew, who was executive editor of the paper. Agnew seemed to be a cold fish, who looked me over pretty carefully. The three of us went to lunch at a restaurant in The Walker House, where they both questioned me. I told them if they wanted to know how I wrote all they had to do was read the sixty-two "Dissent" columns I'd written for the *Telegram*. Their tenure on the newspaper didn't intimidate me; I'd been writing copy for the *Toronto Daily Star*, as a copy-boy, while both of them had been playing in their cribs.

Later I learned that one of the sub-editors who had charge of the "Dissent" columns when I'd been writing them, had made a big pitch for the regular columnist's job. Anyhow, some time later I was interviewed by Doug McFarlane, the editor-in-chief of the paper, who is now the head of the Department of Journalism at Ryerson Tech. Doug and I got along fine, and he took me in to meet John Bassett, the newspaper's owner. Only then did I realize that it had been Bassett who had put up my name for the job.

I told Mr. Bassett I'd take the job as a columnist, but so far nobody had told me what I was to be paid.

He laughed and said, "Doug McFarlane takes care of that. All I worry about is how much the whole editorial page is costing us." As it turned out I was paid more than my predecessor to start with, and received an increase after the first few months.

In one of my early columns I wrote about an early Depression phenomenon: a string of Toronto storefront musical conservatories run by an outfit called the Harris School of Music. The son-in-law of Harris wrote a personal "Dear John" letter to Bassett suggesting that he fire or discipline me for writing it.

Mr. Bassett passed this guy's letter to me, along with a copy of his own reply to it. In a gentlemanly way he told the man to get lost. I don't know what the guy's beef was anyway, unless he'd been passing off his father-in-law as a Canadian Leopold Stokowski.

The short length of the columns was a bugaboo I hadn't taken into consideration. They were less than three hundred words long, a single page of my double-spaced typing, and trying to put a beginning, a middle, and an end to three hundred words is a tough thing to do. Somehow I managed it, and after his initial doubts were laid to rest Andy MacFarlane and I became good friends.

I wrote my weekly five columns on the weekend, which theoretically gave me the rest of the week to write my own stuff. It didn't take me long to discover that having five full days a week to myself didn't work out as well as expected. As soon as I finished writing the next week's columns, and had driven them down to the *Telegram* or mailed them in, I had to start thinking of columns for the following week.

I never found out which of the *Telegram's* editors I was writing for, and my columns were being edited by editorial page writers, each of whom seemed to be given the job in turn of editing my stuff. *The Telegram's* editorial writers, who were just as bland, scared and subservient as most of their kind seem to be, consisted of a little guy, since retired, who wore the mantle of a civic affairs expert, a self-defrocked rabbi who, no doubt due to a trip he'd taken to Israel, was the paper's "foreign expert," and a couple of others who worked the financial and federal politics sides of the street. I disliked any of them editing my copy.

During the same year I was writing my *Telegram* column I was hired by the Province of Ontario Council for the Arts as a short-term instructor in creative writing at an arts-and-crafts workshop in Quetico Provincial Park west of Humber Bay. On the final day of my course I received a phone call from Arnold Agnew who told me they were killing one of my columns and needed another in its place. I thought it was stupid not to just leave the column out for one day instead of calling me when I was a thousand miles away. Anyhow I told him I'd mail him one. I sat in a motel room in Fort William before driving home via Minneapolis and Chicago and banged out something and mailed it in.

Altogether nine of my daily columns were killed during my columnist year. I didn't know whether they'd been found distasteful by the editorial page pedants, any one of five or six editors, or by whom. I had merely written others in their place. Finally one day I wrote a regular column that consisted of the outlines of the nine columns the paper had killed, and the paper ran it.

When my year as a daily newspaper columnist had just a week more to run I went down to the newspaper offices one morning drunk and spoke to Doug McFarlane, the editor-in-chief. I told him I hadn't had any holidays yet, and I was going away for a couple of weeks. He told me that was fine, and I went on a two-week spree. For a couple of days the next week they ran my name in the usual place, and beneath it the news that I was on vacation. I stayed drunk for the two weeks and took another three to recover. By the time I came to, I felt that I'd blown the job, though there'd been no messages from the paper and my weekly cheques had kept coming in. I called Arnold Agnew and asked him if I was still working for the newspaper. He said he'd check. When he phoned me back he told me they'd decided to cut out the column, needing the room for a couple of new columnists—Doug Fisher and Dalton Camp. At times like this I don't need an electric sign to tell me I'm fired.

Actually the *Toronto Telegram* treated me fine, and I retain nothing but affection for almost everyone from John Bassett down. Writing a daily column was an experience I wouldn't have wanted to miss.

When I wrote my novel *Silence On The Shore* in 1959-60, and it was published in 1962, I'd given the name "Gordon Lightfoot" to a middle-aged alcoholic denizen of the Toronto rooming house which is the locale of the book. My reasons for naming him this were quite innocuous, and I'm usually quite careful in naming characters in books or stories. At first I was going to name him Gordon Proudfoot, as I'd known a friend in my youth called Johnny Proudfoot, but then I thought I'd make the name even more less likely to be the name of a real person and call him "Gordon Lightfoot."

When the book came out none of the critics or book reviewers mentioned the name in anything but its context as a character's name. If I'd heard of Gordon Lightfoot the singer and song-writer at that time I don't remember it, and the reviewers' attitudes to the name seem to bear this out. A few years later however I began to realize that the real Gordon Lightfoot was becoming a very famous person indeed, and here I was stuck with his name which I'd given to an elderly drunk. My "Gordon Lightfoot" stayed that throughout the hard cover edition of the book, and was carried over into the Ryerson quality paperback edition, which had been reproduced by offset printing, a process in which the hard cover pages of a book are reproduced by a photographic reproduction as set up in type.

Some high school kids began to ask me why I'd named my character after *their* Gordon Lightfoot, and I had to try to explain what had happened.

When Simon & Schuster brought out six of my books in a paperback edition, the type was re-set, so that I had a chance to re-name my character. I took a hardbound copy of the book, and changed every "Gordon" in it to "George," or thought I did. The other day a man who had just read the book for the first time, in the Simon & Schuster "Pocket Books" edition, told me that though my character was now called "George," he'd come across a couple of "Gordons" in its pages.

I know that using the name Gordon Lightfoot in the book didn't hurt it, and by everything I read it didn't seem to hurt the real Gordon Lightfoot in his singing and song-writing career. It just shows that in naming fictional characters you don't just have to be careful, you have to be clairvoyant.

After finishing my job as a newspaper columnist I became aware of all the new civic centres, city theatres and such that were being built around the country in the affluent nineteen-sixties. So many new theatres needed not only theatrical companies to play in them but plays to perform. I wrote a letter to Peter Dwyer of the Canada Council pointing this out, and telling him that I intended to re-write three of my television one-act plays for the stage as a trilogy titled *Three Women*. The plays would be *Some Are So Lucky, A Trip For Mrs. Taylor* and *The Magnet*. The plays could be played one after the other in a single night of theatre, using a repertory cast which numbered a total of ten actors and actresses as principals. I asked Mr. Dwyer if the Canada Council would give me a grant to carry out my playwriting.

I received a letter from Mr. Dwyer in which he said that my proposal had been studied by the members of the Canada Council, and that they would be willing to give me a playwriting grant. How much did I think it should be? I wrote back telling him that I thought $3,000 was adequate, and he and the Canada Council awarded me the sum I'd asked for.

My play trilogy was sent to and rejected by the following

231

theatre groups: Neptune Theatre, Canadian Theatre Centre, Crest Theatre, Canadian Players, Playhouse Theatre Company, Canadian Plays Committee, Playmakers Theatre Foundation, Manitoba Theatre Centre, Sarnia Little Theatre, and The Arvida Players. The Brockville Theatre Guild turned down the trilogy, but put on *A Trip For Mrs. Taylor,* as a single one-act play, on November 4th, 1966. I considered re-writing *Silence On The Shore* for the theatre, and Esse Ljungh gave me a lot of invaluable advice on how I could lay out a stage setting of the interior of a rooming house on a stage. I intended to do it with a two-floored set, and attic stairs and a cellar landing. I would switch the action from one room to another by blacking out the other rooms and having each room light up in turn. Unfortunately after my trilogy received such a poor reception across the country I gave up my playwriting aspirations for the time being.

In 1967-1968 I rewrote *Cabbagetown* from the one full-length manuscript I had preserved from the 1940's. I took it in to Robin Farr, a new editor-in-chief who had come to The Ryerson Press from the Queens-McGill Press. Robin had it read by the editors, and they brought it out as a hard cover book in 1968. One day as Robert Weaver and I were walking from the CBC radio building to Yonge Street I told him that Ryerson was bringing out a full-length version of *Cabbagetown.* "I'm glad to hear that," he said. "There's so many of you novelists who have old novels stuck in your craws," or words to that effect. He mentioned Morley Callaghan, W. O. Mitchell and a couple of others who had been trying for years to get certain books published.

I was happy about it too, and I thanked God I hadn't destroyed *every* manuscript of the book years before.

When I'd started out as a writer in 1946 my only ambition had been to write a book of good short stories. Actually, the novel hadn't mattered much at all, except as a way to gain a reputation so that I could sell the short stories I had on hand. However, the tremendous difficulties I had in getting *Cabbagetown* published had angered and disgusted me so much that I'd made up my mind to become both a short story writer *and* a novelist, even if it was only to confound the editors and publishers who had turned it down so cavalierly. My determination, yes, and my arrogance, comes from those early years when *nobody* would consider for publication some of the best short stories ever written in Canada. For years when my family and I were existing in poverty and I was supporting us in crummy jobs that nobody should have to work at, just one small cheque or even a few short words of encouragement would have helped me. When I finally broke out as a professional writer I made up my mind to be a full-time one.

Since the age of six Toronto has been my home, and I decided to make that city my writing turf, the locale of most of my future books and short stories. It is axiomatic that a writer writes best about the things he knows best, and I know Toronto better than I know anywhere else. William Faulkner gave his hometown of Oxford, Mississippi the name "Jefferson," and built a fictionalized county around it; Thomas Wolfe wrote about his home town of Ashville, North Carolina; John Steinbeck used California's Salinas Valley and the seacoast town of Monterey as the setting for his novels and stories; John O'Hara set his in the Eastern anthracite region of Pennsylvania, where he'd been born; Willa Cather used Nebraska; and so on through a hundred writers.

My first Toronto book was *Cabbagetown,* followed by two insignificant novels both set in Toronto, *Present Reckoning* and *Waste No Tears.* Another novel with a Toronto setting was *Silence On The Shore,* which dealt with a rooming house in the Annex district of the city. Though *Present Reckoning* dealt with the downtown area, I was anxious to write a novel set in that part of the city's inner core called Moss Park.

While I had written *Cabbagetown* and *Silence On The Shore* as serious sociological studies in fiction of two completely different city neighborhoods, I wanted to depict Moss Park, not only sociologically but featuring its criminal elements, its prostitutes, junkies, and criminals. I thought the best way of doing this would be to write the book as a mystery novel, to be published preferably in paperback.

I wrote the book, titled *The Sin Sniper,* the theme of it being a psychopathic personality who because of childhood traumas has developed an ingrained pathological mysogyny. Using this character, and his police opponents of the Metro Toronto Homicide Squad to carry the plot, a great deal about the neighborhood and its citizens could be revealed in the locales of scenes and the background of the book.

At the time the book was written I was under contract to The Ryerson Press, and under my contract they had an option on the novel. I was labouring under no delusions that they would publish the book, but I gave them first refusal which was what our contract called for.

In a few days I received a phone call from Robin Farr, the Ryerson editor, and I'd hardly got inside his office when he handed me the bound copy of the manuscript as if it were burning his fingers.

"We can't publish this, Hugh," he said.

"Okay."

"We're a lot more liberal in our publishing policy than we were once, but I'm afraid this particular book is not for us."

"Okay, Robin," I said.

We chatted for a few minutes, then I walked out of his office once more free of the shackles of being tied down to a publisher.

Over the next year or two I submitted the manuscript to the following publishing houses, being unaware at the time that there were any branch offices of American paperback publishers in Canada: Doubleday & Co., Longmans Canada, M. G. Hurtig, Anansi Press, and even Peter Martin Associates. They all kept it for varying lengths of time, but none were interested in publishing it, not even Anansi and Peter Martin, who I thought needed money so badly they'd publish anything that would sell, written by an established Canadian author. The only kind word I'd had about the book was from an assistant editor at Doubleday, a young lady whose name unfortunately I forget. She had been a social worker in Moss Park, and thought the book was "right on."

I no longer despaired about selling my books; I knew *The Sin Sniper* was a saleable property, even though Mel Hurtig had sent it down to paperback houses in the United States, and they'd turned it down. In the meantime Robert Weaver of the CBC had it read and bought it to be dramatized on the CBC radio program "Radio Stage." It proved popular on a week-long series, and was subsequently broadcast again on the show, "Theatre Ten-Thirty." It had been directed by Bob Christie, and I believe it was the first radio play he'd ever directed.

At one stage I received a phone call from Westminster Films, and Miss Lee Gordon there held the manuscript for some time, before I went down to her office and picked it up. Luckily for me I'd made some Xerox copies of the script down at The Ryerson Press.

During the summer, while I was instructing at the writers' workshop at Ryerson Tech. I heard that Hugh Kane, formerly second-in-command at McClelland & Stewart had moved into the Macmillian Company as president, with John Gray moving up to chairman-of-the-board.

Having gotten along well with Hugh over the years since I'd

been a one-book McClelland & Stewart author, I took one of my manuscript copies of *The Sin Sniper* with me to my class. When I finished at 10:30 that morning I walked the short block to the Macmillian offices, and gave Hugh my manuscript to read.

I can't remember the whole sequence of events from then on, but I know he sent one copy of the script to England, and I gave him another copy, which he sent to New York. Who read it in either place, or whether it was read at all, I don't know.

In the meantime, some months before, I had written another novel, or part of it, which I'd titled *A Nice Place To Visit*.

This last novel had started out as a short story, but I'd found my theme took up too much space for ordinary short story length, and I couldn't see it as a mid-sized novella. My original short story theme had been that a young man serving a lifetime sentence for murder after being accused of strangling his girl friend, had protested his innocence so much that a friend of his, an older man, in the penitentiary, had decided when he came out to carry out an investigation of the kid's innocence or guilt. He'd found that the boy had been guilty as charged, and his findings had been corroborated by the kid committing suicide.

It was my intention at first to use the ex-con to conduct the investigation, but this would have brought up too many complications in a town the size of the one I had in mind. A lawyer would have been fine, but my knowledge of the law and lawyers is not great enough to use one as a protagonist. Why not an older journalist? Sure, why not? I am an older journalist myself, and my protagonist could be sent to the small town to investigate a two-year-old crime for an exposé magazine. And that was essentially what I wrote about.

When it was finished, and by this time I knew Macmillan were never going to publish *The Sin Sniper*, even though they had two copies of the script, I sold the broadcast rights to the new novel to CBC "Radio Stage." I took another copy of the script to Hugh Kane at Macmillan.

Things dragged on, and on, and on. I began phoning Hugh Kane every week, and he would tell me that they were having an editorial conference on Friday afternoon, and he'd call me back. Then he didn't.

By this time in my writing life I'd learned to tell a publisher's stall when I received one. I knew that Hugh didn't want to publish either book, but didn't like to tell me. God, I'm a guy who has been turned down by every publisher in the country at one time or another! I'm a professional writer; I'm used to such things. They don't fill me with hatred for the man who turns me down. I merely take back my manuscript and sell it somewhere else, especially when I know it is a good one. There was no doubt in my mind that both *The Sin Sniper* and *A Nice Place To Visit* were good books, each in its own way. I also knew, of course, that neither one would set the literary world on fire, and neither one had been written with this in mind; they were merely competent, journeyman novels that would sell.

One morning I took a copy of *A Nice Place To Visit* down to Robin Farr at Ryerson. I'd phoned him first of course and made an appointment.

When I entered his office I found another man sitting there, who was introduced to me as Gavin Clark, the new general manager. I handed my manuscript to Robin, and we sat around talking about books and publishing for a few minutes. Then I bid them both goodbye.

The next day I had a phone call from Hugh Kane, asking me to have lunch with him the following day. I promised to meet him at 12:30 in Les Cavaliers Restaurant on Church Street, not a stone's throw from where The Sin Sniper had lived.

Usually an invitation to lunch by a publisher means he is buying a book, but I knew Hugh wasn't. I figured the lunch was going to give him the surroundings in which to turn down both of my novels. I'm not crazy about steaks or steak houses anyway, and I find them among the dullest places in the world to eat.

That same afternoon I received a phone call, this time from Robin Farr.

"Yes, Robin?" I asked, knowing it was too early for *him* to have turned down *A Nice Place To Visit*.

"I've got good news for you, Hugh," he said. "When you brought your book in yesterday I gave it to Gavin Clark to read. Actually it was the first book manuscript he's ever read. He told me, 'We can't lose this one.' I've been reading it myself, and I like it too. I'll finish it tonight. Can you come in in a couple of days and sign the contract?"

"Thanks, Robin. Sure I can come in."

"How much of an advance do you want?"

"A thousand."

"All right. Will you be in on Thursday?"

"Right, and thanks again."

The next day I had lunch with Hugh Kane.

At first Hugh and I talked about generalities, as he sipped a drink while I drank a ginger ale. I forget what we ordered for lunch, but I know I didn't order steak; I never do. After we had finished eating Hugh said to me over our coffees "You know, Hugh, that our New York and London offices turned down *The Sin Sniper*. I think it's really a paperback, and—"

"Hell, I've always thought that."

"I can send it up to a friend of mine in Richmond Hill, who runs Simon & Schuster of Canada. He can bring it out as a pocket book."

I nodded. I'd missed catching the man's name but now I knew there was a paperback publisher within driving distance of my house.

Hugh went on. "He'll probably offer us four percent royalties, but I'll hold out for six."

"Okay. How about *A Nice Place To Visit*?"

"I don't know about that one yet; I have people reading it now."

"You may as well forget it, Hugh," I said. "I just sold it to The Ryerson Press."

"Good, Hugh," he said. "I'm glad you've found a publisher for it."

"Thank you. What about *The Sin Sniper*?"

"Well of course we wash our hands of *it* now," he answered.

"Good enough."

When we left we found ourselves in the middle of a fooferaw in the vestibule where the coats were hung and the overshoes stored. The Roman Catholic Archbishop of Toronto had had his rubbers stolen, and the restaurant manager and a couple of waiters were in a flap. It seemed like a fitting end somehow to the Hugh Kane-Hugh Garner lunch.

The next day I went down to The Ryerson Press and signed the contract with Gavin Clark for *A Nice Place To Visit*. Robin Farr witnessed the contract for me. Then I accepted an invitation to lunch with Gavin at his club. I think we both had liver-and-onions or some such sensible dish. The only other time I'd been in the Toronto Club, which is strictly Establishment, not like the Granite or the National clubs which are for any parvenu with the membership fee and annual dues, was in the company of Mr. Clifford Sifton, also for lunch. On that occasion we both had lamb stew. Steaks and steak houses are for sales promotion managers and "sales engineers" who flog plastic lighting fixtures. We members of the proletariat and *la haute* prefer stews and liver.

I thanked and said goodbye to Gavin at his club and ran up Bay Street to deposit my advance-on-royalties cheque at my bank.

A couple of days later I phoned Simon & Schuster in Richmond Hill, a dormitory town about fourteen miles north of where I live in Toronto, and asked the switchboard operator for the name of the Canadian president or general manager. She told me it was Mr. James Smallwood. "Of course," I said. "May I speak to him please?"

She connected me, and I told Jim Smallwood who I was, and that I had a manuscript I'd like him to consider.

"Sure thing, Hugh," he said. "Bring it in tomorrow morning."

When we met we talked about people we both knew from twenty years before, a man who had then been sales manager for William Collins Sons, Jack Kent Cooke, and Gordon Rumgay, who had been circulation manager for *Liberty*.

Smallwood said, "I'll lay it right on the line, Hugh. I'll have some people out there—" pointing to the outer office "—read your book, and if we decide to publish it I'll give you a thousand dollar advance, and six percent royalties on every copy we sell."

I remembered Hugh Kane saying, "He'll offer us four percent, but we'll hold out for six," and I was sure glad I didn't have to split my fee with the Macmillan Company.

"Fair enough," I told Smallwood.

"The contract will come from New York, and they keep a royalty fund down there from which you'll be paid twice a year."

Simon & Schuster bought *The Sin Sniper,* and Jim Smallwood and I signed the contract on March 13th, 1970. Gavin Clark and I had signed the Ryerson Press contract for *A Nice Place To Visit* on February 19th. Both books were brought out the following August and September. *The Sin Sniper,* that had been turned down by everybody else, sold 50,000 copies in its first printing.

Incidentally, though I'd forgotten it at the time I sold the book, the name of one of my homicide squad detectives in *The Sin Sniper* was Jim Smallwood. Another case of pure character-naming coincidence, or perhaps a lucky omen. In my next book about the Metropolitan Toronto homicide squad, which I have been writing, on and off, for some time, I have retired that particular detective-sergeant.

When a writer depends for his livelihood on his writing he must, from necessity, begin thinking of writing or publishing something else as soon as his current work is disposed of. Not that this is a constant grind, or what one tri-named lady author once told me was "real physical labor." God, I wish some writers had worked at my early jobs! A writer once he has established himself has plenty of leisure time. This is one of the rewards of the trade.

During the late nineteen-fifties, with our children old enough to take care of themselves, my wife and I began to travel. Our first project was to drive over every mile of Ontario highway marked in red on the road maps, and this we did. We also drove over most of the highways in Quebec and New Brunswick, as we'd done earlier with our children over most Nova Scotia highways. We even circled each one of the Great Lakes one summer, and took weekend trips through the Appalachians.

On these trips, and on many more which I made alone, I picked up short story locales, nostalgic memories of my hitchhiking days, and ideas for articles and columns. On one trip to the Maritimes I found magazine articles for *Saturday Night* in interviews with Lord Beaverbrook and Premier Louis Robichaud in Fredericton, New Brunswick, an interview with the general manager of the Dofasco steel mill in Sydney, Nova Scotia, and an interview with the newly-elected premier of that province, Robert Stanfield.

Some of my articles and newspaper columns came from chance wanderings by car, such as finding the West Virginia town where Mother's Day had been founded by a lady years ago; and, on my return trip from instructing at Quetico Park, visiting the small junior high school in Waukegan, Illinois that had been named after the comedian Jack Benny. Dozens of such things came out of our trips.

During the nineteen-sixties we took longer and longer trips, across Canada, to Mexico City by car during which we drove fifteen hundred miles through Mexico, to Florida several times, New Orleans, to Nassau on a cruise ship from Miami, and finally a trip to Europe, which was the first one for my wife. My final driving project was to drive through every state in the continental United States except Alaska, and this we did over a few summers. We went everywhere in the United States, from Fort Kent, Maine to San Isidro, California, and from Blaine, Washington to Key West, Florida, which is as far as you can go into the four corners of the U.S.

Out of these trips, some of which followed the routes I'd taken as a hobo in my youth, came magazine articles and short stories. Among the stories were "Another Day, Another Dollar," "Step-'N-A-Half," "Brightest Star In The Dipper," "Violation Of The Virgins," and "Twelve Miles Of Asphalt." From our trip to Europe came an article I wrote for *The Globe Magazine,* called "Paris Revisited," which described an abortive student riot in St.-Germain-des-Pres, where we lived in a lovely little hotel next door to the Brasserie Lipp, and across the street from the Café Fleur and Les Deux Magots. A criss-crossing of England, Scotland and Wales, and a trip that included the Riviera and Monte Carlo, with a brief visit to Genoa and Rome, gave me material that will come in useful some day I hope.

To those who may wonder what sort of life-style a writer and loner like me lives, I offer the following. My wife and I have always lived simply, yet we are guilty of flagrant extravagance when we travel. For many years when our children were small we became used to doing without social contacts, and I can only remember two or three occasions when we went out in the evenings, and only once when we had a baby-sitter. We've made up for that since, doing our travelling, once, when our son and daughter were teen-agers, to New York and then for a time taking them with us on trips. Over the past ten years, since they've been married, we've gone anywhere we wanted to go, not waiting for retirement as so many elderly people we've seen, to give us an opportunity to travel.

I used to carry a Diners' Club card but switched to the American Express several years ago. We eat in roadside diners and in Guide Michelin restaurants (two or three-star, never four) with equanimity, and have always taken scheduled airlines rather than charter flights. Our hotels and motels from Las Vegas to the Riviera have been middleclass opulent.

We live now in a one-bedroom apartment in a medium-sized North Toronto apartment house, close to a main shopping street and a short walk from the subway line, which we invariably take to go downtown. Were it not for the fact that my daughter and her family live ten miles from us in the eastern suburb of

Scarborough and my son and his family about twenty miles in the other direction in the town of Brampton, my car, which currently is a six-year-old fairly large Ford compact, would be totally useless.

Neither my wife Alice nor I have any pretentions, social or otherwise. When we met for the first time in 1940, appropriately at the corner of Mountain Hill and the Rue des Matelots (Street of the Sailors) on a first date arranged by her sister Alma, I was sitting on a garbage can. Both of us come from the working class, she the rural French-Canadian Catholic one and I the English-Canadian Protestant urban one. We have few close friends, but with five grandchildren who needs any? Our visits are usually to our children's places or to my in-laws quite a number of whom now live within driving distance in Southern Ontario.

We have no desire for status or prestige, and some years ago gave up purchasing subscription tickets to the theatre. If there's a play we want to see we see it, but most of our relaxation comes at the movies where we manage to see most of the better pictures that come to town. Owning a cottage, boat, snowmobile or any other adjunct to the desperately empty lives of middle-class Canadians is out of our ken but we are liberal enough to grant others these pleasures or escapes just as we are willing to grant others the use of narcotics or any personal escape they wish to follow.

Probably because I moved so many times as a child I have an aversion to moving, and since leaving Toronto Island in 1953 (with one minor spell in the suburbs) we've had only two landlords in the past twenty years. Due to another psychological quirk of mine, but not my wife's, I've never wanted to own a square foot of property and so never have. I want to be free to move at any time if I have to, and with the exception of my car and modest household furnishings everything we own (and we own everything jointly) is in quickly convertible liquid assets.

My only personal vice is very occasionally drinking to excess, while Alice is a frustrated gambler who loves bingo and slot-machines.

Following the sales of *The Sin Sniper* and *A Nice Place To Visit* I had two book projects in mind. One of them was the middle book of a Toronto trilogy which would consist of *Cabbagetown,* the second book, and *Silence On The Shore*. My second project was another paperback mystery, using my Metropolitan Toronto

Police homicide squad inspector, Inspector McDumont, in a murder in the Toronto suburban enclave known as Don Mills.

The way I planned it the second book of my trilogy would be a fairly long novel, bringing Ken Tilling, my protagonist from *Cabbagetown,* out of World War Two, and continuing until his death at the age of forty-seven in 1960. It would also carry forward the lives of some of the survivors among my characters from the depression years in *Cabbagetown,* and introduce some of those whose lives have already been depicted in *Silence On The Shore.*

Because this book was to be a long and serious one I needed a financial guarantee behind me before embarking on it, despite the fact that I'd already written its first three chapters.

The best way to write a novel—Ernest Hemingway once answered a woman's question as to where was the best *place,* by telling her the best place was in your head—anyway, the best *way* to write a novel is to write it without interruption from beginning to end. The worst possible way it seems to me is to break off a piece of creative writing to make a living writing journalism. Not only because the novelist has to keep switching from creative writing to journalese and back again, but because he loses the thread of his story, its continuity, and the rapport he has with his characters.

In 1969 I applied for a Canada Council grant to enable me to write Book Number Two of my projected trilogy. Letters of recommendation were furnished by William French, the literary editor of the *Globe & Mail,* Earle Toppings, who was then employed by the Ontario Institute for Studies In Education, and Robin Farr, the editor-in-chief of The Ryerson Press.

When the literary awards were announced I was not one of the recipients. I received a letter from Mr. Jules Pelletier, Chief of the Awards Service of the Canada Council, explaining that there was a shortage of funds for arts awards that year and that they were holding my application in abeyance until the middle of summer, when extra funds might be forthcoming. I received another letter from Mr. Pelletier in July telling me my application had had to be turned down, but to try again next year.

I wrote him, thanking both him and The Canada Council for their consideration, and wrote explanatory letters to my three referees, thanking them for their recommendations. I decided to postpone the writing of the book.

In the meantime Jim Smallwood of Simon & Schuster had talked to me of the possibility of bringing out several of my books simultaneously, and I gave his firm copies of all my previous books. Simon & Schuster decided to re-publish in a simultaneous paperback series *Storm Below, Cabbagetown, Silence On The Shore, Hugh Garner's Best Stories, A Nice Place To Visit,* and a second printing of *The Sin Sniper.* They were brought out in November, 1971.

During the summer of 1971 I was approached by George Truss, a former advertising manager for The Ryerson Press, who asked me if I had any books that General Publishing-Musson could consider for their paperback series called "Paperjacks." I told him that Simon & Schuster were bringing out six of my books, but that General Publishing-Musson could consider *Present Reckoning, Author! Author!* and *Men And Women.* He made an appointment for us to meet with their Vice-President, Al Knight.

George and I met with Mr. Knight one morning, and he in turn called in the firm's new editor, a young man named Tom Fairley. I left them copies of the three books, and George Truss, who received $35 for each publishable book he brought to the firm, said he'd keep in touch with me. A week later Al Knight left the firm for a destination unknown to me at least, and had been replaced by Tom Fairley, who I suppose took over his desk and his title. This was just another example of literary musical chairs, but lacking any shock effect after the ones I'd survived in the past.

After I'd given him plenty of time to consider the books I phoned Fairley and asked him whether he wanted to publish them. He asked me if I had to sell the three of them as a package, and I told him no, he could reprint only two of them if he liked. I sent him a letter to this effect, telling him I would settle for a smaller advance on royalties than I usually received, and six percent royalties on retail sales.

Fairley told me he wanted to publish *Men And Women* and *Present Reckoning,* but not *Author! Author!* I told him that was all right with me, and asked him when we would sign the contract. He told me he would draw one up as soon as he could find one that was suitable, and was studying various contracts at the moment. I thought this was a funny bloody thing for a publisher to have to do; hell, I could show him a dozen book contracts of my own to choose from. I told him that although a book contract was a piece of legal legerdemain I was prepared to cross out any clauses I might not agree with in the one he finally made up his mind to use. I'd discovered in the meantime that he was a former employee of the CBC, who had taken a year off to go back to university before being hired by General

243

Publishing. Whether he had any literary or publishing background I didn't know, but it does substantiate what I said in a previous chapter about almost anyone being able to get a job in the literary business as an editor.

I kept phoning him for a decision on the contract, and he kept stalling me. I knew that he was either completely in the dark about how to buy book rights, was himself being stalled by the president of the firm, or was just a natural procrastinator. After a few weeks of this nonsense I phoned him while I was drunk, which is as sure a way I know of getting some kind of action. The next day I received the copies of *Present Reckoning* and *Men And Women* by registered mail, along with a short note referring to whatever ultimatum I'd given him over the phone. I phoned him again, and asked him what had become of my copy of *Author! Author!* He told me he'd given it back to George Truss long before that. I then phoned the Truss house, and asked his wife to please have George call me. He never did. If he reads this and would like me to autograph *Author! Author!* I'll gladly do it.

Later I heard from another writer that some publishing houses often find it hard to make up their minds about books and hold off authors for months. That cheered me up a little bit, knowing I wasn't the only one. If a publisher or editor suffers from indecisiveness that's *his* hangup and *his* ulcer he's feeding. I refuse to share them with him.

During the nineteen-sixties, when governments were throwing millions of dollars into the education factories such as universities, and teachers and professors became grossly overpaid to make up for their past years of penury, many institutions of higher learning began buying the notes, manuscripts, and correspondence of Canadian authors. This resulted in some real fooferaws among Canadian writers. I was told by one archivist that a noted Canadian poet had sold parts of his paper garbage to four different universities, and heard of an equally well-known novelist who had begged people to write to him so he could amass a saleable correspondence file. Over the years I had built up a large collection of literary correspondence, first editions of my books, notes, TV scripts, radio contracts, books of press criticism, other trivia, and almost everything pertaining to my trade but original manuscripts. Old manuscripts I had gaily torn up as soon as the books from them had been published.

One day I spoke about my collection of papers to Robert Weaver, for I was aware that such universities as Toronto, York, Western Ontario, McMaster and Sir George Williams, were buy-

244

ing such collections for their libraries and archives. Bob Weaver, besides being my only link with the literati and Academe, is also my posthumous literary executor.

Bob asked me if I had any particular university in mind, and I told him no. He said he'd get in touch with Professor Douglas Spettigue of Queen's University and find out what the score was. He was as good as his word, and one Saturday afternoon he and Doug Spettigue came to my apartment and looked over my collection of thick looseleaf books of correspondence back to 1948, a couple of recent manuscripts I hadn't got around to tearing up, magazine tear-sheets, press clippings, and copies of all my books including the leather-bound copy of my Governor General's Award winner.

Spettigue said he'd report what I had to the aquisitions committee of the Douglas Library at Queen's and let me know what they said. A week later I received a phone call from him, telling me he was passing through Toronto on a certain day on his way to London, Ontario, and would drop in to pick up the material at the price we'd agreed upon. He did this, handing me a cheque, had a light lunch with my wife and me, and drove off.

It was a far different type of operation from the one I'd had with too many publishers, and the money was a welcome windfall. Next to the money was my satisfaction in getting rid of what I'd quite often looked upon as garbage. I felt a slight twinge of sorrow as I contemplated the thousands of dollars worth of original manuscripts I'd so happily tossed in the fire over the years.

Every year now I drive down to Queen's in Kingston, Ontario, and deposit in their archives the past twelve month's collection of letters, manuscripts and assorted *minutiae*. My agreement with the university was for my lifetime's output, and I live up to it. Besides it's one sure way of cleaning out my files.

Last year I received a letter from the Bibliographer of Special Collections telling me they were moving my material from the Douglas Library to the archives, to rest alongside similar stuff once belonging to John Buchan and Donald MacDonald, the president of the New Democratic Party. Whether this was because it had suddenly become important, or was a way of burying it forever, I didn't ask.

Apparently it is consulted by students, for I received a bound copy of a Master of Arts thesis from the University of Waterloo some time ago titled *Hugh Garner and Toronto's Cabbagetown,* by Robert J. Reimer, who once interviewed me at my apartment. This young man's interview deserves a mention, for I've been

245

interviewed and taped by quite a number of people over the years. Some young ladies have sipped glasses of my "vintage" Beaujolais Superieur '69, others have quaffed Johnny Walker's Red Label, newspaper guys and high school Can Lit students have generally been Molson's ale drinkers, while one CBC tape interviewer drank a whole new bottle of Gordon's gin in an afternoon, before he became tangled in his tapes.

I remember Mr. Reimer's interview in particular because he turned down scotch, rye, gin, vodka, beer, imported and domestic wine, and even coffee. He told me he was on his way to Africa very soon, and we got chatting about Europe. I told him that present-day Paris was a lot different from the Paris I'd known in 1937, before Madame De Gaulle had shut down the whorehouses. It was only later that I discovered he'd gone to Africa as a missionary. It still doesn't explain to me why he turned down coffee, or came to see me after getting his material from Queen's.

Before I sold Simon & Schuster five of my old books (six counting *The Sin Sniper* brought out in a separate edition the year before) I sold my fourth book of short stories to McGraw-Hill. My last two books at The Ryerson Press had been novels, and I'd collected enough new stories for a book. Publishers, as I've said earlier, don't like books of short stories, but it wasn't my fault they'd bought Ryerson when they did. Anyhow, because they'd also bought my contracts and five of my Ryerson books that were still in print, they shared the royalties that *Cabbagetown* and *A Nice Place To Visit* received from Simon & Schuster. However, I owned all the subsidiary rights to the other three books that Ryerson had brought out as quality paperbacks.

When McGraw-Hill bought out Ryerson in the fall of 1970 it caused a terrible flap among the ranks of the Canadian Nationalist brigade. Until then nobody had given a damn about The Ryerson Press, it was a moribund and decaying echo of its former position in Canadian publishing. It had been referred to previously, as I've already stated, by Jack McClelland as "being run by the United Church" and anyone who doesn't believe it can look it up in the Douglas Library at Queen's. Jack had used the term in a pejorative sense, as everyone else did, until it was sold.

One day while the sale was being made, and the Ontario Conservative cabinet was debating whether or not to allow the sale, and the papers were full of polemics about "American cultural takeovers," and other such crap, I went down to Ryerson.

There was a group of Canadian nationalists and other screw-balls marching with signs in a picket line in front of the building. When I arrived in the editorial offices I was met by an assistant editor, an Englishwoman, who asked me why wasn't I out on the picket line. I told her I didn't care if the firm had been taken over by a Zulu publishing company, and anyhow it had been running in the red long enough, supported by the dimes from the Sunday school collections of the United Church. This woman was actually angry. Today she is working away at McGraw-Hill Ryerson, sublimating her Canadian nationalism beneath her pay cheques.

A few poets, Al Purdy and Milton Acorn among them, gave up their contracts with Ryerson, and Milton Acorn sent a nasty letter to John Macmillan, the McGraw-Hill Ryerson president, after the takeover. To me such people were off their trolleys. The nationality of a writer's publisher is as irrelevant as the nationality of the guy who blows you up with a bomb. The Ryerson Press hadn't even come close to doing a job for Canadian literature for years, as can be proved by their almost non-existent stable of novelists by the time the United Church sold them off.

After the McGraw-Hill takeover I received a letter from John Macmillan, the Canadian president of the company, welcoming me to the firm, and telling me they'd be glad to consider any of my future work I cared to submit. So one day in early 1971 I dropped into McGraw-Hill Ryerson and had a talk with the president and two vice-presidents. A short time later I dropped into the offices again and Charles Sweeny, who had for some time been one of the international vice-presidents working out of New York, came back to the editorial department to see me. He was the same Charles Sweeny who had bought *Storm Below* for William Collins Sons in 1948.

During the spring of 1971 I gathered together 13 short stories, nine of them newly written but four of them older ones, and submitted them for a book. The final story, "Violation Of The Virgins," was of novella length, the longest short story I've ever written. I had chosen *its* title as the title of the book also, for obvious reasons. McGraw-Hill Ryerson accepted them for publication, and I signed a contract for the book on March 9th, 1971.

Things in this writing caper seem to move in cycles. For a long time after I had been turfed out of the TV panel picture and had once again become a working rather than a talking writer, I was left to myself to write my stories and novels, and this suited me fine. It wasn't too good though from a financial point of view, and I found myself mentally planning alternatives to working as a novelist. I didn't come up with too many good ideas, but I had no great fear of slipping back down the socio-economic scale. I'd started out with no money at all and a young family to support, and that familiar situation of the young had been overcome.

Since the age of forty-eight I'd been a grandfather, and now I had four grandchildren, the two oldest belonging to my daughter and the next two to my son. In my sixtieth year I sometimes paused and wondered how I'd ever survived, and I'm not talking about wars and such things in my youth but the way I'd abused myself with drink through my early middle age. My earlier frenetic drinking, the "let's drink and be merry for tomorrow we die," sort of thing—and believe me I died on many a tomorrow morning—had given way to months of sobriety punctuated with the occasional binge.

From my mid-thirties to the onset of my fifties had been my worst drinking years, on Kingston Road in Toronto's East End and in Don Mills. I'd never excused my drinking, taken the pledge, joined A.A., or gone on antabuse. Drinking was part of my lifestyle, and though I was perfectly aware that I couldn't handle liquor, I never gave up trying. My heavy drinking bouts postponed a lot of writing but didn't succeed in stopping it, and thanks to a strong constitution that I attributed to my deprived childhood and a rough-and-hungry young manhood, I always managed to recover in the nick of time. And *that's* an old man's paragraph, if I ever read one.

It has been much said that drunkenness and writing go together; that drinking is a complement to writing and journalism, or vice-versa. So far nobody has proved this theory, and there are excellent writers among social drinkers as well as among drunks. I've even heard of a couple of writers who were tee-totalers.

A few years ago I was asked by Barry Callaghan, the son of my old friend Morley, who was an English professor at Atkinson College, York University, to go up there one evening and speak to his students. We drove up there in Barry's car, following the heaviest snowfall of the year, and there were only about a dozen students who had braved the elements to attend. I spoke extemporaneously, usually in answer to questions, in a seminar in one of the common rooms. That was the first time I had met Barry, though he had been the book editor at the *Toronto Telegram* when I was a columnist on the paper.

Following this, I fell into a haphazard routine of college speaking engagements: to Doug Spettigue's graduate English class at Queen's, to John Drew's photography class at Ryerson Polytechnic, to an English class conducted by Tony Hopkins at Glendon College, York University, and others. I also made some biographical tapes, for the CBC, for Victor Hoar who was writing a book about the Canadians in the Spanish Civil War, for Mac Reynolds who was collecting Spanish War tapes for the CBC archives, for Earle Toppings at the Ontario Institute for Studies in Education (for whom I also made a filmed interview), and for other groups and individuals, including a filmed interview at Ryerson Tech.

During the early spring of 1972 McGraw-Hill Ryerson arranged two speaking engagements for me at McMaster and Brock universities on consecutive Saturdays. Two speakers were invited, the poet Irving Layton and myself. When I asked them at McGraw-Hill Ryerson what my fees were to be they told me there were no fees. This angered me, for I knew that Layton wouldn't speak without a fee, and the person at my publisher's who had made the deal should have known better than to think *I* would. To make it worse the dual speaking dates were being sponsored by the Ontario Department of Education, under the direction of Mr. Albert State, a department functionary from St. Catherines.

McGraw-Hill Ryerson promised to pay my expenses and also give me a small fee for accepting the engagements, which they did. I was glad to see that all my books, the six from Simon & Schuster and the five from McGraw-Hill Ryerson, were well displayed, and I met quite a number of English teachers at the universities.

During the years 1970 to 1972 I had turned down many invitations to speak in high schools, in Paris, Ontario, Leaside High School, a few blocks from where I live, a high school on Manitoulin Island, and quite a few around other parts of Metropolitan Toronto. I turned down these invitations with genuine regret, for getting to the high school students is much more important for Canadian literature than speaking to a group of undergrads in a university. During the winters I invariably turn down requests, no matter what the fee, to speak at universities.

One day I received a phone call from a student at a high school in the Toronto suburb of Etobicoke, and on a Saturday afternoon he and two of his classmates and a tape recorder came to my apartment. They stayed a couple of hours, and I answered their questions about writing in general and my own books and short stories in particular. A short time before writing this chapter I was in the men's clothing department of a large downtown store when I was approached by a young man who told me he was the teacher of the Etobicoke high school students who had taped the interview with me. He told me that the taped interview had proved to be the highlight of his English classes, which pleased me. It wasn't until later that I remembered an obscene remark I'd made about him on the tape, when one of the students had quoted him as saying something I didn't believe. I hope the kids had had sense enough to erase it, but they probably didn't.

About a month later I received another phone call, this time from a Scarborough high school, but the kid who called me pronounced my name as if it were spelled "Gardner." That was enough to show me that he'd probably never heard of me or read anything I'd written, so I turned him down.

A couple of winters ago, before the FLQ crisis in Quebec, I received a phone call from a young man in Montreal, who told me he was a graduate student at a Montreal classical college. He asked me if he and a friend could come to my place and shoot a short movie of me. He gave me his phone number, and told me that the movie would be used in English classes at various Quebec colleges. I agreed at first, but after thinking it over I phoned him and cancelled the filming. He was quite angry over my cancellation, but I'd become suspicious about him. I reasoned that it could be a group of FLQ people, who could do anything with movie film, setting me up as a typical WASP *maudit Anglais,* editing the film so that I would come out as an idiot, or anything else. Perhaps my suspicions were merely a reflection of my own paranoia, but I was adamant, especially when my original caller told me there'd be a team of five of them coming to Toronto, not just a couple as he'd had me believe at first.

Another university invitation to speak came from Mr. Lloyd Person of the Regina campus, University of Saskatchewan, who told me they would be holding a weekly series of seminars during the fall months of 1972, and asking me my fee and so on to appear at one of these. As this was in the spring, I told him that as far as I knew I'd be able to go out there in Septem-

250

ber or October, and he accepted my suggested fee and expense arrangements. We corresponded during the summer, and he told me he had also arranged an appearance at their Saskatoon campus for the night following the one at Regina. Later on he told me he'd had a request for me to speak on the day following my Saskatoon appearance at the University of Alberta in Calgary. His final letter to me ruined the whole thing. Instead of September or October dates for my visit I'd been put off to December. Nobody gets me out on those Prairies in the winter any more. I wrote and cancelled the three appearances.

The Prairies are wonderful places to visit—for other people. Whenever I go out West I'm either arrested in Vancouver or felled with poisoned booze in Manitoba. I received a request for a prize donation by a service club in Wainright, Alberta, and sent them a book manuscript, which they didn't have the courtesy to acknowledge, but the strangest and most unprofessional deal of all was tried on me by an outfit called Project Canada West. This outfit sent me a request on July 5th, 1972, allowing them to Xerox 50 copies of "A Trip For Mrs. Taylor." They mentioned some imaginary correspondence between myself and a Mr. G. L. Glaicar, whoever he is. This project, allied with the Canada Studies Foundation, wanted me to quote them a reprint fee and also give them permission "to conduct an experiment during the fall semester, 1972, in Campbell Collegiate, Regina, Saskatchewan" . . . and . . . "we request your permission to make 50 copies of the material for the trial period only. At the end of this experiment we will make final selections . . ." In other words, I let them run off fifty copies of my short story, they use it in a classroom—or maybe fifty classrooms for all I know—then they select whatever stories they deem fit, and find a publisher to bring them out in a textbook. Incidentally, it is left to me to make financial arrangements with the publisher who brings out the textbook.

After receiving a second letter of July 19th I wrote them a letter of refusal in which I said, "Regarding 'A Trip For Mrs. Taylor,' it seems to me that using it first as a classroom study, then finding a publisher for the short stories liked or chosen by the students, is doing things ass-backwards . . ."

There was a great upsurge in Canada's interest in its own literature in 1971. During 1972 I was asked for my permission to reprint short stories of mine by a clutch of Canadian publishing houses. The year before most permission requests had come from the United States and West Germany, which illustrates what I've already said about cycles.

251

Early in 1971 I received a letter from Dr. James Foley, Head of English, Port Colbourne High School, in the Ontario town of that name; Jim Foley, probably the only Ph.D. who came out of the old north of Cabbagetown neighborhood during the Depression, and who never uses his doctorate title. He comes from Carlton Street, east of Parliament, the same stretch of street that brought forth Gordon Sinclair.

Jim Foley had made up his mind to feature Canadian writing in his classes at Port Colbourne, and had written to many Canadian writers and publishers asking them either to participate in a day's Canadian literary activities in March, to be called "Canada Day," or send some of their books for display purposes. Most of those to whom he wrote ignored both his request and his letter. I accepted his invitation, sent him a box of my books, and told him I'd be glad to participate in "Canada Day."

For years I'd been listening to the talking writers bitching about the lack of attention paid to Canadian writers—some of whom couldn't hack it here and had taken off for London, New York and Hollywood—and here was a little English teacher down in a small canal town on Lake Erie wanting to do something for them, and they didn't have either the courtesy or the guts to help him.

To make a long story short, "Canada Day" was a huge success, with William Davis, the newly-elected Premier of Ontario as guest speaker and a corporal's guard of poets and writers at the school. Because I was just about the only person who had accepted Foley's invitation, and had told him how to get Canadian books from the publishers for his library, the school library was christened The Hugh Garner Resource Centre, which is just about the finest honour ever paid me.

That first year "Canada Day" received accolades only from the press down in the Niagara peninsula, but in 1972 there were quite a few well-known poets and writers in attendance, and Jack McClelland was the guest speaker. A local service club took over some of the expenses, there were visiting high school teachers from all over Ontario, and even the *Toronto Star* ran a full-page story by Danny Stoffman about the affair. Jim Foley was appointed a sort of roving ambassador of Canadian literature by the Canada Studies Foundation. The James Foley plan, as I call it, is taking off all over the country, as I can tell by the number of textbooks and anthologies of Canadian poems, short stories and essays being published today. Like Mother's Day starting in a little West Virginia village, the appreciation and study by Canadians of their own literature may have begun

252

in a small town Ontario high school, that all the nationalist nuts ignored at the beginning.

In 1971 I received an invitation from D.E.S. Maxwell, the Master of Winters College, York University, to become an Associate Fellow of the college. My name had been put forward by Miriam Waddington, the poet, who is a professor there. When I told an old friend that I had accepted this, without knowing what a "Fellow" was or what he did, my friend broke into laughter. I suppose it *is* laughable that I, high school dropout, anti-intellectual, and professional proletarian, should become a fringe member of academic society. I accepted my first invitation from Des Maxwell, and attended a get-together and buffet dinner at the college. There I met one of my fellow Fellows, whom I had known for years, Eugene Hallman, head of the English-language radio network of the CBC. Gene, who is an Honorary Fellow as opposed to an Associate Fellow, wondered aloud to me who was senior in the heirarchy of college fellowships. I, who don't know the difference between a Dean and a Deacon, and don't give a damn, conceded him seniority.

The professors and other academic people at the dinner were quite friendly, but I felt a little like Mark Twain's Yankee in King Arthur's Court. Having more affinity with Toronto's Don River than with college dons, that was my first and last visit to the college, up to now. Des Maxwell was kind enough to send me a royal blue credit card to the bar of the York Senior Common Room, and I have been invited many times to what I feel sure have been entertaining and enlightening affairs. I'm afraid the halls of Academe are just not my bag, and that for the sake of everyone concerned we should remain forever apart.

Actually my real reason for allowing myself to be appointed a college Fellow was to be able to include it under my name in *The Canadian Who's Who.* Typically, when my entry was sent to me for revisions for a new edition, I forgot all about it.

During the early part of 1972 there was a strike against the CBC by the radio and TV mechanical union, NABET, aided for a while by some announcers, news reporters and others. Before the strike I'd written one short story "Losers Weepers," and Bob Weaver had paid me for a second one, which took me all winter to write.

I've always had great respect for a writer who can depict a

psychotic from his point of view, as William Faulkner did with young Benjy in *The Sound And The Fury,* and Ken Kesey did with his half-breed Indian in *One Flew Over The Cuckoo's Nest.* Though I've used psychotics in two short stories, "The Conversion of Willie Heaps" and "The Sound Of Hollyhocks," I've never used one as my narrator. God willing, some day I will, for I think it is a great challenge to a writer.

My short story "Losers Weepers" has as its protagonist a psychopath. A psychopath is not an insane person, and is often quite intelligent. What separates him from most of humanity is his complete lack of moral discipline or even self-knowledge of this lack in his relationships with others. I tried to depict him in the character Archie Randolph in "Losers Weepers," modelling him on several middle class dropouts I'd known in my Bay Street drinking days.

My second short story, "A Walk On Y Street," was intended to be a story about a square, married, middle class father of two children, who on a Saturday afternoon walk along a downtown street meets up with an old schooldays friend whom he hasn't seen for a great number of years. The boyhood friend turns out to be a homosexual, and during the course of their walk together, the square married man from suburbia finds that he is sexually attracted to the other, that he is indeed a latent homosexual.

I spent a lot of time writing or trying to write this story, but found it impossible. Though as an experienced writer I can put myself into the shoes of a female character, I cannot tell a story from a latent homosexual's point of view. I had to give up the attempt finally, and settle for the square staying square, while slowly becoming aware of his old friend's homosexuality. And that's the way I wrote it.

I'm afraid that trying to write a story from a homosexual's point of view I would only have got either picketed by the Gay Liberation Front or laughed off the bookstands by every homosexual in the country.

But to get back to the CBC-NABET strike.

Because during the length of the strike the CBC could not process radio tapes, etcetera, without the trained operators on the job they had to use material "already in the can" as they say, or at least I hope they do. Bob Weaver ran ten of my old short stories, read by Murray Westgate, on the network program "Anthology." It was a windfall for me, but I'm sorry it had to be at the expense of the guys who were on strike. (My own union, ACTRA, was not supporting the strike for some reason or other.)

As a footnote to what I have said about "Losers Weepers" and "A Walk On Y Street," I received a phone call in October, 1972 from John Moss the editor of *Journal Of Canadian Fiction* in Fredericton, New Brunswick. John told me that his Halifax printers had refused to set up a short story for an issue of his book that was due to go to press, because they were afraid of or objected to the story's obscenities. I sent him copies of my two stories and he used "A Walk On Y Street." Strangely, about a week later I received a note from David Helwig, a Queen's University English professor, who asked me if I had a story to send to him as the editor of an annual Oberon Press anthology of Canadian stories, their third. One of my stories had been included in their first anthology, so I sent him the only unprinted story I possessed, "Losers Weepers," which I'd written for the CBC. It is to be printed in September, 1973 in an anthology titled, 73: *New Canadian Stories.*

What I laughingly call my "Address for All Occasions" is a catch-all piece I wrote and re-wrote several times to meet the needs or interests of many audiences, from high school and college students to would-be writers and professors and teachers. Finally, in 1972, the poet John Robert Colombo phoned me and asked if I'd be one of the weekly speakers of a group of six poets and short story writers-novelists who would address public meetings in a room of the Royal Ontario Museum that spring. I said I would, providing my fee was as high as anyone else's.

Colombo, who moonlights from his poetic endeavors as a sort of literary jack-of-all-trades and entrepreneur, said, "Good, Hugh, I know the audience will love to hear you read a couple of your stories."

"You mean you want me to read my *stories!*"

"Sure. The poets will read from their work, and you, Hugh Hood and Douglas LePan will read from your fiction."

I thought to myself, Colombo, you've finally slipped your trolley.

Poetry readings are one thing but short stories or extracts from novels are not written to be read by their author. Though Colombo doesn't know it, the modern short story is not a folk-tale to be told inside an Indian tepee, or something one stoned-out-of-his-gourd acid freak reads to other members of his coffee-house tribe. "Okay," I told him.

I was the final speaker of the six scheduled to speak to the museum audience, so I cased both Douglas Lepan and Hugh Hood's platform performances. To be as charitable as I can be to both these gentlemen, they were lousy. LePan read from a novel of his in a bored academic mumble that must have put hundreds of university students to sleep over the years. Hood, another academic, was much better in his delivery, but when he finished reading one short story and began another I still thought he was reading more of the first one. Those members of the audience who were seated along convenient escape routes left LePan standing there with egg on his face ten minutes after he'd begun, while a slightly lesser number escaped from Hood's presence halfway through *his* reading, including me. I was now convinced, more than ever, that if I tried the same caper I'd probably lose *all* of my audience while still on page one of the first of my opuses.

I've never minded being a public drunk, but I was damned if I was going to become a public fool. I revised my set speech already used another occasions, and to Colombo's consternation, and I hope his satisfaction, I read *it* to the museum audience. I kept a weather eye on those at the rear of the room, and if they had egressed en masse, as we public speakers say, I would have joined them immediately. I noticed only one or two illiterates—or perhaps they were women's libbers hurrying home to put the TV dinners in the oven—fleeing the scene. I read my piece, and answered some audience questions, including a curve ball from a string-haired broad who tried to engage me in a discussion about Kafka and Dostoyevsky. I was, let's say, a qualified success.

My speech, in order to preserve it in something more durable than the aspic of public utterance, follows.

Creative writing cannot be taught, yet it takes a great deal of learning. To me "creative writing courses" are cruelly misnamed, and I say this despite the fact that for the past several summers I have conducted writing classes in various educational factories around Ontario. There are good "how-to-write" courses, such as those taught by writer-professors like Wallace Stegner and Walter Van Tilburg Clark in the United States, but most of them are bug-outs or holidays for teachers and students alike. All the beginning writer can learn in such classes are the elementary techniques of the craft, not its creativity.

The beginning writer, like the neophyte in any branch of endeavor, is searching for a confirmation of his talents. He does not want criticism, constructive or otherwise, and resents it when it is given. What he really wants is fulsome praise.

256

When this is given by a teacher for a bad piece of work, the student is cheated and the teacher has revealed himself as a timid or sycophantic jerk.

Let's begin this polemic by admitting that anyone who can put four words together into a sentence is an incipient writer, and that everyone's life is a prospective novel. Unfortunately most lives, no matter how dramatic, adventurous or plain bathetic they seem to the person who's lived them, are not a saleable literary commodity.

Artists such as painters, sculptors and composers have to lay out a lot of money to rent a studio or purchase the tools of their craft. The writer, unlike the musical composer, does not need to buy a piano—or even a guitar—all he needs are pencil and paper. There is no need for him to study anatomy, perspective or counterpoint; his instructors are on the public library shelves and his characters pass him by on the street.

It is perhaps the fact that almost anyone can compose a sentence or even write a letter that is responsible for the wide proliferation of amateur writers. I guess they say, "Hell, if some bum like so-and-so can become a professional writer anybody can." And in many cases they are absolutely right.

But I'm not here to talk about amateur writers, who enjoy the same status in the literary world as the amateur hamburger-stand chippy enjoys at a convention of professional call-girls.

The only person who can teach a writer to write is himself, and if he's a bad teacher or a lazy pupil he'll end up as a bad writer, or as no writer at all.

If, during his self-imposed apprenticeship, the hopeful writer finds he can't write at all, he's only wasting his time as both teacher and pupil and may as well quit before the sheriff or the ulcers get him. It's still surprising to me, after twenty-five years in the business, how many really hopeless writers still plod along, living on their wives, husbands or parents, chasing that elusive chimera of fame or fortune that their lack of talent keeps from them. Like the donkey following the carrot on the stick.

Now the inevitable question is asked. "How do I know if I'll ever become a professional writer or not?" I think the answer lies within yourself, and is both instinctive and philosophical. The answer also lies in the consensus of those who have read your work, and have criticized it honestly. If you are certain you're a writer, and so are those strangers who have read your work, the chances are you might be. If you are doubtful of your talents, and becoming a writer is not the main thing in your life, the chances are you're probably not one. And if everyone but you thinks you're not, you either prove to everyone that you are, or give up the pretence. The world is as full of people pretending they're writers as it's full of people believing they're reincarnations of Napoleon.

We are always hearing or reading about someone who is, quote, "working on a novel." This brings to my mind a picture of a young man or woman, after a hard day in the stenographic pool or on the shipping floor, sitting at their typewriter or at the kitchen table trying to hammer out a readable book on their portable or put one down on paper with a 19¢ ballpoint pen. Usually however it means that the clown who gives this simpering psuedo-prestigious answer to a television host is a phony who couldn't write, "The cat sat on the mat," without first spelling it out on his fingers.

To assuage the ladies who resent me using the male designation "he" to cover all writers, let me state that there are probably as many failed male authors as female, though, thank God, they're not as visible. Many frustrated women however take out their hang-ups either on the telephone or the typewriter, giving Canada more telephone users than any other country, per head of population, and I would guess more would-be lady novelists.

Though it may be true that women are more creative than men, at least in that highest of creative tasks, the creation of human life, it is not true that they write the most songs, poems or novels. Neither does their intuition help them, for it has no place in writing anyway. And if intuition is such an infallible psychological fact, how come so many women tie themselves down to the wrong guy, or are so often disappointed in love?

I don't want to dissuade anyone from becoming a writer, if they have the urge to and have developed the talents for it, men or women. Among this country's best novelists and short story writers are Ethel Wilson, Alice Munro and Margaret Laurence. All became professional writers while bringing up families at the same time. This means they had to work at two careers at once, but so have many male authors who have had to support their families with a workaday job while becoming writers in their spare time. I think it works out about even.

A frequently used book-reviewer's cliché is "he is a born writer," which often proves only that it would have been better if the subject had been born a paper-hanger. Another critical cliché is "he is sincere," though sincerity, as Bernard Shaw pointed out, does not prevent the person in question from being a blithering idiot. This latter piece of literary pap is frequently offered by kindly and scared old book-reviewers as the critical equivalent of "Don't shoot the pianist, he's doing his best."

All literary craftsmanship is not art, but when it is it is a *tour de force* that evolves from the professional skill of the writer. Ernest Hemingway once wrote "How can anyone think that you can neglect and despise or have contempt for craftsmanship, however feigned that contempt may be, and then expect it to be at your service when you must have it." Craftsmanship is careful, patient technical competence, and as William Arthur Deacon, ex-book editor of the *Globe & Mail* once put it, "There is no good writing, only good re-writing."

Creativity is a manifestation of pressures and aspirations that arise within the artist's psyche, or are forced on him by ambitions, hang-ups and urges as varying and various as are the number of writers. Creative writing, being more cerebral than manual, demands of its practitioner certain intellectual capabilities. All of the arts need imagination as well as the acquiring of certain techniques, but I believe that writing demands a greater and more diffused intelligence than some of the others. A writer not only has to form or paint a word picture of his subject, but he also has to explain why he has done so within the work of art itself.

Next to talent, which is the honing to a fine point of whatever skills and techniques he has acquired, the writer must create his people, scenes and situations as if he were a god. This godly —or ungodly—omnipotence and omnipercipience may be the psychological reason for his becoming a writer to begin with. In other words what he is unable to do himself, as a human being, he can live out vicariously with the people and situations he has created with his pen. Creative writers—to separate them from interpretive writers such as journalists—are a strange breed of cat in any event. They may be correctly viewed with a great deal of validity as neurotic offshoots from the "normal" run of the population.

Besides the overwhelming urge to write, and his creativity, an author must have a general knowledge of his language's composition, punctuation, syntax and vocabulary, though some very good writers indeed have been deficient in one and sometimes all of these literary requisites. Correct spelling is also a great help to an author, though F. Scott Fitzgerald reached early fame and fortune with the spelling ability of a ten-year-old rather than that of a college man.

To become a literary craftsman does not necessitate the acquiring of a great deal of formal education, unless one wishes

259

to re-write *Tom Brown's Schooldays* or *This Side Of Paradise*. If I may inject a personal note here, I dropped out of a technical high school on my sixteenth birthday, in the tenth grade. High school was a futile waste of time in preparing me for the trade I've followed professionally for the past twenty-five years, and university would have only compounded the waste. The things I needed to learn to become a writer I should have learned— but unfortunately didn't—in public school. These were spelling, composition, grammar, syntax and vocabulary.

I was awful in grammar in public school, and still am today. Though I don't know what a gerund or a participle is, and don't want to know, I can use them correctly in a written sentence. I'm like a self-taught jazz pianist who can't read a word of music but knows the black keys from the white keys, and which ones to press. And I can also spot an ungrammatical sentence most times, my own or somebody else's, and I know how to change it.

Almost as important to a writer as *how* to write it down is *what* to write down, and sometimes what to leave out. These things cannot be learned in any school. What a writer needs more than anything else is a shallow knowledge of a great many things. This widely diffused but cursory knowledge of anything and everything is something he stores in his memory bank from the moment he begins to think, and he adds to it every day of his life. It comes partly from whatever formal education he's had, but much more so from the erudition he's acquired from reading, the experiences he's gained from living, and the observations he's made and stored away during his lifetime.

The United States has had six Nobel laureates in literature: Eugene O'Neill and Sinclair Lewis, who seem to have acquired university degrees; John Steinbeck and William Faulkner, who were college dropouts from Stanford and the University of Mississippi after short periods of attendance; Pearl Buck, who went to Randolph-Macon Women's College, and Ernest Hemingway who was a Grade Ten dropout from an Oak Park, Illinois high school. The varying lengths of their formal educations is not reflected in their work as literary artists, for who can seriously claim, for instance, that Pearl Buck was a better writer than Faulkner or Hemingway.

All these six winners of the Nobel Prize for Literature learned most of their trade in the streets. John Steinbeck received the education necessary to write *The Grapes of Wrath* from ten weeks on a WPA project picking beans in California's San Joaquin Valley. Pearl Buck picked up her most notable material from the streets of Chinese cities. William Faulkner hung around the town square of Oxford, Mississippi, and wrote some of his books on the back of a coal shovel while tending boilers in an electric power station in his home town. Eugene O'Neill wrote *The Hairy Ape* from his experiences as a fireman on U.S. merchant ships. Sinclair Lewis wrote a series of books from his observations of his fellow citizens of Sauk Centre, Minnesota. Ernest Hemingway, whose training came mainly from early interpretive journalism, learned his trade on the *Kansas City Star,* the *Toronto Star Weekly,* and in bordellos, bistros and bars from Key West to the Paris Latin Quarter.

Of the six, O'Neill, Lewis, Faulkner and Hemingway were alcoholics. Steinbeck was a non-alcoholic heavy drinker, and only Pearl Buck seems to have controlled her drinking, if she drank at all. The point to all this is that a slight smattering of education can help a writer, but being an alcoholic is almost a necessity if you want to win the Nobel Prize for Literature.

This may be as good a place as any to give a cursory study of the short story as a literary art form.

The differences between the novel and the short story are many and manifold. The short story has been defined in many different ways by many different writers. Edgar Allen Poe declared that "in the whole composition there should be no word written, of which the tendency, direct or indirect, is not to one pre-established design." Anton Chekhov held that a story should have neither beginning nor end (a notion, incidentally, that has been carried to a silly extreme by the *New Yorker* magazine for the past several years). Chekhov also reminded authors that if they described a gun hanging on the wall on page one, sooner or later somebody must fire it. H. G. Wells defined the short story as any piece of short fiction that could be read in half an hour, while another English critic and nitwit once described a short story as "a story that is not too long."

Edgar Allen Poe, who along with Nicolai Gogol around 1830 invented the modern short story, was right with his aphorism, as was Anton Chekhov when he wrote about the gun hanging on the wall. The others were engaged in what probably passed for literary humor in their particular circle.

The modern short story is a distinct art form, which may follow a hundred different courses from beginning to end, but has a few inflexible rules, as has the fugue in music or the sonnet in poetry. The novel has no rules at all, except the rules that cover prose writing in general.

Most good modern novelists have also been good short story

writers, but there are many novelists who cannot master the short story at all. On the other hand there are writers who have made their reputations with the short story, but have been unable to write a longer piece of work.

A talk like this is not the place to review the rules of short story writing, but I can tell you what a short story is not. It's not a chapter or an incident cut from a novel. It's not a descriptive piece of writing, an anecdote, episode, vignette, a piece of journalism or a brief revelation of its author's uptightness. None of these should be served up to the public as stories, and the author's hang-ups should be saved for his psychiatrist, clergyman or marriage counsellor.

The short story can trace its beginnings back to the folk tale told in a medieval hall, or earlier still to pre-historic man and his warming fire. It has come down to us through the phases of myth, legend, fable and parable. The account in Genesis of the conflict between Cain and Abel is a short story, as is the parable of the Prodigal Son. The stories of Ruth, Judith and Susannah are examples of a folk art that was already old and highly developed some thousands of years before Poe and Gogol structured what is now the modern short story.

The main reason behind the birth and popularity of the short story in the 19th Century was the growth and distribution of the weekly and monthly periodical. From that day to this— when many magazines have disappeared forever and those that are left feature journalism over fiction—they were the natural home of the short story. With the demise of fiction-carrying consumer magazines the list of short story writers has also diminished.

Believing as I do that fiction is written and read primarily as entertainment, and that the short story is a viable entertainment medium, I also believe that the best years of the short story were those of the first half of the 20th Century. My own all-time favorite short story writers were Ernest Hemingway, John O'Hara, Irwin Shaw, Somerset Maugham, Dorothy Parker, A. E. Coppard, Scott Fitzgerald, James Joyce, Guy de Maupassant, and the Russian-Jewish writer Isaac Babel.

In Canada the short story comes down to us from the early and middle 19th Century stories of Joseph Howe, Thomas Chandler Haliburton, Edward W. Thomson, and the later ones of Duncan Campbell Scott. The flowering of the Canadian short story didn't really begin however until well into this century with the internationally-accepted stories of Morley Callaghan. With a couple of notable exceptions I think all the better Canadian short story writers are still alive today. I refuse to name them of course; I have simpler ways of making lifelong enemies than that. Anyhow, telling you what I myself like to read is like finding out who cuts your barber's hair. It's an exercise in trivia.

Despite the lack of consumer magazine markets in this country today the short story is not yet dead, and indeed is flourishing. It is kept alive by such magazines as *Canadian Forum, Chatelaine, Fiddlehead, Quarry, Queens Quarterly, Tamarack Review,* and a brand-new addition, *Journal of Canadian Fiction.* Mr. Robert Weaver and the CBC radio network have done more than anyone or anything to keep the Canadian short story alive. Other short story markets are supplied by many college quarterlies and spontaneous little magazines.

The spreading use of Canadian novels, anthologies and textbooks in this country, especially among high school students, has suddenly made Canadian literature acceptable. This has given the Canadian writer a bigger sales potential than he's ever enjoyed before, but we still have a long way to go. The increase in Canadian paperback books, grants to both authors and publishers by the Canada Council, and the increase in Canadian Literature courses in schools, have all contributed to this trend.

But let's get back to writers and writing.

A popular misconception about writers is that they must also be intellectuals. Let me quote to you from a *Time* magazine essay of May 21st, 1965. Quote: "In the creative arts, the merely popular practitioners are excluded from intellectual status— but so are most of the really great talents. J. P. Marquand was no intellectual, but neither were Hemingway, Faulkner or Thomas Wolfe. The critic, on the other hand, is almost automatically an intellectual, at least in his own view." Unquote. The only Canadian writer I've met who is also a certified intellectual is Lister Sinclair, who once flourished in this country as a first-class radio dramatist.

In form and structure the history of writing has always been dynamic rather than static. Here are some extracts from an article I stole from *Playboy* recently—along with the nude centrefold. I've also edited it a bit. Quote: "Consider for example the changes in every aspect of modern life. Religion. Sex. Clothes. In the 18th Century the novel was a story of adventure, of the great migrations from the country to the city, the churning of urban and rural classes, Richardson's *Pamela* and *Clarissa,* Smollett, Defoe. How in the 19th Century it changed to provide stories of the new middle class, the manufacturing class, the new world of Dickens, George Eliot, Arnold Bennett, William Dean Howells. It told readers about the new people, how they lived, what they wore, how vicars sat down to tea, what lawyers did at the office—and furniture, boy, how they described furniture!

"The 20th Century novel, while admittedly still struggling with the furniture, is not quite sure where it's going, finding narrative shot away by the movies and TV. It still moves toward telling us what we intuitively need to know about our world, about the inside of people's heads, about how men and women act in bed together, how they really are; how, at any rate, they think they are." Unquote.

Creative writing has taken various blind alleys in its development from the epistolary novels of Samuel Richardson to the present day. The letter-writing style of course was resurrected by Ring Lardner with his *You Know Me, Al* stories of my youth, in the *Pat Hobby* stories of Scott Fitzgerald in *Esquire* magazine, and John O'Hara's *Pal Joey*.

Proletarian writing was a 1930's Depression phenomenon, of which nothing much has survived. Clifford Odets' play *Waiting For Lefty,* was one of the finest examples of the genre, with Irwin Shaw's *Bury The Dead,* and the short stories of Michael Gold, Albert Maltz, Alvah Bessie and others, of whom a few were very good indeed. World War Two killed, among much better things, proletarian fiction.

With the loosening of religio-moral censorship in the early 1960's, the bookstore shelves became filled with so-called pornographic novels. Actually the early ones were not pornographic at all but naturalistic, following in the steps of such earlier naturalistic authors as Henry Miller, Emile Zola, Theodore Dreiser and Erskine Caldwell. Far removed from their artistic predecessors, a great many third-class novelists rushed into print with pornographic and scatological junk.

Here in Canada—one of the last bastions of puritanical literary hypocrisy—some worthwhile realistic and naturalistic fiction was produced and published. To my knowledge at least, the first time *the* four-letter word (beginning with F) was used in a Canadian novel, was in Hugh Hood's *White Figure, White Ground*. The publisher was The Ryerson Press, a subsidiary of the United Church of Canada.

In the mid 1960's we were treated to a spate of homosexual and hard-drug culture novels, among them *Last Exit To Brooklyn, Naked Lunch* and *City Of Night. Last Exit To Brooklyn* was not only a homosexual novel, but was a direct descendant of the proletarian novels of the Depression years. It contained the best fictional treatment of an industrial strike I have ever read. My favorite homosexual novel, however, is James Baldwin's *Giovanni's Room.*

But to get back on the track again.

In his introduction to a book called *Writers At Work,* a compilation of interviews with sixteen famous authors made by the *Paris Review,* Malcolm Cowley says, "The sixteen authors have come from the ruling class, the middle class, or the working class of five different countries. They are Catholic, Protestant, Jewish or agnostic; old or young, married, single or divorced. They had all sorts of education, from those who never finished secondary school to those who are university professors or fellows . . . About the only thing most of them agree on is that they're not overly fond of other writers." And he goes on to say, "Authors are sometimes like tomcats; they distrust all the other toms, but they are kind to kittens."

Most writing doesn't take place at a typewriter but in the author's thoughts, days, weeks or months before he sits down at his machine. Or, on the other hand, it comes to him in a revelatory flash that he has to immediately transfer to paper. In either case it is what is commonly called "inspiration." I happen to be an inspirational writer, and I don't believe those who advocate the sitting down at a typewriter and typing away until something sensible comes out. All that generally comes out is what Norman Mailer calls, "writing words."

The average author cannot describe from experience the thoughts of a person on the gallows, of a scientist who has made an earth-shaking discovery, or those of a mother looking on her baby for the first time. This is where his imagination comes into use, as well as a little deception.

The author—unless he's a woman scientist who's had a baby but is then hanged for shooting her husband—has to make up what he believes such characters in such situations would be thinking. For this he relies on a combination of lifelong percipience, his brainbank of diffuse knowledge, and his creative ability. And this is what creative writing is.

There are many important facets to a short story or a novel, not the least of which is its title. I have written many banal titles myself, but not as many as some editors have tried to force on me. I like alliterative titles or those that are eye-catching or thought-provoking. Two titles I *didn't* write but wish I had are *How to Cook a Wolf* and *The Night the Old Nostalgia Burned Down.*

For short stories I generally write the title first, sometimes months before it suggests a story theme to me. I understand from one of my young friends that many youthful song-writers do the same thing. A title of mine that took me a couple of years to find a theme for was "E Equals MC Squared," Einstein's famous equation.

The names of fictional characters are sometimes very important. I used to just think them up until I had a traumatic experience with the name I gave to an alcoholic middle-aged character in a novel, *Silence on The Shore,* back in 1959. The book was published in hard covers in 1962 and then as a paperback first in 1968. The process used to transcribe it from hard covers to paperback is called offset printing, that is, to simplify things, photographing each page and reducing it in size. This precludes changing anything as it's possible to do when new type is set. At the time I wrote the book the name I gave to this particular character had no significance at all, and no critic or book reviewer even mentioned it. By the time the paperback came out however the name of the drunken character was well known indeed. He is an internationally-famous singer-composer called Gordon Lightfoot.

A second paperback edition of the book was reprinted last year, and I went through the original hardcover book and changed every "Gordon" to "George." Luckily new type was set for that edition, which allowed me to change the name.

Today I take all my names from the Toronto telephone book, either using a name that is in the public domain, like John Smith, Mary Jones, Walter Jennings and so on. In the case of names I hope are offbeat—like Gordon Lightfoot—I generally pick a name from the phone book, change one or two letters of the last name, then add a different Christian name. For the names of ethnic characters I find a name that sounds indigenous to his or her nationality, change a letter, and add a fictitious first name. For French-Canadian names I generally use common ones such as Tremblay or Levesque.

Someday I'm afraid even the phone book is going to let me down, and I'll cop an instant plea of insanity. Speaking about phone books reminds me of the poor little drunk who, much the worse for wear, staggered into a public library and picked up the first book that caught his eye, which happened to be a phone book. He took it to a table and read it with interest until it was time for the pubs to open. When he took it back to the checkout desk he said "Say, lady, this is quite a novel! It seems to have a lousy plot, but boy what a cast of characters!"

The people easiest to write about are those who most resemble their author, not necessarily physically but in age, personality, background and outlook. The characters more difficult to write about are those of the opposite sex, those occupying a different social stratum than the author, and those engaged in an occupation that will be all too familiar to many readers but is known only by hearsay to the writer. The male writer, for instance, must use his imagination and the memory of what women have told him to describe the thoughts of a female character. This gives memory an importance equal to imagination and erudition.

The characters I find most difficult to depict from their own point of view are psychotics and homosexuals, though I have depicted both in short stories and novels. I have tremendous admiration for a William Faulkner who wrote parts of *The Sound and the Fury* through the twisted thought processes and observations of the cretinous boy Benjy. Also for Ken Kesey, who wrote *One Flew Over the Cuckoo's Nest* from the point of view of the Indian half-breed schizophrenic in the Oregon mental hospital.

Strangely, the lives of quite ordinary people are very difficult for some writers to make interesting. I have been writing about ordinary people all of my professional life, so I was not aware that this difficulty existed until it was pointed out to me twenty odd years ago. The writer who cannot depict believable or interesting ordinary people is forced to fall back on eccentrics, hysterics and picaresques as his characters.

Writing style is something that develops naturally in an individual from childhood, and no author should try to change his style to conform with trends or to imitate another writer. As both editor and reader at various times I have read manuscripts that attempted to imitate successful writers from James Joyce to Jack Kerouac, with terrible results.

My own literary mentor was John Dos Passos, though fortunately I never tried to copy his style. I did copy his realism, that is to call a can of soup on a shelf a "can of Campbell's soup." As a consequence I became what is known as a realistic writer. I am amazed and disconcerted when English majors ask me about the symbolism or allegory of scenes in my books or stories. If they find any, believe me, they were placed there quite unconsciously.

Dialogue always came easily to me, though I picked up its varying nuances and differences from many writers, either purposely or subliminally. The two who come most quickly to mind are Ernest Hemingway and the man I consider to have been the best dialogue writer of them all, John O'Hara.

My teacher in the field of young romantic love was the novelist and playwright J. B. Priestley. Learning how to write about sexual love was a job I kept for myself.

Literary innovation in creative prose is so rarely a popular success that the names of only two real innovators in this century come to mind: James Joyce and Ernest Hemingway. Joyce invented the stream-of-consciousness or interior monologue technique, or at least popularized it, while Hemingway brought to a high art the leaving out of all unnecessary modifiers in his sentences.

Kildare Dobbs, the *Toronto Star's* literary editor, said not too long ago, "In literature there are no great leaps forward, no break-throughs, no real novelties. The entire possibilities of an art form may be present in its first masterpiece. After *Don Quixote,* the novel doesn't go anywhere. But neither does it go away. If we're lucky we get other masterpieces in the novel form. We get, so to speak, *Don Quixote* again."

What about the market for Canadian writers? It is my belief that though the short story market has dwindled in all countries, the market for novels was never better in Canada than it is at the present time. There are not only more Canadian publishing houses than there used to be, but more of them are willing to publish works by Canadian authors.

We have a tendency in this country to denigrate our arts, especially in comparison to those in the United States. The following statistic may be an eye-opener to some people. Recently Truman Capote, the American novelist, said in a TV interview, "Each year there are 22,000 books published in the United States, and out of these only about 600 are even reviewed." I think our ratio between numbers of books printed here, and the number reviewed in Canadian periodicals is higher than that, if that's any consolation.

The best information I ever received about writing short stories was at a cocktail party my publishers held on the publication of my first novel some twenty-four years ago. It came from a young Canadian writer who was a regular contributor to the *Saturday Evening Post.* He said to me, "The best advice I can give you is always make your stories seventeen pages long." And I generally have.

This is page seventeen, so I guess it's time to quit. So I will.

In 1972 I received a Senior Arts Fellowship from the Canada Council, which allowed me, among other things, to write this book.

It was around this time that I enjoyed two happenings that were more than somewhat unusual. The first was the acceptance of a medal given by the City of Toronto every year "for distinguished public service." My only contribution to the city, besides making it the locale of most of my fiction, had been to shovel snow from the downtown streets during the Depression. The putting up of my name to the annual Awards of Merit Committee was the work of an old friend, Mrs. Georgeanna Hamilton, a former Ryerson Press public relations manager.

The second happening was a run-of-the-mill event that happens to many authors, but of course ended up being a typical Garner gaffe.

Among my invitations to speak at universities around that time had been one from Dr. Glenn Clever of the Department of English, University of Ottawa. Actually, in his initial letter of March 15th he had asked me if I was interested in becoming writer-in-residence at the university, and when I would be available to talk things over with him and his colleagues. I told him that I intended to visit Queen's University in April, to deposit some material at the library there, and also to take some library books, that I'd saved up during the winter from book reviews I'd done, to Joyceville Prison north of Kingston. I could drop up to Ottawa then and see him.

In his next letter he asked me if I would speak at the university during my Ottawa visit, and we agreed on a date. He reserved me a room at the Chateau Laurier, which is only a few blocks from the downtown university campus, and I drove to Ottawa one Sunday, with the last of the snow still piled along the fence-lines of the Eastern Ontario fields. (I had delivered my collected material to Queen's, and my collected books to Joyceville, on a separate trip a few days before driving to Ottawa.)

I checked into the hotel and invited my sister June and her husband, to the Chateau for dinner. We had a good meal, and we laced it down with Beaujolais '69. That day went fine, but it was practically the last day of my trip that I remember. The next morning I phoned Michael Macklem the president of Oberon Press, whom I had corresponded with a year before about a short story of mine that David Helwig, a Queen's professor, had included in an Oberon Press anthology titled *Fourteen Stories High*. Macklem invited me out to his house at 555 Maple Lane, from which he publishes the Oberon Press books. I think it has the loveliest address of any publishing house in Canada.

Out at his house Mike Macklem, his wife and myself had a

few ales and when it came time to leave he called me a cab. I had purposefully taken a taxi for the instructions for getting to his house were much too complicated for me to attempt driving there.

That evening, armed with my "Address For All Occasions" I went down to the University of Ottawa, and was taken to a lecture room by Dr. Clever and one of his colleagues, where I put aside my prepared talk and enjoyed a question-and-answer session with the audience. At least I *think* we had a question-and-answer session, though I'm not quite sure of what transpired. Following the ale-priming at Oberon Press I'd probably got into the sauce at the hotel, and was travelling in my private dream world about one foot off mother earth.

Like Scott Fitzgerald, Dylan Thomas and Brendan Behan before me I'd proved myself to be a pretty risky speaker at any college, unless I carefully curbed my drinking beforehand. My wine-drinking of the evening before, followed by my morning's beer-drinking at the Macklems' house, had proved my undoing. However I don't think I did much damage, either to the literary lecturing caper, to myself, or to the University of Ottawa, except that my answers to the questions by the audience may have been a little fuzzy. I don't suppose I have to assure those who heard me that my dissertations on whatever I disserted upon were completely uninhibited and extemporaneous.

I was supposed to drive home the following morning, but it was a couple of days later that I was driven home to Toronto by my sister, who had rescued me from the hotel. Where I'd been in the meantime, whom I'd spoken to, joked with, or insulted are things I'll perhaps never know, or even want to know. A few days after arriving home I received a visit from a representative of the Canadian National Railways claims department, and with the insane, post-alcoholic fear that somehow I'd managed to derail an Ottawa-Toronto train or something I read that I'd fallen through or kicked in a large plate glass panel of the revolving front door of the Chateau Laurier Hotel. Having no recollection whatever of the incident I finally paid a bill of $42 and change. The hotel also sent me a Xerox copy of a counter cheque for $20 I'd filled out during my stay, which I guarantee looked like a Chinese laundry ticket that even Mao Tse Tung couldn't decipher. I was also the proud possessor of a twelve or thirteen dollar receipt from an Ottawa government liquor store, which covered the purchase of, I presume, two 26-ounce bottles of Walker's Special Old Canadian rye whiskey, which is my usual alcoholic tipple. Up to then I didn't think an Ontario government liquor store, under any circumstances, furnished receipts to drunks. I must have been very persuasive in telling the cashier I needed it for an expense account.

As far as my expenses went I ended up, after paying my hotel bill with my American Express card, paying for the broken front door, paying my sister (after my wife had already done so) for driving me back to Toronto, and other incidentals, about $150 in the hole, after the University of Ottawa sent me my speaker's fee.

I remember having breakfast one morning in the hotel coffee shop seated at a table next to the Roman Catholic acting Archbishop of Toronto, Philip Pocock. Unlike the time however when His Excellency had lost his rubbers in the Toronto steakhouse, while Hugh Kane and I were discussing the fortuitous turndown of *The Sin Sniper*, things didn't turn out so well for me. At least I can thank my stars that unlike Dylan Thomas I didn't make a bet to drink fourteen straight bourbons in a row, only to end up dead in St. Vincent's Hospital in Greenwich Village. Nor did I, like Brendan Behan in a visit to Toronto, end up drying out in a small private alcoholic hospital called Stein's in the west end of my city. My own drying out had to wait until I reached home.

Before leaving for Ottawa to see the professors about the writer-in-residence offer I'd phoned an old professional writer-in-residence friend, Irving Layton, to ask him what the job should pay and what my duties would be. Irving has been writer or poet-in-residence at George Williams University and for a semester at Guelph University.

Irving asked, "Is it a university or a college, Hugh?"

"A university."

"Okay. Ask them for twenty thousand, but don't take less than fifteen."

"What do I do as a writer-in-residence?"

"Whatever you want to do. You make your own hours, read students' manuscripts, do whatever suits you. In my two appointments I ran poetry lectures, but that's my ordinary work anyway. When Mordecai Richler was at George Williams he did fuck-all."

I told him that I'd been invited to visit Margaret Laurence when she was writer-in-residence at Massey College, Toronto University, and she had apparently been imitating Richler, writing a book, or perhaps even reading students' manuscripts.

"Sure. They hire you for the prestige it gives them to have a known writer there for a year. You don't have to do anything, really. But don't forget, twenty grand is the going fee."

I guess I must have asked Ottawa for twenty thousand, but

271

I don't remember it now. Anyway the job didn't materialize, much to my, and the university's, relief. I read somewhere later that they'd hired a young writer from the Maritimes.

A short time later I received a phone call from the English Department of the University of British Columbia, offering me twelve thousand a year to teach creative writing. I turned it down politely, not wanting to try to teach creative writing anywhere, and knowing that twelve grand a year in Vancouver wouldn't even pay my drunk fines.

I have come to the conclusion that there are some Canadian cities that I should avoid.

A couple of years before my last caper at the University of Ottawa I'd been invited by my union, ACTRA, to fly there on a charter flight, along with thirty or forty fellow unionists from our Toronto local, to appear before the government's radio and television commission to plead our case for more Canadian work on radio and TV.

I'd left Toronto with a couple of drinks under my belt, sharing a seat with a well-known Canadian actor who was disgustedly eating his breakfast on the plane. We were transported from the airport by bus to the commission hearings, which for all I remember may have been held in the Skyline Hotel. Not knowing any better, and not caring anyway, I'd made my way to the front row of seats where I'd sat down along with such professional speakers as Fred Davis, Bill Walker (Timex, Mercury cars, et al), Pierre Berton, and others. Some time during the proceedings I'd made my own personal plea for the Canadian actor and writer. All I remember about that was Bill Walker's comment, "How do I follow *that?*" and the sight of Pierre Juneau, the commission president, asking Harry Boyle who I was. Later on I sat farther back in the room with Pierre Berton while the Montreal local made their pitch.

After the meeting I wandered up to a bar or two, had my picture taken with Adrienne Clarkson, then blacked out. I was told later by Paul Siren, our union business manager, that he'd last seen me sitting in a bus with a lady member of the commission. He also told me that when the plane left I'd been among the missing, and Pierre Berton had said, "Don't worry about Garner. Nobody can kill that bastard." Which is true enough, providing you don't include me among my killers.

Anyhow, I made both the Ottawa General Hospital (where they X-rayed my skull following a gash I was wearing on it—at least I hope it was for that reason), and a small two-cell jail, which I shared with another guy. The next morning I paid the usual fine to a justice of the peace.

After I got back to Toronto—and don't ask me how—I received a congratulatory letter from our union president, Victor Knight, in Montreal, about the wonderful speech I'd made. Too bad I didn't hear it myself.

In the summer of 1972 a man named Rolf Kalman called me up, said he'd seen a play of mine, "Some Are So Lucky," on TV, and asked me if I'd ever written for the stage. I told him I'd adapted three of my half-hour TV dramas, "Some Are So Lucky," "The Magnet," and "A Trip For Mrs. Taylor" into one-act plays for the theatre, under the overall title *Three Women*. I told him the three could be played in a repertory trilogy, using ten principals, and making up two hours or more of theatre.

He in turn told me that in 1971 he'd published a book of Canadian plays, and was going to publish a second volume at the end of the year. He also told me, very apologetically, that he could only offer a hundred dollars as an advance on royalties on the book. Mr. Kalman told me he published his books under the imprint of his own publishing company, Simon & Pierre, and gave me his home address and phone number, and also the post office box number of his publishing company.

My three one-act plays had been turned down years ago by most of the theatrical companies in Canada, and had been lying in my filing cabinet almost forgotten by me ever since. I had nothing to lose by sending him a copy of them.

Mr. Kalman had told me he worked on the Toronto docks as a longshoreman, and this didn't faze me, for the modern American philosopher Eric Hoffer was also a longshoreman on the docks in San Francisco. However, because I could contact him at his desk by phone, I knew he was something more than a guy slinging cargo. What he actually was, or is, I don't know to this day, and it's his own business.

I called up a couple of well-known playwrights and asked them if they knew Mr. Kalman, but neither of them did. Len Peterson told me there were all sorts of people wanting to publish books of plays, from which the playwright received little or nothing, even if the books were eventually published. I ignored this, and sent Mr. Kalman copies of the first two plays, the last ten pages of the final play having been removed by a director or somebody when it was staged by the Brockville Theatre Guild some four years before.

In a few days I received a second call from Mr. Kalman, who told me he liked the two plays, and asked me if I would please fix up a copy of the third one, and send it along to him. I told him that the originals of all three were in the Douglas Library at Queen's, but I would re-write the last ten pages or so of the third play, using a CBC TV shooting script that I had of it at home. This I did. He in turn promised to send me a copy of his first book, which he did. He didn't mail it but sent it by a messenger service, so that I knew whatever else he might turn out to be he wasn't niggardly about expenses. This little gesture on his part impressed me.

His first volume of six Canadian plays turned out to be a beautiful book, elegantly printed, bound, illustrated and everything else, that retailed for $9.95. Out of the hard cover volume each of the plays had been printed as a separate entity in soft covers, but the same size as the hard cover volume and with the same printing and illustrations. This proved to me that the proposition was legitimate.

I went out of town for a few days, and when I returned I found Mr. Kalman's cheque for $100 waiting for me.

During the next weeks I met him, and we had a few drinks at the King Edward Hotel, he came to my apartment and shot some 35 millimetre pictures of me, and I wrote him an introduction about myself for his volume number two. He also, at my request, left me a page of his publishing firm's letterhead and a second sheet, upon which I drafted our oral agreement, over his pre-inscribed signature. I gave up all royalty rights on the hard cover book, but we agreed to split the royalties fifty-fifty on the soft cover reproduction of my trilogy, which I'd titled years before and copyrighted as *Three Women*.

Until fairly recent times the fees paid for reprint rights, for textbooks and anthologies in Canada, were scandalous in the extreme. Lately they have risen, in some cases to equality with those paid by American reprint houses. In my own case the fees I'd received for reprint rights twenty years ago had been low because in those days I needed the exposure, and I had no literary clout with which to bargain with tight-fisted publishers. Today this has changed, and I demand reasonable fees from all textbook and anthology publishers.

For a long time after *Hugh Garner's Best Stories* won the Governor General's Award for Fiction, and the subsidiary rights to the book were held jointly by The Ryerson Press and myself, there were quite a number of requests for permission to reprint the stories, most of which I didn't even see. This was because the woman in charge of Permissions for The Ryerson Press had been there it seemed since before I was born, and was fast approaching both her pension time and spinster senility. Finally

I spoke to the editors, and had her instructed that I was to be consulted on all fees before they were accepted. Later on, after the book sold out, all subsidiary rights reverted to me, and I did the bargaining.

It was to gain full ownership of the book that I bought the 970 copies of another book of short stories, *Men And Women*, some years later, as I've already mentioned.

All publishing houses have somebody, usually a young lady, who arranges permission to reprint the works of their authors, and it is in this particular phase of the writer-publisher relationship that many young and inexperienced authors fall down, especially those who, like me, do not have an agent. To me, outside of assigning copyright and subsidiary rights, this is the area in which most writers are knowingly gypped and defrauded by publishing houses.

The old maid at Ryerson was replaced by a young lady, Pat Pierce, who is one of the most knowledgeable and conscientious women holding down such a position in Canadian publishing. When McGraw-Hill bought out The Ryerson Press they were smart enough to obtain her services in the deal. McGraw-Hill also hired the managing editor at Ryerson, who is the soul of honour but happened to forget being a witness to the agreement giving me *all* rights to the stories in *Hugh Garner's Best Stories* when Ryerson reprinted it as a quality paperback, as he also forgot that he had signed the letter turning over all rights to *Men and Women* when I bought out all the remaining stocks of the book.

In 1971 an English publishing house, Blond Educational Publishing, asked McGraw-Hill Ryerson for permission to reprint my short story "Red Racer." The story had been offered to them for fifty dollars by mistake while the permissions editor was on vacation, although I control the subsidiary rights. When Mrs. Pierce returned to work she had to write Blond Publishing and me and explain what had happened. I thanked her but told her to let things stand.

August and September, 1972, were the two busiest months I can remember as a writer. I wrote a couple of chapters of a novel, and there was a great deal of rewriting and additional writing to this autobiographical work, but most of my work was in the business end of my trade, not the writing end.

To begin with there were the negotiations, and the rewriting of the last half of my third play for the trilogy, *Three Women*. Besides this were the meetings with Rolf Kalman, and my writing of the biographical and bibliographical introduction to my plays. Then I wrote my own contract with Mr. Kalman's firm, Simon & Pierre, which incidentally is named after his pair of cats.

During the early part of the summer Doug Fetherling, a young poet and writer and a friend of several years, had told me he had been commissioned by Coles, "the book people," to write a monograph about me for Coles' "Canadian Writers & their Works" series. He came to my place for supper, and I gave him quite a bit of biographical material, including about 140 pages that formed the basis for this book. I had written it originally to straighten out all publicity people, and especially all anthology editors, who didn't seem to have a clue about even the chronological order in which my books had been published. I took the fair copy of the script to my publishers, made two copies of it, which I charged to the promotion department, and gave a copy to the promotion girl who had moved to McGraw-Hill with the purchase of The Ryerson Press by McGraw-Hill. She took the manuscript from me and dropped it in the clutter on her desk top.

After Doug Fetherling finished his monograph for Coles and left, with a friend Jim Christy, on a Jack Kerouac safari to the Yukon in an ancient truck, his girl friend sent me a copy of his monograph.

There were few corrections to make, not by me at any rate, although his hurried, uncorrected and ink-corrected script would pose a problem for any publisher's copy-editor. Fetherling's typescripts are typical of dozens of scripts written by young people, and may even have been typical of the writers of my early days: full of typographical errors that the author can't seem to stop writing long enough to correct. An old editor friend of mine recently told me that he still remembered my own scripts, which were the cleanest ones he ever received. He told me too that he'd been surprised when reading a biography of Robert Benchley that Benchley's scripts had always been meticulously typed. I suppose neatness is a compulsion shared by Benchley and me, the same as our affinity with the bottle.

Before leaving on his Odyssey, Doug took me to lunch, and over my coffee and his drink told me that he, Jim Christy, and another man were thinking of starting a small publishing house. He asked me if there was anything in my contracts with McGraw-Hill Ryerson and Simon & Schuster to stop them launching their firm with this book, then titled *The Writing Years*. I told him that McGraw-Hill Ryerson had been in possession of the original copy of this manuscript for months, but nobody had come forward with an offer to publish it. As for Simon & Schuster my contract with them covered only paperbacks.

He told me that they would be launching the firm on a shoestring, and couldn't afford much of an advance on royalties. I told him what other publishers paid me, but that for him I wouldn't hold a gun to his head. Just to keep him honest however I'd take two hundred dollars. We shook hands on it. In turn he told me he wanted the finished script by August.

During August I took two of my old books, *Present Reckoning*, a short paperback novel published in 1951 by William Collins Sons, and *Men And Women*, a collection of fourteen short stories published in 1966 by The Ryerson Press, up to Simon & Schuster, and asked Jim Smallwood and his editor, Jock Carroll, to read them with an eye to bringing them out as paperbacks. A short time later I withdrew *Present Reckoning*, feeling that it was too short and too inconsequential as a novel to publish again. I told Jim Smallwood however that I'd like to see *Men And Women* in paperback, though fourteen stories made a pretty thin book. I suggested to him that I add six stories, four from my first short story collection, *The Yellow Sweater*, and two brand-new stories that I'd written for the CBC the winter and spring before.

Not having a copy of *The Yellow Sweater* I had to go down to the main branch of the Toronto Public Library and get a copy—the last one they have I think—on my library card, and from it Xerox four of the stories. I had a fair copy of one of my two latest stories, but had to re-type a fair copy of the other from a carbon in my files. I rearranged all the stories, putting two strong stories at the beginning of the book, two equally strong stories last, and mixing up the others as best I could with an eye to their content, whether or not the protagonist was a man or woman, and sometimes even by their titles. Having done this with four collections to date, I think I know a little of how it's done.

Many writers and editors know nothing at all about putting together a short story collection or anthology. I've read many such books in which the best stories have been hidden away somewhere in the middle, with weak stories in the lead-off position and another weak one placed last, in the places that call for strong memorable stories. Knowledge of this important fact seems to be one of the things that writers and editors seem to overlook.

My own rule of thumb, including the placing of strong first and last stories, is to alternate male and female stories, not bunch together stories whose first title word is either the articles "A" or "The," divide the stories as often as possible according to length (that is, separate two long stories with a short one, if this is possible), and try to relieve a sad story by following with a happy one. If the book is to take its title from one of the stories, let it take a title that is odd, offbeat or eye-catching. For instance, my first collection took its title from the lead story, "The Yellow Sweater," which is really a nothing title. The book had much better story titles to choose from, and much better stories to place in the lead-off position.

Violation Of The Virgins, my last collection, was given the book's most eye-catching title, which is also the title of the final, and longest, story of the thirteen that make up the book.

I have approached each collection of my short stories as if it were to be my last, and this was the case with *Men And Women.* Because I did not foresee a short story sequel to it I included one story, "The Moose And The Sparrow," which unlike every other story in the collection does not involve the male-female relationship. I put this story in to give it hardcover permanence, and to the couple of reviewers who mentioned it, that's the reason for its being included.

Anyhow, to get back into some sort of chronology, I received a phone call late in September from Jock Carroll, the book editor of Simon & Schuster of Canada. Because we'd had an argument over the phone a week or two before, he called me "Mr. Garner" instead of by my first name which he's been using for twenty-five years. (Sure, I have fights and arguments with every editor I've ever worked with; writing/publishing, like law, is an adversary occupation.) Jock asked me if I'd sign a contract with the firm for the paperback publication of *Men And Women,* and I said I would, after I read the contract.

Men And Women, though not my best collection of short stories, didn't get a break at all from The Ryerson Press. As I've already written, I was forced to buy up the last 970 copies of it just to get it off Ryerson's shelves. My subsequent sale of these copies didn't do much for the book's Canada-wide image, and I'm hoping that the countrywide exposure that Simon & Schuster's "Pocket Books" are given will at last give the stories a break.

Before this Jim Smallwood had phoned me from Simon & Schuster and had told me he'd heard once more from a young New Yorker, Jim MacCammon. This young man had read a copy of *The Sin Sniper* while on a flight from Toronto to New York, and had been impressed by its film possibilities. On his next trip to Toronto, prior to settling here, he'd got in touch with both Jim Smallwood and myself about the possibilities of buying the film rights. Now, more than a year later, he'd phoned Smallwood to make another movie offer.

One evening the previous winter I'd attended a meeting between the writer members of ACTRA and some movie producers. During the coffee break Johnny Bassett, the movie-making son of my old boss at the *Toronto Telegram,* had asked me if a guy called Jim MacCammon owned any part of my book. I'd told him that Simon & Schuster and myself were the sole owners, on a fifty-fifty basis, and that nobody else had negotiating rights for it, including movie options on the book. Now Jim MacCammon, who had made nothing but empty promises to Smallwood and me before, was at it again. As I say, I refused to believe it.

I was very much surprised then a week later when a young woman named Pat Stewart, who works for Jim MacCammon & Associates, Film Production Co-ordinators, with a prestigious downtown skyscraper suite address, phoned Jim Smallwood and read him a tentative contract. The contract however contained a clause giving MacCammon not only a movie option on *The Sin Sniper* but options also on my twenty-four stories in *Hugh Garner's Best Stories.* Smallwood told her that that clause had to come out, for he didn't own any part of my other books except a five-year paperback deal. I think Miss Stewart then phoned me, and I corroborated what Jim Smallwood had said —quite emphatically.

A couple of days later there was a knock at my door, and a man told me he was Jim MacCammon's accountant. At the time I was talking with Ronald Side, a teacher at the Hamilton Teachers College, who was visiting me to discuss a multiple book deal involving my books that he was negotiating with a Toronto publishing house. I excused myself from Mr. Side and asked MacCammon's accountant his business. He took three copies of an option contract from a manilla envelope, and a certified cheque. I read the contract, and, satisfied that it was legitimate and there was no hanky-panky about other books or stories of mine, signed all three copies, having them witnessed by Mr. Side, who had been an interested observer of this little literary deal.

When the contracts were signed I told the accountant I'd keep them, and take them up to Jim Smallwood to sign the next morning, for in my *The Sin Sniper* contract, Simon & Schuster and I split movie rights down the middle.

The accountant told me he had been instructed to bring all

copies of the contract back to Jim McCammon & Associates, and also the cheque. I asked him if he thought I looked crazy enough to sign a contract and then return it to the other party, plus a certified cheque. I assured him I'd have the copies signed by Simon & Schuster the next day, and ushered him out of my apartment. A few minutes later he returned to my door and begged me to give him one copy of the contract at least, so I gave him one.

The next day I took the other two copies up to Simon & Schuster, Smallwood agreed that the contract was a good one, signed our two copies and gave me a Simon & Schuster cheque for my half of the option fee, and that was that.

A couple of weeks later Miss Stewart drove up to Richmond Hill and had Mr. Smallwood sign the Jim MacCammon & Associates copy. She once again brought up the subject of my short stories, and Smallwood told her again that I owned all the subsidiary rights. She said she'd have MacCammon phone me. Instead she phoned me herself a couple of weeks later, and asked me if I was willing to negotiate the sale of the movie rights to my book of short stories. I told her I would only negotiate each story individually.

In the meantime things had been happening back at my other publishing house, McGraw-Hill Ryerson. Ron Side had told me he'd bought a hard cover copy of *A Nice Place To Visit* in a Hamilton bookstore for a dollar, and I'd been hearing from Jim Foley in Port Colborne about the remaindering of what was left of my Ryerson quality paperbacks. In one of his letters to me Dr. Foley told me he'd purchased 150 copies of my *Best Short Stories* and 150 copies of another book, I think it was *Silence On The Shore*, "at a ridiculously low price," selling them at the same price to his students. I thought I'd better go out to McGraw-Hill Ryerson and see what their sales department was doing.

I drove out to the publishing house one afternoon, my cheque book in my pocket, and called on the trade book sales manager. He was on a sales trip to the Maritimes. I then went along the hallway to Frank Flemington's office, but found he had just left on his vacation. The vice-president in charge of trade books, was also away.

By this time I was not only angry but frustrated. I chatted for a while with the editor-in-chief, who following a literary cocktail party one evening had come to my place and helped me kill a quart of scotch. He was busy, and I suppose was getting tired of my bitching about the way his firm was shafting me. He told me to go see the sales manager's assistant, which I immediately did.

This woman, an ex-Cabbagetowner, told me that the firm still had 464 copies of *A Nice Place To Visit* and 84 copies of *Cabbagetown* in its warehouse. She told me that no copies of *Cabbagetown* had been remaindered, but read me some figures about the remaindering of *A Nice Place To Visit*. Britnell's bookshop in Toronto had bought a thousand copies, Palm Publishers of Montreal had bought some, as had International Books of Ottawa, and Coles. She had no figures on the remaindering of the paperbacks.

I told her I'd buy every copy of *A Nice Place To Visit* at its lowest remainder price, and every copy of *Cabbagetown* at the author's discount of 40% off the list price. I wrote her a cheque for $162.40, or 35¢ apiece, for 464 copies of *A Nice Place To Visit*. My author's discount on *Cabbagetown* would be $4.77 apiece, or a total of just over $400. I told her to put this on my royalty account.

The shipping department placed the bundles and boxes of books on the shipping ramp, and a young man and I loaded as many as I dared into the trunk and back seat of my car. I had to return the next morning for five remaining packages of books.

This whole series of events must sound screwy to the reader, but it is a manifestation of my personality. I suppose that one of my dominant and dominating traits is my impatience. I can't stand waffling or an inability to get things finalized and out of the way, and so those who frustrate me and disturb my sense of accomplishment, or throw my self-imposed schedule out of gear, can expect a wild-eyed visit from me. At times the consequences of this have been deleterious to my relationships with publications and publishers, but at least it's kept me from getting an ulcer.

Here I was, unable to make a start on a novel because I felt I had to clear up the other business first. Five (actually four, though I didn't know it then) of my books were being remaindered behind my back, I was waiting for a movie option deal involving a guy I didn't trust, I'd promised a non-book—the original of this one—to a friend whom I was doubtful could set up a publishing firm, a book of my short stories was lying on Jock Carroll's desk up at Simon & Schuster, while in my view Jock was awaiting word from the Almighty before getting around to reading it. To top it off I still wasn't sure about the eventual publication of my trilogy of plays. To say nothing of

281

having to sell the copies of my books I'd bought from McGraw-Hill Ryerson.

To begin with I sold the copies of *A Nice Place To Visit* and *Cabbagetown* to Peter Martin Associates for Peter's Reader's Club of Canada. Peter didn't have the money at the moment to buy them from me, so they were stored in my basement storage locker in the apartment house. Finally, in November, the Canada Council came through with a grant that Martin had been waiting for, and we completed our transaction.

One by one, by practicing a painful patience and writing some letters, I began eliminating my possible ulcer agents. Jim Smallwood had Jock Carroll phone me and tell me they were bringing out a paperback of my twenty short stories; I wrote the biographical introduction to my trilogy of plays, and told Rolf Kalman to use one of the pictures he'd taken of me; I also consoled myself with the fact that whether or not a movie was ever made of *The Sin Sniper* I had been paid my share of the option money. My neurasthenia became merely mild paranoia.

I read, and made a few small corrections to Doug Fetherling's monograph. Though it was a hastily-written document it had been written out of friendship, and, like some published theses on my work, it was both an acknowledgement of my *persona*, as the critics say, and a fair-to-middling account of what made my writing and me tick.

One day in mid-September as I stood outside the CBC radio building talking to a couple of friends, Doug Fetherling came out and we chatted for a minute or two. He told me he was sorry about missing the deadline he had given me for August, but promised some action during the first week of October.

Finally I wrote a friendly letter to Mr. John Macmillan, the president of McGraw-Hill Ryerson, outlining my objections to the firm's remaindering of my books, and pointing out some of the misinterpretings of my Ryerson Press contracts. Mr. Macmillan phoned me, and we made an appointment to meet in his office, which we did a couple of days later.

Sitting around a low coffee table, Mr. Macmillan, Bill Darnell, one of the firm's vice-presidents, and I came to mutually satisfactory agreements about the contracts, the remaindering of the books, and other things. My paranoia had disappeared, and I now suffered only a vague apprehension.

Less than two weeks later I received a contract from Simon & Schuster for the paperback publication of the enlarged *Men And Women*. It turned out to be a Canadian contract (unlike the U.S. hardcover contract I'd originally signed for *The Sin*

Sniper), and I was content with it. The arrival of my advance royalty cheque wiped out my apprehension. Most of my worrisome business deals had now been taken care of, and I could return to my normal state of mild neuroticism.

Over the next two weeks I received visits to my apartment from several people, among them a young writer named Juan Butler whose second novel, *The Garbageman,* I'd picked up at Peter Martin Associates. Mr. Butler asked me to be a referee to an application he was making to The Canada Council for an Arts Grant. Because I thought his novel was an excellent one, though of course almost ignored by the panjandrums of the literati, I willingly agreed. The day after he and a girl friend had visited my place I wrote my letter of reference for him.

One evening two young men rang my bell, and one of them introduced himself as the editor-to-come or something of a new nationalist Toronto weekly newspaper which was being backed by somebody or other. I plied this young man, and his friend, who apparently works for *Who's Who In Canada,* with beer and scotch respectively, and listened to the promotion scheme he outlined to me. Apparently he or someone else connected with the paper wanted me to write the odd column. I told him that I was not a nationalist, which not only cooled his ardor but also stopped him drinking. Anyhow, I mention this incident only to lead up to the fact that despite my overwhelming, and to some, overbearing sense of personal privacy, there are occasions when I do entertain.

In the meantime, after allowing two weeks to go by since Doug Fetherling's October deadline for coming to an agreement about the short autobiography, I went down to his apartment and picked up his copy. Since the previous spring it had grown to the book you are reading now. Doug and I chatted about this and that, and parted good friends, me with my Xeroxed script under my arm as I left. When I arrived home I dropped the script down the garbage chute. Then I phoned the editor-in-chief at McGraw-Hill and asked him if I could bring in the completed book for him to read and for McGraw-Hill Ryerson to publish, if they wished.

After innumerable interviews over the course of my writing years I've come to the conclusion that is has not been so much my bad answers as the bad questions which has made some of them banal. I remember once walking down the street from the CBC-TV studios with my old friend Frank Tumpane. We had just made guest appearances on Nathan Cohen's live panel show "Fighting Words." Frank, who was a good newspaper columnist, first on the *Globe & Mail* and later on *The Toronto Telegram,* said to me, "I'm always mad at myself after a show like that. I can think of a million scintillating things I should have said, and didn't."

I'm the same way, but in most cases it has been because I was not asked the right questions.

Once, being interviewed on a tape recorder by John Moss of the *Journal of Canadian Fiction,* he asked me if I'd ever written for the academics. I forgot now what my answer was, but what I should have said was, that, first, I've always written for myself, second for the editor whom I wished would buy the book, article or story, and third for the public I hoped would read it. Somewhere along the line I've also wished that the reviewers or critics, academic or not, would like what I'd written.

Yesterday, October 17th, 1972, was the twenty-seventh anniversary of the day I was formally discharged from the navy at the end of World War Two. I suppose it should have been the day when I had to make up my mind what I was going to do for the rest of my life.

Imaginary questioner: *Did you?*

No. I toyed with a couple of job or career ideas, but continued as a beer parlour philosopher until my money ran out. Two months later I began writing my first novel.

Are you satisfied with what you've done with the last twenty-seven years of your life?

Not entirely. I've committed many sins, usually sins of omission. The years have contained a series of happy surprises though.

What do you call "sins of omission?"

I think I should have written some novels during the nineteen-fifties. I regret now that I didn't write a novel or two in those days.

What about "happy surprises?"

I've been living with the same wife for thirty-two years, have brought up two nice children and watched them raising five children of their own. I've had a lot of fun, been a reckless happy drunk, won some honours, travelled quite a bit, and made enough money—except for the first couple of years at my trade—to keep us in relative comfort.

Do you think you've followed a path of vertical social mobility?

I haven't followed any conscious social path. I think all artists, or writers if you will, are classless people. Anyhow all social mobility is vertical; either up or down. Horizontal social mobility would mean staying at the same social level.

Most of this book seems to be concerned with writing as a business rather than writing as an art. Why?

The art of writing defies accurate description. It begins when a creative writer sits down at his desk or typewriter and ends when he gets up from it. Getting what you have written published is a pretty important part of writing, and this is the business part.

You've conducted creative writing seminars and classes. How do you describe creative writing?

I don't. All I can tell budding writers are the business and technical things about the craft. How can I describe to anyone how my ideas, story lines and twists, dialogue or characterization occur to me, and are then transferred from my brain to the typewritten page? Or, for that matter, how one or more incidents or a few lines of dialogue change craft to art? The answers to those questions are what all students of writing courses and workshops seek, but there are no answers. Creative writing cannot be explained, it springs out of a union of talent and sweated craftsmanship.

Do you consider yourself a novelist or a short story writer?

Both, I'm happy to say.

But what do you call yourself, a novelist or a short story writer?

You're really worrying that bone, aren't you? I generally call myself a writer, no qualifications, just a writer. When I made much or most of my living from journalism, I called myself a journalist. And sometimes I've called myself a journalist when to call myself a writer would have brought forth a lot of questions that would have been as boring to me as my answers would have been as embarrassing to the questioner.

Do you consider yourself a commercial or literary writer?

Both. They are not antithetical terms. I write from literary compulsion and motivation even when my writing has a commercial end in view. As I've said earlier, I've written in different styles depending on whether I was writing a novel, short story or something else, but I didn't say that I didn't try to write as well as I could in all of them. I've always tried to write at the top of my talent. Nobody in his right mind sits down consciously to write a work of art.

Then what makes some writing become art?

285

The writer is a craftsman, and if he has developed his talents and craftsmanship to their fullest, some of what he writes may become art. Craftsmanship only becomes art through critical acceptance and public consensus.

What is the difference between talent and craftsmanship?

Craftsmanship is how a writer uses his talents.

You've told us, briefly, about your marriage, your family, and your comparative success as a writer, but what about literary satisfaction?

All success is relative, and familial, financial and literary success, to oneself, are equally important. At least they are to me. My literary satisfaction is very personal. I once told someone that the best feeling a writer gets is when he types "The End" to a short story or a novel, and knows that he has just created something wholly satisfying and unique. It is the best feeling, regarding his work, that he will ever experience.

Besides that, what is the most important thing writing has done for you as a person?

It has allowed me to live my life on my own terms.

THE END

Sources of Biographical Material, and a
Compilation of Literary, Dramatic and
Journalistic Works, 1949 to winter, 1973.

BIOGRAPHICAL SOURCES

The Canadian Who's Who. Toronto: Trans-Canada Press.
Literary History of Canada: Canadian Literature in English,
Carl F. Klinck (ed.). Toronto: University of Toronto Press,
1965.
The Oxford Companion to Canadian History and Literature,
Norah Story. Toronto: Oxford University Press, 1967.
Canadian Writers/Ecrivains Canadiens, Guy Sylvestre (ed.).
Toronto: Ryerson Press, 1967.
Creative Writing in Canada '55, George Whalley (ed.) Toronto:
Macmillan, 1956.
The Author's and Writer's Who's Who. London: Mercury House.
Hugh Garner and Toronto's Cabbagetown, Robert J. Reimer.
Waterloo: University of Waterloo Press, 1971.
Journal of Canadian Fiction, an interview with John Moss.
Fredericton: University of New Brunswick, Volume I, 1.
"On the Road in the Thirties," in *The Dirty Thirties*, Michiel
Horn. Toronto: Copp Clark, 1971.
Hugh Garner and his Writings, Doug Fetherling. Toronto:
Coles', 1973.
"*Garner's Good Ear*," an article in Canadian Literature, Miriam
Waddington.
Douglas Library, Queen's University, collected notes, press
clippings, first editions, newspaper columns, TV scripts, manu-
scripts, etc.
University of Western Ontario (tape) Spanish Civil War.
McMaster University (microfilm) TV Dramas.
CBC Archives (voice and video tapes) biography, Spanish Civil
War.
Toronto Star Weekly, 1960, three part biographical article, "A
Spanish Loyalist Returns to Spain," 1959.
Toronto Telegram (book page column) 1950, "How *Cabbage-
town* was Written."
Tamarack Review, Dec. 1969, an interview with Allan Anderson.

MISCELLANEOUS VIDEO AND VOICE TAPES

Canadian Broadcasting Corp., various voice and video tapes.
CTV Television Network, videotapes.
CHCH-TV, videotapes.
Screen Gems (Canada), interviews by Pierre Berton.
Ontario Educational TV Network, videotaped interviews.

Ontario Institute for Studies In Education, interviews by Earle Toppings.
"Writing Biography," 9 voice tapes with Allan Anderson, CBC.
Toronto Public Libraries, videotape.
University of New Brunswick, biographical voice tapes.
Xerox, University Microfilms, Ann Arbor, Michigan.
Ryerson Institute of Technology, videotaped interview.
"1930's Revisited," Victor Hoar, University of Western Ontario.
'The Day Before Yesterday," CBC videotape, autobiography.

AWARDS

The Governor General's Award for Fiction, 1963.
First Prize, short story, *Northern Review*, 1951.
Canada Council Senior Arts Fellowship, 1959.
Canada Council Playwriting Grant, 1964.
Canada Council Senior Arts Fellowship, 1968.
Canada Council Arts Award, 1972-1973.
Award of Merit, The City of Toronto, 1972.
Associate Fellow, Winters College, York University, 1971.

PUBLISHED BOOKS (In chronological order)

Storm Below, Toronto: William Collins and Sons, 1949.
Cabbagetown, Toronto: William Collins and Sons, 1950. Reprinted Toronto: Ryerson Press, 1968.
Waste No Tears, Toronto: News Stand Library, 1950.
Present Reckoning, Toronto: William Collins and Sons, 1951.
The Yellow Sweater, Toronto: William Collins and Sons, 1952.
Silence on the Shore, Toronto: McClelland and Stewart, 1962.
Hugh Garner's Best Stories, Toronto: Ryerson Press, 1968.
Author! Author!, Toronto: Ryerson Press, 1964.
Men and Women, Toronto: Ryerson Press, 1966.
The Sin Sniper, Toronto: Simon and Schuster, 1970.
A Nice Place to Visit, Toronto: Ryerson Press, 1970.
Violation of the Virgins, Toronto: McGraw-Hill Ryerson, 1971.
Three Women, 3 One-Act Plays, Toronto: Simon and Pierre, 1973.
One Damn Thing After Another, Toronto: McGraw-Hill Ryerson, 1973.

ANTHOLOGIES, TEXTBOOKS, ETC., CONTAINING
SHORT STORIES, ESSAYS AND ARTICLES

Alienated Man, Eva Taube (ed.). New York, Hayden Book Company, 1972. "One, Two, Three Little Indians."

Best American Short Stories, Boston: Houghton Mifflin, 1952. "The Conversion of Willie Heaps.'

The Book of Canadian Prose, Volume 2, A.J.M. Smith (ed.). Toronto: Gage, 1965. "One, Two, Three Little Indians."

A Book of Canadian Stories, Desmond Pacey (ed.). Toronto, Ryerson, 1962. "One, Two, Three Little Indians."

Canada and the United States, Continental Partners or Worried Neighbours? R.P. Bowles et al (eds.). Toronto: Prentice-Hall, 1973. "I Love Americans."

Canadian Literature: Two Centuries in Prose, B. Rita Mickleburgh (ed.). Toronto McClelland & Stewart, 1973. "E Equals MC Squared."

Canadian Short Stories, Paderborn, West Germany: Ferdinand Schoningh. "One, Two, Three Little Indians."

Canadian Short Stories, Robert Weaver (ed.). Toronto: Oxford Univesity Press, 1966. "One, Two, Three Indians" and "One Mile of Ice."

Canadian Short Stories, Second Series, Robert Weaver (ed.). Toronto: Oxford University Press, 1968. "One, Two, Three Little Indians," "Hunky," "E Equals MC Squared."

Canadians and Their Society, Allan Skeoch and Tony Smith (eds.). Toronto: McClelland & Stewart, 1972. Excerpt from *Cabbagetown.*

Canadians at War: 1939-1945, D. How, G. Ronald and C. Smith (eds.) Monteal: *Reader's Digest,* 1969. Extract from *Storm Below.*

Canadische Erzahler. Switzerland: Manesse Verlag. "One, Two, Three Little Indians."

Cavalcade of the North, George E. Nelson. Garden City, New York: Doubleday, 1958. "Some are So Lucky."

The Centennial Food Guide. Weekend Magazine and McClelland & Stewart co-production. "Restaurant Euphemisms."

A Collection of Canadian Plays: Volume Two. Toronto: Basset Books, 1972. "Some are So Lucky," "The Magnet," "A Trip for Mrs. Taylor."

Compass 11, Lee Davis et al (eds.). Glenview, Illinois: Scott, Foresman and Company, 1971. "A Trip for Mrs. Taylor."

Contemporary Voices, Donald Stephens. Toronto: Prentice-Hall, 1972. "Red Racer."

Curriculum Guide, New York: State University of New York. Excerpt from "One, Two, Three Little Indians."

Dance of the Happy Shades, Alice Munro. Toronto: Ryerson, 1968. Introduction.

Die Kinder-Kultuuru. South Africa. "A Trip for Mrs. Taylor."

The Dirty Thirties, Michiel Horn. Toronto: Copp Clark, 1971. "On the Road Through the Thirties."

Douze Ecrivains, Douze Nouvelles, Hubert Aquin (Trans.).

Les Editions "Ici Radio Canada." "Les Secrets des Roses Trémières."
Editura Pentru Literatura, Rumania. "One, Two, Three Little Indians."
Encyclopedia Canadiana, Toronto: Grolier Society, 1970. "Undertaking," "Cemeteries," "Cremation," "Burials."
English Through Experience, G.A. Nelson. Toronto: Copp Clark, 1968.
Erzahlungen Aus Kanada. Munich: Langewiesche-Brandt. "Eins, Zwei, Drei Kleine Indianer."
Essays of our Time, B. Webber, L. Hamalian and E.L. Volpe (eds.). Toronto: McGraw-Hill, 1967. "My Day with the Head-shrinkers."
The Evolution of Canadian Literature in English, 1945-1970, Paul Denham (ed.). Toronto: Holt, Rinehart and Winston, 1973. "One, Two, Three Little Indians."
Fighting Back, Graham Fraser. Toronto: Hakkert, 1972. Excerpts from *Cabbagetown*.
Forum. University of Toronto Press, 1972. Excerpt from *Cabbagetown*.
Fourteen Stories High, David Helwig and Tom Marshall (eds.). Ottawa: Oberon Press, 1971. "The Happiest Man in the World."
Great Canadian Short Stories, Alec Lucas (ed.). New York: Dell, 1971. "A Trip for Mrs. Taylor."
In Search of Ourselves, Malcolm Ross and John Stevens (eds.). Toronto: Dent, 1967. "One, Two, Three Little Indians."
International Reading Lab 3a. Educational Kit, Toronto: Science Research Associates, 1972. "I Hate Dog Lovers."
Invitation to Short Stories, H.L. Willis and W.R. McGillivray (eds.). Toronto: Macmillan, 1958. "A Trip for Mrs. Taylor."
Kaleidoscope, John Metcalf. Toronto: Van Nostrand, Reinhold Ltd., 1972. "The Moose and the Sparrow."
Language Comes Alive, John E. Smallbridge and Philip J. Linden. Toronto: Dent, 1967. "Manitoba: Keystone Province Holiday."
Literature in English for the French-Speaking Canadian, Frank X. Stever and Douglas W. Veitch (eds.). Toronto: Dent, 1969. "A Trip for Mrs. Taylor."
The Mackenzie-Papineau Battalion, Victor Hoar. Toronto: Copp Clark, 1969. "Letters from Spain."
Man in Revolt, Eva Taube (ed.). Toronto: McClelland & Stewart, 1970. "One, Two, Three Little Indians."
Man in Society. Toronto: McClellend & Stewart. Excerpt from *Cabbagetown*.
Modern Canadian Short Stories. East Germany: Verlag fur Internationale Literatur. "One, Two, Three Little Indians."
Modern Canadian Stories, G. Rimanelli (ed.). Toronto: Ryerson, 1966. "The Yellow Sweater" and "One, Two, Three Little Indians."

New Canadian Stories. Ottawa Oberon Press, 1973. "Losers Weepers."

The New Romans, Alfred W. Purdy (ed.). Edmonton, Hurtig, 1968. "I Love Americans."

Northern Lights, George E. Nelson (ed.). Garden City, New York: Doubleday, 1960. "A Trip for Mrs. Taylor."

The Open Window, P. Daniel and W.F. Langford (eds.). Toronto: Longman, 1961. "One Mile of Ice."

The Oxford Anthology of Canadian Literature, Robert Weaver and William Toye (eds.). Toronto: Oxford University Press, 1973. "Hunky."

The Pleasures of Fiction, Gerald Camp and Gerald Gray (ed.). Reading, Massachusetts: Addison-Wesley, 1972. "One, Two, Three Little Indians."

Readings in Canadian Civics, John S. Moir, T.T. Ferris and G.A. Onn (eds.). Toronto: Ryerson, 1968. "The Jury: Many are Called but Few Are Chosen."

Safaris 3, J.W. Chalmers and H.T. Coutts. Toronto: Dent, 1970. "A Trip for Mrs. Taylor."

See/Hear/Now. Educational Kit. "On the Road."

Short Story International. New York: Universal Publishing Company, 1965. "The Nun in Nylon Stockings."

Sixteen by Twelve, John Metcalf. Toronto: Ryerson Press, 1970. "The Yellow Sweater."

The Study of Man, Eva Taube. Toronto: McCelland & Stewart, 1967. "The Father."

Talking Books, D.J. Mackenzie. Scarborough, Ontario: Scarborough Public Library, 1972. Stories from *Hugh Garner's Best Stories.*

Telling Tales, Gray Cavanagh and Ken Styles (eds.). Toronto: McClelland & Stewart, 1973. "One Mile of Ice."

Temper of the Times, R. Side and R. Greenfield. Toronto: McGraw-Hill, 1969. "Artsy-Craftsy" and "Black and White and Red All Over."

Ten for Wednesday Night, Robert Weaver (ed.). Toronto, McClelland & Stewart, 1961. "Hunky."

Tigers of the Snow, James A. MacNeill. Toronto: Thomas Nelson and Sons, 1972. "The Sound of Hollyhocks."

The Time of Your Life, James Henderson (ed.). Toronto: Macmillan, 1967. "A Manly Heart."

Tuned In, Grace Mersereau (ed.). Toronto: Macmillan, 1970. "The Father."

What do You Think? C.M. Worsnop. Toronto: Copp Clark, 1969. "One, Two, Three Little Indians."

MAGAZINE ARTICLES AND ESSAYS

436 articles and essays were published between September, 1949, and February, 1971, the majority between 1950 and

1960. The major magazines using Hugh Garner's material were: *Canadian Broadcaster, Canadian Forum, Canadian Home Journal, Caravan, Chatelaine, CBC Publications, Dale's Magazine, Encyclopedia Canadiana, Everybody's Digest, Financial Post, Globe Magazine, Industrial Advertising, Journal of Canadian Fiction, Liberty, Maclean's, Mayfair, Montreal Standard, National Home Monthly, Quarry, Royal York Magazine, Saturday Night, Star Weekly, Tamarack Review, The Canadian, Toronto Daily Star, Toronto Telegram, Woman's World* (U.K.)

Reprints have been used by:
Addictions (Ontario Alcohol Research Foundation), *Associated Australian Papers, Atlantic Advocate, Belgium Newspapers,* Canadian Broadcasting Corporation, *Canadian Press, Chicago Sun-Times, Concorde* (in French), *Dartmouth Free Press,* Dutch Newspaper Syndicate, *Everybody's Digest, London Daily Express, Maclean's, Magazine Digest, Milady* (South Africa), *Newark Evening News, Ontario Hotel Magazine, Pix Magazine, Reader's Digest, Vancouver Sun, World Digest.*

SHORT STORIES

In addition to the volumes and anthologies already mentioned, short stories have been used by the following CBC Radio programs: "Anthology," CBC International Service, "Centennial Stories," "Commonwealth Stories," "Perspective," "Radio Stage," "Stories with Drainie," "Sunday Night," "Take 30," "Tuesday Night," "Wednesday Night."

TELEVISION DRAMA SCRIPTS

A Couple of Quiet Young Guys: Used by CBC "On Camera" and "Eye Opener."
A Trip for Mrs. Taylor: Used by CBC "On Camera," June 3, 1957; BBC, July 12, 1957, Australian TV, October 1957.
Aftermath: Used by CBC "General Motors Presents," and Associated Television in the United Kingdom.
E Equals MC Squared: Bought by CBC "To See Ourselves," and not used.
Murder in the Suburbs: Used by the CBC "The Serial."
One, Two, Three Little Indians: Filmed by the CBC for "To See Ourselves."
Silence on the Shore: Used by the CBC "The Serial."
Some Are So Lucky: First production used by CBC "On Camera," December 17, 1956 and the BBC, January 12, 1957. Second production used by CBC "First Person," August 17, 1960; CBC "Summer Circuit," August 10, 1961; CBC "Studio Pacific," October 3, 1966. Third production used by CBC "To See Our-

selves" and the BBC Regional Network.

The Father: Used by CBC "On Camera," February 10, 1958, and the BBC, May 5, 1958.

The Guardeen Angel: Used by CBC "First Person," November 9, 1960.

The Happiest Man in the World: Used by CBC "To See Ourselves."

The Lost Cause: Used by CBC "Playdate."

The Magnet: Used by CBC "First Person," June 15, 1960, and CBC "Studio Pacific."

Wish You Were Here: Used by CBC "The Play's the Thing."

STAGE SCRIPTS

Three Women (a trilogy of one-act plays) made up of *The Magnet, A Trip for Mrs. Taylor* and *Some are So Lucky. A Trip for Mrs. Taylor* was presented by the Brockville Theatre Guild, November 4, 1966.

RADIO DRAMA SCRIPTS (not author's adaptations)

The following were broadcast by the CBC "Radio Stage": "Aftermath," 1959; "The Magnet," 1965 and repeated; "A Trip for Mrs. Taylor," 1964; "A Visit with Robert," 1964; "Some are So Lucky," 1964; "One, Two, Three Little Indians," 1964; "Silence on the Shore," 1966 with repeat in 1967; "A Manly Heart," 1968; "Cabbagetown," 1969; "Storm Below," 1969 and 1970; "The Sin Sniper" 1970 with repeat; "A Nice Place to Visit," 1970.

Take 30 broadcast "A Trip for Mrs. Taylor" in 1964.

MOVIE SCRIPTS

The Sin Sniper: Six-month options sold to Jim MacCammon & Associates, and to Monitor Productions.